Remember to Forget

Amelia V. Sinclair

Copyright © 2022

All rights reserved, including the right to reproduce, distribute or transmit or store in a database or retrieval system this book or portions thereof in any form whatsoever, without the express written permission of the publisher. Contact address avsinclair7@gmail.com

Printed in the United States of America

ISBN 979-8-218-03791-8

Library of Congress Control Number: 2022913832

Permissions
Mac Eaton, signed consent dated August 27, 2012
Pia Mellody, signed consent February 27, 2012

Cover by Fiverr, Cal5086

The past hanging thickly over us
 needs to be remembered
  in order to be forgotten.

Paul Wilson Brand, M.D.

To
>   David, my beloved
>   >   Mac, unrivaled therapist
>   >   >   Marc, forever friend

>   Beacons of light on my shadowed
>   pathway to safety and wellness

PROLOGUE

Without the fragments of memory linked together into a full picture of our traumatic past history, we may be doomed to remain helpless victims. It was surprising to me that it wasn't until I was in my thirties that I began to awaken to my history. It was then that I started earnestly trying to organize the chaos of my own trauma-filled past. Why? Not only because I was an insecure person, an anxious person that frequently fell into the role of victim, but because suicide loomed as a serious threat.

Remember to Forget brings to completion my effort to capture and organize my elusive history; throughout the later chapters the reader will discover my pathway that has resulted in my healing. In the process, questions emerged: Why did my mother burn down the family home at age fifteen? What happened to Buddy, Jr.? Why did the gynecologist find scaring in my vagina even though I was a virgin?

My mother, Edna, is central to this dramatic story that is told through my experience of living with her as a child and relating to her as an adult. The story begins before my mother conceived me and terminates at her death with places and events ordered from what I have remembered and what other have told me.

A series of forgotten memories were eventually recovered in therapy. Some memories are so traumatic, they become shattered-fragmented pieces the mind seems unable to reassemble. What cognitively I could not remember of the trauma, my body retained. My body memories presented as involuntary muscle contractions which replicated the original physical trauma, often accompanied by painful emotions. *Remember to Forget* includes details of body memories I have personally experienced.

These early experiences were very frightening. I searched for books written about body memory. I searched for information of someone who had gone through a similar experience. Other than a life-saving tape my therapist gave me that held Pia Mellody's insight into this strange new experience, I could find nothing else on the subject of body memories. As a result, I wanted to share my own story but it was too emotionally difficult to seek publication when the manuscript was completed in Spring of 2013. But by changing most of the names in the story, my feeling of vulnerability has lessened and publication is motivated by thinking my story may help others.

EDNA ROSS SCHREIBER HALL

Maiden Name: Ross
Parents: Lowell (Jack) & Pansie
Siblings: Eva, Pansie's daughter
            Angie her half-sister
        Jim, wife Evelyn
        Ralph, wife Della
            one child: Billy (M)
        Mary
        Nettie, husband Fritz
            two daughters. Lisa, Gena

Husbands:
    Schreiber, Vernon
        Daughters, Verneda and Vernetta
        Siblings: Herman, wife Mary
                    Hannah, husband
                          Kenneth
                    Clarence, wife Mae
    Hall, Norman
        Daughter, Glenda
        Children from previous marriage:
            Harold
            Robert "Bobby"
            Susan

Lovers: Ferd, married, no children

"Bud", single
    Son, Buddy, Jr. aka Larry
        Mother: Edna
Siblings:
    Vi Lee, Roy, husband
      "Adopted": Buddy, Jr./Larry
    Dewey, wife, Grace
    Al, wife, Blanche

Friends

Lucky, Larned, KS

Grandpa Hoffman, SLC
    Clifford, son
    Maxine, daughter
        Ray, husband
        Tudy/Dale, son

Red Getchel, took Edna to Jarbidge

Glen and Vi of Albert, KS

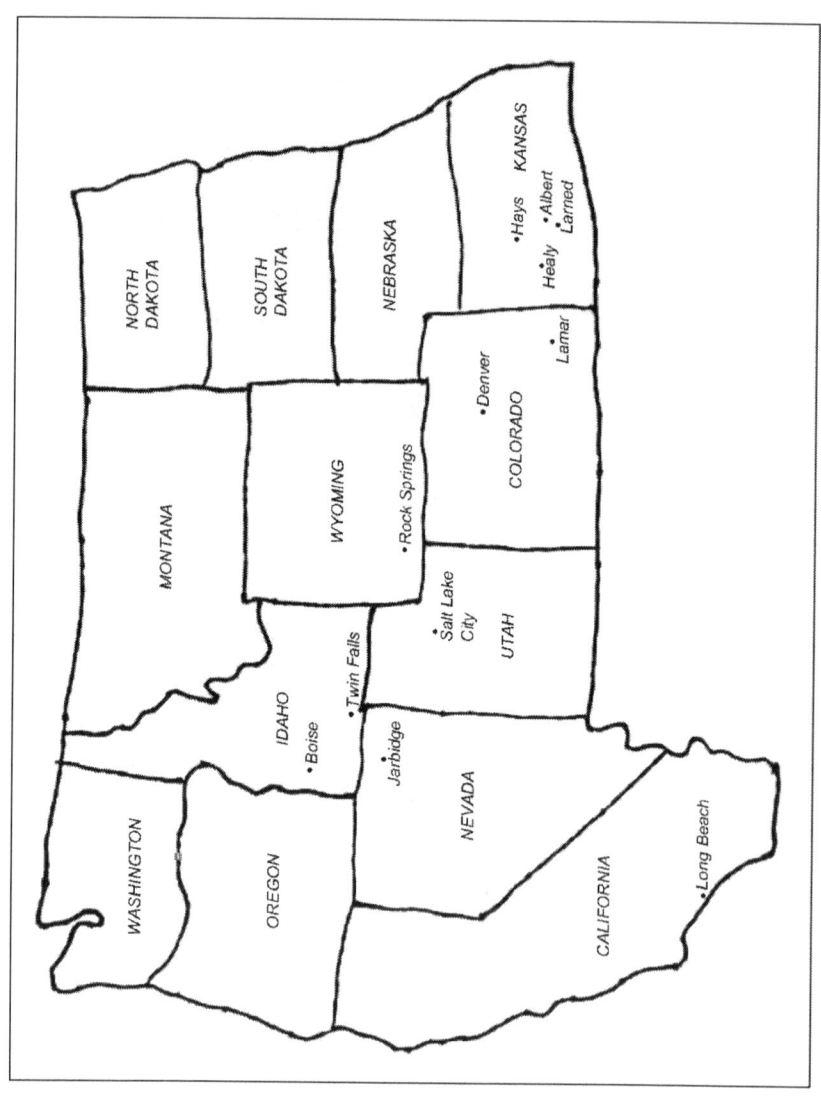

Chapter 1

California
1986

What's urging me to see her today? I questioned again as I turned right at the bottom of my driveway. It's been seven years. I haven't seen her for seven years. Five years ago since she hung up on me. I tried to avoid feeling a twinge of pain that came with the memory. A fragment of what my sister Verneda had said distracted me, "She's livin in a fifth-wheel out in Lake Elsinore."

Nagging discomfort threatened my intention as I continued thinking and driving away from my home in Redlands. She'll never contact me; she'll never get in touch with me, I reminded myself. Silence between us until the day she dies if I don't go to see her. That's not what I want! The needle on the speedometer caught my attention. Twenty miles over the speed limit, better slow it down I told myself.

Lake Elsinore next exit, I read aloud. I could almost hear the tone of Verneda's voice, "...livin' in a fifth wheel out in Lake Elsinore." It's really happening, almost there. What makes me think I'm ready to find her? I anxiously considered. My years of therapy with Mac, I reminded myself. Yes, and I think I can offer her my love without asking for anything in return. Am I fooling myself? I questioned, as I exited the freeway.

Why did they move back to California, I wondered, as I turned my El Dorado into the campsite at Lake Elsinore. I guess I don't really know why they moved to Kansas in the first place. Looking for their fifth wheel, I passed rows of trailers and fifth wheelers parked in the permanent section. A familiar lifestyle for them, I thought as I had a brief memory of living with Mom and Norm in a small trailer during fifth and sixth grade.

Mom was sitting at a built-in table looking out the window. When I came through the door, lack of affection in her face and the coolness of her few sparse words greeted me. She looked at me as if I'd recently been there and what do I want now. Was I anticipating more? Maybe even an embrace simply because she hasn't seen me in seven years, I asked myself.

I sat down at the table across from her; the faded pattern of the placemats caught my attention. Next to Mom was a plastic yellowed lampshade askew on the lamp where it sat precariously perched. A large nicotine-stained glass ashtray overflowing with smelly cigarette butts took up space on the table. At least Mom never smoked, I thought to myself. Dust sat tall around the clutter on the shelves. A few breezy cobwebs swung in random places from the ceiling. A multi-colored afghan was thrown on the back of the small sofa that went across one end of the fifth wheel. Had Mom made it, I wondered. The blatant colors clashed against each other making a noise that bothered my eyes.

"What brings you here?" she asked. I was relieved to hear a non-threatening tone in her voice.

"I came to see you!" I said, smiling as I looked at her. "Haven't seen you for such a long time. Seven years."

My words were lost to her fixed gaze out the window. "There goes the neighbor with that damn dog that's been tryin' to get at our cat. They keep him out there tied up, but he gets loose," she said with a familiar sound that momentarily frightened me.

"Where's Norm?" I asked, finally aware he wasn't there.

"Gone to the store. I usually go with him."

I waited for her to say more, thinking how fortunate I was. She had stayed home. I'm not sure how long we sat in awkward silence.

"So, how have you been, Mom?"

"Been doin' fine," she answered as she reached for a little round mirror that lay on the table. I watched her look into the mirror to pick at a blemish on her face. She still has her long fingernails, I silently observed. "Would you like to take a walk down by the lake?" I invited.

"Norm's gonna be home soon. I don't wanna be gone."

"So you decided to move back to California?"

"Norm wanted to get away from them hard Kansas winters," she said.

I sat watching her pick at her face. Finally, I asked a question for which I already knew the answer. "Didn't you have your own second-hand store in Garden City?" I asked, hoping her response would offer details about herself and her experience beyond what I already knew.

"Yes, I had a little store I run by myself down on Main Street. Lookie there, just like I told ya. That dog has got off the leash," Mom said in disgust as she placed the mirror back on the table. "Good thing the cat's in here."

"Where is the cat?" I asked, disappointed that she had changed the subject, "I don't see it."

"Up on our bed sleepin'."

After spending slightly less than an exhausting hour with her in a space I found oppressive, I became restless. "I need to go, Mom. Tell Norm I'll see him on the next visit when David and I come back together. Wonderful to see you again," I said as I stood.

"Nice to see you, too," she said quietly with some sincerity I thought as I gave her a good-bye kiss on her cheek.

Mom and I sat at that same table several months later on one of my weekly visits. She started talking about a trip they wanted to take or needed to take back to Kansas, but they didn't have the money. She placed a beautiful gold pocket watch on the table. "This belonged to Aunt Emma. If you could give me five hundred dollars you can have it."

My grandmother Pansie had received an inheritance from her Aunt Emma when I was a very young child. I had never seen this beautiful gold watch even though I remembered seeing a lovely cameo pin that once belonged to Aunt Emma. I sat stunned. I wanted to ask, "You've had this since I was a girl but you've never shown it to me! Why?" I wanted to ask, but the risk of alienating her was too great.

"Mom, you don't have to sell me your watch. I'll give you the five hundred dollars. You keep the watch."

"No, I want you to have it, but we need the money so we can go back to Kansas."

"I would love to have the watch and of course you can have the money you need for the trip."

"Eva took the chain that goes with that watch when Momma died. I used to wear that chain as a necklace. It was gold. I don't know who it has now," she said with deep sadness dusted lightly by anger that reflected in her dark brown eyes.

Mom's remorse over the loss of the chain kept coming into my thoughts many years after her death. It pricked at me until I finally searched for it. I remembered Mom said that Eva, her half-sister, Pansie's only child from her first marriage, had taken the chain when Grandma died. But Eva died years ago. I thought of her half-sister Angie--maybe she has the chain–but I had no idea where to find her.

Why would I want to find the chain? I asked myself. What's so important about that? Sentiment perhaps, a feeling I had that the watch was incomplete without its chain when a jeweler examined it and said, "This is a very fine watch," then opened the back and found inside an inscription: Emma 1888. But maybe it was the look in my mother's eyes or the sound of her voice when she told me about the lost chain. Or might the lost chain represent my experience of repeated losses in childhood and my inability to retrieve what I had lost? Whatever the reason, I eventually found Angie. And what did she say when I asked about the chain? "Eva had it. I found it among her things when she died."

"Could I buy it from you?" I asked.

"No, you can have it" she answered quickly. She left momentarily but returned and placed the precious chain in my hand.

It's hard to understand the significance of how something that is so insignificant can burrow into our minds, a seed that germinates into a tyrant driven by desire. When Mom told me of the lost chain as I sat across the table from her, I felt her sadness, but I never imagined myself driven to find it years later.

But the gold watch and the lost chain were nowhere in my thoughts late in the summer when I went with Mom and Norm to the Loma Linda Medical Center because she hadn't been feeling well. Sitting behind his desk, the doctor began to share his findings. "It appears that you have multiple myeloma, Edna, a form of cancer in the bone marrow." I looked at my mother and saw no change in her expression. The doctor continued, "We'd like to get a bone marrow sample." As he described the procedure, I allowed his voice to fade away. I tried to avoid the visual image of what he described: a large needle inserted into the bones of my mother's sternum to extract the sample. He concluded, "There is a possible three-year life expectancy."

As she listened to the doctor indicate that she may have only three years more of life, I sensed in her no anxiety or dreaded anticipation. There were no words, no facial expressions to indicate otherwise. I experienced her as not truly present, a characteristic of hers that I had experienced and observed since childhood. In the past, it had seemed to me that my mother lived in a state of numbness. Now as she received her diagnosis of cancer and life expectancy, I felt this dwelling place of numbness was a safe haven for her.

Away she went for her sample extraction while Norm and I sat in the waiting room. He leaned over to pull his wallet from his back pocket. Fumbling through his cards, he took one out and looked at it. "We have cancer insurance," he said flatly.

During the following year, we made many trips to the doctor for chemotherapy. On one of those trips Mom said to me, "The neighbor lady came and said a prayer for me." It was obvious that the neighbor's prayer had a deep significance for her. I was surprised. There wasn't even a hint of God in her life beyond her frequently saying 'goddamned this or goddamned that.' She had sent my sister and me to Sunday school when we were children, but that was years ago.

I didn't think you had much use for God, I almost said to her as I looked at her sitting there. Instead, I told her something else that was on my heart. I love you, Mom. And you are always in my prayers, I said to myself.

It was almost a year after her cancer diagnosis that my mother placed on the table a crumpled, time-stained cardboard box filled with photographs, negatives and an album or two. Regrettably, the significance of this monumental moment escaped me until much later. This was my mother passing on to me the only tangible legacy she had, her photographs. "Take whatever you want. The rest goes to Terry. I don't think Glenda wants any."

Terry is my only real sister, my senior by three years and nine months. When I was very little, I called her Nee-Nee until I could say her given name, Verneda. I remember I was in the seventh grade when she decided to be Terry instead of Verneda. To me, she will always be my sister Verneda. I don't want that to change. There were already so many changes in our lives by the time I was a seventh grader, her name change was a giant step I didn't take.

Glenda was the child Mom and Norm had together, the child who got the same last name as theirs, my half-sister ten years and nine months younger than I. It seemed to me at age eleven, when Glenda slept in a bassinette, that we already had enough people in our eight-foot by twenty-four-foot trailer with no toilet and no shower. What did we need with a baby in a bassinette that made it almost impossible to get from the living room to the kitchen? We don't really have a close relationship, probably because she was only five when I left home just before my sixteenth birthday.

Mom handed me a hard backed photo of a very young child sitting on the lap of an older woman. "That's my mother when she was a little girl." I looked at the beautiful little girl.

"You mean that's Grandma?" I asked.

"Yes, that's my mother. Her name was Pansie."

"Oh, I remember her name was Pansie. But who is the older woman?"

"That's the woman that raised Momma."

I picked up another photo of Pansie and the woman who had raised her. "Look; this one is dated 1894! I'd like to have all of these," I said to Mom as I looked through several very old but well-preserved photos of my grandmother in various stages of childhood.

Mom poked around in the cardboard box of loose pictures until one caught her attention. "This here is a picture of the Healy, Kansas farmhouse where I was born and raised." I looked at the picture. In the foreground was a pen with several very large hogs. Standing outside the hog pen was a woman I recognized as Grandmother Pansie. "Who is that standing next to Grandma?" I asked.
"Oh, that's me," Mom answered.
"You? I didn't recognize you. Are you about thirteen or so?"
"Not sure. 'Bout that probably."
"That's a nice house in the background," I said in admiration.
"I burned that house down when I was fifteen," Mom answered without hesitation. I sat there, next to her, astounded. She had almost never shared any personal details of her life with me and now nonchalantly she mentions she burned down a house. "Why?" I blurted out. "Why did you burn the house down?"

Without looking at me, she answered matter-of-factly as she continued sorting through the pictures. "Just decided to burn it down." There must be more to it than that, I found myself thinking but said nothing. Something had to be radically wrong for her to burn down her family home at fifteen, but what was the reason? It's one of those questions that burrows into the psyche until the "why" is satisfied.

Almost immediately, she handed me a picture I hadn't seen in a very long time, a baby in a checkered sun suit. "You know who that is?" she asked. For a moment, ripples of the past found their way into the present. "That's Buddy, Jr., isn't it?"

"Yes," was her brief reply, followed by a long period of silence.

Remembrances came to mind of what my sister had told me: "After Mom gave Buddy, Jr. away, she used to cry and cry and cry. When Mom got drunk, she'd cry and say to me, 'You find him. Promise me when you turn eighteen that you'll find him.' She kept that up until I left home. Then when I was an adult, every February eleven, Mom would call me and say, 'You know what day this is? Buddy, Jr.'s birthday.' I knew what day it was without her crying and reminding me."

"I guess Verneda promised to find him when she turned eighteen," I said to Mother but she didn't respond. "I guess she wasn't able to look for him." Still no response. I searched my mother's face and in it I saw what I thought was sorrow, maybe longing.

"July 27, 1941 is when they took him from me," she finally said as she picked up a wallet-sized plastic folder, a folder I hadn't seen since I was a child. Inside was a picture of Bud on one side, a picture of my youthful mother on the other side and a picture of baby Buddy, Jr. floating freely between. A single thought escaped my deeply emotional response. She has carried this with her since leaving Jarbidge, Nevada forty-six years ago.

Bud   Edna

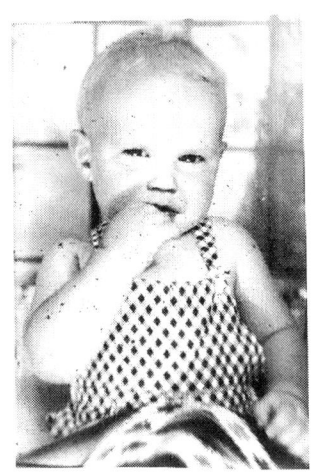

Buddy, Jr./Larry

Vernon and Edna

Chapter 2

Kansas to Idaho
1932 – 1937

When my mother took my sister and me to live in Jarbidge, Nevada, March of 1940, I was about two years and six months old. But long before I was born, long before Buddy, Jr. was born, my mother's destiny came chugging up the long, dry road to the Healy, Kansas farmhouse, sitting behind the wheel of an old borrowed-model T disguised as a handsome young man who called himself Vern.

"We'll be goin' over to Kenneth and Hannah's," Vern said. "They invited us for supper." Edna liked Hannah, although she had only met Vern's sister a few days earlier.

"That'd be nice to have supper with them," Edna said.

The feeling of Vern's arm around her waist as they walked toward the car sent warm tingles to unimagined places. "Slide on over here by me, honey," Vern said after they had gotten into the car. A somewhat shy seventeen-year-old, Edna hesitated but slowly inched her way closer to him.

Vern opened the door to Kenneth and his sister Hannah's home. "Go on in," he said, patting her on the rear end as she walked by.

"But there ain't nobody here; I thought you--" but Edna stopped mid-sentence when she felt Vern's hand slide under her dress. "No!" she yelled at him, trying to push him away. Easily he forced her onto the couch. "You're hurtin' me!" Vern, intent on one thing only, paid no attention to her painful cry or her protests.

Although taken advantage of by Vern on their first date, my mother married him six months later in February 1933, unaware that at age seventeen, she had set the course of her life in a downward spiral. It was the era of the Great Depression, a time of hardship for most people but especially the uneducated, which included Vern and my mother. In January of 1934 they added a new baby girl, their first child, to an already difficult situation. They named her Verneda, after her father.

Vern took Mother and Verneda from Healy, Kansas to Twin Falls, Idaho sometime in 1936 to escape the devastation of the Dust Bowl. They settled in a one room, tarpaper shack next to the Snake River on a bluff in South Twin next to his brother Herman and wife Mary. The tiny shack sat side-by-side with identical ones, housing built for the poorest of the poor during the Depression. Each shack had a wood-burning stove, which served as the cook stove as well as the source of heat. The only bit of landscaping surrounding these humble one-room spaces were piles of wood used as fuel for the stoves. An extraneous feature were the chickens who scratched their way around in the dirt and left tiny piles of chicken poop where the children played.

At a dance in Twin, Vern met Kae Hicks, ten years his senior, in the early months of my mother's pregnancy with me. Kae and my mother both had dark hair, but the similarities ended there. Maybe it was her bra size that gave Kae the edge. Maybe Kae had the advantage when it came to kids because hers had babysitting jobs or paper delivery jobs; they could take care of themselves. Maybe Kae had the advantage because she knew how to manage the small amount of money she and her three children were able to earn. Money she was willing to lavish on Vern.

But whatever the reason, Kae definitely had the advantage over my mother. He began yo-yoing back and forth between the two women. Vern was with Kae in one of his "gone phases" when I came home from the hospital with my twenty-one-year-old mother.

My sister told me she watched as the big black car stopped to let Mom get out of the car with me in her arms, her new baby sister, Vernetta. Verneda tugged at Mom's coat. "What the hell do you want," snapped Mom.

"Mommy, I'm hungry," cried my sister. Mom didn't say anything as she walked into the tarpaper shack and lay down with me on the bed. Eventually she told Verneda, "Go over and borrow some potatoes from Aunt Mary. That son-of-a-bitch Vern, he's over at that goddamned Kae Hicks eatin' steak and we're here eatin' nothin'." Verneda came back with the potatoes, holding onto her bottom.

"Why in the hell are you holdin' your bottom?"

"Mommy, I gotta to go pee-pee."

"Well what do you want me to do about it? You know where the toilet is."

"But Mommy, I'm scared of the dog." Vern and Uncle Herman usually kept their big white pit bull tied to a woodpile.

"Oh for Christ's sake." That ugly look on Mom's face always frightened Verneda. She ran to the door and peeked out. She saw the big pile of wood, but she couldn't see the dog. "Go on out there; that dog ain't gonna git you." Mom gave her a shove out the door and closed it. Verneda banged on the door with her fist and yelled, "Mommy, that dog might git me."

As Verneda stood outside the shut door, she started thinking about the other day when the big dog got loose, chased a little dog, caught it, had it in his mouth then shook it and shook it then dropped it limp on the road. Just thinking about the dog caused a little trickle to start down her leg.

"Mommy will be mad if I potty my pants." Turning from the door of the shack, Verneda started to run toward the outhouse. As she darted past the woodpile, the dog suddenly appeared, pulling the rope taunt when he lunged for her, snapping at her face. Verneda's startled scream pierced the air. The dog fell back as suddenly as he had appeared. She ran safely past as fast as she could go.

"You old barkin' dog, you sound like my Daddy," Verneda said when she peeked out through the knothole in the outhouse door trying to see what the dog was doing. She started thinking about the angry words her Daddy yelled in the car, 'I oughta kill you.' This is all she could remember her Daddy yelling. "I oughta kill you right now and lay that kid right out beside you." These were the words she had forgotten.

Why was Daddy so mean? she wondered, poking her finger through a little hole in the wall, feeling again how frightened she was when Mom jumped out of the moving car holding her so tightly it hurt.

"Anybody in there?" The outhouse door opened. It was Aunt Mary coming to take her safely back.

For a while, Verneda watched Mom put clothes in a big suitcase to the sound of my bawling. "Why don't you take that damn baby back where it come from?" Verneda shouted. Mom paid no attention but said to her, "Grandpa is sending us a bus ticket."

A bus ticket home: that's what my mother wanted. A ticket home to Poppa and Momma, home to the farm where she was born--miles away from Twin Falls, Idaho to Healy, Kansas. And that's what her Poppa sent her, a bus ticket home to a haven that promised temporary relief.

Chapter 3

Kansas
Early December 1937 – Late January 1938

What was once a model farm on the plains of Southwestern Kansas had been remorsefully changed. The magnificent Healy, Kansas home where my mother had been born, she burned to the ground one evening in late October 1931. A secret shared with no one but her sisters until the last days of their lives.

Now its replacement, a basement-like structure, sitting down in the earth with its windows just above ground level and barely visible on the landscape except for its roof, was the home of the Ross family. This is where my sister and I came with our mother to stay with her Poppa and Momma in Healy.

The Ross family at the basement house

"Why in the hell do you let that son-of-a-bitch run you around like that?" Mom's father Lowell yelled at her.

"Now Poppa, don't start on me, I'm not up to it."

"He dumps you, leaves you high and dry with a new baby. Just when you start makin' a go of it, he's back and messes you up. I told you to kick the bastard out and never let him back. No, you wouldn't listen to me, so look what you've gone and done. Had another baby you can't take care of!"

Mom turned away from her father. It was hard to hear the truth but even harder to hear it in harsh tones of criticism. She changed the subject, "I've gotta do some washin'. Where's Momma?"

"Don't know, probably still in bed. Been stayin' in bed again."

"I hoped Momma could help with the kids while I did the wash. I got sheets to hang and more dirty clothes to wash."

"Come on, Edna; sit for a minute," he said.

"Gotta take care of changing Vernetta's diaper," she said, avoiding his invitation. Get me that diaper over there," she said to Verneda. "I'm takin' you out to the washhouse after I change Vernetta. You can play out there in the buggy and watch your sister."

"Look what a big girl I am, Grandpa," Verneda said, holding up the diaper. "I got it for Mommy."

"You are a big girl and Grandpa loves you," he said, bending down to kiss her on the cheek.

Verneda was Lowell's first grandchild. She was extra special because my mother, his first and favorite daughter, had given birth to Verneda. He had other daughters. Eva was his stepdaughter, Pansie's only child from her first marriage. Eva was his most vigilant adversary. His second daughter was Mary, usually ignored by him except when he focused his anger on her after he'd had a drink or two. His youngest daughter, Nettie, had especially delighted him since age ten.

The washhouse, one of many outhouses on the farm, was right out the door of the basement house, just across the dirt driveway near the windmill. Mom already had sheets washing in water she had heated on the wood stove, water she had poured into the huge tub of the old washing machine that sat, I imagine, like a sentinel with its attached wringer rollers towering above the tub, as if on guard for trespassers.

"Climb up into that buggy," she told Verneda when they got into the washhouse, "You can play with them wooden clothespins but keep an eye on Vernetta, she'll be fallin' asleep soon." Verneda loved playing with the wooden clothespins that had the shapes of armless wooden dolls.

Mom took the sheets out of the washing machine, rolled them through the ringer to get the water out and put them in a basket. Verneda watched as Mom dumped the dirty clothes into the tub of water then pulled on a long arm that set the washing machine into motion. The old machine rattled and spit as the clothes got sucked under the churning water.

"I'm goin' out to hang these sheets." Mom was out the door faster than Verneda could say, "Mommy, it's makin' too much noise." Verneda stood up in the buggy and called again, "Mommy, Mommy," but no answer. "Stop that bawlin'," she yelled at me, her screaming baby sister.

"This old thing is too noisy!" Verneda said as she reached across to push a button she saw. The wringer rollers started going round and round. Everything got noisier. She put her hand on the wringer to try to stop it but instead, it drew her hand in. She tried to stop it with her other hand, but the wringer sucked it between the rollers as well. Now both hands were between the two moving rollers.

"Mommy, Mommy!" she screamed.

Mom, who was already on her way back to the washhouse came running, but when she saw Verneda's arms pulled in up to the elbow, she forgot about the roller release button. Instead, she pushed the reverse button, which caused the wringer to roll back over her arms in the opposite direction. "Mommy, it hurts so bad," four-year-old Verneda cried.

Mom looked at the two little red, bruised arms. The familiar numbness that often shut her off from feelings too overwhelming to experience helped deaden her pain, a comforting numbness that since childhood had come to her rescue. A casual observer might mistakenly think of her as not caring. Sometimes, however, it was anger that came to her rescue. An anger that kept at bay those feelings of helplessness she feared, hated most of all, feelings of desperation with no promise of relief beyond accepting the unacceptable.

"What's the matter, Edna," Pansie called from the house, awakened by the screams. Mom ran as she pushed the buggy that held a crying Verneda and a screaming Vernetta.

"Got to get her to the doctor!" she yelled.

With town only four miles away it wasn't long before the doctor was soothing away their worst fears. "Nope," the doctor said with finality. "No broken bones here. But we'll put your left arm in this little cradle until it gets better." With a smile on his face, he slipped Verneda's left arm into a sling as he said to her, "This will help you feel better and get well quicker."

"Vern called while you was gone," Lowell said to Mom when she returned. "He wanted to talk with you to tell you he's comin' to Kansas. I told the bastard to go to hell."

"When is he comin', Poppa?" Mom asked.

"Said something about next week to see you and Hannah. I told him you don't want nothin' to do with him. He's in and out of your life like some damn weed ya can't get rid of," Lowell shouted, like one in a jealous rage. "Thinks he can have ya any time he wants, treatin' ya like shit."

Mom didn't respond to her father's ravings. I'm sure she had her own mixed feelings to deal with. Lowell stormed up the basement stairs. She heard the car door slam, then the sound of the engine followed by crunching gravel on the driveway. "I guess Poppa's goin' into town." Pansie had gone into her bedroom, not hearing the despondent tone in her daughter's voice or the ringing of the phone.

"I need you to come home," she heard Vern say immediately after picking up the receiver. "Hannah will buy you a bus ticket. You can get on a bus and come back."

As always, whenever Vern made another one of his entrances into my mother's life, begging her to come back, she went back. Why didn't she take her father's advice? Was it love, or a lack of vision, or maybe an inability to see other choices when she told Vern, "We'll be comin' back soon. I'll talk to Hannah but don't call here again." With repeated assurances from Vern, she returned to Idaho. But Vern, he was still holding on to her and Kae at the same time, waiting for some internal voice to tell him, "Choose this very one."

Chapter 4

Idaho – Kansas – Idaho – Kansas – Idaho
End of January 1938 – November 1939

A drunk Vern picked up Mom, Verneda and me at the bus station. Mom hadn't been in the car long enough to get her seat warm before Vern got nasty. "So ya found yourself a boyfriend in Kansas!" he said accusingly. Before Mom could deny this untruth, he grabbed a handful of hair on the back of her head, pulling her painfully in his direction. He tried to slam her forehead into the dashboard, but Mom jabbed her elbow into his rib cage. Little Verneda screamed at him, "You stop hurting my Mommy." My crying joined the chorus of agonizing sounds.

"You're nothing but used goods, Edna," Vern said angrily. He swung the car over to the curb, leaned across Mom. Fumbling with her door handle, he yelled, "You ain't nothing but a goddamned whore! You ain't good for nothin'." He got Mom's door open. Nothin, ya hear me?" He gave her a shove. "Go on, git outta the car and take them two brats with ya."

Vern drove off, leaving my bewildered Mom with Verneda and me alone at night. A recessed storefront provided shelter for the three of us until morning when Mom turned to the only resource she had, Vern's brother Herman and his wife Mary.

"You stay with us until you can get back on your feet," Aunt Mary said. "We'll make do with what space we have." Uncle Herman often went along with whatever decision Mary made because for the two of them, she was the provider. "I think I can help you get a waitress job where I work," Aunt Mary added.

The following months must have challenged Mom almost beyond her ability to cope. What else might have motivated her to take the course of action she chose? When I was about thirteen months old, she contacted her parents in Healy. "Can I send the girls to you, Momma?" she asked on the phone. A long uncomfortable silence followed.

"Well how would you get them here?" Pansie said at last.

"I figure by train," Edna said, not knowing what her mother would think of the idea.

"By train! You think them little girls can travel alone almost 800 miles by *theirselves*?" Pansie asked in disbelief.

"I don't know what else to do Momma," Edna said, "I got no job. I can't git one and take care of the kids too. Verneda's almost five; she'll take care of Vernetta."

"There's a train change in Denver. Is Vernetta walkin' yet?" It was a gentle confrontation to bring some sense of reality to the proposal.

"Oh yeah, she started walkin' last month."

"I'm gonna put Poppa on the phone," Pansie said, overwhelmed by her daughter's predicament.

"What the hell's goin on Edna?" Lowell asked.

"Poppa, I need to send the girls home to you and Momma." Lowell heard the desperation in her voice.

"Well, Momma says we can do it. If you get 'em on the train, we can pick 'em up at Shields."

Our mother took Verneda and me to the train station with a small package she handed to Verneda. "You take care of your sister. Change her diaper like I showed you. You gotta get on a different train when ya get to Denver. The train man will help you."

Lowell and Pansie, along with their oldest son Jim and his wife Evelyn, sat in the car at Shields waiting for the arrival of the train. "Guess they're gonna have to flag the train to stop it," Jim said. "The train doesn't stop unless they do."

It wasn't long before the light of the train could be seen coming toward them through the darkness. "Let's wait out there on the platform," Evelyn suggested. The train came to a stop with a great hissing sound as if sighing in relief.

The porter stepped off the train with me held in his arms and Verneda by his side. "Are you Lowell and Pansie Ross?" he asked.

"Yes sir," Grandpa said as he took hold of Verneda's hand, and the porter handed me to my grandmother.

"Can I sit in the front seat by you, Grandpa?" Verneda asked, looking up at him.

"You get right on in there by me," Lowell answered as Pansie got in the front seat with me in her arms.

Verneda sat between her grandpa and grandma. As they started to drive toward Healy, she said, "Grandpa that man in that place where we eat--"

"Where was that?" Lowell asked.

"That place where they put us in another train to come to you."

"Well, that was Denver. What did you eat?" he asked.

"We had pancakes and sausage."

"That was a nice meal."

"Grandpa, I jist reached over and tapped the man next to me and asked him if he'd cut mine and sister's up. We didn't know how to cut it up." That man told me, 'Why sure I'll help you little girls out.'"

"That was a nice man, wasn't it?" A tired Lowell responded rather vacantly.

"I told him thank you, Grandpa."

"That's what a little lady should do," he said. Lowell lowered his window to let the freshness of the night air take away the drowsy feeling he had.

Evelyn was the first to see it after they got into the house and turned on the lights. "My God, them kids have got sores on their heads. That's the worst case of impetigo I ever saw in my life!" she said in disbelief. "We're gonna practically have to cut off all their hair to get rid of it."

"Chicken poop," Pansie said.

"Chicken poop?" Lowell asked.

"Chicken poop. Edna said them kids play out where the chickens poop. Causes impetigo," Pansie said.

About three months later in the month of February, Mom brought Verneda and me back to Twin Falls at the urging of her parents, living again close to Uncle Herman and Aunt Mary in one of the tar-paper shacks that overlook the Snake River at 410 Bell Street.

"Stay here with Vernetta while I'm gone and don't touch that stove, it's hot," Mom told Verneda as she crammed the last piece of wood into the big black stove. "I'm gonna go talk to Aunt Mary."

Verneda, five-years old, and I, sixteen months old, lay together in bed, across the room from the single door of the shack. There wasn't much else in the room other than some orange crates that Mom had nailed to the wall and, of course, the big black wood stove that sat on the left side of the door.

The first small lick of fire that danced on the wall of the shack didn't catch Verneda's attention. It wasn't until it had traveled up the wall behind the stove that she saw it. The flames momentarily mesmerized her as she watched dazzled by what she saw. But then, calmly walking over to the door, she opened it to look outside. "Nobody there," she said. Then, as if guided by a guardian angel, she went back to the bed.

"Common Netta, we gotta git outta here."

Verneda pulled me to the edge of the bed, wrapped her arms around my chest and with one last pull, off the bed I came. Verneda, put her arms once again around my chest. The shack had filled with fire and smoke, but my sister struggled backward with me toward the burning doorway where, still holding tightly to me, she fell backwards over the burning threshold.

Hearing the screams of neighbors, attracted by the dense smoke, Mom ran toward the fire just in time to see Verneda pull me out of the burning shack.

"Ouchie, Mommy, it hurts!" Verneda cried.

"What hurts," Mom asked as she took me in her arms.

"My foot."

"Let me see," Mom said. "Your foot got burned. It's gonna be all right. It's gonna be all right," Mom said again.

The shack stood burned and charred beyond livability, with the contents badly damaged or destroyed. Fire Chief Fred Perry informed Mom, "The blaze was apparently caused by an overheated stove located too close to the wall of the cabin." He looked down at Verneda and patted her head, "You're a little heroine. You saved your sister from the fire."

She looked up at him and said, "I just picked up my sister and walked out."

Mom left Verneda and me with our Aunt Mary that night. She went out to drink and dance away the nightmare of the day, her usual way of dealing with the pain in her life.

"Have you seen the paper, Edna?" Aunt Mary asked as she handed the newspaper to Mom the next day. "See, there's an article about the fire!"

"Well I'll be damned," Mom said as she read the bold title out loud, "5-YEAR-OLD-HEROINE SAVES SISTER IN FIRE." Mom started to read the article.

"Oh my God, they printed that: 'The husband, a WPA laborer, was at work at the time.' What if Vern reads that?"

"He don't live here, I just told that to the fireman," Mom said.

"Don't worry, Edna. It doesn't matter if he does. What does it matter?" Aunt Mary asked.

"The bastard might come over here and beat on me!" Mom said. "He comes over here drunk and beats the shit outta me, for no good reason. Whenever he feels like it!"

Aunt Mary didn't know how to respond other than telling her, "You and the girls can stay with us until you figure out what you're going to do, Edna."

But about two weeks later Mom told Mary, "I can't stay in Twin. The fire ruined everything. I got nothing! I'm takin' the kids and we're goin back to Kansas." A source of security, though distant, Kansas continued to draw my mother home.

Aunt Mary didn't try to dissuade her. "Do you want us to tell Vern where you are when he comes around asking?" Aunt Mary wanted to know.

Vern came around unannounced, less frequently now but when he did come, drunk or sober, a jealous rage usually came with him. My mother was a good-looking woman with dark curly hair and dark eyes to match. She stood about five feet four inches tall, with a beautiful figure. Attracting men came to her naturally just like the curl in her hair. Vern knew this and it made him jealous. He didn't want anyone else to have her even though he still didn't know if he wanted her. Through his brother Herman, Vern knew her every move, especially any boyfriends she might have. His sister Hannah unwittingly disclosed information to him whenever my mother was in Kansas.

"So, what do you think, Edna? Shall we tell him you went back to Kansas? Aunt Mary asked again.

"Tell him if you want, I don't give a damn."

Arrow points to shack that burned

Edna's farewell to Mary and Herman

Shortly after the fire in early March, Mom took us back to Kansas but the trip home to her parents was different this time. The many government loans taken out by Lowell and Pansie during the Depression against the Healy, Kansas farm were now coming due, but they had no money to pay. It was only a matter of time before they would lose it to foreclosure. As if to escape the inevitable, they had left the farm. Their oldest son, Jim and his wife Evelyn continued to live there until foreclosure forced them out.

Lowell and Pansie had moved to Larned, Kansas; the town where Pansie was born and raised. Here they worked and lived at the Larned State Hospital for the Criminally Insane, Pansie as a cook, Lowell as a guard. They had a very small apartment, much too small a living space to include Mother, Verneda and me.

Hannah, Vern's sister who lived on a farm in Dighton about an hour from Larned, told Mom, "Edna, there's a local farmer Kenneth and I know who needs a cook and maybe some cleaning. The job is yours if you want it. The girls can live on the farm with you."

Within weeks of taking the job to cook and clean for the farmer, after a phone call from Vern in late March my mother shoved me down hard in the highchair. "You goddamned big bawl baby, if you don't stop cryin', I'm gonna give you away," she threatened.

My sister, who had often heard such threats from our angry mother, paid no attention. But within a few days, Mom borrowed the farmer's car to drive over to Utica to talk with a woman she knew. Utica is a small town near Mom's childhood home of Healy and a reasonable drive from the farm where she now worked in Dighton. She took me with her but left Verneda with the farmer's wife. I was much too young to understand what was about to happen. It was a short time before my mother's death that she told me how she had given me away to a "nice lady in Utica, Kansas." Following is an elaboration of the sparse details Mother shared with me, along with memories my sister had of the event.

The Utica woman, whose grown daughter still lived at home, heard a knock on her door. Opening it, she said, "Well, Edna what a surprise to see you! And who is this standing on my porch with you?"

"She's my daughter, Vernetta."

"Well, isn't she a cutie," the woman said. "I heard about you and Vern. I'm so sorry."

"I'd like to come in to talk with you," Mom said with all the pleasantness she could muster.

"Why sure," the Utica woman responded, ushering Mom and me into the living room.

I'm sure Mom wanted to get right to why she had come but when asked about her parents, about the foreclosure on their farm, and about her brother Ralph, she politely answered as briefly as she could. She was relieved when the Utica woman said, "Now what was it you wanted to talk with me about?"

"You know I'm tryin to raise two little girls by myself. Vernetta's my youngest and needs someone to take care of her. I can't work and take care of her too. I wonder if you could keep her. Her sister can take care of herself while I'm workin'."

The Utica woman was not sure if she understood what Edna needed so she asked, "You mean you need me to take care of her for a few days?" Mom hesitated before she spoke, "No, I was wonderin' if you'd like to have her."

The woman was well acquainted with Edna's circumstances as well as that of her mother Pansie. She knew Pansie was unable to take in her own grandchild. With but a brief time to think about it, the woman answered, "You leave her with me, Edna. We'll see she's taken care of."

Very little was said before Mom walked out the door, leaving me behind. She had gotten rid of her burdensome "bawl baby". Pregnant with me when Vern met Kae; and abandoned by him from the time of my birth, I probably held no special place in her wounded heart.

When she returned alone, Verneda asked, "Where's my sister?"

"She's stayin' with some nice people." To distract Verneda from thinking about me, Mom told her, "You go get ready, we're gonna go see your Aunt Hannah."

At bedtime, Verneda asked again, "When is Netta comin home?"

"She's not comin' back for a long time. Now stop askin' me." Mom told her.

Verneda, a few months short of being six, didn't understand why I couldn't come back. It was only a day or two when once again she asked, "Is my sister gonna come back today?"

"No, she ain't comin' today," Mom said angrily.

Verneda started to cry, "I want her to come home."

A storm of anger escaped Mom's mouth as she shouted, "Shut up that bawlin'! She ain't comin' and I don't wanna hear another word about it."

Verneda stopped asking about me, her baby sister. Weeks ran to months, but Verneda hadn't forgotten. One day she told Mom tearfully, "I want my sister back. You go git her." Ignored by Mom, or so it seemed, Verneda became relentless in her crying and continued asking her to bring me back until late in October.

Shortly after my second birthday Mom said, "I don't know if we can git her back." That was the day Edna borrowed the farmer's big black square car and drove to Utica with Verneda in the backseat.

"Can I go in?" Verneda asked when Mom parked the car.
Mom said, "You wait in the car."
Verneda insisted, "But I wanna go in too."
"Shut your goddamned mouth and do as I say," Mom said in that angry voice that frightened her. After Mom went into the house, Verneda opened the car door and sat alone on the big back seat, waiting.

"Well, Edna; Vernetta has been with us for so long now, we don't see how we can let her go." I don't know how Mom convinced the "nice lady of Utica" to give me back, but eventually Mom made her way to the car with me in tow.

Verneda sat eagerly waiting for me to come. I climbed into the back seat and then scooted clear to the other side where I buried my face in the very far corner. My disappointed sister asked, "Why is Netta mad at me?" But Mom didn't answer. She simply started the car and drove back to the farm.

Edna 1939   Verneda and Vernetta 1939

The harvest was over, and the fields almost prepared for winter; soon the farmer would have no further need of Mom's help. Although her prospects were bleak, she couldn't turn to her parents, whose circumstances prevented their ability to help.

In dire straits she looked to help from a most unlikely source. "Mary," Mom said on the phone, "Have Vern call me."

"I'm gonna be out of a job with no money to take care of the kids. We ain't goin' to have a place to live. You need to send me some money," Mom told Vern boldly when he called. Back and forth they went until Vern finally conceded.

"I'll help support you and the kids if you come back." With no place else to turn, she once again misplaced her hope in Vern and returned to Idaho with my sister and me.

"That son-of-a-bitch Vern promised to give me some money to help with the kids if I'd come back, and he hasn't given me a dime! He's over there livin' high on the hog with that goddamned Kae Hicks." Usually not one for many words, Mom flooded Aunt Mary with a torrent of frustration.

"Let him go Edna," Aunt Mary said. "Try to get on with your life as best you can. You can't look to him for help. He's been comin' and goin' between the two of you for almost two years and kept your life in an uproar. Might be time to face it: Vern's gonna stay with Kae and …

"Yeah," Mom interrupted, "and the bastard hasn't given me a dime to help with the kids," she repeated with anguish in her voice.

Jarbidge, Nevada

Edna

Red Getchel

Chapter 5

Nevada
February 1940

In mid-February, about three months after Aunt Mary advised Mom to forget about Vern, Mom left my sister and me with Uncle Clarence and Aunt Mae because Red Getchel, a man she had met at the New Year's Eve dance in Twin Falls, extended an invitation. Many years later, Red's best friend, Roy Lee, became the source of details about the people, the mine, and the stores of Jarbidge as well as what he knew about my mother, my sister and me beyond my own memories of living in Jarbidge.

"Would you like to go to Jarbidge and keep house for me and my boy?" asked Red, a miner from Jarbidge, Nevada. A talkative man, Edna thought, but a nice kind of guy. Once happily married, Red's restless search for gold had caused him to leave his wife behind too many times. Now it was just Red and his eight-year-old son.

"Never been to Jarbidge," Edna answered without looking at Red, hoping she was wrong about his intentions. "I've been a lot of places but haven't been to Jarbridge." Red hesitated, then said, "It's called Jarbidge. Don't feel bad, most people who haven't been there call it Jarbridge. They want to put an "r" in it but there ain't no "r". It's just Jarbidge."

"I don't know, Red. Where in the hell is it?"

"Well, it's about ninety-two miles south from here just across the Idaho border into Nevada. Pretty drive all the way there this time of year. It's a little jewel of a mining town that sits down there in the canyon out of sight and far from the real world full of all its troubles."

He had Edna's attention, especially that part of "being far from the real world and its troubles." She was ready to let go of Vern and all the troubles connected to him. Edna thought that by leaving Twin Falls behind, maybe she could finally leave Vern behind, too. Opportunity with the face of Red Getchel on it was asking her to go to Jarbidge.

"Whatdya say, Edna?"

"Why hell, Red, I'll go to Jarbidge with ya if there's any chance of getting' a job and a place to live. I don't know about keeping house for ya. I kinda want my own place."

Red was quick to respond, "You know you can stay with me and my son 'til you know for sure you like Jarbidge. 'Til you get yourself settled if you decide to stay."

A few days later, Mom left my sister and me with Vern's brother Clarence and his wife Mae in Twin Falls. She left with Red to go to Jarbidge.

"I think you're gonna like Jarbidge, Edna," Red said.

"Are there a lotta people livin' there?" Edna asked.

"Nah. Used to be nearly twice as many people in the *big* minin' days but we only got about two hundred people in Jarbidge now. Most of 'em work at the mine, some of 'em run the stores in town." Red went on talking about the mine. "Gray Rock Mining Company runs the mine. Been in there since they sunk that three-compartment shaft, a shaft that goes straight down." Red paused, took a quick glance at Edna then continued, "I can tell you more about the mine, if I'm not borin' you."

"We got nothin else to do but drive and ride," Edna responded which Red took as encouragement to continue.

"That main compartment is for the skip, the men call it the bucket. That bucket's used to haul the men, ore and everything else up or down that shaft with a big cable. They got a ladder comin' up that second compartment so the men can get outta that mine in an emergency. On the other side of that shaft is a bunch of pipes like air pipes, ventilation pipes. Pumps: well them pumps! They got their own place, sittin' in a recessed side room," Red said, pausing to take in the scenery.

"You sure know a lot about that mine!" Edna exclaimed.

Red smiled at Edna, "Sure is nice of you to say that. We're almost to Rogerson where we turn off Highway 93. We'll be drivin' through the valley floor. Kinda deserted but I think you'll like the view. You can see the mountains in the distance. Kinda pretty. Do you like mountains?" Red asked.

"Have ya ever been to Kansas, Red? We ain't got any mountains. But I been through the Rockies. Is them the kind of mountains you're talkin' about?"

"No, you'll see 'em off in the distance, not as jagged or high. We'll be getting' to where we start goin' down into the canyon. Can't see it from here yet. Looks like we'll keep drivin' right through a flat desert, doesn't it?"

"Sure does look flat out here like there ain't nothin here but more of nothin," Edna said.

For a minute, Red got a faraway look in his eyes as he told Edna, "Jarbidge ain't a town you happen to stop at as you drive through on your way to somewheres else. Jarbidge is a place you go to deliberately. A *gold* minin town," he added.

Soon they began a gradual descent into the canyon. Eventually, they passed a beautiful dam whose waters sparkled in the sunlight. The canyon widened the further they went.

"Look there, Red, a river!"

Pleased with Edna's show of interest, he told her, "The Jarbidge River flows side by side with the road, right on into Jarbidge. Yeah, the river's gonna follow us right into town and keep on a flowin' right past the stores, the houses and even the mine, 'cause the mine sits close to that river on the other side from the houses."

The last gentle curve of the dirt road took Red and Edna into the bustling mining town where Red parked his truck in front of Johnny Insuenza's Bar. "Now sit a minute and I'll get that door," Red said as he ran around to open the truck door for Edna.

"Why are we stoppin' here, Red?" Edna asked as she looked around at the small conglomeration of wood buildings on either side of the road.

"This here's Johnny's. You can meet the whole town in here," Red said with a laugh. "Let's go in and get ourselves a beer." Immediately, Red spotted Kap Perkins talking to his best friend Roy Lee.

My mother didn't know that Roy Lee, the man she was about to meet, would become a part of her ongoing history for the rest of her life, along with Roy's wife, Vi and her brother, Bud. Though of less significance, she would meet Vi and Bud's brother Al Johnston who also worked the mines in Jarbidge.

While they waited for Kap to leave, Red told Edna about his friend, Roy. "He's an easygoing fella. Knows the comings and goings of people in Jarbidge because people like to talk with him. He's been the mail carrier here in Jarbidge since 1938, the same year he met and married his wife Vi then took her to live in Twin Falls. On Monday, Wednesday, and Friday, he comes all the way from Twin to deliver the mail, and a passenger or two, and then spends the night and part of the next day before goin' back to Twin. He still feels a part of the mine because the year before he got the mail contract, he helped sink that thousand-foot mineshaft." Red paused to see if Kap had a foot out the door yet so he could introduce Edna to Roy. "I guess Kap's gonna talk all afternoon," Red said then continued his story.

"Before Roy brought in a picture show machine, Jarbidge had only two entertainment choices: getting drunk or going to the dance. But when Alan set up his picture show machine in the Community Hall on Friday nights, he "packed the people in."

Kap Perkins was finally getting up to leave, so Red and Edna went right over. "Roy, I'd like you to meet Edna. She's gonna stay at my place 'til she decides if she likes it in Jarbidge and then try to find some work if she stays."

"Glad to meet you, Edna. This here is a pretty good guy to be associating with, but you probably already know that," Roy joked a bit, then in all seriousness he told Edna, "You know this is a rough little mining town, not really a place for a single woman."

"Now stop that, Roy," Red interrupted, "You'll plumb scare her away." Laughter relaxed the momentary tension. "Edna's got two little girls she'll be bringin' here before long if she stays," Red added, then changed the subject. "I'll be showin' her the sights after we have a beer."

Roy wished them well before he excused himself, "I'll be seein' you later."

"Are you ready for the tour?" Red asked when he saw that Edna had finished her beer.

"Won't take long." Edna said.

Red laughed. "Yeah, and don't need to drive to see it!" Red added.

"Right across the street is the Community Hall." Red pointed to an attractive wood building. That's where Roy has his picture shows on Friday nights, in one of the rooms. The big room is used for the dances. I know you like to dance!" Red teased with a silly grin. "We hire a live orchestra to play for the dances; means everybody chips in to help pay the cost. I'm warnin' you, if there is a dance goin on that night, you better be getting' yourself to it cause otherwise, they'll come to your house and get you, so you better go."

"Guess they like to dance same as us, Red."

"That there's the town jail." Red said as they walked past it next to the Community Hall. Remember that man talking to Roy? He's the jail keeper!"

"Why do they have a jail?"

"Cause them damned miners get drunk as skunks and get into brawls, so Kap throws them in there till they cool off and sober up."

Red stopped in front of another storefront, "This is the main store in town, run by Mrs. Beatty. Kinda like a grocery store but it's stuffed with everything and anything. Mrs. Beatty is an old timer, been here since the 1920's. Mr. Barry has a dry goods store right there next to Mrs. Beatty's store, mostly sells clothes. He's a little Jew with a big sense of humor. One of the miners came into his store one day and said, 'Mr. Barry, how much are your dollar watches? Mr. Barry thought a minute, 'Dollar and a half.' Red roared with laughter, but Edna stood with a confused look on her face.

"You get it?" he asked.

"Sure, but it don't seem very funny."

Red continued unfazed, "Notice the boardwalks in front of them stores? That's to keep the dirt and mud from the miner's boots outta the stores cause when it rains, we got lotsa mud." Red especially liked telling Edna, "The only place in Jarbidge to eat away from home is Mrs. Irvin's Boarding House. It's a café really, doesn't have no sleepin' quarters. There it is, right there across the street, backing up to the river. A lady or two in the town work there to help Mrs. Irvin run it."

"Maybe I could get a job workin' there."

Red didn't seem to hear Edna. "On up the road are places where people live. Some are small cabins, and some are a little fancier." He paused a moment, "My place is on the other end of town where we come in."

"Can we go on up the road to see them cabins," Edna asked.

"Sure!" Red said. "Then I can show you the mine. It's right across the river from the back side of the houses." It didn't take long to see the variety of small homes that lined each side of the street.

"Now this is the best part of all!" Red exclaimed as they approached the area of the mine. "That hole is a thousand-foot underground, a thousand foot," Red repeated as they stood looking down into the mineshaft. "One guy has the job of lowerin' the bucket that takes four guys into the mine at thirty miles per hour. Yeah, he lowers you down at thirty miles an hour and raises you up at thirty miles an hour."

Red stressed the last "thirty miles an hour" then looked at Edna to see if she was impressed but she just kind of shook her head and shrugged her shoulders a little and said, "Well, I'll be damned."

Red continued, "That mine is goin' full blast. We're workin a twelve-inch vein of gold ore there," Red paused, looking Edna in the eye as he punched out the last word, "gold." Thinking somehow to impress Edna even further, Red lowered his voice and said, "That mine is so wet, if you're workin down below and them pumps go out you better be figurin' on gittin' a way out of there because it's gonna flood and its gonna flood fast 'cause it's right down here on the river."

Edna tried to get interested in what Red was saying, but she wished he would stop talking. However, like the constant flow of the Jarbidge River, the stream of words continued to pour from his mouth. "Well, the mine shaft would fill with water if they didn't have them bunch of pumps runnin' to pump that water out. They pump that water from a thousand foot at the bottom up to the six-hundred-foot station and then on out to keep it from floodin'. If it weren't for them pumps, that hole would fill up with water and drown everybody in it."

Red's last few words suddenly caught Edna's attention. She listened intently as he explained, "Now if you hear a loud whistle blow during the day or night, don't be scared. It's only a Power Bump. When the power in the mine suddenly shuts off, a whistle blows. That means there's a power failure and them pumps have stopped workin'. That whistle signal tells the guy on duty to get down there pronto to start that standby electrical - those big diesel engines that feed power to the pumps - to start them up again, so the mine don't flood. We don't want no men drownin' down there in that hole."

Edna was relieved when Red dropped her off to spend some time with Blanche Johnston. "She's Roy Lee's sister-in-law and she's real nice. I think you'll like her. She's married to Al Johnston, a guy I work with in the mine; has a younger brother here, name's Bud, workin' the mine too. I told her you know how to pin curl hair."

Blanche was easy going. Edna liked listening to her talk as she made curls in Blanche's hair and secured each one with a pin. "You ain't been to the dance yet, Edna so let me tell ya. If there's a dance, you better go.

"Yeah, Red told me about that."

"You have to get used to that crowd in here. There ain't too many of us in Jarbidge that is really married like Al and me. Some of 'em go to the dance, see someone they like better, swap and go home together. That's just the way they do it here. Even the guy that runs the mine, him and his wife aren't married either and he's the head of mining here!"

"Well hell, Blanche, I'm stayin at Red's place. People will probably think we're shackin' up. I guess I fit right in." They both laughed.

"Edna, you wanna go out to Twin with me to git groceries? You could go in with me when I go 'bout onct a month," Blanche offered.

"That'd be good Blanche. I'd like that."

Two weeks later, Edna was pretty excited to tell Red her good news when he came home from the mine. "Mrs. Irvin gave me a job helpin' out at the Boardin' House. So, I guess I'll be stayin' in Jarbidge."

"You know you can stay with me at my place as long as you want."

"Blanche said there's a little cabin for rent. We're gonna look at it tomorrow, maybe rent it then pick up my kids next week."

"We can still go to the dance Saturday night, can't we?" Red asked. "That orchestra we like is comin'."

"Yeah, we're still goin' to the dance, Red."

When they arrived late at the dance Saturday night, things didn't go as Red and Edna might have expected. Edna, who always paid special attention to her hair, makeup and dress, looked especially attractive as Red moved her out onto the dance floor. One of the young miners, who had already danced with the few ladies that interested him, stood leaning against the wall, watching. Who is she? he asked himself because he knew all the women in Jarbidge. This one, he had never seen until now.

The music ended. He sipped his beer, shifted his weight, keeping his eye on her.

"The next one will be a slow one, ladies and gents," the orchestra leader announced. "So grab your partner while you can still see cause we're a-turnin' the lights down low."

Red took Edna out on the dance floor but soon felt a tap on his shoulder. "Hey Red," the young miner said, "Mind if I steal your woman away for the rest of the dance?"

Red stepped aside.

The young miner enfolded Edna in his arms, "I'm Bud. Bud Johnston. Nice to see such a pretty face come to town." As Bud glided her smoothly around the dance floor his embrace merged their bodies as if one in motion to the music. He kissed her softly on her face then whispered to her, "I don't know your name." Looking up to tell him her name, Edna's eyes met his. Without words, each one knew they were going home together.

Bud and Edna left the dance. Red went home alone. It was just as Blanche had said, "Go to the dance, see someone, and go home together."

Chapter 6

Nevada
March 1940 – July 1941

Rounded hills encompass Jarbidge, crisscrossing each other at different levels with one of them running right behind our tiny cabin; the cabin where my mother brought Verneda and me to live with her and a stranger named Bud. It was small, even to me, a child of almost three.

A large, upholstered chair sitting against a short, solid partition challenged anyone who came in the front door. Behind this partition was a double bed sitting opposite a small window where Mom and Bud slept. A second partition separated the main sleeping area from a cook stove and the canvas army cot where my sister and I slept, right next to the back door.

About two months later, when spring came to Jarbidge in May, fragrant purple flowers bloomed on a bush in front of our cabin. "Nee Nee, I got you a present," I said, handing her a branch I had taken from the bush.

"Those are lilac flowers. Mom told me," Verneda said. "Mom might get mad if you pick 'em."

"But I like 'em sooo much."

"Yeah, but don't *pick* em!" she ordered.

"What's wrong Mom? Are you sick?" Verneda asked a few weeks later as she watched Mom vomit into a bucket.

"Go on! Leave me alone!" she ordered. The next morning, it was the same thing, Mom vomiting.

Verneda dared to ask again, "What's wrong Mom?"

But before Mom could answer, she heaved into the bucket then looked up at Verneda and yelled, "Goddammit, I'm pregnant, I'm gonna have a baby! Now leave me alone."

"We got a new barber in town." Bud said to Mom the next morning. "He's been workin' with my brother Al in the mine during the day and he'll be cuttin' hair in the evenings pretty soon."

"So I won't be cuttin' your hair anymore?" Mom teased. Bud gave her a little kiss.

"The barber greases the pumps. Al's been tellin' the guy to walk the plank instead of jumpin' across the shaft, but he keeps on jumpin' across," Bud said.

An unbecoming scowl accompanied the irritation in Mom's voice. "Why are ya tellin' me?"

"I don't know, thought you might be interested in hearin' what goes on in the mine."

She watched him go out the door; whispering to herself, "Just a kid of twenty, don't wanna get married and I'm gonna have his baby! What am I a gonna do?"

About midway through that summer of 1940, the mine horn screeched its sharp, piercing cry: accident in the mine. Men, women and children came running, including my sister and me. As Al came up out of the mine, one of the miners asked him, "What the hell's goin' on, Al?"

"That barber, he jumped across the shaft. The crosshead come down and cut him right in two, and both halves of him dropped clear down a thousand foot to the bottom of the mine. He should have had better sense than that. Cut him right in two. I kept telling him to walk the plank instead of jumpin' across that shaft!"

Before Al could say anything more, a blood splattered Shorty Shaws came up out of the mine. Shorty was crying and talking at the same time, repeating himself over and over, "Cut him right in half. Cut him right in half." Al was the only one who was able to calm him enough to hear the rest of Shorty's story.

"I was workin down at the bottom when I saw something comin' right at me. Half of him dropped on one side of me then the other half almost landed on me. Cut him right in half, right in half. Some of the men are sending him up in the bucket." As soon as Shorty said the word bucket, a volcano of puke spewed out of him.

My sister and I along with other children watched them bring up the barber from the mineshaft. Because he was wrapped in a tarp or because people were too occupied, no one shooed us away. Men at the top of the shaft lifted the deceased barber out of the bucket and placed him on a stretcher.

"That's the doctor making sure he's really dead," Verneda whispered to her friends Ernie and Amy when one of the men bent over the stretcher to make certain the body was secure and well covered before the others lifted it into a truck to remove it from the area.

Edna

Later that day, Verneda, Ernie and Amy decided to play-act the accident next to the clothesline in the side yard of our cabin. "I'll be the barber," Verneda announced. "You can be the doctor," she told six-year-old Ernie and "I guess you can be a nurse," she decided after looking at five-year old Amy for a while. But Ernie had decided for himself the role he wanted to play. As they reenacted the scene, with Verneda lying on the ground to imitate the deceased barber on the stretcher, Ernie plopped down on her to create the second half of the barber who had been cut in two. Verneda was just about to tell Ernie "Get offa me!" when Mom came out the back door of our cabin with clothes to hang.

My pregnant, unmarried mother saw Ernie lying on top of Verneda. A vicious anger deeper than any child could comprehend exploded in Verneda's direction. "You goddamned kid, git your ass in here," she said as she hit Verneda on the side of the head. She shoved my sister into the cabin with a force that knocked her down onto the floor. She yanked her up by the arm and dragged her over to a belt that hung on a hook by the bed. "I'm gonna beat that shit outa you," she said as she raised the belt again and again against the back and bottom of my helpless sister.

"What did I do Mommy," cried Verneda.

Mom threw the belt on the bed then grabbed Verneda by the shoulders and shook her so hard that her head flopped back and forth on her neck. "You dirty little thing, you was doin' sex," Mom accused her.

My sister sobbed almost in a whisper, "No Momma, I didn't. You can ask Ernie."

Mom stormed out the back door. A frightened Ernie probably shook his head vigorously, saying yes to any and all questions our angry mother posed, because she soon returned and continued her tirade.

"That boy said you was doin' sex." She slapped Verneda across the face, "You git on that bed and don't you move from there 'til I get back!" Out the door she went, slamming it hard. Only the intermittent sobs of my sister broke the quietness that remained.

The events of summer were eclipsed by the coming of September. My sister was getting ready for her first day of school as a first grader. My mother took a picture that captured the two sisters: Verneda with her Shirley Temple curls wearing the sweet dress my mother had sewed and me standing beside her, clinging to her arm, my hair short and straight but poking up at odd angles willy-nilly.

First day of school

"You stay away from that school, ya hear me!" Mom warned me with voice, face, and hand when Verneda started walking up the road toward the school. "That teacher don't want ya there and she'll be mean to ya," Mom added before she went back into the cabin. With my fingers in my mouth, I stood at the fence post, watching my sister walk up the dirt road toward the school without me.

"I gotta go back to work," Mom told me when she came outside again. "You go on in the house now," were her final words before she walked away toward town. But I stayed by the fence post for a long time before I scuffed my way through the dirt of the yard and up onto the wooden porch. I opened the cabin door but quickly shut it, ran off the porch, past the fence post and up the dirt road to be with my sister.

I stepped into the doorway of the school. "Well, who do we have here?" the teacher said as she smiled at me. She knew very well who I was because everyone knew everyone else in Jarbidge, including the children.

Verneda jumped up and said, "She's my sister."

"Would you like to come in? the teacher asked me.

With my fingers in my mouth, I shook my head a vigorous yes.

"Come right down here on the front row. I'll give you a picture to color."

That day I fell in love with school. It was a warm safe place to be.

When Mom left me on the worn wooden porch that ran across the length of the tired, old farmhouse, I didn't know we were somewhere between Wakeene and Twin Falls at the home of Bud's brother Dewey.

A man with a large black bag went up the steps to the porch where I, almost three and a half years old, stood watching him on a cold February day in 1941.

"What's in your bag?" I asked him.

"I'm bringing the baby for your Mommy," he answered as he pulled open the screen door and knocked. I stood thinking of the baby in his bag as he walked into the house and the door closed behind him. I went over to the window next to the door where the man had gone. It reached low enough for me to see into the room where my mother lay in a big bed all by herself. I wanted to see the man open his bag and pull out the baby. "Why don't you come away from the window little girl," a nice lady said as she took my hand.

Later, I stood at the doorway of the room I had seen from the porch. Mom was still in the bed only now her hair was very wet, and she had a baby in her arms. Mom said to the man with the black bag, "We're gonna name him Buddy, Jr., after his father Bud."

When Buddy, Jr. was about two months old, my seven-year-old sister Verneda was left to take care of us, as she often was. How long Mom was gone, I'm not sure. I was too little to know where she had gone or why. The river was already swollen from the melting snows of spring when a steady rain began to fall. As the day wore on, the rain continued until the river overflowed its banks with waters that reached across the road almost to the front of our cabin.

"We can't stay here by ourselves," my sister said as she put the baby on the bed to change his diaper.

"What we gonna do, Nee Nee," I asked. She didn't answer. She bundled up the baby in her arms and opened our front door. Water was starting to creep toward our porch. "I'm scared!" I cried when I saw water everywhere.

"C'mon," my sister ordered as she stepped off the porch into the water. "We gotta walk in the water to get down to the stores." The baby started crying. "Stop cryin, Buddy," Verneda wailed. I started crying almost louder than Buddy, Jr. as water swirled around my ankles. "Ya gotta shut up that bawlin' and keep goin'," she insisted. It was hard to move very fast in the waters that flowed down the empty street toward the stores. "Where's everybody?" Verneda said out loud, with no answer from me.

Water lapped at the boardwalk that ran in front of the stores. We stopped at Mrs. Beatty's grocery store. The door opened before we could knock. We stood looking up at Mrs. Beatty. "Can we come in? We're scared of the water."

"Git on in here!" her welcoming voice boomed.

A fearful vision of cougars followed us in early summer a little after my sister finished first grade. She didn't know what a cougar was and neither did I. She heard Mom talking to someone about cougars.

"The weather is so bad, the cougars are comin down out of the mountains." Even though she didn't know what a cougar is, Verneda didn't ask Mom. She just thought about it. She had made a connection in her mind that cougars are gorillas, maybe by watching one of those picture shows Roy Lee showed on Friday nights like King Kong or Mighty Joe Young.

Cougars must have been on her mind the day we climbed the hill that sat behind our cabin. Weeds grew there this time of year taller than I was, but I followed my sister and her friend up the hill. We'd gone only a short distance when she suddenly darted past me running full speed with her friend right behind. They were both screaming, "Cougar, cougar!"

"Nee Nee, wait for me!" I yelled after her.

She ran ahead of me along the ridge of the hill, but before she started down, she turned and yelled again, "Cougar!"

"Wait," I cried. "Wait for me!" I ran in the tall weeds as fast as I could, but she was gone. I reached the path that led down off the hill, then sat on my bottom to scoot as fast as I could to get away from the cougar.

"You didn't wait for me!" I said, crying. "Why didn't you wait?"

"Because I was scared the cougar would get me," my sister answered. Always my keeper, fleeing in fear for herself, she had left me behind this time.

Soon after the cougar scare on the hill, my sister was taking care of Buddy and me at night when she became frightened again about the cougar.

"Wake up," she said as she shook me. "We're getting out of here."

"But it's dark time, Nee Nee," I said.

"I'm scared. I'm scared the cougars are gonna open the windows and come in to get us." Now I was frightened and started to cry. "Don't be a big bawl baby," she said as she got a blanket off our mom's bed. "Help me with the blanket. I gotta get the baby."

"It's dark; I'm scared," I told her, trying not to cry.

"We're gonna go outside where the lights are. We'll be okay out there where it's light."

My sister picked up Buddy, I carried the blanket, and we went out to the middle of the street under the light of a streetlamp. She lay the baby down in the dirt of the street then spread out the blanket.

"Now get on the blanket," she told me as she picked up the baby. "We're sittin' here 'til someone comes."

It was a hot summer day late in July of 1941. For a while, I watched the empty baby bottle roll around on the backseat floor of the car. Then I watched the fields go by, wondering why we couldn't have our baby anymore.

"Where's my baby brother?" my seven-year-old sister asked Mom.

"They took him away from me," Mom said.

"Who took him away?" Verneda asked.

"Vi took him, Bud's sister."

"But she can't have him, he's my brother!"

"She threatened to take you kids away too if I didn't let her have him," Mom said.

Verneda didn't ask any more questions. Mother offered no further discussion, no explanation. My baby brother, Buddy, Jr., was suddenly gone after being with us six months. Not quite four, I found a place to put such things, deep within myself. Unintentionally, that's where I put the memory of my brother. As time passed, that place became like the great waters of the north when winter comes. It simply froze over. Access to this frozen wilderness of myself lay unreachable for many years.

Chapter 7

Idaho
Early August 1941

Mother had a pattern. Peace and calm prevailed for a period of time followed by a crisis, which catapulted us off to somewhere else, either with her or without her. This time, soon after Buddy, Jr. was no longer a part of our lives and Bud had disappeared as well, she took us with her to Pocatello, Idaho. A friend from Jarbidge, with her six-year-old daughter, came to Pocatello with us. We all moved into a cheap hotel on the wrong side of town where Mom got a job working in a bar across the street and down the block from the hotel.

My sister's seven-year-old imagination worked overtime when it came to figuring out how to spend our days, left alone in the hotel room on the third floor.

"Help me move this mattress," she said to the six-year-old girl and me. That mattress floated off the bed and onto the floor with no help from me. "Now let's shove it over there," and shove it we did until it was right under the window. "We're gonna get this open so we can see down there," she said as she and the girl struggled to get the big double-casement window open just enough for us to stick our heads out.

"Nee, Nee I don't wanna look down; it's too scary," I said, as I ran to the other side of the room.

Down below was a man from the kitchen in a white dirty apron, smoking a cigarette. "Hey," my sister said. "Let's throw some water down there on him." She ran to the sink and filled a glass with water then stuck her arm out the open window. "Bombs away!" she yelled as they watched to see the splashing water hit the ground below. The guy looked up to see where the water came from and yelled back at us. "You kids stop that!" Verneda laughed her head off.

While she was throwing water on the kitchen employees, I was sitting on top of the box springs mattress playing with a bottle I had found.

"Gimme that," Verneda said as she grabbed it from me. "That's a bottle of whiskey. You found a bottle of whiskey," she said excitedly. "I better give it to the hotel clerk." So, she ran downstairs with the bottle and gave it to the clerk.

"That bottle of whiskey was mine," our mother said angrily when we told her the story.

The dog wash Verneda managed to set up in front of the hotel didn't last long but that didn't faze her because she was never without an idea of what we could do next.

"We're gonna go under the viaduct to those nice stores and see what they got."

I never had a choice. My sister was my keeper and where she went, I went. I followed her faithfully. In the store, she picked up things, looked at them, put them down.

"Pretty rings," she said as she picked up one, put it on her finger admiringly and slipped a few others into her pocket. I passively followed her to look at little decorated jeweled boxes. A store clerk approached Verneda.

"You know, that cabinet over there was full of rings a while ago. I think you better put them back."

"I was gonna put them back," my sister said defensively. She took the rings out of her pocket.

"I want you to come in to see me every day," the clerk said.

"Okay, I will," Vernetta said. Once outside, she took off at a run.

"Wait for me," I called after her.

"I ain't ever goin' back in that store!" she said, when we were under the viaduct on our way back to the hotel.

But the idea of stealing things stuck in her mind. "We can make money by stealin' things and sellin' em and you can help me," she said. By the time we had implemented her plan, we had quite a few things set up on the shelf of a ticket booth which sat in front of an abandoned movie house right across the street from the hotel. One of the most curious items was a little goldfish swimming in the water of a small glass bowl.

"Where in the hell did ya git this money," Mom asked when Verneda offered her the proceeds from our sales. Mom was always harping about money so that's why Verneda came up with the idea to sell stuff and give her the money.

"Some man jist gave it to me when we was goin' under the viaduct."

For some reason, that satisfied Mom. She had probably had one too many and any response would have made sense to her.

"Netta, ya gotta come with me. I forgot and left our stuff at the ticket booth," Verneda said to me as she shook me awake.

"I don't wanna go," I told her.

"No, ya hafta go with me. We gotta git our stuff." So I ran across the street with her but when we got there, everything was gone. Someone had stolen our stolen things.

"C'mon, we gotta git back," she said as she darted out between parked cars in front of me, right into the path of an oncoming car. The brakes squealed then I heard a thud. I froze between the parked cars when I saw my sister under a big black square car with a tire right at her head.

"Where's your mom, kid?" the man said to me when he got out of the car.

I shrugged my shoulders. "I don't know. Did you kill my sister, mister?" I cried. Verneda groaned as the man helped her get out from under the car. "Oh God, you're bleedin'! Let's get you to the hospital." A few stitches to her head later, we were back at the hotel. Mom was gone, working at the bar or out dancing.

"What are you doin? Can I help?" Verneda stopped cutting crepe paper and turned around. A scruffy looking man with greasy hair covering his ears stood uncomfortably close. "Can I help?" he asked again.

Even though she was in the hallway right outside our hotel door, she was scared. She has seen him before. She thought he lived at the end of the corridor. She fumbled for words that finally came. "Oh, we're gonna make some grass skirts so we can dance the hula."

"Anything I kin do to help?" he offered a third time, scratching at his crotch. Verneda didn't respond. Something

50

about him gave her the creeps. She was happy when he turned and walked away.

Our paper for the hula skirts was in beautiful bright colors. We shredded it part way and then tied the remaining solid section around our waists.

"We can hula dance by our ticket booth and maybe people will give us money," my sister said hopefully as she wrapped mine around me. Not long after we started our hula dance in front of the old, abandoned movie house, it began to rain.

"Jist keep dancing," she told me and so we did, as wet strands of crepe paper bled their colors in beautiful streaks down our legs.

Wooden benches with a decorative front sat at one end of the hotel corridor. Nearby on the wall was a little red box with glass on it. "It's a fire alarm thing," she told me after reading the sign. I think my sister was bored staying in that hotel day after day with me tagging around behind her, because this day as we walked down the corridor, she turned to me and said, "I'm gonna set off the fire alarm. Get ready to run under that bench."

Suddenly there was a loud clanging sound. My sister yelled at me, "Run for the bench." She scrambled in under the bench with me close behind where we watched to see what would happen. People came running out of their rooms and raced down the corridor. She laughed quietly and whispered to me "There goes that creepy man. Look at him run!"

"If those kids of yours do one more thing, I'm kickin' you out of this hotel!" the clerk shouted to my mother.

A few days later, my seven-year-old sister and I waved goodbye to Mom as we looked out the window of the Greyhound Bus that would take us back to our grandparents in Kansas. In the darkness of night, I could see her silhouette and that of a man who stood next to her. Feelings of indifference comforted me.

Children experience time differently from adults. What seems an eternity to children may in actuality be but a short time. Mom had taken us from Jarbidge directly to a brief stay at the hotel in Pocatello, but time stretched out for my sister and me to a length difficult for an adult to imagine. As that Greyhound Bus took me away from my mother once again, I was too young to be aware that I would never return to Jarbidge as a child, and I would never again return to Pocatello. I sang a song for myself as I watched the lights of the city disappear into the darkness of night -

"There'll be blue birds over
The white Cliffs of Dover
Tomorrow, just you wait and see.
There'll be love and laughter
And peace ever after,
Tomorrow just you wait and see.
The shepherd will tend his sheep
The flowers will bloom again
And Johnny will go to sleep
In his own little room again.
There'll be love and laughter
And peace ever after,
Tomorrow, just you wait and see."

Chapter 8

Kansas: Mid-August 1941 – Mid-November 1941
Wyoming: Mid-November 1941 – End November 1941
Idaho: December 1941 – End of February 1942
Utah: March 1942

It was in early August after Buddy, Jr. was no longer with us that Verneda and I rode away on the Greyhound Bus, once again returning to Kansas to stay with our grandparents. But my usually excellent memory noticeably forgot that I lived this time with my grandparents for at least three months on the grounds of the Larned State Hospital for the Criminally Insane. Many decades would pass before I understood for myself the possible significance of my forgetting.

A yellowed letter handwritten by my grandfather and found among my mother's things partially illuminates my forgotten span of time. The following uncorrected letter is exactly as he wrote it.

Larned Kans
Nov 3, 1941

Mr. John Elling

Dear sir and friend

I have notice of your garnishement and will say if you had written me you wouldn't had to do this. I was going to make up the two payments I missed this month. **I have had my two little grandchildren to take care of for about three months and I have gotten behind on everything that V. Shibers children they are going back home soon** if this goes through I may loose my job and one payment all you would get until I get another job and they are scarce for a man of my age. Now John I can borrow the money from a friend hear and send you the $6.00 I owe   and agred to pay Gus Noltie if you will stop the garnihe and let me no by return mail as I will send it so you could release my check without any further cost if this goes through I am afraid I will loose my job and winter coming on I don't think their will be much cost. I hope not.

Yours truly

LD Ross
State Hospital
Box 58

Kansas with Grandma and Grandpa

Maybe it was the threat of war that delayed my mother sending for us, not her own raging personal wars. Japan had bombed Pearl Harbor. Germany was marching its armies across Europe. With the instability of life deepening, my sister and I stayed longer with our grandparents in their tiny apartment on the grounds of the hospital.

My Mom and her half-sister Eva have a bond of tension between them, but if Aunt Eva hadn't eventually come to Larned from Rock Springs, Wyoming to visit her mother, Pansie, I don't know how much longer we would have stayed with our grandparents. "I'm tired, Eva. These girls need to go back to Edna," Grandma said as all two hundred pounds of her five-foot two-inch frame collapsed onto her upholstered chair. Eva thought for a moment. "I could take them back home with me. Edna can pick them up or send for them," she suggested.

Verneda watched as Aunt Eva started packing our clothes in a suitcase. "You're going to go home with me to Rock Springs," Aunt Eva said.

"Why are we gonna do that, and where is Rock Springs, and will Mom know where we are?" she demanded. Aunt Eva was a kind, intelligent woman who understood a child's need for information and explanations.

"Kansas is a very long distance from where your momma is in Idaho. I live right next to Idaho in Wyoming. It'll be easier for your momma to pick you up at my house." Once in Rock Springs, however, we stayed with Aunt Eva from the end of November through a cold, barren January and February of 1942.

"My goodness, Vernetta, you're so constipated. I'm going to give you something that will help," she said as she reached for a dark blue bottle. Aunt Eva's remedy for constipation was a healthy drink of Phillips Milk of Magnesia. "Now it doesn't taste real good, but you need to take this," she said as she handed me the glass. That nasty, chalky taste went down hard in my four-year old throat. "Here, honey, have a drink of water to wash it down," she said to me in a kindly tone. Even as a child, I experienced the contrast between Aunt Eva and my mother, who terrified me with various threats and actions until she was satisfied that I was potty trained.

Wyoming   Edna and Bud, Idaho

55

When Mom was finally willing or able for us to come to her, Aunt Eva put us on a bus to Boise. Leaving Rock Springs, in the southwest section of Wyoming, we traveled northwest about four hundred miles to Boise, but distance in miles was not a concept I understood. The names of places I had lived began to accumulate in my memory as if they were anchors to hold onto: Twin Falls, Larned, Jarbidge, Pocatello, Rock Springs. How each place related to the others geographically was also beyond my comprehension. But I did understand that a bus was taking me to my mother.

The attraction for Mother in Boise, Idaho was Bud. She had gotten back together with the love of her life, the father of her son, Buddy, Jr. The attraction for Bud to Boise was his brother Dewey, who lived there with his wife Grace and their three sons. Mom and Grace both worked together at a laundry close to a small house Mother rented. One day, Grace said to Mom, "Vi doesn't approve of an older divorced woman shackin' up with her little brother."

Even though Mom hadn't seen us for almost six months, there was no "huggy-kissy" reunion on our arrival. My mother rarely hugged or kissed Verneda and me. There was almost no tender physical contact between us but when she was angry, unwanted physical contact was a certainty.

Within a month of joining mother in Boise, Verneda and I along with Mom and Bud left for Salt Lake City with Clifford Hoffman, a man Bud had worked in the Jarbidge mine. The two men came to the agreement sometime around March of 1942 that Clifford would take us to his father's home in Salt Lake some three hundred miles away.

Mom was probably aware of the extra miles this move would put between her and Bud's sister Vi, who still had Buddy, Jr. and had renamed him Larry Gene. Maybe Mom didn't mind moving away because of what Grace said, "Vi doesn't approve of an older-divorced woman, shackin' up with her little brother." Roy Lee agreed with Vi, his wife. Years later, Roy talked with me about his personal experience in Jarbidge of Mom, my sister and me which helped partially explain their disapproval. One description lingers, "A drinkin' woman with two little girls, little girls who run hand in hand down the street with dirty, snotty noses, not taken care of at all." The tone in his voice suggested concern and sympathy more than judgment.

When we arrived in Salt Lake City, Bud, Mom, Verneda and I moved in with Clifford's father, Edward Hoffman, and his sister, Pat. Their modest house was at Fifth South and Second West, within walking distance of Temple Square. Clifford's father had his own room on the back porch off the kitchen. Pat had her room off the dining room. A double bed was set up in the living room for Mom and Bud. My sister and I slept end to end on an army cot in the corner of the dining room next to the kitchen door. The house had one tiny bathroom accessed from the kitchen.

Bud and Mom both got jobs right away at Huntsman Tin and Shield because Maxine, Edward Hoffman's other daughter, helped get them hired. But their new-found bliss was short-lived. One day in late March or very early April Vi, along with her older sister Mickey, came all the way from Twin Falls to Salt Lake City to shop, Vi innocently claimed. But it seems that her real intention was to talk her brother Bud into going back to Idaho with her because that's what happened. "Vi was a very persuasive woman, especially when it came to Bud," her husband Roy Lee reflected as we talked together about the past many years later.

Maxine, who became a childhood friend and continues to be a friend in my adult years, shared with me, "Bud was young, some would also say, unstable. It was easy for Vi to talk him into leaving. That afternoon, Bud left Salt Lake City with his sister Vi. He left your mother with no warning, no goodbye. He walked out on her and his new job without saying a word. For a time, your mother frequented the bars to try to mend her broken heart."

But the painful emptiness she felt must have driven Mom to a new plan. She sent my eight-year-old sister and me back to our grandparents shortly after Bud left. They still worked at the Larned State Hospital in Kansas, known by the locals as "The Bug House." They still had the same jobs: Grandma worked in the kitchen and Grandpa was a guard on one of the wards for the

Criminally Insane. Once Mom was free of the responsibility for us, she returned to Boise where she managed to get back together with Bud.

Edna, Vernetta and Verneda
Utah

Chapter 9

Utah
May 1942 – December 1942

    Our country was at war. Uncertainty hung over everyone's lives. Out of that uncertainty, Bud confided in Mom, "I joined the Navy today. I report to Salt Lake next week the twenty-eighth." Mom wasn't taken by surprise because for a period of days, she had argued against his volunteering for the Navy. Now she answered with a quiet reserve, "We'll go back to Salt Lake together." Bud and my mother traveled from Boise to Salt Lake City where on April 28, 1942, Bud officially became a sailor in the U.S. Navy.

    After Bud left, Mom stayed again in Salt Lake with Edward Hoffman in the same place we had stayed when we first came to Salt Lake with Bud. Mom had always called him "Pa" because that's what he wanted.

    "You stay with me, Edna," he told Mom after Bud reported for duty.

    "But I don't have any money to pay you. I need a job, Pa," Mom told him in earnest.

    "Ray could check at Burlington to see if they need any help," Maxine suggested when she stopped by to visit her father on the weekend. As a result, Mom got a job cleaning buses for Burlington Bus. Then in May, she received a letter from her father, reproduced here as he wrote it, without corrections. "Little girls" refers to my sister and me.

                          Larned, Kans   5-5-42

Dear Daughter
    We just got your welcome letter sure glad to hear from you sure hope you get that good job in Laundry. How are you anyway you old dear? I guess Mom wrote you everything and if you get that job will you have anything to keep house with sure wish we had some money so we could help out.

    But have been hear 3 years and 3 months and haven't saved anything. May quit some of these days and try something else. I will be 59 and 10 of this month. If I don't make it some of these days, it will be the Poor house for me. But I am a pretty lively old stiff. I like to dance. Mom said I never would grow up. I hate to quit hear because I don't do anything and haven't for 3 years. Don't know if I could work or not. I got to weigh 231 have come down to 218 have been dieting. We have been thinking of coming out that way this fall. I could sit in a Bug House most any time. Mom wants to quit she is tired of this **if you can take the little girls we will try and help a little.** I am paying on my operation. I am going to have my teeth pulled only a few left. Well Edna will close for this time. Be a good girl. Is there any work I could do out their what kind of work is their. If I had money to go in a restaurant or a Joint of some kind maybe we could make it. Well by by from your dad with love be sure and write I sure think of you a lot. Now be sure and write.

By the third week of May 1942, Mother arranged for us to join her in Salt Lake City. Some of my separations from Mother I remember vividly. Others I've forgotten, skipped over like rocks flying across the surface of a pond, nothing in between but blank spaces. Although I know I was with my grandparents a second time in Larned at the State Hospital for the Criminally Insane, I have no memory of it, forgotten the same as the first time - twice forgotten. But memories surrounding periods of forgotten time remain crystal clear, such as my experience of Edward Hoffman when I returned to Salt Lake City.

Grandpa Hoffman and Tudy
Verneda and Vernetta

"Call me Grandpa," he said to my sister and me as we sat at his kitchen table where he served us freshly baked bread with peanut butter and honey. He was really Tudy's grandpa, not mine, though I was the one who got to live with him. Tudy, two years younger than I, was lucky to have Maxine for a mom. She was just as kind and sweet as her father who was now my new grandpa, but not my real grandpa.

To me, Grandpa in his kitchen was a wonder to behold. I stood watching as flour puffs fell from his hand and covered the table in white.

"Grandpa," I asked, "do you have a wife?"

He poked around in his bread dough, "I had a wife," he gave a little whistle that made me laugh, "but she left a long, long time ago."

He wasn't much bigger than I, but I still had to look up when I asked him the question, "How old are you, Grandpa?"

"Why don't you guess," he said with a broad smile on his slightly wrinkled face. "I don't know, ya got white hair. Does that mean you're old?"

"Not necessarily, my little sugar plum," he said.

"Good, cause I didn't think you're old cause you're so fun," I said.

His room was right off the kitchen. I walked around his bed with wonder and amazement the first time I saw it. "Steps!

You got to climb steps to get on your bed," I said with glee. "How's come, Grandpa?" Grandpa's bed was lifted very high by large wooden blocks of wood he had placed under each leg.

"Used to be wasted space under there, my little pumpkin, but now I have a place to store things."

At the end of the kitchen counter, sat a wooden chair. "Vernetta, you got your goddamned shoes on the wrong feet again" my mother said as she picked me up and shoved me down on the chair. Monty, her new boyfriend stood behind her, watching. "Now git those shoes and socks off," she said with that ugly look on her face that told me she hated me. I got one shoe off. "My God, gimme that." She impatiently yanked at the other shoe, almost pulling me off the chair as she raged on at me. "Are you too stupid to know which shoe goes on which foot?" I didn't look at her. She jabbed at me with one of my shoes, "See if you can get this on the right foot."

There was no escape. I put a shoe on my bare foot.

"For Christ's sake," she said. "That shoe goes on the other foot." I carefully took the shoe and put it on my other foot. Of course, I knew on which foot to put the remaining shoe.

"Ya see that? That's right. Now take em off and git your socks back on."

My heart sank. I sat in fear. I wanted so much to ask, "Do the stockings have a right and wrong foot too?" I didn't know, but I didn't ask.

When I came to live with Grandpa Hoffman, he had already built an enormous tepee in the backyard. It was his way of storing the long pieces of logs and lumber he liked to collect. But it created an exciting place to play. One day I was in the backyard playing, or most likely, I was following along behind Verneda and her friends, when suddenly I had a strong urge, but instead of going into the house, I ran into the teepee. My sister came in shortly after.

"P-U-eeee" she said as she ran out yelling, "Grandpa, Grandpa come see what Vernetta did in the tepee."

At four and a half, I was young enough to be innocent but experienced enough to feel frightened that I had done something terribly wrong. Also, it hadn't been that long ago I had sat on the wooden kitchen chair with my shoes on the wrong feet.

When Grandpa came to see what I had done, much to my relief, he wasn't ugly and angry with me. Instead, he took me gently by the hand and led me out of the tepee. He didn't make me feel naughty or bad. There, as I stood outside the tepee, he knelt in front of me and in his German dialect clucked out sweet sounds of comfort and admonishment.

"Netta," he said, his big, round, grey-blue eyes looking seriously into mine, "now you know our tepee isn't a place for potty." The tears began to roll down my cheeks. Grandpa reached for his handkerchief and as he softly patted my cheeks dry he said, "There, there, Grandpa loves you."

A few days later, Grandpa was out in his backyard whistling and building.

"What are you makin'?" I asked.

"A surprise for you and Tudy, you watch and see."

I watched as he quickly built a large square open box of wood. Then he took a bicycle wheel and attached it to one side, right in the middle. Next, he put another bicycle wheel on the opposite side in the middle. He took two long boards and put one above each wheel. I laughed.

"Those look like arms, Grandpa." He hammered some more.

"There she is, all done." He wheeled it off the porch, placed it on the sidewalk then lifted me into the box. "It's a cart," he said proudly.

"But what does it do?" I asked. He stepped into the space between the arms and the cross bar he had hammered into place. With his back to the cart and his hands on the bar, he began an easy run. He pulled me out to the front of the house and back.

"When Tudy comes today," he said smiling at me, "I'll give you both a ride."

"Grandpa, can you take us for a ride in that thing you made?" I asked after Tudy came in the afternoon. With a broad smile on his face he said, "You and Tudy come to the backyard with me." After he took the cart from where he had leaned it against the fence he told us, "Now climb on in there." All Tudy did was stand there and say "Wow!" over and over.

"C'mon Tudy. Get in!" I shouted. But Tudy just stood there.

"Did you *make* that Grandpa?" he asked.

"Sure did. Now go on and get in. Grandpa's gonna take you and Netta for a ride."

Tudy and I giggled all the way from the backyard to the front of the house. When Grandpa began to pick up speed as he turned onto the main sidewalk that ran in front of the house, we held on tight. We flew past house after house, watching grandpa bounce up and down as he ran. Tudy and I bounced up and down as well when the wheels bumped over the lifted sidewalk parts but that's when we laughed the most. Grandpa made a turn at the end of the block to bring us back home.

"We wanna go some more, Grandpa," Tudy called.

"Grandpa is getting tired. We'll go again next time you come, Tudy," he said. "Promise," Tudy yelled.

I chimed in, "Promise, promise, Grandpa," Tudy and I sang in chorus.

After that, whenever Tudy came to play, Grandpa put the two of us in the cart and pulled us about the neighborhood for joyous, memorable rides.

In early September, the peaches Pat had left in the kitchen a week earlier were still sitting in the kitchen.

"Them peaches are gonna spoil," Mom said when she came home from cleaning buses. "I'll put them peaches up," she said to Grandpa who was just pulling a loaf of his bread out of the oven as I watched, hoping to get a piece while it was still warm.

"And if you leave that oven on," Mom said to Grandpa, "I'll bake you a peach pie." After telling Grandpa she'd bake him a peach pie, she turned to me.

"Here," she said as she handed me a red beret of felt, "I found this on one of the buses I cleaned today. You can have it." I loved her very much that day, she was so nice, almost happy, but that was my difficulty. I never knew which way Mom would be on any particular day, nice or mean.

"Wake-up!" Grandpa whispered loudly in my ear one wintry December morning, "Jack Frost was here last night!"

"Who's Jack Frost?" My eyes blinked away the sleep as Grandpa's face came sharply into focus. His full head of pure-white hair, his round red cheeks and his usually happy eyes always reminded me of Santa Claus. But this morning the red of his cheeks had a glow and the grey of his dancing eyes read blue.

"Let's go see what he left us," he said.

Grandpa swooped me up in his arms and carried me into the bathroom, whistling one of his tunes. As he whistled, Grandpa didn't just walk because Grandpa seldom walked. You might say we scurried into the bathroom.

"There it is!" Grandpa whispered in tones of awe fit for a cathedral. "Look at all the icy stars and shiny gems Jack Frost has left on our window."

While held in his arms, I saw for the first time the wonder of Jack Frost. Grandpa traced with his finger the meticulously carved ice-crystal beauties. The tiny bathroom had become transformed into a magnificent art gallery featuring one Jack Frost masterpiece. Grandpa became quiet while together we gazed at the window.

With Grandpa, I experienced myself as valued and loved. He became my security in the midst of my mother's personal turmoil. He was my father for a short time in my fatherless childhood.

"It's gonna be Christmas soon," Mom said as she handed Verneda a small rubber doll dressed in red velvet. "Here's yours, Vernetta," she said as she handed mine to me. "I sewed them dresses for the dolls." She continued, "We're goin' to Kansas to live with Grandpa and Grandma. You can play with your dolls on the way."

Mom was taking us back to Kansas to live with my real grandpa, grandma too, of course. I had to say goodbye to Grandpa Hoffman, Maxine and Tudy. In leaving them, perhaps for a time, I went to a place of numbness similar to where my mother lived.

Chapter 10

Kansas
December 1942 – April 1943

In the back seat of the taxi that drove us at night from the train station to Albert, sat my mother, my sister and five-year-old me, holding onto my doll. Monty didn't come with us.

Albert was a quiet town set amid Kansas wheat farmers. Main Street, about two blocks long, ran straight through it with a few tired and worn stores on each side. Humble homes sat at one end of the stores with a few homes beyond the alley behind the stores. Mother's parents, the Grandpa and Grandma Mom always sent us to stay with in Kansas, had left their jobs at the State Hospital in Larned, about thirty miles away, to run their newly purchased business, a bar masquerading as "The Albert Café."

Albert Café   Edna

Grandpa served the beer and whiskey from the long side of the L-shaped counter. "C'mon up here," he said when he saw me, "Grab one of them pickled pig's feet." A big old jar of pickled pig's feet sat on Grandpa's side of the counter. "Climb up there on that stool and sit your little-self right on the counter, honey. Go on," he urged, "Stick your hand right in that jar and pull one out." I sat on the counter eating, watching Grandpa. A question popped into my head.

"Where did all your hair go, Grandpa?" I asked him, noticing his bald head with only a little patch of hair that went from one ear, around the back of his head, to the other ear.

"Don't know. If I did, I'd go get it," he answered in pensive-serious tones I gullibly believed.

"Grandpa, if you find out where your hair went, I wanna go with you to get it back," I said after sitting there thinking and watching him. He moved over near the entry door to the cash register where he pushed a button. The drawer jumped open, "Do that again, Grandpa," I giggled, but Grandpa didn't pay any attention to me; he was counting his money.

Grandma, the Albert Café cook, came out of the kitchen with some plates, moving in the direction of one of the tables that sat in the floor space beyond the counters.

"I've got your eggs ready, Lowell," she told Grandpa. "Vernetta, you want a pancake?" she asked but didn't wait for me to answer. "Run up to the apartment and tell Verneda breakfast is ready." We all lived together in the small upstairs apartment, accessed from inside the café or from an exterior door on the front of the building. Either way, steep stairs challenged anyone going up to the apartment.

Grandma continued bringing food to the table, including grapefruit halves for each one of us.

"Grandma, do you like to cook?" I asked when she gave me my grapefruit.

"Go on, eat your grapefruit," she told me. I took a bite, scrunching up my face and swallowing quickly to get rid of its zing.

"I swallowed a seed," I cried out fearfully. Grandpa picked up on my fear.

"That seed is gonna go down in your tummy then it's gonna grow and grow then it's gonna come out your nose, your mouth, and your ears."

My five-year old imagination experienced every step of the germination and growth of that seed. I sat unrelieved of my terror as breakfast conversation shifted elsewhere. Looking at the remainder of the grapefruit on my plate, I pushed it away. No one noticed.

After breakfast, my sister asked me, "What's wrong with you. You've got that long face again!" I started to cry.

"The grapefruit seed is gonna grow and come out my ear." She interrupted my crying with raucous laughter.

"That grapefruit seed ain't gonna grow. Grandpa was teasin' you."

"He was?"

"Yeah, forget about it!" she told me then went running off.

Verneda and I were never alone in Albert because my grandmother was always there. But despite her constant presence, almost nothing about her comforted me, including the way she moved her short bulky frame with a heaviness equal to her girth, or her dark hair she pinned tightly in curls to the top of her head, or the way she looked at me with magnified brown eyes through her rimless glasses. When it wasn't serious or stern, her face was rather blank which was most of the time. She kept her words and her hands to herself.

I didn't know she didn't hug and kiss my mother and tell her she loved her when Mom was a little girl. Aunt Mary told me when I was all grown up, "No, uh uh, she wasn't that kind of person." I didn't know about the ulcer that troubled her because I was only a child. I didn't know she had already raised six children, and what a burden my sister and I must have been to her the great number of times Mom left us in her care, sometimes months at a time.

It was World War II. Air raids and blackouts were common across our country at that time. The practice of blacking out an entire area was an effort to thwart enemy planes from hitting targets, should they get over our country.

One evening Grandma went around turning out all the lights. I watched in curiosity then asked, "Why are you turning out the lights?"

"It's a blackout," she finally answered, probably to shut me up.

"What's a blackout Grandma?" I asked.

"We have to make it dark so the planes can't see us," she told me without emotion or concern as she pulled down all the shades. The room was dark except for the dim light coming from the kerosene lamp she had lighted.

"Take that flashlight and go get me your crayons," she said, "and bring me an old jar lid from the kitchen." I didn't know why she wanted these things, but I came running with them. "Put that jar lid on the floor furnace," she said. "Pick out one of your broken crayons and put it in the lid." I watched, not knowing what would happen.

"It's melting," I said in surprise.

"You can add one of a different color," she said. I watched in delight as swirls of colors melted together. Grandma had given us a bit of herself that evening.

"Grandma, Grandma!" I called as I ran past the counter in our café into the kitchen where she stood in front of the big black stove. She looked at me blankly, spatula in hand.

"I got a song I can sing! Do ya wanna hear it?" She didn't respond. "Do you wanna hear it, Grandma?" I asked again. She nodded her head. The kitchen filled with music from my heart.

"A sunbeam, a sunbeam, Jesus wants me for a sunbeam,"

"A sunbeam, a sunbeam, I'll be a sunbeam for Him."

I waited in silence. Grandma's eyes stayed fixed on the pancake. She put her spatula under the pancake then placed it on a plate. I stood looking up at her, expectantly. For a moment, just before she turned away and walked to the sink, she looked at me with a faint smile that brought tenderness to her somber face. Water flowed from the faucet. I ran out of the kitchen.

The child that ran out of the kitchen, after singing to Grandma, didn't know that Grandma had taught that song to my mother when she was a little girl. When I learned this as an adult, I wondered why Grandma didn't tell me? Why would that even be important to think about? I asked myself.

"Where's Grandpa?" I wanted to know when I got to the counter where he usually stood. "I'm gonna sing him my song."

Grandpa was a good audience for a song. He liked to pick me up and sit me down on the counter. "Now sing your grandpa a song," he'd say, smiling at me through his rimless glasses that looked exactly like Grandma's.

Sometimes Grandpa would drop a coin in our jukebox, select a song and then say to me, "Sing along with the record, honey. Grandpa wants to hear you sing." But that morning, I couldn't find him until I heard noise coming from the stair area. Just as I was about to go investigate, Grandpa came through the door and opened the cash register.

"Hey, what are you doin', Grandpa?" I asked.

"I'm tryin' to find something in the basement. You wanna come see?" We went out the door, past the bottom of the stairs leading to our apartment and through a door straight ahead.

"What is this place, Grandpa?" I asked.

"We store our stuff down here," he answered as he started going down a few stairs while I stood at the top, watching. A large plastic beer icon of a yellow crescent moon with a lady sitting on it caught my attention.

"Wow, a lady riding on the moon," I squealed in delight, "and a big giant peanut man with a black hat!" The rest was unattractive clutter to my young eyes. "I don't like the smell, Grandpa. I'm leavin'," I told him as I left the musty old basement and ran up the stairs to our apartment.

When I got to the apartment, Aunt Mary was talking to Mom. "There's something that looks like a roll of underwear on the stairway. Whose underwear and what's that doin' on the stairway?"

"That's Poppa's. He went out last night and got a mess of crabs." Mom's answer didn't make sense to me.

Surprised later to see my mother on the kitchen floor of our apartment with scissors and newspaper, I asked, "Watcha doin, Mom?"

"I'm cutting out a pattern," she said without looking up.

I skipped on through the kitchen and out the back door, not knowing what a pattern was. Saturday night before Mom put me to bed, she washed my hair then rolled it in curlers. My sister often had ringlets in her hair, but Mom usually let mine go straight, except for when she was going to have a special picture taken of me.

"Tomorrow," she said, "it's gonna be Easter."

"The Easter Bunny came last night. See if you can find what he left," Mom said when she woke us the next morning. My sister and I raced around the small apartment. I looked behind the couch where I saw a beautiful colored basket with candies and a stuffed toy. My sister found hers behind Grandma's chair.

"Now let's git you bathed and dressed," Mom said. When we came out of the bath, our bed was covered with new dresses she had made for each of us. They were full of gathers and beautiful colors.

"What's this," I asked as I picked up something in a plain dark color with a red lining.

"Them is capes I made for you kids," she explained. "Put your dress on, then put the cape on your shoulders." I loved my cape so much, but I loved my mom even more. "Get your capes on, then we're goin' outside; I want to take your picture." Verneda and I, with curls in our hair, wearing the newly stitched dresses and capes Mother had made for us, stood side by side, smiling happily at her. Mom snapped a picture.

Verneda and Vernetta

Chapter 11

Kansas
May 1943 – May 1944

Fairly soon after our arrival in Albert, Ferd came into our lives. He was a well-to-do farmer whose wife, home and land were not far from our café. His wrinkled skin had been sunbaked into crevices by the hot Kansas sun as he rode for hours on his tractor working the land. A deep red inverted triangle with the texture of a turkey neck sat unnoticed on his chest until he took off his shirt. Then it looked rather silly to me against the rest of his saggy white skin.

"He's an ugly old man," I told my sister, "Why does Mom like him?"

"It's none of our business!" she yelled back at me as she rode away on her bicycle.

Ferd led my mom, Verneda and me through the back door of his house into the kitchen. He stepped ahead of us into a bedroom right off the kitchen and turned on the light. "You kids can sleep in here," he said, pointing to a large double bed covered with an inviting floral-patterned spread. This was the first time I had ever been in Ferd's house. I wonder if Mom has been here before, I thought, walking into the bedroom. After we were alone, I turned to my sister and almost whispered to her.

"Gosh, this feels weird. Where's his wife?"

"How do I know!" was her curt response.

Late that night, the silent darkness was suddenly interrupted by the banging sound of the back door. Lights went on in the kitchen. I sat straight up in bed.

"Verneda, wake up! There's a woman throwing plates!"

"Probably Ferd's wife," my alarmed sister guessed as we watched the woman throw plates from the cupboard in the direction Mom and Ferd had gone when we went to bed.

Mom screamed at us as she flew past our room, headed in the direction of the back door, "Git yourselves outta there; we're leavin'!" Plates flew about our heads while screams and yelling filled our ears as we fled to follow Mom.

"Run, goddammit!" she yelled to Verneda and me. She ran for the tall wheat of the nearby field. I was the last one to catch up with her. "Sit down and shut up," she ordered, "and stay down." We watched from a safe distance in the darkness of the field. We waited quietly, almost frozen, until the lights in the house finally went out.

"Can we go?" Verneda dared to ask.

"I'll tell ya when we're gonna go," Mom said. At last, Mom took us through the wheat field to the nearby highway where a passing truck picked us up and dropped us at the Albert Café.

I'm not sure how Mom met Glen and Vi who lived close to Albert. Glen was also a farmer. Compared to Ferd, he and his wife Vi lived a meager existence. The old broken boards of his rundown farmhouse were hungry for repair and paint. It was a perfect picture of poverty. But Mom and Ferd liked to go there to drink with Glen. My mother was good at finding people to leave us with who had no children. Once again, she hit the jackpot with Glen and Vi.

Glen and Vi

"C'mon over here, Glen said to me, "I want to show ya something." He took a box down from the cupboard then pulled a fist full of saltine crackers out of it. "Now watch, 'cause I'm gonna show ya how to make something good to eat!" He smiled while energetically crunching the crackers up in a bowl. "The next thing ya do is put a lot of sugar on it, like this," he said, as if preparing a delicacy. "Then the last thing ya do is put enough milk on to cover the crackers." I watched as he added the milk. "Here," he offered, handing me a spoon - "Try some."

I took my first bite. "Mmm, that's good," I said. I was a kid who was really into sugar.

After my lesson on how to make a delicious bowl of crackers and milk, I wandered into the bedroom to see Vi.

"What's that?" I asked as I pointed to something on her bed.

"That's our featherbed," she said. "Would you like to try it?" I wasn't frightened of Vi. I could ask her questions, or I could tell her what I wanted, and she wouldn't get angry with me.

"Sure," I said. She put me up on the bed. "Now lie down. See what happens." I sank down into the featherbed with giggles of delight as it puffed up in great billows all around me. Getting off the bed, I pinched my nose. "Yuck, I smell something yucky." Vi reached down under the bed.

"Oh," she said casually. "That's our thundermug. I forgot to empty it." I looked at the smelly round pot filled with a mixture of brownish liquid and solid, swimming in soggy paper. "This is our indoor plumbing we use at night," she teased, then removed it from the room.

"Please, please," Verneda begged, when she found out Glen would be harvesting wheat. "Can we ride in the combine today?" Vi overheard the pleadings.

"Well, I don't know if it's safe."

"I wanna go, too," I chimed in, even though I hadn't the slightest idea what riding in a combine meant.

Glen and Vi went back and forth, then finally agreed. "If you promise to be really careful, you can go. You gotta hang on real tight. Don't go shootin' out the bottom," Glen warned. "Go on, climb up in there," Glen instructed Verneda when we got out to the field where the tractor was hooked to a strange contraption.

"Let me help you in there," Glen said as he lowered me down into the large round metal drum perfectly smooth inside with nothing to hold onto. I grabbed the top edge of the metal drum when Glen started the tractor. It wasn't long before the cut wheat poured into the top of the drum, swirled around us, flowed over us and almost completely covered us. It swished around in the large drum, then went pouring out the large hole in the bottom, threatening to whirl us down and out the treacherous hole.

"Them kids coulda been killed," I heard Grandma say when Mom told her about Verneda and me riding in the combine.

"Can't ya slow down," Mom said to Verneda after we came home from Glen and Vi's. "Poor little Vernetta, runnin her legs off tryin to catch you on your bicycle!" It surprised me that Mom even noticed.

My sister blasted me later. "I'm tired of you followin' me everywhere I go! You're nothin' but a tag-along. The faster you run the faster I'm gonna pedal. You'll never catch me."

It was only a day or two after the bicycle incident that Verneda had me alone across the street in a neighbor's house. "You're so stupid!" Verneda yelled at me then slapped me in the face.

"I didn't do nothin'." I started to cry.

"If it wasn't for you, I wouldn't get in trouble with Mom," she accused angrily, yanking on my hair. "Shut up that cryin', you big baby," she demanded, pinching me on my arm. I stood by the dining room table, trying not to cry, but I couldn't control the deep intermittent catch-breath sobs. "If ya don't shut up, I'll hit ya again," she threatened.

Truly, my sister owned me, a continuation of the many years I was in her care. Ownership continued that summer when she took me out to the garage, where distance from the café and our apartment created a safe zone for her clandestine ideas. An old round metal tub hung almost flat against the wall of the garage. She reached up to pull it away from the wall. "Look out the door to see if anyone is comin'," she said.

I peeked out the garage door and looked in the direction of the building. "Nobody comin'," I said as I ran back to see what she was doing. She reached into the tub with one hand, still holding it away from the wall with the other. "There, got it," she said as she pulled out a package of cigarettes.

"Wow, whatcha doin' with them?" I asked.

"Gonna smoke em, dummy, whatdaya think? You're gonna smoke one, too," she added. After she opened the package, she pulled out a cigarette and handed it to me. "You're gonna smoke this so you can't tell on me, 'cause you smoked too."

"But I don't want to," I protested.

"Then you have to take a puff, 'cause if you tell on me, I'll tell Mom you smoked too, and you'll be in trouble." I was trapped for sure, I thought. I took a puff of the cigarette because I innocently believed everything she told me.

Her ideas escalated into the realm of sex, probably helped along by Vernon, the boy who lived down the street. Across the dirt alley from our garage sat an old, weathered outhouse. Indoor plumbing had found its way into a lot of homes, rendering some of the outhouses as unused relics that no one bothered to tear down. This outhouse may have fallen into that category, but it was a nice two-seater that was reasonably free of debris and cobwebs.

"You have to come in, too," she said to me, opening the door of the outhouse as Vernon went in ahead of her. "Stand in the corner," she insisted when I got inside. Dutifully, I took my place in the corner. "Now pull your pants down so he can stick it in," she said. It was the same story as the cigarettes. The "I don't want to" from me was followed by "Ya gotta, 'cause then you can't tell Mom what I did, 'cause you did it too." She was a lot bigger than me, sometimes scary, too. I pulled my pants down. I stood there while Vernon poked at me with no success. "You can go but you better not tell Mom." I ran out of that outhouse as fast as I could, leaving my sister and Vernon behind. But it wasn't long before Vernon was taking me by myself to our garage.

"Let's get in the back seat of your grandpa's car," he said to me. Once we were inside the car, he asked, "Can ya take your overalls off?"

Overalls are pants made of denim with a bib on them, like farmers wear. Straps come up over the shoulders with metal eyes to slip over buttons on the bib. Vernon, at least four years older than I, started fumbling with the hooks on my bib.

"Lay down on your back," he said. After he had my overalls and my panties down around my feet, he got on top of me. I couldn't see what he was doing but I could feel it. I liked it very much, but he kept popping up and down to look out the back window of the car to see if someone was coming. Then after a while he said, "We better stop, before someone catches us." I got quite good at undoing the bib of my overalls in the backseat of Grandpa's car. "Here," he said one day when he took my hand, "put your finger right here."

"I don't know where to put it," I said.

"Let me show you." He put his finger on the shaft of my clitoris and wiggled it back and forth. "You try it," he said, "Doesn't that feel good."

Vernon gave me a thorough lesson in how to pleasure myself, but it never occurred to me to ask him, "How do you know all this stuff?" I was an excellent student despite how stupid Mom and Verneda kept telling me I was. Now I had two methods to make myself feel good, suck my thumb or pleasure myself. I was five.

"Some night, I'm gonna come up the back stairs to your place and I'm gonna come into your bedroom and fuck you," Vernon promised me one time when we were in the car. I thought it was a great idea.

Later that day, my mother told us, "You kids go git in the car. I'll be right there." My place was the back seat because my sister was always in the passenger seat next to Mom. This time, I didn't sit behind Mom's seat as usual, but I scooted over so I could see between the two front seats because I was eager to tell them something. I waited for Mom to get in the car then announced my good news, "Vernon's goin' to come to my bedroom some night to fuck me."

My mother turned on me with the fury of hell. "YOU DIRTY LITTLE..." began an endless stream of threats and obscenities fired at me. 'IF I EVER...," and "DON'T YOU EVER LET ME HEAR YOU SAY THAT WORD OR..." She threatened me as only she could threaten. Up the stairs she dragged me into the apartment, pushed me down the hall and into the bathroom. She said as she reached for the bar of soap, "Put this in your goddamned mouth..." The taste of soap was mild compared to her wrath. I got left behind that day to think about my crime. "Filthy" is what Mom said. I concluded that the word is dirty, the act is dirty. Why else would Mother be so upset?

I took one more trip to the car with Vernon after that. "Take off your pants," he directed as always. But I sat motionless, stared out the window, and didn't look at him. "C'mon," he paused for a moment, "Don't ya wanna do it?" I didn't speak but shifted my gaze to the back of the front seat. He reached out to take hold of the button on my overall bib. I pulled away. Vernon got out of the car.

Summer and Vernon came to an end about the same time I would start first grade, September of 1943. That's when my mother said, "I'm takin' you kids to get some shots before school starts and I don't want no damn bawl-baby, Vernetta. I'll git ya something if you don't cry," Mom promised me.

"I'm not a big baby. I'm not gonna cry," I assured her.

The building where the vaccinations were given had been an old store on Main Street. Now empty of its contents, it looked gigantic to my not quite six-year-old eyes. Children and people were everywhere. A nice man said to me, "You're such a pretty little girl. I'm going to put this right here," he pointed to the top and inside of my left leg, "where it won't show." I heard him explain to my mother how the smallpox vaccination would make a little circle with bumps in it. I watched as he rubbed my leg with some smelly cotton then reached for a needle. I quickly looked away, biting my lip when the stinging needle pierced the skin of my leg. I didn't cry, not because I didn't feel like crying, but because I wanted Mom to buy me something.

When we left the building where I got my shot, she was true to her word. Next door at the drugstore, I spotted three or four highchairs for dolls sitting on the highest shelf. "Can I have one of those?" I said, pointing up to the highchairs. My Mom nodded to the storekeeper. He climbed up a ladder and brought down two. One of them had a padded red seat and the other one had a plain wood seat.

"I want this one," I said without hesitation, as I placed my hand on the marvelous red seat.

"This one's jist as nice," Mom said with a scowl on her face and ice in her voice when her hand touched the plain wood seat.

"But I like this one best," I said, my hand still on the red seat.

Mom paid the man for the highchair with the red seat but when she got me out of the store, she let me have it. "Goddamned kid, gotta git the one that costs the most. What the hell do ya think, I'm made of money?" She opened the door on her side of the Coupe, pulled the seat forward and shoved me in the back as she snarled at me, "You're jist like the Schreiber's," comparing me with her first husband and in-laws. I slunk down behind the driver's seat so she couldn't see me. My sister was probably glad it was all directed at me instead of her. Mom bitched about the choice I had made most of the way home. At least, it felt like it.

School started with Verneda in fourth grade and me in first grade, both of us in the same room. "Class," the teacher began. "Your schoolbooks are stacked here in the front. I'll call one row at a time to come forward to pick up your books."

A student raised his hand. "Can we take them home?" he asked.

"Yes, these are your very own books for the school year," the teacher responded.

"We don't have books at our house," I told my new teacher when my row went to the front.

She patted me on the head. "Now you have some books of your own."

"Can you come sleep at our house Friday night," Rosita, a school friend of my sister asked within the first week of school.

"Yeah, if my mom will let me."

Mom didn't care, but she told Verneda, "You can go if Vernetta goes too." So, my sister and I went across the street to have a sleepover. When it came time for bed, Rosita's mother led the six of us into one bedroom. "You three girls sleep in the double bed against the wall," she said, indicating the two youngest girls and me. "Verneda, you can sleep with Rosita in this bed. Manuel will sleep in his bed."

After the lights were turned out and we were all talking and giggling, Manuel went over and got into bed with Verneda, and Rosita moved into his bed. When I saw him on top of my sister, I decided not to pay any attention. I lay in the dark wondering, why didn't she include me to make sure I'd keep my lips sealed.

A few days later, Verneda and I started scratching at our heads. "Come over here, let me see your head," Mom said to me. "Those goddamned Mexicans give ya lice," she grumbled. Mom poured stinky stuff all over our heads to kill the lice and their eggs. Mom put newspapers on the living room floor. "Stand on them newspapers," she ordered, "Bend over and hang your head down."

What an ordeal, practically standing on my head while Mom brushed lice out of my hair onto the newspaper. "Oh, shut up; I'm not hurtin' ya," she said when I complained. Not only was it a high price to pay for a sleepover, but I found out that Mom didn't think much of Mexicans. I wondered why she let us go there if she felt that way.

Two things came in the spring of 1944, hollyhocks and my Uncle Ralph. I must say that I prefer hollyhocks. Uncle Ralph, Mom's older brother, was on leave from the military. One of the siblings decided a family photo was needed. There was talk about it being dangerous to take a family photo because tragedy was known to strike after the photo of a whole family is taken. But whoever started the thought, lost out to those who decided to go ahead with the picture.

Everyone that wasn't there already showed up at Albert. Aunt Eva, Grandma's daughter and the oldest, came from Rock Springs, Wyoming. Uncle Jim, Grandpa and Grandma's first child, came from Rock Springs with Aunt Eva. Uncle Ralph, their second child, got drunk early in the morning and caused a commotion right up to the moment the picture was taken Edna, my mother, was their third child, their first daughter. Aunt Mary was the fourth child. Her conversation always included two subjects, money and her health. She had come from Dighton. Aunt Nettie was the fifth and last child. Where she came from, I'm not sure, but she was on her way to Maryland to join her husband Fritz who was in the military. The photo included Grandpa Lowell and Grandma Pansie, Eva, Jim, drunk Ralph, Edna, Mary and Nettie. No one else was invited to be in the picture. I didn't mind because I didn't want to take a chance on tragedy striking me down.

Front row: Ralph, Lowell, Pansie and Jim
Back Row: Eva, Mary, Nettie and Edna

Chapter 12

Kansas
June 1944 – February 1945

Patterns of sunlight and shade rippled up and over the front of the car, some danced their way through the windshield as I sat between Grandpa and Grandma in the front seat of the car watching rows of trees flow by on a late August day.

"Could you put that cigarette out, Lowell?" Grandma asked. "The smoke is making me feel sick."

"Me too, grandma. I feel sick to my stomach," I added. Grandpa threw his cigarette out the window. Everyone was happy, not because of the cigarette Grandpa threw out the window but because of what I heard the grown-ups talking about. "Now you won't have to stand on your feet for hours cookin'," Mom told Grandma.

"Movin to Larned is gonna be better for all of us," Grandma responded, almost cheerfully, I thought.

I didn't know the reason we left the Albert Café and moved to Larned, my grandmother's childhood home not quite 30 miles away. I didn't know it was because my grandma's rich Aunt Emma had died, leaving her a splendid sum of money.

Pansie and Lowell   Edna, Verneda, Vernetta

83

Grandpa opened the door of our new home on the corner of Fourth and Santa Fe, a small white house that to me looked like a mansion. With Grandma in front, moving so slow I thought she'd fall over, I couldn't see anything until she finally got through the door where she collapsed into a large, upholstered chair immediately inside the door on the right.

I wanted to run through the house to see everything, but Grandma cautioned me, "Wait 'til I catch my breath, Vernetta, then I'll show you the house."

Grandpa spoke up, "Come see my new radio," he beckoned. He turned a knob on a big brown thing sitting under the front room window. The sound of music filled the room. "That there is my new Philco console radio," he proudly announced, then sat in an upholstered chair next to it.

I ran over to the sofa and bounced on it a bit. "Better not bounce on that sofa," Grandma said. I noticed I could see into a bedroom when I sat on the sofa but something else caught my attention.

"What's this?" I asked, running excitedly across the room to a little fake fireplace that sat diagonally in the opposite corner from Grandma's chair. "Let me show ya," Grandpa said enthusiastically, lighting a match. Flames of fire filled the face of the little stove. "Now isn't that pretty!" Grandpa declared.

"I like it!" I squealed in delight.

The doors of glass next to the fireplace distracted me. I ran my hands over the bevels of the glass. "These are so beautiful!" I said in awe. Grandma pointed into the room beyond the glass doors.

"That's the bedroom where you kids will sleep."

"Can I go in there?" I asked her. She nodded yes as she continued to sit in her chair.

"Oh my! It has a big bed. Is that for Verneda and me to sleep in?!"

"That bed is for the two of you," Grandma confirmed. I looked out the window next to the bed.

"Our yard is so big and look at all those trees!" I whirled around in the room past the huge mirror sitting on top of a vanity, past the chest of drawers sitting almost in the corner near the French doors, whirled past the French doors and came to a stop at a small, closed door. "Is it okay if I open this door, Grandma?" She could see me from her chair pointing to the door.

"That's the door of the closet. You can open it." I peered into the empty closet, then saw a stream of light at the far end, to my right.

"Wow, the closet is like a long hallway!" I called out before I started running toward the light.

"Boo!" Grandpa said when I got to the other end of the closet. "Surprise!" Grandpa said. "Now you know where Grandma and I sleep. This is our bedroom."

"Grandpa," I said in surprise. "I went into the closet in my room then came out of the closet in your room!"

"That's just what you did, honey," he said.

"Where's the bathroom? I need to go pee-pee."

"Well, it's right here," he said, showing me the tiny bathroom within their bedroom.

"There's a silly window in that room, Grandpa." I said when I came out.

"Yeah, it is. If you were really tall, you could look through that window to see into the kitchen!" he teased.

Grandma appeared in the doorway. "Vernetta, this is a very special cabinet." I looked at the exquisite glass cabinet sitting next to her new vanity filled with all shapes and sizes of cats created in various materials. "You must stay away from it," she said with a stern look on her face.

"Can I play with one of the cats?" I inquired.

"Oh no!" she said. "Those are not toys for children. You must never touch them!"

I wandered out of Grandpa and Grandma's bedroom thinking about the serious consequences if I dared touch one of Grandma's fake cats and found myself in the dining room. Though separate from the living room, an opening almost as wide as the room itself connected the two.

"There's a kitty under the table," I called to Grandma.

"His name is Smokey. Better leave him alone 'til he gets used to you."

"He sure is cute and fluffy, looks like a big puff of smoke," I laughed.

"Now be careful around this table, Vernetta," Grandma cautioned once again, 'It's new and I don't want it scratched, or the sideboard," she added.

"What's a sideboard, Grandma?"

"This long piece of furniture here," she indicated the cabinet that sat against the common wall between the dining room and her bedroom.

The phone started ringing. It was in the dining room too, sitting on a little table that had a seat attached. I started to run to answer it, but Grandma said, "I'll get it." A few moments later she told me, "That was your mom. She and Verneda will be comin' soon."

"Where's Mom gonna sleep? On the couch in the living room?" I asked.

"No, your mom is gonna sleep in a room off the back porch."

"Can I see it?" I pleaded.

"Don't matter to me," Grandma said as she headed to her bedroom.

"But how do I get there?"

"Go on through the kitchen, out to the screened porch – there's a door into her room." The small room on the back of the house wasn't hard to find but it held no particular beauty that enthralled my six-year-old enthusiasm for our new home.

Grandma was in the kitchen when I came back into the house. "We're gonna have some lunch when your mom gets here. You can put the forks on the table."

At lunch, Mom told Grandma, "I got that waitress job at the Blue Goose."

"That's right close to home," Grandma said.

"Only two blocks down the street. I can walk to work." I was contemplating how happy Mom and Grandma looked when suddenly without warning, my sister kicked me under the table.

"Ouch!" I yelled. When I looked up, she made a face at me. Mom and Grandma kept talking. I went back to enjoying the happiness I saw on their faces, hoping my sister would quit bugging me. Despite the aggravation between Verneda and me that occasionally appeared from nowhere, happiness filled our home long after second grade started.

The week before I started second grade, Grandpa called to me from the dining room. "I want to show you how to plant beans."

"Where are we gonna plant beans, Grandpa?"

"Right here in this coffee can, honey," he proclaimed, holding up a large red can with soil in it. "Now take one of them lima beans outta the bag," he said, "Then put it right down in that dirt and cover it up."

"How's that?" I asked.

"Fine. Now take one more and stick it in there and cover it." When I finished planting the two beans, Grandpa told me, "Put that can on the windowsill there that looks out on our rain barrel, where the light is."

"What's it gonna do?" I asked.

"Pretty soon little sprouts will come up, then the vine will start to grow. We're gonna let it grow right into the little holes of the curtain and we'll train 'em to go in and out," he proudly revealed his plan for our beans. When Grandpa told me we would train the vines to go in and out of the little holes he was referring to the crisp new white-lace curtains that hung at the windows of the dining room.

The next day, Mom took Verneda and me downtown to buy our schoolbooks. In this small store, the perfume of new books filled the air. Books were everywhere we looked, books on shelves that went almost to the ceiling. Mom bought all the books I would need for the second grade and the ones Verneda would need for fifth grade.

"We're gonna go across the street to the drugstore," Mom said without telling us why.

"It's a soda fountain!" I said, jumping up and down when we went inside, "but it's bigger and better than the one in Albert."

"Let's sit over here, Mom suggested, moving us in the direction of a round table. What do ya want?" Mom asked.

"I'd like a chocolate soda, if that's okay," I said.

We sipped on our sodas, smiling at each other. It was a rare experience to be on a pleasant outing with our mother; she never once got mad at us for anything that day.

School began the day after Labor Day. My second-grade class shared our room with the first-grade students. It was near the end of the school day when it happened.

"Students, please stand at the side of your desks," the teacher instructed the first graders. She then told them, "John will lead you through the cloakroom. Be sure to pick up your coats and lunch pails. I'll stand at the classroom door where you will pass in front of me on your way to the stairs to go home."

I sat and watched row after row of students leave. Not understanding, I looked around at the second graders, still sitting, and I thought, well you can sit here but I'm leaving. I followed the last first grader through the cloakroom, past the coats and lunch pails, but as I started to walk past the teacher, she took hold of my arm.

"It isn't time for the second graders to go yet," she said, as laughter came from the sitting second graders. "The first graders leave earlier," she explained.

"Is Edna ready?" Ferd asked when Grandma opened the front door. I saw a scowl on Grandma's face when she answered him.

"It's best you don't come to the house, Ferd. You're a married man. I'll send Edna out if you don't mind waiting in your truck." Grandma shut the door.

We watched Ferd walk down the sidewalk, back to his truck. Larned was an easy drive for him from Albert and now that the harvest was over and his fields were prepared for winter, Ferd came to see Mom any time he wanted.

Late that night when Verneda and I were asleep, the lamp in our bedroom went on. Mom was sitting on the edge of our bed crying. She picked up a little round music box that sat on the vanity. "I'm just the black sheep of the family," she cried as she turned the key on the bottom of the box. "The black sheep of the family," she repeated as she removed the round lid of the music box, then took out the pink powder puff tucked inside. She stroked her face with the puff and the tinkling music of the box slowly came to a stop as once again she repeated, "Just the black sheep of the family."

I wondered, what does it mean, the black sheep of the family? I didn't know, but I was sad because it made my mother very sad.

"What's wrong with Mom," I asked Verneda after she left the room.

"She's drunk. Go back to sleep," she ordered, turning away from me.

I understood, 'Mom's drunk.' I lay in the dark thinking about my mom.

On the weekend, Grandpa took me with him four blocks down Santa Fe Street, the brick road that ran past our house, to the rental property on Eighth Street that he and Grandma had bought with some of Aunt Emma's money.

"This here is my granddaughter," Grandpa said to the renter who, at the time, I didn't know would eventually become my mother's closest friend.

I looked at her jet-black hair and then her facial features and skin color. "You look like an Indian," I started to say to her but before I could, she said to me, "Hi, I'm Lucky. "I've got a daughter Shirley just about your age."

"You got three daughters, don't you?" Grandpa inquired.

"Jerry and Pat's my two oldest," Lucky said, kind of proud, I thought.

"Probably about the age of my oldest granddaughter, Verneda." It was all very boring to me, and I was glad when Grandpa announced, "Time for us to head home."

When we got home, Grandpa took out his wallet and began taking everything out of it while I sat on the ottoman and watched. "I told ya you could have this, if ya want it," he said, continuing to empty the contents of his wallet. "But ya can't have it for nothing," he continued. "Ya have to sing me that rain barrel song."

I was excited about the wallet and more than willing to sing for Grandpa to get it.

> "Oh Playmate, come out and play with me,
> And bring your dollies three
> Climb up my apple tree
> Look down my rain barrel
> Slide down my cellar door
> And we'll be jolly friends
> Forever more."

I stopped singing. "Now sing that other part," Grandpa insisted.

> "I don't want to play in your yard
> I don't like you anymore
> You'll be sorry
> When you see me
> Sliding down our cellar door.
> You can't holler down our rain barrel
> You can't climb our apple tree
> I don't want to play in your yard
> If you can't be good to me."

"Here you go, honey. The wallet is all yours." I gladly took it, then skipped my way to my Tea Cupboard, sitting in the dining room right next to the kitchen door.

Mom had taken two wooden orange crates, set them on end, then added a third one horizontal across the top of the other two. Across the bottom she hung a lovely curtain that she had made herself.

"You can put your play dishes in here," Mom had told me after it was all done. I wanted to give her a big hug and kiss, but Mom wasn't much for hugs and kisses.

"I don't understand it," I heard Mom say to Grandma in the kitchen, "Vernetta plays so well by herself, but put the two of em together...". She was talking about Verneda and me. I listened as I continued playing with my Tea Cupboard.

"Well, better git back to the Blue Goose," I heard Mom say to Grandma.

"Bye Mom," I said to her as she passed me on her way to the front door.

After Mom left, Grandma sat in her chair to crochet. That's what she did when she wasn't in the kitchen. Tired of playing in my Tea Cupboard, I went into the living room. Smokey came and sat on the arm of Grandma's chair. He batted at her thread with one paw. Grandma had tender exchanges with Smokey, spoken too softly for me to hear, but the cat must have heard it because his purring was so loud that even I could hear it. I sat perplexed on the living room floor as I watched Grandma crocheting and talking to her cat.

"She has so much to say to her cat," I thought, "but nothing to say to me. Or anyone else as far as I can tell. But I'm only a second grader, what do I know?"

Sometime in October, I woke up late at night. "I'm sick!" I cried. I called out, "Mom" but no one came. I poked at my sister, "I'm sick."

Just as Mom came through the French door, I sat up in bed and spewed vomit onto the wood floor. "Why in the hell didn't ya git to the bathroom?" Mom asked. She grumbled something about "middle of the night...goddamned kid." Then she raised her voice, "The next time ya git sick, git your ass to the bathroom." As she cleaned up the vomit, she continued to bitch at me, "I gotta git up early to git to work." She stormed out of the room. This is probably one of those times she was thinking about that "Son-of-a bitch Vern" and the fact he didn't send even a "dime" to help her with us kids. But, I blamed myself that night for vomiting on the floor.

The house was empty except for Grandma and me when Grandpa came home late in the evening. "You're drunk,

Lowell," Grandma said. He flopped down on the bed and passed out. I watched her start to untie his shoe.

"I'll help, Grandma," I said. As I moved to untie the other shoe, an enormous, big sole looked me in the face.

"Careful, he might kick ya." I sure didn't want to get kicked, but it didn't seem like a problem to me because Grandpa didn't move a muscle once he flopped down on the bed. Grandpa and Mom sure do like to drink, I thought as I watched Grandma try to undress him.

The next morning, snow from the mild winter storm of the night before covered the school grounds with fresh flaky deep whiteness.

"C'mon!" Steve Fox, my best friend in second grade, called to me. "Let's make a snow angel." He fell backward into the white softness and lay flat on his back as he moved his arms in wide arcs up and down at his sides. When he carefully got up, he said to me "It's a snow angel!"

"Let me try," I said as I copied what I had seen him do, then stood up, filled with wonder at our angel creations.

"We don't have to come back to school until Christmas is over but maybe you can come over to go sledding."

"Sledding?"

"Yeah. They shut down my street for sledding on the hill." Sledding with Steve and our friends from school brought us to the brink of Christmas.

Mom came out of the kitchen with a plate full of cookies. "You kids want a cookie?" she asked. "You can only have one cause the rest are for Santa Claus." Our Christmas tree with its colored balls, its silvery foil icicles and its beautiful colored lights stood in the front window of the living room, next to the console radio. Mom placed the cookies on the coffee table. She smiled at me.

"Santa Claus comes tonight. The milk and cookies are for him." That night, Mom slept on the sofa. Happiness filled our hearts as we went to sleep with high expectations of what morning would bring.

On Christmas morning I was the first one to dash into the living room. There by the coffee table my dreams had come true. The dolly bed I had wanted with a new dolly baby sleeping under soft flannel blankets of pastel colors was right there, in my living room. "Look what Santa brought, look! Oh, no cookies. Santa ate all the cookies!" I yelled as my sleepy Mom watched.

By contrast, February was not fun. A lot of the children in our area were having surgery for tonsil removal, and in February my sister and I were wheeled into surgery. The process didn't seem scary, probably because I was too young to visualize the procedure. First came what felt like a toilet plunger put over my nose and mouth, followed by an awful smell, which I later learned was a gas called ether. I woke up in a "cage," a bed with tall bars all around it, in a very dark room. My sister and I groaned in harmony as we experienced the rawness of our throats.

"They won't be able to eat for a few days," the doctor said to my mother, "but the cool of milkshakes will help sooth their sore throats.

The milkshakes were almost the best part of having my tonsils removed. The very best part was the gift of two Golden Books. I'm not sure who gave them to me, or if they knew I was a second grader who could read quite well. But after reading them over and over from cover to cover, I said to my grandma who was sitting in her chair, "I wish I had some more books to read!" I'm not sure if she heard me.

Chapter 13

Kansas
Mid-March 1945 – Mid April 1945

Satin ribbons of contentedness connected one day to another for a month or so until Monday evening March 12, 1945. After our move to Larned, my mother's frequent absences hadn't been noticed too much by my sister and me because our grandmother was always with us. But on the evening of March twelve, change came with an argument that started in the dining room.

"Come on!" Mom yelled at my sister and me from the dining room, "We're gittin' outta here."

We scrambled out of the bedroom in time to see Mom headed for the back door with Grandma right behind. Across the screened porch and out into the yard they went with Grandpa, Ferd and us kids following close behind. Words flew like sparks of flashing fire. Mom slapped Grandma hard in the face; her glasses fell to the ground.

The content of the argument between Grandma and Mom, the reason they argued, became lost to me in a blur of emotions. Grandma would only have had to say some small something of a truth for it to sting its way into Mother's feelings, provoking the rage she had felt toward Grandma that evening. I had learned from living with Mom the need to tiptoe carefully around whatever the subject might be when talking with her. The least little thing could earn easy access to her anger. I don't know what the last angry words were that Grandma heard from my mother as we left her and Grandpa standing in the side yard.

Ferd drove us to Albert where we stayed with Glen and Vi. The next morning, Tuesday, March thirteenth, Mom took us to the one-room country school outside of Albert, enrolled us, then left us there. After school, we walked three miles on a dusty road to Glen and Vi's. The next day at school, Wednesday, March fourteenth, the teacher came to my sister after lunch.

"Take this message home to your mother, she said. "Mrs. Ross is in the hospital.'"

When we got back to Vi's from school, Verneda told Mom, "My teacher said to give you the message that Mrs. Ross is in the hospital."

"No, No! For Christ's sake, you got it wrong. They don't mean Mom; they must mean Dad." She turned to Vi, "Dad was goin to git some tests done in Wichita. They must've found something."

Since there was no phone at Vi's, Mom left to go to town. She didn't come back for us until Sunday morning, March eighteenth. "Grandma died," she said unemotionally, "I'm takin you to the funeral today." She discussed it no further.

"We're stopping by the house to change your clothes," she said when we arrived in Larned. As she parked in front of the house Mom gave us a non-negotiable order. "Eva is sittin in her car on the side of the house. I got the house locked so she can't get in. Don't let her in."

Verneda and I knew better than to say anything, but it was hard to keep back the question, why can't Aunt Eva come in, Mom? I ran into my bedroom to look out the window. Sure enough, Aunt Eva was sitting out there in her car, parked on Santa Fe Street. I like Aunt Eva. I wish we didn't have to lock her out of our house, I wanted to say to Mom.

We got to the funeral parlor early. My grandmother lay in the open casket at the center front of the room. An abundance of fragrant flowers covered the casket with beauty. The metal folding chairs put orderly in their place still sat empty, waiting. Aunt Hannah and I sat down in the second row.

While Mom and Aunt Nettie stood at the casket looking at Grandma, I said to Aunt Hannah, "I'm gonna go up and see Grandma too." Nettie was saying to my dead Grandma, "Now no one will ever know, Momma. No one will ever know." I wasn't sure what "no one would never know" but when Mom and Aunt Nettie went over to talk with a man I had never seen, I looked into the casket to see my grandmother.

I looked at her black hair, neatly rolled as usual into the familiar tight curls that always surrounded her face. She's wearing glasses, I almost said out loud. I thought Mom broke them, I whispered to myself. At age seven and a half, I had never seen a dead person. She lay so still, so quiet as if asleep. I touched her arm. I turned in surprise and shock, quickly running back to my Aunt Hannah, saying as I went, "She's cold, Aunt Hannah, she's cold!"

My words and voice caught Mom's attention. She yanked me by the arm.

"You sit and keep your goddamned mouth shut," she ordered as she pushed me down onto the chair next to Aunt Hannah. My body stayed sitting on the chair despite my wish to be somewhere else.

"We're leaving now, Vernetta," Aunt Hannah said an eternity later. "You come with me."

"Where are we goin', Aunt Hannah?"

"Up to the cemetery, honey."

Everyone, except Uncle Ralph, who was still in the army and couldn't get leave to come home for his mother's funeral, went to the Larned Cemetery located at the top of the hill a mile or so from our home.

The casket was surrounded with people listening to the pastor, who was saying nice things about my grandmother. I snuggled against my Aunt Hannah.

"The Lord is my shepherd," the pastor began as the coffin was slowly being lowered down into the earth. "I shall not want."

I stayed close to Aunt Hannah's side, a little wooden stick that shed no tears, too young to contemplate the reason. Maybe I felt that I had lived on the outside of my grandmother's heart or maybe only an empty shell resembling me stood there at the graveside.

"And I shall dwell in the house of the Lord forever. Amen," concluded the pastor.

Lowell, Jim, Mary, Edna
Nettie, Eva

    The people flowed right off the top of that hill into our house. It quickly filled with relatives, then emptied by evening as if no one had ever been there except Lisa and me. There we were, Lisa, a baby, and me a second grader, alone midst the remains of the day. Lisa began to cry. I tried to remember what Mom had said, "Here's the diapers, the bottle is in the fridge. We'll be at the bar." Because Lisa was her baby, "Aunt Nettie said, "I better give her the number, Edna."

    Lisa cried louder. I went to the fridge to get a bottle. I held the nipple to Lisa's mouth. She sucked long enough to get a good drink of cold milk then shoved the bottle away. "If you don't want the milk, maybe you're wet," I said.

    The diaper was a large cloth triangle. I wasn't sure how to make it work. The old diaper must come off first, I decided. A large safety pin was on either side of it. "I can't get the pin open," I said to Lisa who was still crying. The cloth of the diaper was thick and in-the-way, but eventually I got the pins opened and removed. I placed naked Lila on the new cloth triangle, took the pin and shoved it into the cloth. That pin went straight through the cloth and right into Lisa's skin. Ear piercing screams shattered my efforts. I looked at the big scary-red welt on her side and then went running for the telephone.

"Jo's Bar," the man at the end of the line said.

"Can you get my mom on the phone," I asked, trying not to cry.

"I stuck Lisa with a pin, it's all red, she's cryin and cryin, can you come home?" I wailed to Mom.

"Oh for Christ's sake, you shoulda put your hand behind the pin!" She didn't come home and neither did Aunt Nettie.

A week later, on Sunday, when the flowers on my grandmother's grave were still fresh, Mom drove my sister and me back to Albert where she left us for two months with Glen and Vi to finish the school year.

"Would you like to color a picture with me," Vi asked, with a coloring book and a large box of crayons in her hands on Sunday, after Mom had left us to go back to Larned.

"I don't know," I mumbled.

"We'll have fun. It will help you feel better."

"We're just fine," Verneda said with a scowl on her face.

"I do like to color," I admitted to her, edging in her direction. Vi had already started coloring a picture. I lay on my stomach on the floor and began coloring the picture opposite her page. Soon we were laughing together. It was the first of many times that Vi and I colored pictures together on the floor of her living room. It was a simple gesture on her part, but she was probably unaware that I experienced it as a profound act of love. Mom never came into my world in that way.

"You girls go on in and get ready for bed," Vi suggested Sunday evening. "I'll tuck you in when you're ready."

"She's really nice," I said to Verneda as we were getting undressed.

"Yeah, she's nice," my sister said in a soft voice. Sure glad you aren't feeling huffy and mad anymore, I wanted to tell her but kept my mouth shut. Let sleeping bears sleep, I thought.

"Which end do you want?" I asked her before getting into the single bed where we would sleep end to end.

"I'll take this end," she said and climbed into bed.

Above us on the wall was a picture of an angel with wings that reached toward the heavens, hovering over two little children who were crossing treacherous waters on a rickety bridge. After Vi tucked us into bed, she pointed to the angel in the picture. "This is a Guardian Angel. Did you know that each one of you has a Guardian Angel?" she said to us. "Your Guardian Angel is with you all the time, wherever you go to keep you safe." She kissed each of us on the cheek. "Goodnight, sleep tight," she said as she left the room. A soft illumination flowed into our room through the partially open door, casting a glimmer of light upon the picture. I fell asleep thinking about my Guardian Angel.

Verneda was completing the fifth grade and I the second grade in the one-room country school of about twenty students who ranged from grades one through eight.

"Remember you have to wait your turn for the teacher," Verneda told me. "That's what she did last time we were here." Finally, my turn came.

"Vernetta, we'll work on multiplication," she said, taking a piece of paper and writing as she talked. "Two times two is four. Do you understand?" In my mind, I added two and two.

"Yes, I understand."

"Now what do you think two times three is?" she asked.

I confidently answered, "Five!"

"Three times two is six," she said with a smile. I didn't see anything to smile about because when I added up three and two it only came to five. How in the world did she get six? The more the teacher tried to explain, the more confused I became.

I wanted to scream at the teacher, "I don't get it and don't try to teach me this stuff cause I have other things on my mind. My grandma died! Mom slapped her and then she just died. Then Mom left us again. I don't even know when she's comin' back. I hope she's comin' back but I don't know. What's gonna happen to me next? I don't care that two-times three is six not five. Leave me alone! I hate math!" Of course, I didn't say this to the teacher. I didn't say it to anyone.

Later my multiplication despair yielded to joy when the teacher said, "Students, please come up to the front, we're going to sing a song. If you don't know the words, just listen to the children who do, and you'll catch on quickly." As she played, music rolled out of the piano and something inside of me danced up and down shouting, "Yippee!" The others started singing, "Give me land lots of land under starry skies above, Don't Fence Me In."

I couldn't sing the song because I didn't know the words. But it didn't take long to catch on that "don't fence me in" was stuck in there over and over and I joyfully sang those four words every time they came around again. After that, I could hardly wait for music time.

One fun song the teacher taught us went like this:
"Mairzy doats and dozy doats and liddle lamzy divey
A kiddley divey too, wouldn't you?"

I had no idea what the words meant for they ran together like frightened sheep. They were only nonsense sounds to me. Little did I know that the lyrics were purposely written to be nonsensical. Maybe we didn't sing the part that would have unraveled the mystery of the foolish words we were singing, I don't know. If we did, I simply didn't catch on to their real meaning: Mares eat oats and does eat oats and little lambs eat ivy...

School continued to be a safe haven for me, even in spite of what I called the "Math Monster."

"When's Mom gonna come to see us?" I asked my sister as we walked the dusty road home to Vi's.

"I don't know and don't keep askin' cause I don't care," my sister said as she ran ahead of me.

Easter Sunday came on April Fool's Day but passed us by as if in jest. We didn't see Mom until the middle of April when she drove us to Larned. "You kids clean up the house," she said when we got out of the car just before she drove off.

"I'm not stayin' here," Verneda said. "I'm goin over to my friend's house."

But Mom'll be mad at you," I warned.

"I don't care!" she yelled back at me as she walked away.

What's all that junk, I wondered on my way to the bathroom when I passed by the dining room table smothered in clutter. Cutting across the corner of my grandparents' bedroom to get to the bathroom, I stopped suddenly. Grandma's glass display cabinet where she kept her precious collection of cats sat with its door gaping open. The glass shelves that had once displayed an assortment of Grandma's beautiful cat collection were starkly bare, except for the very few that were left.

"Where did all the kitties go?" I said to the almost empty cabinet. The special ones were gone. One little cat lay turned on its side, as if a careless hand had knocked it over. I reached in to place it upright but then I remembered Grandma telling me, "You must never touch them." I withdrew my hand. I stood staring into the cabinet, at that age not seeing it as a metaphor for my own world, turned upside down without my grandma.

The light of day changed to the dark of night. I rummaged aimlessly through the stack of things on the dining room table, wondering what had happened to Smokey, Grandma's real cat. A fat brown bag intrigued me. When I opened it I found a nutcracker sitting on top of nuts in their shells. I stood there midst the clutter, aware of the empty house and the darkness outside, cracking and eating almonds, thinking about my grandma and my mom, until the bag was almost as empty as the house. I wandered into the front bedroom and put myself to bed.

"That goddamned bunch of vultures jist come in and took it all," I overheard Mom say to Lucky the next morning. "That Eva and Mary was the worst! I'm a tellin' you," Mom ranted on and on to Lucky. According to Mom, her sisters had swooped down on this sacred shrine of cats that Grandma had created, desecrating it as they took what they wanted, which was almost everything.

"What are *you* lookin' at?" Mom said when she saw me standing there listening.

"Nothin'. I didn't know what happened to Grandma's cat collection. Now I know."

"Go on and get your things together. Soon as Verneda gets home, I'm takin' you back to Albert."

We drove in total silence from Larned to Albert until Mom turned off the main highway toward Glen and Vi's place.

"School gets out the end of May," Mom said. "I'll bring you home then."

Chapter 14

Kansas
June 1945 – September 1945

"It's so different without Grandma here," I tried to tell my sister after Mom brought us back from Albert, but she didn't pay any attention to me. "I miss Grandma, don't you?"

This time, she looked at me. "You better get used to it cause she ain't comin' back."

A perforated ulcer, peritonitis, then death. Did Mother's slap of anger across the face of Grandma cause her ulcer to perforate? Or might the cause of her death be hidden behind the declaration heard beside her casket, "Now no one will ever know, Momma." Would her ulcer have perforated in spite of the slap or the secret? But knowing the truth would not have brought my grandmother back into my life in Larned, Kansas. And so, for almost two years after her death, the following events unfolded one upon another, covering us in an ever-deepening blackness.

Mid-afternoon of early June, I skipped from the front door through the living room into the dining room. When I got to Grandpa's bedroom door, I came to a dead stop. Our neighbor lady was in his bed, lying on Grandma's side, looking at Grandpa, watching him come into bed with her. No one noticed me, momentarily frozen within view. I quickly moved past the door. I knew what they would do together, in Grandma and Grandpa's bed. I left the house through the kitchen, careful not to bang the back porch screen door.

This is the only memory I have of my grandfather after my grandmother died, even though I lived with him for almost two years following her death. All memories of him were totally forgotten, as if he didn't exist. This is the third period of time I have a memory loss relating to my grandfather.

"Ferd and me are gonna be gone tonight. I bought you kids some sparklers you can light when it gets dark," Mom told Verneda, handing her a box.

My sister and I sat alone that evening on the front porch of our house, not saying much to each other. June bugs flew into the porch light, their brown bodies sometimes falling to the porch, wing tips sticking slightly out the back.

"Here," Verneda said, handing me a lighted sparkler then lighting one for herself. The sparklers danced and sizzled as we wandered back and forth on our front sidewalk with them, but they did nothing to relieve the profound loneliness of the night or to heighten our sense of celebration on this Fourth of July 1945.

On a hot summer evening near the end of July, Mom said, "Ferd and me are takin' you kids to Great Bend. Get yourselves ready."

"Why is she taking us?" I asked Verneda as we were getting dressed because Mom usually left us home.

"How do I know? Just shut up and get dressed."

After driving twenty-five miles through flat Kansas farmland to Great Bend on a two-lane paved road, they dropped us off at a roller-skating rink. "We'll be back to pick you up," Mom said before they drove away.

Hours later, the rink was closing but no mom and Ferd. "What are we gonna do?" I asked Verneda.

"I don't know," she said as she flopped down on the curb. "I guess jist wait."

The lights of the roller rink went out, so we moved to sit on a curb under a streetlight.

"Here they are, finally!" Verneda grumbled.

"Go on, git in the car," our tipsy Mom said. Why Ferd decided to take the back roads home, I'm not sure.

Riding along through the dark countryside, we fell asleep until we heard the sound of Mom's voice, "Wake up! Verneda, Vernetta," she yelled. "Wake up!" Next, she yelled at Ferd, "Stop this goddamned car, Ferd. I'm getting' out." Profanities came out in a steady stream. I looked out the car window to utter darkness. Ferd gave in to Mom's demands. He pulled up and stopped on the long dark narrow road.

"Git your asses outa this car," she ordered us as she headed around the back side of the car, across the road, under a barbed fence and started out across a dark field.

104

My sister could keep up with her, but I was trailing far behind when I heard Ferd call out, "Come back, Edna, that's swamp land out there." Horror shot straight through me. At the movies, I had seen a big man slowly sink into quicksand right up to his mouth, then his nose, over the top of his head and he was gone! To me, swamp was a synonym for quicksand.

Trailing behind in the dark, frightened to the point of terror, I called out, "Wait for me; wait for me, Mom!" She was hell bent for a farmhouse that sat across the other side of the field; I got no response.

One more time the voice of Ferd filled the night with sound. "Edna, come back; it's a swamp."

Just at that moment, I stepped into something soft. My foot sank. I shrieked at Mom, "I'm sinking. I'm sinking in quicksand!" My desperate cries for help didn't slow Mom from her intent nor did she respond. I realized no help would come from her. Ferd drove away, taking the light from his car with him. Now totally alone in the dark field, I ran as fast as I could with a determined effort to get myself across the dark unknown that I feared could swallow me whole. When I caught up with Mom, she was knocking at the door of a farmhouse. Somehow, she got us a ride back to Larned. Home at last, I looked at my shoe. I had stepped in a soft cow pie.

Ferd wasn't entirely back with my mom after the night we drove back from Great Bend but there was no short supply of men. Mom moved my sister and me out of the front bedroom onto a double rollaway in the corner of the dining room, right across from the door to Grandpa's bedroom and within easy sight of the front door. I was sleeping on the rollaway when, late on a warm summer night, I was startled awake by the front door opening with a bang. I watched as a strange man dragged my mother across the threshold. I got out of bed and crossed over to the floor furnace. What are you doing with my mother? I wanted to demand, but I only stood there and watched.

"Go back to bed, little girl. Your Mommy is fine. She had a little too much to drink and passed out."

"But where is her shoe?" I asked. The man looked at Mom's feet.

"I'll find her shoe, don't worry. Go back to bed," he said, continuing to drag Mom into the front bedroom.

I went back to bed, but I was worried about Mom. I wanted to yell at him, "Get away from my mom!" I wanted to push him away from her. I lay there in the dark imagining myself throwing rocks through the windows of liquor stores aimed at bottles of whiskey. Smash, Smash! – I wanted to smash every whiskey bottle in the world.

It happened again later that month. I woke to hear Mom in the front bedroom laughing and pleading, "Stop, stop." A man's voice said something I couldn't understand.

I shook my sister awake. "Listen to Mom," I said in disgust.

Verneda turned over, away from me. "Oh, go to sleep," she said.

Shame on Mom, I thought. I lay there emotionally flooded, another strange man in her bed. Strange men get close to her. I wonder why I can't, I asked myself. For it seemed that she was far, far away from me although she was in the nearby front bedroom.

Mom slowed down her activities with men long enough in mid-August to take me with her to Great Bend where she was scheduled for gallbladder surgery at the end of the month. St Rose Hospital, Sisters of St. Dominic in charge, was a Catholic hospital. After our visit to the doctor, Mom and I went into the enormous Catholic church next to the hospital. A nun in habit talked with us about the presence of God. "He dwells with us here," the nun explained as she pointed to a small gold square container. I wasn't sure how God could fit into that small container, but I didn't ask her to explain.

I was surrounded by articles of remarkable beauty that stimulated my senses: statues, stained glass windows, burning candles. I gazed around in awe, enthralled by the image of Jesus hanging on a wooden cross. "This feels like a holy place," I whispered.

Recently, I had seen Loretta Young playing a nun in the movie, "Come to The Stable," showing at the only movie house in Larned, The Electric Theater. She was so beautiful in her habit and oh so spiritually able to move the hearts of gangsters and others to make God's wishes take place against all resistance. That movie planted in my young heart the fantasy of becoming a nun. Fuel for my fantasy was my very own, real and personal visit with a nun from the order of St. Dominic, who gave me a St. Christopher medal. I'm going to be a nun, I said to myself, imagining how beautiful I would look in a habit, just like Loretta Young.

When we returned to Larned, I converted the space in the corner of the front bedroom, where the French door meets the dresser, into a prayer closet. It was a daring act in the face of the critical magnifying glass Mom and sister normally placed on any of my activities, especially any activity that digressed from what they considered usual. I knelt in my prayer closet with the St. Christopher medal hanging from my neck, twiddled with the beads of my rosary while I talked to God and fantasized that I would someday wear the clothes of a nun. Mom and Verneda totally ignored me.

When it came time for my mother to go to the hospital for surgery, Aunt Hannah came from Dighton to take us home to her farm where we stayed while Mom was in the hospital. Driving along with me in the back seat behind her, Aunt Hannah and I began to talk about my St. Christopher medal.

"I'm gonna be a Catholic nun someday," I said.

"You don't want to be a Catholic, Vernetta," she said. "Those nuns have babies with the priests, then they throw them into big acid baths to kill the babies." She continued to talk vividly about why I shouldn't become a Catholic, especially a nun. With my splendid imagination, I was able to visualize the details of her descriptions. She successfully struck a fatal blow to my dream of becoming a nun.

"Now you take that medal from around your neck and throw it out the window," my Aunt Hannah said, leaving little room, I thought, for further discussion. I liked Aunt Hannah a lot, but I liked my St. Christopher medal almost as much. I didn't want to throw it out the window. Because I had delayed in complying with her command, she repeated, "Now go on, throw it out the window."

I took the medal from my neck, rubbed it between my fingers, and with one toss, it was gone. With that toss, both the medal and my fantasy of being a Catholic nun went out the window. Aunt Hannah seemed relieved and clucked soothing sounds like those of the chickens she had in her backyard.

"You want to come with me, Vernetta?" Aunt Hannah asked. "I'm going out to the back yard to get some chickens to cook for the harvest hands' lunch."

I watched her pick up the first chicken. She twisted and twisted its outstretched neck then put it back on the ground where it flopped around the yard a bit. Three or four more chickens were chosen for the same fate. Next, each chicken got its turn at the chopping block, just like my St. Christopher medal. She struck a blow at each neck, separating the head from the body. The final act, before throwing the chicken carcass into the hot oil of the frying pan, was to stick it into a pot of boiling water, then pick the poor bird naked. My Aunt Hannah was a whirlwind at this procedure.

The farm hands filled the chairs that went around the kitchen table. Uncle Kenneth has the same kind of red turkey neck that Ferd has, I thought. In a slow drawl, he said, "Pass the chicken."

The chicken disappeared off the plate, with my help. I didn't question what I had watched Aunt Hannah do to the chickens before they were passed around all crisp and brown on a plate for us to eat.

It was fortunate for me to experience Aunt Hannah and her world because it contrasted greatly with the world in Larned I returned to after Mother's surgery. I was so happy to see her as she lay there on the couch in a pretty, new robe. I ran over to sit on the couch beside her because I wanted to give her a kiss and a hug, but she pushed me away. "Watch out! You're gonna git on my stitches. What the hell do you think you're doin'?"

Mom was still recovering from surgery when, about a week later, Uncle Ralph, his wife Della, and their two-and-a-half-year-old son Billy came to visit. Ralph had been away in the service during World War II. Now here he was in our living room arguing with Mom, who was lying on the couch still in her robe. Suddenly, he grabbed Mom and wrestled her from the couch down to the living room floor. I started crying.

"My Mom just had surgery; you're hurting her!" I screamed. Profanities filled the room as they rolled over and over.

"I'm gonna shut your ass up in this goddamned sofa," Ralph said to Mom.

I turned crying to Aunt Della, "He's gonna hurt my mother, he's gonna hurt her."

"No, she'll be OK," Aunt Della tried to reassure me.

Ralph repeated his threat, "Gonna shove your ass in this sofa." The sofa had a storage area one could access by lifting the seating area. It was in this large storage area that Ralph threatened to stuff my mother, but he didn't make good on his threat. Anger resolved into a quiet truce. Mom returned to the couch.

That night little Billy slept in the corner of the dining room on the rollaway bed with Verneda and me. My sister was asleep on the inside against the wall. Billy was between us, lying partly on my pillow. I was lying next to him on the outside.

"Suck me," he said, pointing to his penis.

"What!"

"Suck me," little Billy repeated.

"I'm not gonna do that, Billy! You move over there and go night-night," I said, then turned away from him toward the dining room table, pondering the strangeness of his request.

Uncle Ralph, Aunt Della and Billy went away almost as quickly as they had come. We waved goodbye to them before I started third grade, the day after Labor Day.

Chapter 15

Kansas
September 1945 – May 1946

"I'm sure glad Mom didn't send us back to the country school in Albert," I said to my sister as we walked up the hill to the school where we had been when Grandma died last spring.

Verneda ignored my comment about the country school. "Next year I'll be at a different school after I finish sixth grade. You'll still be here but I'll be with the older kids," she said with a snooty tone, I thought.

"And what grade are you in?" the nice woman at the top of the stairs, who was standing close to the room where I had attended second grade, asked me.

"I'm a third grader."

"Mrs. McVeigh will be your teacher. She's standing right there by your new classroom." She pointed to a small woman wearing glasses who stood at the classroom door.

"Hello, and what is your name?" Mrs. McVeigh asked me as I approached her.

"Vernetta Schreiber."

She looked at her list of names. "I think you are in third grade."

"Yes, I'm in third grade."

"You may sit across the room in the last row next to the windows. Why don't you take the fourth seat," she suggested. I liked her nice smile and her brown hair with soft curls that almost reached to her shoulders.

In spite of Mrs. McVeigh's pleasant ways, most of third grade, I was hardly present. Oh, I was physically present, but I sat at my desk in a daze, emotionally adrift in tune with those who had lost their way, my mother and my grandfather. Uncertainty had become the foundation of my days. One morning, feeling especially absent from myself as I gazed out the windows and watched the trees, I put my hand in my panties and stroked myself as Vernon had taught me in Grandpa's car. Mrs. McVeigh never said a word about it.

"You're gonna be eight in a few days," Verneda said, "I'm planning a birthday party for you."

"You are?" I said in disbelief.

"Yeah, Mom will be too drunk to do anything for you." It was a special party with friends and fun games like blowing on a feather to see which team could keep it on the opposite side. My birthday party was unlike the parties Mom started having at our house around the same time.

Men and women with a glass or a bottle in their hands filled the living room furniture to overflowing. Dirty jokes rolled out of their mouths on rising puffs of cigarette smoke, saturating the room, clogging the air. I stood listening when Wes, Lucky's boyfriend, came to the punch line of his joke, "…and I found out what that hole in my ass was for." People laughed. The line embedded itself in my mind.

At some stage of her drunkenness Mom called my sister and me in to be the entertainment. "Go git them grass skirts Ralph brought you from Hawaii. Put em on."

"But we don't want to," Verneda said.

"You'll do as I tell ya! Put em on and dance the hula for us!" she shouted across the room. "Ya wanna see 'em dance the hula, don't ya?"

"Let's see ya dance the hula," one of the drunks said as he stood up to swing his hips but lost his balance, falling back on the couch into someone's lap.

When we returned, dressed in our grass skirts and halters, people whooped, hollered, and even whistled. We stood in front of the fake fireplace as our stage area, gyrating our hips round and round, making motions with our arms and hands as we had seen on the movie screen at the Electric Theater.

Dressed to dance

    Placed in this situation time after time by Mom, we had no concept of our vulnerability to those drunken men who watched my sister and me, young grade schoolgirls, compelled to dance for drunks in our hula skirts.
    One drunken party seemed to blend with the next until February, when I was surprised to see my school friend's father sitting on our couch as I watched from my bedroom. His hand started to fondle the breast of the woman sitting next to him. She leaned over, kissing him as she unbuttoned her blouse. "They're all yours, honey," she said at the end of the long kiss, tossing her head as she sat back, her generous breasts fully exposed.
    "You got nice tits," I heard him say as I turned away, sick to my stomach.
    That's not your wife, I wanted to yell at him. But what I really wanted was to be somewhere else.

    Mom was slightly tipsy when she and Ferd picked me up late one Saturday night.
    "C'mon," she said, slurring her words. "You're gonna go Honky-Tonkin' with us." That's one thing I hadn't experienced with Mom yet and I didn't know what it was. "You stay here, don't git outa the car," she ordered as she left to go into the first bar. No way could I tell her, I don't want to sit out here alone in

the dark. I watched her disappear into the bar where the neon Pabst Blue Ribbon beer sign hung in the window, casting a lonely blue light into the darkness.

At the next bar, after they had been gone for what felt like hours to me, Mom opened the car door. "Here, I got ya some potata chips and a pop," she said as she handed them to me then left again. Gee, that was nice of Mom, I thought as I quickly crunched my way through the entire bag of chips. Eventually, I fell asleep in the back seat, not aware of how many bars we went to that night, but I learned firsthand what it meant to go "Honky-Tonkin.'"

Aunt Mary and Uncle Herman came to see us in Larned a few weeks later. "We're gonna drive over to Sterling to visit with Aunt Annie. Can we take Vernetta with us?" she asked Mom.

"It don't make no difference to me," Mom said. "How long ya gonna be gone?"

"We'll have her back in time for school on Monday," Aunt Mary assured her. It was settled. I got to go with Aunt Mary and Uncle Herman.

First, they took me to the drugstore downtown on Main Street where I had seen some pretty things I liked. There was a small glass display counter that held bracelets made of silver with turquoise settings. "Can I have one of those, Aunt Mary?" I asked.

"What do you think, Herman?" Mary asked.

"Um hum," he said as he nodded. She helped me pick out a slender one that had about four pieces of turquoise.

"Oh, it's the most beautiful one of them all," I said.

She smiled and said as we left the drugstore, "Now let's get you a new nightgown.

"I love this one, Aunt Mary, the pink flannel one."

"The little flower print is very pretty and it's nice and long to keep you warm."

We arrived at Aunt Annie's place toward late evening. We entered the back door of her home into the hot, hot kitchen. All the doors inside her home were closed because she had staked out her kitchen as the only room in the house to heat. After greeting us, Aunt Annie moved toward a chair near the warmth of the old, black woodstove. As she sat down on the chair, her body flowed over it until it seemed to me, she sat in mid-air. At long last, she showed us where we would sleep, in a very cold room that had only one bed.

"I guess we can all three sleep in here, together," Aunt Mary said as she turned to Uncle Herman. "What do you think, Herman?"

"Um hum," he responded as he nodded his head the same way he had in the drugstore. Uncle Herman doesn't talk much, I thought, but he doesn't give Aunt Mary any trouble.

After I got into my new flannel nightgown, Aunt Mary told me, "You slide in against the wall; I'll sleep in the middle." It didn't seem to me that the three of us had been in bed very long before I heard Aunt Mary say to Uncle Herman, "Lift up."

I guess he didn't hear her because he said, "What are you sayin'?"

"Lift up," she said with a bit more vigor.

Uncle Herman and I caught on about the same time what she had in mind. I decided to pretend I was asleep but almost stopped breathing, waiting to hear what his answer would be. "No," he replied. She tried to negotiate but he didn't budge from his unwillingness to have sex with Aunt Mary that night. I took a deep breath. I was sure glad Uncle Herman didn't say, "Um hum."

Do other kids have as much sex in their life as I do? I found myself wondering after the episode with Aunt Mary and Uncle Herman. I especially wondered after what happened when Steve Fox and I were lying on a grassy slope enjoying the warmth of a spring day in April of our third grade. Opportunity knocked again as it had in Albert.

Suddenly, Steve said as he pulled little blades of grass from the slope, "I want to F you." Totally surprised, I silently froze in place. My Albert experience and life in Larned after Grandmother's death had taught me clearly about the F word. I knew well what Steve wanted to do to me, but silence was my only reply to him. He changed the subject, never to bring it up again and neither did I, but for whatever reason it became a remembered moment. I didn't mention it to anyone else. Not because it was a secret, it just didn't seem that important.

    I came home from school one Friday late in April to find a lovely dress Mother had made for me, laying on the back of the sofa. I knew she had been making it, but I didn't know when it would be finished. Now there it was, a beautiful spring dress with ruffles instead of sleeves at the shoulders. I stood in the empty house holding my lovely dress. I wish Mom was here, I said to myself when I thought of how sweet she could be sometimes. I'd rather be with her than wear the dress she made me, I said to no one but the empty house.

    I'll wear my new dress to church on Sunday, I decided, without asking Mom. The warm spring sunlight bathed my back as it came through the window of the Sunday school classroom. I was seated with other third graders at a wood rectangle table on chairs that were just the right size for us. The teacher, seated at the end of the table, held up a picture. "Do you know who this is?" she asked.

    One of the kids answered, "It's Jesus!"

    I chimed in, "I know a song about Jesus wants me for a sunbeam!"

    The teacher smiled at us then began telling us stories about Jesus. She pointed to the picture of Him knocking at a door, "Jesus is knocking because he wants to come in; he wants to come into your heart. Jesus wants you to come to the door of your heart and open it for him." I wanted to open the door of my heart for Jesus to come in, because when I heard the stories about Jesus, I fell in love with him.

    Mom never went to Sunday school or church with me, but she said, "If you don't go to Sunday school in the morning, ya can't go to the movie in the afternoon." It started to dawn on me, because I was finally old enough to clearly understand, that Mom lives by rules different from the ones she has for Verneda and me.

Monday, when school was over, I started home, an easy walk two blocks down the street from the school and then turn and walk two more blocks down the hill to my house. Walking, looking around and fondling a little chrome key, I popped it in my mouth about the same time that I looked straight up into a tree to take a closer look at a bird's nest I thought I saw. The key slid right down my throat. More surprised than scared at the time, I ran the last three blocks to get home.

Vernetta and "The Key"

"Mom, Mom!" I called when my feet hit the wooden boards of the screened back porch. I called again as I raced through the kitchen into the dining room. "Mom, are you home?" All was silent, no response, because no one was home.

I ran out the front door and turned in the direction of town. Maybe she's working at the Blue Goose today, I thought. "No, your mother has the day off," the woman working in the café told me.

I hurried across the street then down a short distance to the alley I detested crossing when I came home from the movie at night. The alley was a convenient way to get into the bar without being seen from the entrance on Main Street. At first, I couldn't see very well because my eyes hadn't adjusted to the darkness of the bar but in a moment, I found my mother sitting in a booth with Ferd. It was my lucky day; she wasn't drunk yet.

"What do you want?" she asked, then surprised me with a second question. "Would you like a bottle of pop?" Normally, I would have told her yes, but I was pretty anxious about the key and since she was in a good mood, it was the perfect time to tell her.

"I swallowed a key." I also wanted to say, I'm really scared, but Mom didn't like to hear stuff like that.

"What the hell were you doin' with a key in your mouth? How big was it?"

I decided to leave the first question alone and deal with the second one. "It was little," I said holding up my fingers to demonstrate the length.

"Well hell, that ain't nothin' to worry about.

"Hey kid," Ferd said, "You want a quarter to go see a movie tonight and buy yourself some popcorn?"

"Sure, I guess," I told him as I held out my hand for my quarter. I wasn't sure why, but Ferd or whatever man Mom might be with often gave me money. "Here kid, go see a movie and buy yourself a treat," each of the different men parroted, as if rehearsed in agreement. I often saw each movie that came to town at least twice.

"Go on home now," Mom urged, rather nicely I thought. I didn't ask her when she'd be home. Don't take a chance on spoiling her good mood, I told myself. As I left the bar I thought, Mom didn't get mad at me or tell me how stupid I am like she usually does. But I wasn't sure what to do about how scared I was to have that little key somewhere inside of me.

The next day Mom said, "I'm takin you to get an x-ray."

I walked down the long hall beside the doctor as he explained to me what it means to have an x-ray.

"Mrs. Schreiber, can you describe the key to me?" the doctor asked as he turned to my mother.

"I don't know, its jist a key she had."

"Well," the doctor said. "Tell me what the key looked like."

"It was just a little key," I said, shrugging my shoulders.

"Did it have anything sharp on it?" asked.

"I don't think so," I said getting frightened and anxious.

"You see, Mrs. Schreiber, the main concern is that the key doesn't damage the intestines on its way through the colon. If it is smooth, then it should go completely through, causing no problems to her whatsoever."

After the x-ray had been taken of my stomach, the doctor talked to my mother again. "You will need to check her stools each day to see if she has passed the key. This is very important," he added. "I will then be able to determine if the key or the projection on the end of the key could have snagged or torn her intestine."

When we got home, Mom handed me a large tin coffee can. "You can poop into this can out on the screened porch, then look for the key," she told me, then walked away. She had no further involvement. None until she saw me one day sitting on the coffee can as she passed through the screened porch. Opening the back door to go into the kitchen, she paused long enough to say, "You'll never find anything in them little goat turds."

I didn't know what "goat turds" were, but from the sound of Mom's tone of voice I knew it wasn't good. "Never find anything in them little goat turds" went through my thoughts again. But I kept with my vigil to find the key until one day, I exclaimed, dancing up and down, "I found it, I found it!"

I quickly ran to the sink, washed, and inspected it carefully. "The key is smooth!" I declared.

An important lesson learned from swallowing the key: Mom is not always right. Of course, I also learned it's best not to put small objects into my mouth!

At lunchtime a few days later, my drunk Mother picked me up at school. "We come to git ya to give ya lunch." It was a car I didn't recognize with three more drunks inside, waiting for us.

"Git right in here, honey," the man said to me, pointing to a place right next to him, "We're takin ya to lunch."

"Go on," Mom insisted as she pushed me into the front seat next to him then got in beside me. Off we went for lunch: potato chips and a candy bar.

"Do ya wanna drive," the man behind the wheel asked me.

"Sure," I said without hesitation.

"Climb right up here on my lap," he said. "You can drive yourself back to school." Everyone laughed at a third grader driving. I happily sat on the man's lap to steer us up and down the steep brick streets of Larned. Eventually, we stopped at the curb next to my school. Mom's arm waved from her window as they drove away. She probably didn't know that the school day was almost over.

Although Mom was rarely home, she must have thought of Verneda and me because occasionally when we came home from school there might be a can of Campbell's soup sitting on the kitchen counter with a note, "Have this for dinner."

Sometimes, right before she left, she would put us in charge of a pot of beans she had started cooking. "Now watch them beans," she would tell us before leaving. We weren't any good at cooking beans, but my sister and I excelled at burning beans. If Mom came home that night, she'd yell at us, "You goddamned kids can't do anything right! Want anything done right, I gotta do it myself."

She repeated this sentiment so many times that I believed her. It was impossible to figure out that she was really talking about herself, not us, so we just accepted what she said. "I can't do anything right," became one more personal belief I included along with several of Mom's negative opinions of me that had become my own. I believed her but I never once questioned why she continued to ask us to "Watch them beans."

In early May, before the end of third grade, Mrs. McVeigh brought each student to the old upright piano. "Get up on the piano stool," she instructed, "and sit very still." The light from the window cast a shadow of our silhouette onto a piece of paper. "I'm drawing around your shadow," she explained.

When she had finished each student's silhouette, she told us, "After I've transferred your drawing to heavier paper, you can take it home to your parents."

The time came when Mrs. McVeigh passed up and down the rows, handing out our drawings. "Here's yours Vernetta."

"It looks like me from the side! I like it a lot," I said. I liked Mrs. McVeigh a lot too. I guess she liked me because that summer she wrote me a letter and even included a picture of her with her baby boy. I looked forward to fourth grade in the fall because she would be my teacher again.

Chapter 16

Kansas
June 1946 – August 1946

Mom moved my sister and me to her bedroom off the back porch. "This is where you kids can sleep this summer," is all she said with no explanation of why she had moved us into her room.

One time when I was alone, I decided to see what was in the bottom drawer of a big chest. "Mmm, this is nice," I thought, stroking a satin pillow that had "Sweetheart" stitched on it. What's this rolled up thing? I wondered as I dropped the pillow to pick it up. A picture of a bunch of sailors on a big ship! I said in surprise as I unrolled a long narrow photo. Wonder why Mom has it. I looked up and down the rows of sailors at each of the different faces when suddenly, I recognized the man squatting on the front row with a big smile on his face. It's Bud! It's Bud from Jarbidge! Rummaging around further, I found what I thought was a small wallet but when I opened it, I saw a picture of Mom on one side, a picture of Bud on the other side and a loose picture of a baby floating freely between the two of them.

My sister came in. "What are ya doin' in Mom's drawer?"

"Nothin, just lookin'," I said. "But see what I found!"

She looked at the pictures and the satin pillow. "Yeah, I know. Bud sent them to Mom."

"Is that Buddy, Jr.?" I asked, pointing to the picture of the baby. "Is that a picture of our baby?"

"It isn't our baby anymore. Now put it back or you'll be in trouble."

The back porch bedroom turned out to be a pretty good retreat from the goings on in the main part of the house.

"Please Mom, please, I want to go."

"I told ya, you're not goin'."

"Why not?" I demanded.

She raised her voice and glared at me. "Because I said so," meaning end of conversation. That was her usual response. "Because I said so." It was never enough for me. I wanted to hear something that made sense, a good reason why I couldn't do what I wanted to do, a discussion, maybe even a negotiation. But she had the power.

As I sat forlorn in Grandma's chair, the sadness I felt showed itself in my lower lip, which apparently fattened then protruded. "You're gonna trip on that lip," Mom said in a nasty tone. "It's gonna freeze stuck out there on that long face of yours." I thought it best to take my ugly self to the back porch bedroom where no one had to look at me.

Other offerings waited for me there, like playing the toy piano Aunt Hannah had given me, or embroidering flowers on flour sacks. Some well-intentioned, elderly relative saw me stitching one Sunday. "You're gonna have to take out each one of those stitches with your nose when you get to hell cause you're stitching on Sunday," she said in a raspy voice with the certainty of a god.

But I had come a long way since the frightening lie Grandpa told me, that the grapefruit seeds I swallowed would sprout and grow out my ears. I no longer believed everything a grownup said. I momentarily contemplated what she had said, then resumed my stitching.

It was in this back porch bedroom that my sister and I started to read the Old Testament in bed before we went to sleep. It was our goal to read the entire Bible through from cover-to-cover, all sixty-six books. Someone at Sunday school had given my sister the inspiration. Now she shared it with me. We got to the book of Leviticus. It might as well have been written in a foreign language because we couldn't make any sense of it. But we felt quite successful to have gotten as far as we did, completely through Genesis and Exodus, the first two books of the Bible.

Freedom on wheels came as a gift to me at the end of June from Aunt Mary and Uncle Herman in the form of a bicycle. My sister took charge of my new shiny-blue bike and me.

"I'll show ya how to ride it," she offered without my asking. She wheeled it out to Santa Fe Street, the brick paved street that ran past our side yard. "Stick your leg through," she ordered. "Sit on the seat with both feet on the pedals. Now I'm gonna push you and you pedal," she instructed as she placed herself behind the back wheel.

"But don't let go," I pleaded.

"Nah, I'm not gonna let go," she assured me, "just pedal." When I started to pedal, the bike wobbled a little. It frightened me.

"Keep pedaling!" she yelled at me. The bike went faster when I pedaled.

"Don't let go," I repeated, not knowing that she had already let go.

She was standing half a block away by the time I fell over with my new bike. "I told you not to let go!" I yelled at her when I picked myself up. She was laughing so loud she probably didn't hear what I said and probably didn't care anyway.

Along with summer came good news and bad news. The good news was that the drunken parties in the living room had nearly come to an end. The bad news was that mom was almost always away from home, gone somewhere else to drink with her friends. This change meant that I was frequently alone in an empty house because my sister was now old enough to be gone, like Mom, with her friends. The pleasure of swimming and going to the movies helped balance my aloneness, my loneliness.

Kansas summers are hot both day and night which meant that the water of the Larned Olympic-sized swimming pool stayed deliciously warm all summer. Shirley, Lucky's youngest daughter, and I were buddies that summer, born only five days apart in the same year. Shirley was much shorter than I, but "tough." We were at the pool almost every day. Lifeguards sat perched above us, keeping watch.

After graduating from the kiddy pool, I spent many hours in the middle section of the pool getting burned and blistered by the hot Kansas sun as we played game after make-believe game. We especially liked playing "Heil Hitler." Mimicking the German soldiers, we had seen in the newsreels at the Electric Theater, we marched stiff-legged across the deck with arms outstretched, then goose-stepped off the edge of the concrete into the water, shouting "Heil Hitler!" When out of breath and tired, I took a rest on the warm concrete surrounding the pool, where I listened to the gleeful sounds of children's voices all mingled together. A feast on candy bars or ice cream bars or potato chips completed my day at the pool. I was free in a big way.

The Electric Theater was my magic carpet to life outside the walls of our little bookless house where anger and drunkenness were the main features day after day, month after month. But some of the movies I saw at the Electric Theater took me beyond the mental and physical confines not only of my home but the little world of Larned, Kansas as well.

Mom never went to the movies but, as with church, she had no problem sending us there. I was given money to see them again when the new movie hadn't yet replaced the old. It didn't matter what the movie was about or that it was night, and I was alone. I was sent to the movies.

The parade of movies recorded their impressions on my not quite nine-year-old imagination. I watched zombies in horror as they walked toward me from the screen, saw cowboys ride or sing their way into the sunset after doing in the bad guys, tapped my way through musicals with Betty Grable and Carmen Miranda. I absorbed Esther Williams moves so I could repeat them at the swimming pool the next day. I cringed as Olivia de Havilland went crazy in "Snake Pit" to the tune of the New World Symphony. I laughed at Bob Hope and Bing Crosby in the road pictures, Abbot and Costello with their "Who's on First" routine.

When it came to the movies, there was the worst and the best for me in what I watched. The best for me was any movie that had Barbara Stanwyck. She became my role model: a strong woman in charge of her destiny. The worst of it was when, in ignorance, I purchased a ticket to see Frankenstein and later a ticket to see the Wolf Man. I wish the ticket person had come out of her booth, hugged me as she said, "Honey, don't see this movie, it will scare you real bad."

It did scare me "real bad," almost as bad as the Wolf Man. This movie was about the full moon and what happened to a man when he looked at it. His face began to grow hair, his teeth became ugly, large and jagged; his hands turned to claws. Instead of a voice when he spoke, he growled when he opened his mouth. Once he was transformed into this loathsome creature, he went about preying on people until the sun came up.

After the Wolf Man movie ended, I had to walk home in the dark, alone. I came out of the theater, passed by the bar, and passed a couple of stores before I turned right to go up the hill to our house. The dreaded alley lay a short distance in front of me. I was sure the Wolf Man was hiding in that alley. I stopped at the last building. I peeked down the alley. A light shined on trash cans up against the wall across from the alley exit of the bar. Something banged against a garbage can. I ran as fast as I could past the alley. I hurried up the hill to my home, out of breath from running. The empty house was dark when I got home.

One evening towards the end of summer Mom said to Verneda, "I'm leavin' and you stay here with Vernetta." Mom's motive for telling her to stay home may have been concern about what Verneda would do while Mom was gone rather than concern for my being alone. Mom made it clear that my sister was supposed to stay home.

But the minute Mom left, Verneda declared, "I'm goin' to the park with my friends," and away she went.

About an hour later, Mom came through the front door. "Where's your sister?" she demanded.

"She went to the park with her friends."

"C'mon," she said. "You're goin' with me to git her." Outside, a strange pickup was parked in front of our house. "Git in!" Mom yelled at me. She gunned that pickup, left rubber on the road as she spun a U-turn, and headed to the park next to the swimming pool. It didn't take long for her to spot my sister next to the swings, lying on a blanket with a couple of her friends.

"You git your ass in this truck!" she yelled as she jumped out of the pickup, grabbed Verneda by the hair, pulled her to the truck then shoved her into the seat next to me. Mom cussed at her all the way back to the house. When we got home, Lucky was there. Mom pushed my sister down on the couch. "Git them jeans off!" she shouted as she went toward Grandpa's room. Verneda wasn't fast enough because Mom was back with a belt before she got her jeans off. "Goddamned kid, you're gonna learn to do what I tell ya," she said, yanking on the leg of the jeans so hard that Verneda fell off the sofa onto the floor. "Git your butt over the end uh the couch," Mom ordered.

My sister dutifully draped herself over the arm of the sofa with nothing on but her panties. "I'm gonna teach you a thing or two." Mom laid the first strike of the belt across my sister's back then raised the belt and slapped it down hard again and again.

"You're gonna kill that kid, Edna," Lucky said. "She's not gonna cry." Mom didn't seem to hear. "You better quit, Edna," Lucky said more urgently. This somehow broke Mom's rage. The beating stopped.

"You leave the house again, you'll git it again," she promised my sister. "Let's git outta here, Lucky." Mom stormed out the front door with Lucky on her heels.

Edna and Lucky

Verneda turned on me, "I hate your guts!" She raised her hand to strike me.

"It wasn't my fault. Mom told you to stay home," I cried.

"You're a big baby. I'm sick of takin' care of you!" she yelled at me. "If it weren't for you, I could be at the park with my friends! If it weren't for you, Mom wouldn't beat on me!" It was impossible to convince her that I wasn't the reason she got beaten. In her mind, I was to blame for the beating she took for disobeying Mom.

In the following few days, doing the dishes with her became an experience of aggravation, frustration, and downright harassment.

"You dry, ninny, 'cause I'm gonna wash 'em," Verneda said in a sassy tone. She purposely piled the dishes as fast as she could on my side.

"I can't rinse and dry that fast," I complained.

"Well, what do you want me to do about it, slow-poke!"

I hurried as fast as I could while she played with the soap bubbles in the dishwater. I finished rinsing and drying the stack of dishes. Now I had no more dishes to rinse and dry. I stood there while she played in the water. "Aren't you gonna wash the rest of the dishes?" I asked.

"Yeah, when I feel like it," she sneered.

"I'm not gonna stand here waitin' for you. You can dry them yourself," I threatened.

"Sure, go on. They'll be sittin' there with soap dryin' on 'em and then Mom can beat the hell out of you. So sure, go on!" She always gets the best of me I thought, as I stood waiting for her to wash the next dish.

Verneda spent Friday night of Labor Day Weekend at Lucky's on Santa Fe Street. She and Pat were asleep on the double bed in the middle bedroom.

"I woke up and Wes had his hand on my private parts," my sister told me the next day in a bland tone of voice.

"Wow! What did you do?"

"I just moved over on the other side of Pat where he couldn't reach me and went back to sleep."

"But what about Pat? What did Wes do to her?" I asked.

"I don't know, I went back to sleep."

Lucky had been "shacked up" with Wes for many years, at a time when society looked down on unmarried couples living together. Wes was a tall man with brown hair, dull eyes and a reddish prominent nose. When he worked, he painted signs. The rest of the time he hung out with Lucky, smoking and drinking.

Wes was usually at the drinking parties Mom had at our home. I don't know what he was thinking when he watched Verneda and me do the hula or what his thoughts were at the party Mom had Saturday night of Labor Day weekend right before I started fourth grade. Maybe Lucky knew what Wes had on his mind, or maybe she didn't.

The couch and chairs were filled with strangers and a few people I knew. The ones I knew were Ferd, still my mom's main boyfriend; Big Swede, Ferd's brother; Big Swede's girlfriend; Lucky and Wes. Ferd motioned for me to come over to him.

"Here's some money for you and Shirley to go to the movie," he said as he handed it to me.

"Yeah," my mom said loudly. "You kids go on ta the movie." She made a wide sweeping movement with her arm toward my sister and Lucky's two oldest daughters, Jerry and Pat, "You kids all go ta the movie." Mom and the rest of them had all been drinking long enough to be a bit tipsy.

"Wait just a goddamned minute," my mom told Verneda. "I hear you was gonna git drunk on coke and aspirin."

My twelve-year old sister denied it. "I never said that."

Mom ignored her. "If you wanna git drunk, I sure as hell will let ya git drunk."

"No, I never said I wanna git drunk," my sister insisted.

But Mom and Lucky picked up three small bottles of Coca Cola and passed one to Wes. "Drink'er down a ways, then we'll fill 'er up with whiskey." The three of them--Mom, Lucky and Wes--tipped up the small glass bottles of Coca Cola.

"Gimme that open bottle uh Four Roses, Wes," Mom said. She filled the partially empty bottle of Coca Cola to the brim with whiskey then handed it to my sister. "Go on, take it." At the same time, Jerry aged 13 and Pat 11 each took their bottle of Coca Cola mixed with Four Roses Whiskey.

I watched my sister take a big drink followed by a spray of liquid from her mouth that landed on a few of the partygoers who roared with laughter. Someone shouted at her, "Bottoms up, honey!" Eleven-year-old Pat was out of the running. She dumped hers into the sink.

My sister put the bottle to her mouth again and took a big gulp. "I don't like it!" she said and ran to the kitchen to dump it down the sink. In a short time, when that big gulp of alcohol took effect, Verneda experienced a new world. She sneaked over and took a drink of Mom's booze, which was sitting on the ironing board, still standing in the dining room from earlier in the day. She liked how it made her feel. She went into the kitchen.

"I'm gonna drink it right outa the bottle," she told me as she picked a new bottle of Four Roses Whiskey from the case that sat on the kitchen floor. I watched her struggle to get the lid off. "Bottoms up," she said echoing what she had heard earlier, drinking undiluted whiskey straight from the bottle. She ran into the living room transformed by alcohol into the "life of the party."

The partygoers laughed and egged her on as she ran leaping over the floor furnace, cussing and swearing as she ran. "And I ain't scared of you, Mom. I ain't scared anymore," she shouted at our laughing mother. Suddenly, Verneda stopped dead center between the living and dining room, all eyes on her. "I feel sick."

Vomit spewed out of her mouth onto the floor. I was surprised at how tenderly Mom took care of her after that. She wasn't angry about cleaning up the vomit. "Git that mattress off the bed. Put it by the bathroom door," she ordered Ferd. She led my sister to the mattress.

"Git on here. If ya half ta vomit, git yourself over to the toilet." She turned and saw me watching. "Go on, git outta here." I left with Shirley to go to the movie.

"I feel so sick," my sister complained to me faintly the next morning. Then she looked at me and said in amazement, "That was the first time I wasn't afraid of Mom. I wasn't afraid of her. I could cuss in front of her, but I wasn't afraid of her when I was drunk." It surprised me that she remembered not being afraid of Mom.

Verneda

Chapter 17

Kansas
September 1946 – January 1947

Unlike my sister, I missed the opportunity to experience the sweet bliss of not being afraid of Mom. In my non-inebriated state, I remained fearfully respectful of her.

In September, a different scene between Mom and me, without the assistance of Four Roses, played out in our living room.

"That son-of-a-bitch Vern and that goddamned Kae Hicks!" she said. "They got money but don't send a dime for you! She paused, glaring at me coldly. "He kin live high on the hog while I work my ass of ta pay for you!"

I guess Mom thinks it's my fault I don't have any money to pay my own way, I decided after she got done ranting. But I didn't know Vern, the man I was told was my father. I had never met the man. I had to take Mom's word that he was "a son-of-a-bitch livin' high on the hog."

At another time, when I was sure she detested me, she said, "You're jist like the Schreibers." That was Vern's last name; that was my last name too. Probably she doesn't like any of us Schreibers, I said to myself, but just to be on the safe side, I didn't ask her.

At times it was hard to avoid getting in Mom's way. She had brought Ferd home in the middle of the day, but I didn't know it. I dropped my bicycle at the front of the house when I got home from school the first week in September and went into the dining room. For some reason, I decided to look for something I wanted and thought it might be in the top drawer of the sideboard. It was filled with all kinds of junk, a mishmash. I poked around for a while in the first drawer. When I opened the other drawer, I heard Mom and Ferd's voices coming from Grandpa's bedroom. I continued rummaging in the drawer but planned to inch my way toward the bedroom door to take a peek at what they were doing.

I heard Ferd's voice say, "That kid's out there!"

Mom came flying out the bedroom straight for me. With a hand on each shoulder, she shook me and demanded, "What the hell do you think your adoin' out here?"

"Nothing, I'm not doin' nothing."

"You ain't got no business bein' in here." I went out the front door thinking, if it weren't for Ferd, maybe things could be different between my mom and me."

Edna with Ferd wearing Ralph's military hat

It happened about a week after I was about to peek into the bedroom to see what Ferd and Mom were up to. That day, I seemed to forget the importance of being vigilant. After coming home from school to an empty house, I sat relaxed in Grandma's chair sucking my right thumb when in walked Mom.

132

She took one look at me as she came through the front door and said, "I'm gonna cut off your goddamned thumb if you don't stop sucking it!"

I quickly pulled my thumb out of my mouth and put my arm behind my back as I looked up at her, silently frozen.

"Goddamned eight-year-old and you're still suckin' your thumb. "I oughta cut off your whole damn hand!" she said, leaning down into my face with hers.

I had sucked my right thumb since I was a baby. Over the years she had tried a few things to break my habit. Painting "nasty tasting" stuff on my thumb didn't work, putting a glove on my hand at night didn't work, nothing worked. I was still sucking my thumb in September, a short time after I started fourth grade. When Mom threatened to cut off my thumb, then escalated the threat to include my hand, I visualized the experience right then and there, sitting in Grandma's chair. I believed she was capable of carrying out her threat. I thought the best thing I could do for Mom and me was to stop sucking my thumb. Maybe that would make her happy. Once I set my mind to it, it was easy. I simply quit. Mom didn't yell or threaten me when I bit my fingernails so at least I didn't have to give that up too.

School became my safe harbor against the storms of life that raged with Mom in our little white house on the corner of Fourth and Santa Fe Streets. School, my security blanket throughout the years I lived with her, my constant balance against a teeter-totter existence of uncertainty.

Although I was in a foggy daze most of my third grade, I was wide-awake in the fourth grade with Mrs. McVeigh in a room I loved. I loved it partly because Mrs. McVeigh was there, partly because it was familiar, but certainly because the big square room with its tall abundant windows allowed me to watch the trees. I watched them when the wind wrestled leaves from their branches, tossing them wildly down to the ground or floated them dreamily far, far away; watched them when they stood gracefully undressed, black against the winter sky; watched threatening bolts of lightning flash at them after the grumble of thunder. I watched the magic of snow gently drift down upon their branches dressing them in coats of white; watched flurries driven by mad wind with its own intentions for the heavenly whiteness against the dark bark of the trees. I marveled in spring as fresh new leaves once again dressed the bare branches in green.

"Ask your mom if you can come to my house after school tomorrow," Steve said.

Steve Fox   Vernetta
Fourth Grade, 1946-47

Steve and I had become the closest of friends. "I'm pretty sure I can come," I said, knowing Mom didn't pay much attention to what I did or didn't do most of the time.

After school the next day, we walked down Fifth Street to his house, only half a block from our school and on the same street that was closed off during the winter for sledding.

"You live in a really nice house," I told him as we walked up the five broad steps to a generous porch that ran across the front of the house.

"Let's go in," Steve said, opening the front door. Ahead of us was a flight of stairs that led straight upstairs to the second floor. "You can wait in the living room," he told me as he raced upstairs for something.

"A piano!" I said excitedly, running over to touch the white keys. With the sound of voices coming from nearby, I stood frozen by the piano afraid I might be in trouble for touching it. A lovely woman and a man came through the dining room as Steve bounded down the stairs holding a ball.

"This is my friend from school, Mom."

Mrs. Fox smiled at me. "Hello Vernetta. Steve told me you would be coming over this afternoon."

"Come on," Steve yelled as he ran out the front door.

"Goodbye Mrs. Fox," I hurriedly called, rushing out the door after him to throw balls through the basketball hoop behind his house.

"I like your piano, Steve," I said as I watched him toss the ball.

"Yeah, it's okay. I take lessons from the lady down the street."

Walking home from school, I started thinking of his piano and how very much I would like to play the piano. As I scuffed along on the sidewalk, I thought about when I had seen my first piano. I could almost see the room where it sat when Mom took us with her to visit a lady in a big house. That's when I fell in love with the piano.

"You kids wait in here," I remembered her saying. She closed the pocket doors of the parlor where a huge grand piano sat.

"What is this, Nee Nee?" I asked.

"It's a piano! Don't you know what a piano is?"

I put my finger on a smooth white key, pushed on it ever so slightly and a sound came from the piano. It was magical. I was enthralled as I pushed key after key to hear the sound it would make. After doing this for a while, I decided to play two keys at once. "Nee Nee, listen. It sounds so pretty," I said.

I started thinking again about Steve. Lucky him, he has a piano, I said to myself, skipping the rest of the way home. The next day after school I told Steve, "You're so lucky! I really want to play the piano, but I don't have one."

Steve said, "You can play mine! Hey, maybe you could even take lessons from my teacher!"

"But I need a piano I can practice on," I said.

Steve came up with another idea. "I'll ask my mom if you can practice on ours." He went into the house and returned a few moments later. "My mom said you can practice at our house and my teacher said we could come to see her about lessons after school tomorrow."

The following day, Steve and I hurried down the hill on Fifth Street to talk to his piano teacher, who lived in a tall, narrow two-story house. We stepped onto her large wooden porch and knocked.

"Well, Steve, so this is your friend. Come right in," she said kindly as she took us to a small alcove off the living room where an enormous upright piano stood. She took her place on the bench, "Come here, dear, and let me see your hands." After looking at them, she asked, "Can you put your fingers on the keys, like this?"

"I think so." I placed my fingers on the keys trying to imitate what she had done.

"Very good. Yes, I think I can teach you how to play the piano."

I smiled up at her, "I hope my mom will let me take piano lessons."

The first phase of our plan was successfully completed. I could practice on Steve's piano, and I had a teacher, but I shuddered when I thought about the second phase of our plan. "Now I gotta ask my mom," I meekly told Steve.

What mood will Mom be in, if she's there, I thought as I walked toward home. If she's angry today, I won't ask. I opened the front door and there on the living floor sat Mom with two of her friends. She gave me a nod. It seems she might be nice today, I thought, even though I could tell she had been drinking.

Rare was the opportunity to talk with her alone, so I decided to sit down beside her.

My wish flew out of my mouth before my bottom touched the rug. "Can I take lessons with Steve's piano teacher? His Mom said I could practice on their piano. I wanna take lessons so bad. Could I please take piano lessons?" I begged, as I began to fidget with a button on her dress.

"You want that thing," she laughed, as she took hold of her breast, joking with her friends about it. I pulled away when she started to unbutton her blouse. "Ya want it?" laughing again, as she said it.

I pressed her again for an answer. "Please let me take lessons, Mom."

"That woman don't want you practicing on her pi-ana!" Mom said.

"Please!"

"I said 'No!' Now that's final." There was no further discussion, ever.

"Hey Edna, let's go down to the bar, see what's happenin'. What do you say?" one of the women sitting on the floor suggested. A few minutes later, they were gone.

Left alone, sitting on the living room floor with Mom's "No" sitting heavy on my heart, I didn't know that my mother had taken piano lessons when she was a child. Never in my entire life did she mention it to me. I didn't know until after my mother died and her sister Mary caught me by surprise when she told me, "Piano lessons. Momma just pounded that into us. Yes, Momma was an accomplished pianist." I felt a hollow void as I recalled the afternoon when I asked my mother if I could take piano lessons.

On Wednesday afternoon of the following week, I heard Mom, Lucky and Wes in the kitchen. Wes had a wooden crate sitting on a tall stool. He had fashioned a projector by putting a light bulb in the crate. A large picture of a woman was projected onto the kitchen wall. From her waist down, she had on a grass skirt. From the waist up, her naked breasts sat exposed. An uncensored disapproving sound escaped my mouth. My mother grabbed me and dragged me into the dining room,

"Who in the hell do ya think ya are? Huh? Huh? Why I oughta…" she raised her hand. I thought to slap me. Fortunately, she only gave me a push then walked away.

A new friend at school invited me the next day to stop at her house on my way home. Unknowingly, she delayed my return home, a place I preferred not to go. She lived a short distance beyond the tree where I had swallowed the key. Her brick house with its diamond-shaped windowpanes enthralled me. When we stepped inside, it was as if I had entered the scene of one of my favorite movies; all was beautiful and elegant. In the ornately bricked kitchen, her grandmother was dipping candles in a large, round wooden vat. Some of the finished candles hung by long wicks over a line strung across the length of the room.

"Why don't you children go and play in the garden," the kindly woman said. I was drawn into this beauty as a revelation to myself that life could be lived in many different ways, a lesson I had already started learning from my seat at the Electric Theater.

Sometime in October Mrs. McVeigh introduced the class to the verb "to do": I do, you do, he does, we do, they do. "Here is a sentence that uses the verb in its contraction form," she said as she wrote it on the blackboard: *He doesn't want to work today*. "Now class, it is incorrect to say, He don't want to work today. The correct way is what I've written on the board."

I ran home from school, filled with excitement about what I had learned, eager to share it with my mother. I was so sure she would be happy to learn it too. "Mom, Mom, guess what I learned today." Mom was sitting in Grandma's chair staring blankly out the window with the palm of her hand against her mouth as she often did.

"The teacher told us not to say, "He don't." We're supposed to say, "He doesn't." It's wrong to say, "He don't."

Mom stared at me. She got an ugly look on her face and said in a familiar gruff voice, "I been talkin' this way all my life and I ain't gonna change now."

I decided that day that it was best not to share with Mom what I learned at school.

In the middle of a Saturday morning early in November, Mom and her friends were in a frenzy. It took me a while to figure out what was going on because it wasn't in Mom's nature to have conversations with me or to explain situations. I was either invisible or in the way. This morning, I watched as they frantically moved from one area of the house to the other talking about where she might have put the jewelry. I stood watching at the doorway of the kitchen as I saw Ferd yank the cookstove chimney out of the wall.

Mom reached her hand into the black hole and pulled out a white handkerchief. "My God, this is where I put it," she remarked in surprise, opening the handkerchief filled with jewelry. Ferd and Mom and the rest of them laughed.

"Edna, ya gotta watch what ya do in them blackout times, you're gonna lose your ass if you aren't careful!" Lucky snickered.

So, I thought, Mom had another blackout. Mom drank so much again, she passed out. On this day, I learned something else about her blackouts. She couldn't remember what had happened to her or what she had done.

Her drunkenness continued to color the quality of our lives through the rest of November and into the New Year. Her celebration of the New Year lingered in consequence at our house. I overheard the adults talking about what happened to her. A heated woodstove stood against the back wall of the bar where she was drinking. In her drunkenness, she had fallen against it and severely burned her arm.

Mom stood on our floor furnace to warm herself with Ferd at her side. I wanted to stand by her, but I couldn't get close. I wanted to put my arms around her and give her a big kiss and say, I love you. I wish you weren't hurt. I feel so bad about your burned arm. I wish I could take care of you to keep you safe. I wanted to, but I didn't know how.

Chapter 18

Kansas
February 1947 – July 1947

For Valentine's Day, Mrs. McVeigh taught us how to make large envelopes out of red construction paper. After we decorated them as we pleased, she hung them from the eraser holder on the side blackboard right next to the outside row of desks where I sat. For the next two weeks, I watched the envelopes get fatter and fatter with valentines.

"All right children, go to the board now to get your envelope. You may take it to your seat to see what's inside," Mrs. McVeigh said. Squeals of delight and other joyful sounds filled the room.

Mrs. McVeigh had become an important person in my life. I had never been afraid of her. I had learned to trust her; I felt safe with her. But in March, I saw a Mrs. McVeigh that frightened and disappointed me. Barbara joined our fourth-grade class late in February, too late for Valentine's Day. She was tall for her age, almost skinny in appearance, as neat as the average student, a full head of shortly cropped black hair but a posture and a demeanor that announced her shyness to even the most insensitive of our classmates.

Barbara may have repulsed Mrs. McVeigh simply because of her person but Mrs. McVeigh's disapproval of Barbara and an intention to change her demonstrated itself in two ways. Barbara's desk was most untidy. It overflowed with wadded up paper, pieces of which Barbara was known to sometimes put in her mouth to chew. Mrs. McVeigh asked me to help Barbara clean out her desk.

"What a mess this is," I said to myself, but I felt compassion for Barbara. She projected the message that she had suffered. It wasn't anything she said. She kind of wore it, like part of her dress.

Mrs. McVeigh must not have registered Barbara's pain. I was certain that the Mrs. McVeigh I loved would never cause harm to anyone in her classroom and that's why I didn't understand what she did next.

"Barbara, come up to the front of the class, please."

Barbara dutifully made her way to the front of the room where the rest of us stared at her awkward, uncomfortable body. Mrs. McVeigh stepped over and handed her a wadded-up piece of paper.

"Here Barbara, put this in our mouth," the teacher told her, "and chew it." But Mrs. McVeigh didn't stop there. She added a second and a third piece of paper to the dreadful nightmare, instructing each student in the room to watch. I sat horrified.

Further humiliation of Barbara took place not long after. It was rumored that Barbara had been sucking on rocks she picked up in the playground. Once again, she stood in front of the class.

"Barbara, I'm going to break you of the habit of putting rocks in your mouth," Mrs. McVeigh told her, along with the third and fourth graders who watched. "I have asked Barbara to gather rocks from the playground. Now Barbara, take a rock from your pocket and place it in your mouth."

Barbara took a rock from her bulging pocket without saying a word and put it in her mouth.

"Now another," Mrs. McVeigh said. Again, Barbara obeyed. Mrs. McVeigh had her add another and yet another. Barbara stood in front of us, her mouth stuffed with rocks. Her humiliation became mine. Barbara was with us for a brief period of time, then she was gone. I had a longing in my heart that I didn't fully understand. My sorrow for Barbara was all mixed up with my conflicted feelings toward Mrs. McVeigh.

Following the death of my grandmother, Mrs. McVeigh became a very important person in my life; first as my teacher, then as my friend. But the safety she had provided during my third and fourth grade at a time when I felt extremely unsafe, she destroyed with how she treated Barbara. In standing Barbara at the front of the class, belittling and humiliating her, Mrs. McVeigh became just like my mom, a person I didn't trust, a person that wasn't safe.

Something I said to Mom when I got home from school provoked another onslaught. She looked at me hatefully. "You," she said, elongating her vowels, "You think you're sooo smart!"

I was totally mystified. Why was she so angry; what did I do; what had I said that made her turn on me?

"No, No," I tried to explain. "That's not what I mean."

But she didn't understand, no matter how hard I tried. There was no reasoning with her. After that, I tiptoed around her, trying not to throw her into a rage by what I said. Sometimes, I messed up and she would hurl those sickening words at me, "You, you think you're sooooo smart!"

I rode away on my bicycle, away from Mom and her anger, away to where the deep, green grasses of spring covered the rolling field. The wheels of my bicycle left small tracks in the grass as I rode to the hill where a tall wooden tower stood. I climbed the ladder to reach the top of the tower. The sun danced in and out as if to purposefully make shadow play. I breathed the sweet fragrance of spring grasses that filled me with adventurous dreams, obliterating the nightmare of mother's rage. A sense of joy was mine, but I was not consciously aware at this point in my life, I had developed a strong self-dependence. Sitting in the tower, looking out across the green, I made a clear decision. I don't want to be like my mother. Maybe this decision was a result of how she had treated me earlier that day, but more likely, it was a conclusion arrived at from years of living life with her, an accumulation of experiences that resulted in my important life decision.

Surprisingly, Mom said directly to my sister and me, "Grandpa's in the hospital over in Great Bend." The reports came in, "...he's got dropsy." "...he's got an enlarged heart." On March 26, 1947, Grandpa died in the St. Rose Hospital where my grandmother had died two years earlier. I was but a few months from being ten years old, but I have no memory of the event of his death, my feelings about his death or the funeral services I'm told I attended. And my memories of him since the time of Grandmother's death remained forgotten, except the one time of seeing him go to bed with the neighbor lady.

The fabric of our lives continued to unravel, as it had since Grandmother's death, until the end of May. My sister and I were asleep in the living room on the couch that had been made into a bed. I'm not sure why Mom had us sleeping there instead of the front bedroom or the back room or the bed that had been in the corner of the dining room, places we had slept at different times, also for reasons unknown to me.

Mom, a strange man, and Lucky woke us up by their noise that night when they came in the front door. "Lock it," Mom told Lucky.

Almost instantly, there was a loud banging on the door and by the voice that shouted, "Edna, Edna, let me in!" I knew it was Ferd. His pounding got faster, harder, "Edna, Edna, don't do this." He continued to bang on the door, pleading with my mother.

I looked over at the man standing next to her, Ferd's replacement, I thought to myself. Mom stood motionless while Ferd continued to pound on the door. Then suddenly, silence. Mom and the strange man stayed their positions by Grandma's big chair. Lucky went to the window to peek out.

"He's getting in his truck. He's drivin' away." Mom looked as if she was starting to relax, Lucky was still at the window.

"Here he comes again, Edna. He must have driven around the block. Why hell, he's laughin'," Lucky said starting to laugh herself as the tension subsided.

Ferd drove out of our lives that day, four years after he had been invited in. His wife will probably be happy to hear he had broken up with Mom, I thought as I lay on the couch looking at the strange man who stood next to my mother, with no way of knowing that this one was a "keeper."

His name was Norman Hall, married with three children: a boy named Harold who was about two years my senior, a boy named Robert one year my junior and a little girl named Susan who was about three. It didn't put him in my favor when I learned he was here instead of with his wife and children.

"At least Ferd didn't have any children," I grumped to myself. I remembered how Mom would bitch about "that goddamned Kae Hicks" who had stolen Vern away from her.

Did she think of herself as "that goddamned Edna Schreiber" who stole Norm from his wife and children," I wondered.

The major event of Ferd's departure was overshadowed by the mega event of our home on Fourth and Santa Fe Streets completely stripped of everything except a bare mattress placed on Grandma's bedroom floor, next to the bathroom. All the furniture had been on our front lawn, publicly auctioned off on June 2, 1947, one piece at a time, including my grandpa's Chevy coupe.

Drunk Aunt Nettie was flopped down on the bare mattress and with slurred speech told me, "Look in that bathroom cabinet. I think I put a pint in there."

When Aunt Nettie went home to Hays, Kansas, Verneda and I went with her. One thing about staying with her made me happy, I got to sleep on the couch all by myself. The couch was simply a couch, no multiple features, no folding out flat to make a double bed. My sister wanted to sleep on the living room floor, which was a good arrangement for me because the two of us weren't getting along very well.

I didn't let anyone know that I sucked my thumb at night. At the end of two weeks, I wrote a letter to Mom, (the original found among her things after her death).

June 13, 1947

Dear mother,

I miss you a lot. I wish you and Norman would come up and stay. Verneda is writing to you to. I didn't even get to say hello when you phoned. I miss Shirley too! How is Tuffey and Smokey. We are going to bring Friskey home with use. Verneda wrote to Carley today. How is Norman? Lisa makes fases and bals at the least little thing. Tell Norman hello. Lisa gets mad at Friskey and kickes him and everything. She says she dosen't like him. Verneda took a comb and almost beat me to death then she slaped me in the fase and called me a lier a Dirtey lier. We went to the show last night. We are listing to Queen for a day. Verneda got her a new swimming hat. Uncle Fred went fishing last night but the river was up to high. Well I all close.

>With All my love
>Vernetta
>xxxxxxxxxxxxxx

>And one big kiss just for you
>x x
>x X x
>x x x

I was happy to leave Aunt Nettie's place for a lot of reasons. One of them was because there wasn't enough food on the dinner table.

It was night when we got back to Larned with Mom and Norm, but I knew we were on the "wrong side of town where the Mexicans live." According to Mom, and now Norm backed her up, "Mexicans and Niggers" were the worst no-good-no nothings.
"You kids sleep in here" Mom said as she took us through the tiny living room into the only bedroom in the house where an old white-metal bedframe sat under the glare of a bare light bulb which hung dangling from an ugly twisted-black wire in the middle of the ceiling. "Norm and me is goin' out to stay at his place." We heard the front door close then listened as the whir of the engine grew faint.
Morning shed light on our surroundings. Tall weeds, dried by the hot July sun, stood thick and deep in colors of yellow in a yard that swallowed up this tiny house, which was covered in tar tiles of red, creating the failed illusion of bricks. The single-seat outhouse in sagging posture sat encompassed by its own assortment of dried weeds almost my height, outside beyond the kitchen door. No pathway beaten through the weeds to the relief it offered.
In the kitchen was a relic I had never seen before, an icebox with two doors. Behind the small door sat a block of ice; behind the large door were multiple bottles of beer, no food. A

large white porcelain sink, companion to the icebox next to it, was suspended from the wall. Pipes hung down below as bare as the light bulb in the bedroom.

"We're takin ya out ta Norm's place," Mom told me, maybe days later. Thirteen-year-old Verneda was left in town to stay alone at the little red house on the wrong side of the tracks. I'm not sure why. Maybe because she and Mom got into it when they were together. I don't know, but Verneda had inherited a slice of freedom away from Mom.

Verneda

Norm's place was a farm a few miles out of town. When we got there, no one was there, except for the three of us.

"We gotta go do some things," Mom said to me. "You stay here." She didn't say what things she had to do or why I couldn't go with her or when she would return.

I pulled back the stiff laced curtain just in time to see them drive away. Flies buzzed against the glass of the window in the Kansas heat. I wandered through the emptiness of the house. I waited. The incessant buzzing of a fly irritated me. I looked out the window again. Nothing to do. No way I could get into town to go swimming or amuse myself with a movie. When would they come home? Wait.

Night came and with it a car on the driveway. "They're home!" I ran to the door to greet Mom. They looked past me, grunted, and moved around me. They went into the living room where they lay on the couch and snuggled in each other's arms. I sat on the floor at an indifferent distance but then slowly inched my way over until my back touched the front of the couch. But they still didn't see me. Eventually, they took me back to town. At least now I could go swimming again.

"You're gonna git a permanent," Mom said to me. I wanted to know why but I didn't dare ask. "I'll pick ya up from the swimming pool this afternoon."

My hair was long and straight, I liked it the way it was. "Is she gonna cut it?" I asked.

"She's gonna cut it and she's gonna put a perm in it," Mom repeated.

I reluctantly got out of the water when she came to pick me up. I didn't want to go someplace to get something done to my hair when I thought it was fine the way it was. Most of all, I didn't want to get out of the pool. But what I wanted didn't count. Mom dropped me off at what looked like a house.

As the lady put tiny rollers in my hair, she asked, "Do you like to swim?"

I went on and on about how much I loved to swim.

"Well, you won't be able to swim after I give you your permanent," she told me with an air of authority in her voice.

I don't know what else she said to me because I wasn't listening, I was thinking. I decided to give myself permission to keep on swimming. I also decided I wouldn't tell Mom that the lady said, "You can't go swimming, or you'll ruin your permanent."

"There ya go, honey," the lady concluded and spun me around in the chair so I could see myself in the mirror. My beautiful long straight hair was now short and fried into crispy little wavy kinks.

"I look like someone else," I said. I kept it to myself that I hated what she had done to my hair, that I hated getting out of the swimming pool to let her do this terrible thing to me and no permanent was going to take away my swimming pleasure.

The last thing she said to me was, "Now remember, don't go swimming."

The next day, I went swimming as usual. By the end of the day, my frizz lay limply on my head and around my face. "What the hell happened to your hair!" Mom questioned. If only I could be invisible today like I usually am, I thought to myself.

I lied and shrugged my shoulders, "I don't know."

"You're goin' right back to that beauty parlor. That's the worst permanent I ever seen. That woman has to fix it." I shuddered at the thought but stood firmly silent.

The lady lifted my limp hair by the palm of her hand. "Did you go swimming?" she asked. I denied that I had. She met my lie with a lie, "I'm gonna snip a piece of it off to send in to have it tested. They can tell if you went swimming."

Once again, I stood my ground in silence. Finally, she gave up and said to me with determination, "Now I'm gonna try to fix your hair to make your momma happy."

I don't know what she did to my hair, but when Mom came back my life became unbearably miserable.

"Did your girl go swimming yesterday?" she asked Mom.

"Ya" Mom nodded.

Then all hell broke loose when the lady said, "I told her not to go swimming, it would ruin the perm."

"You goddamned kid!" she yelled when she got me outside. The sting of her hand hit hard against my face. "Git your ass in that car," she said, shoving me into the back seat. "Who the hell do you think you are, goin' swimmin', ruinin' that perm! That perm cost money! What do you think: I can shit money?"

I cowered in the backseat until finally she left me alone and drove us back to the little red house where she yanked me from the car by my arm.

"You stay in this house. If you leave and I find out about it you'll git the lickin' of your life. You're goin' to Idaho with your sister, and I don't want your hair lookin' like shit. You stay away from that swimmin' pool if ya know what's good for ya!"

After a few more threats she went out the door with Norm, adding, "Git in there and clean that kitchen."

She and Norm got in the back seat of the car that was waiting out front. I thought they were laughing as I watched them drive away. It felt for a time that the sky Chicken Little warned about had actually fallen on me. Alone in the little red house amid a sea of yellow dried weeds, I decided it was better than being with Mom.

Dutifully, I went into the kitchen where I was greeted with a repulsive but familiar odor. It was the smell of beer and whiskey mixed with the remains of cigarette butts floating amid garbage left on dirty dishes. This floating smelly mess filled the sink and plugged it from draining. It didn't occur to me not to clean the sink. That didn't seem like an option, going against Mom's orders. But satisfaction was my reward as I looked back at the cleanness of the empty kitchen sink on my way to the living room to dance to music from the record player.

Without explanation a day or so later, Mom handed me one of the old grass skirts, "Put this on, I'm gonna take your picture."

"What shall I wear for a top?" I asked.

"Ya don't need a top." The halter-tops that came with the skirts were gone, lost or given away.

"I feel naked without a top,"

"Ah hell, don't worry about them little mosquito bites." I tried to express my embarrassment at having my picture taken with nothing on except the grass skirt.

She pulled a plastic lei from the box and threw it at me. "Here. Put this on and shut your goddamned mouth. Git out there by that tree; I'm gonna take your picture."

Leaning against the tree that stood out front, I crossed my arms in front of me, trying to cover my nipples.

"Git your damned arms down," Mom ordered. I slid my arms down. "Smile, dammit," she demanded, but never told me why she wanted to take the picture.

Vernetta

    Mom brought some suitcases in and put them on the bed of the little red house,
    "Pack up your things. Norm and me is gonna drive you kids to Denver to catch the train."
    Verneda asked her, "Where are we goin'?"
    "You're gonna go stay with Clarence and Mae or Mary and Herman in Twin Falls."
    "Idaho!" Verneda said in disbelief. The Verneda's anger didn't find a target until we reached Denver. We drove off in the back seat of Norm's car July of 1947, never return to Larned, Kansas as children.

Edna and Norm

Chapter 19

Idaho
July 1947 – October 1947

In Denver Mom and Norm got us a cheap hotel room. Norm handed Verneda a couple of dollars. "Here, you kids go see a movie."

My thirteen-year-old sister protested, "But I don't know my way around this town."

Norm proceeded to give her directions. "Now go on and take Vernetta with ya."

On the sidewalk outside the hotel, Verneda's pent-up anger found its target in me.

"I'm sick of always havin' to take you where I go." She turned away from me and walked as fast as she could.

"Wait for me," I called after her, but she rushed on. I ran, trying to keep up with her but it was useless. I watched her turn a corner, which took her out of sight. The fear of being lost and alone in a strange city spurred me to run as fast as I could to the corner where she had vanished out of sight. "There she is," I said, watching her disappear around another corner. I continued turning where I thought she turned until I caught a glimpse of a theater about half a block away on the right-hand side. There she was, waiting for me.

"Here's your ticket, but don't sit next to me," she ordered, then went inside.

I knew better than to say anything to Mom when we got back to the hotel about Verneda trying to lose me. My first reason was that I was about to go on a long train ride, alone with my sister. The second reason was that it wouldn't do any good.

The next morning Mom gave Norm a camera. "Here, I want ya ta take our picture." So I, with my frizzy perm, stepped into the doorway of the train, Mom stood in front of me, and Verneda was next to her, standing on the platform. Norm took our picture. I waved to her until the train took us out of sight, not knowing when I would see her again.

The train sped along to Twin Falls. My sister and I covered some of the same miles that we had traveled alone when she was a mere five years old, and I was but a toddler. On this trip, we were alone again but at least now, she could take better care of us because she was thirteen and a half and I was almost ten. On the map, the distance between Larned, Kansas and Twin Falls, Idaho is approximately eight hundred miles. In child miles, Larned is a continent away from Twin Falls.

Aunt Mary and Uncle Herman, Uncle Clarence and Aunt Mae met us at the train in Twin Falls. Although I had not yet met Mom's first husband, Vern, I had lived with his two brothers, Herman and Clarence and their wives, intermittently during the early years of my life. This connection was one way in which my mother unknowingly provided some sense of security.

The decision was made that Verneda and I should stay with Uncle Clarence and Aunt Mae since Mae was home during the day. The experience I had of living with kind, simple people who didn't drink acted as an antidote to the frightful aloneness I drove away from when I left Larned in the back seat of Norm's car.

Uncle Clarence and Aunt Mae lived in a small cinderblock house where Jackson Street dead-ended into a pasture. The humble house had a small living room with a linoleum-covered floor. A door on the right led to the kitchen with a view to the pasture through a window over the kitchen sink. The only bathroom was off the kitchen at the back across from the back door. Stairs to the unfinished attic went up toward the back of the living room then turned as they continued to the top. The four of us slept in the attic, which was strung with ropes where blankets hung as room dividers. Our bed was a mattress on the floor toward the front of the house under a window.

Across the dirt street and parallel to the house was a fresh-water canal that flowed freely on its destination to I didn't know where. Under the blue of the Idaho sky, shielded from the summer sun at times by billows of white clouds, I lay on the wood-planked footbridge that crossed the canal. With the warmth of the sun on my back, I watched cloud reflections ripple over the water. I let my hand dangle in the water to feel its coolness as it rushed around my fingers to continue its course. I watched the water skippers as they darted in and out, skating gracefully on the water's surface, a wondrous mystery to me.

Almost every evening, Uncle Clarence put the same record on the player then sat back in his chair in the corner of the living room and we listened. "On the Jericho Road, there's room for just two. No more or no less, just Jesus and you. Each shackle He'll bear, each sorrow He'll share. There's never a care, for my Jesus is there."

Uncle Clarence and Aunt Mae took Verneda and me to church, not on Sunday, but on Saturday. This seemed odd to me. I had never heard of anyone going to church on Saturday. The first Saturday I went to what they called Sabbath School in a room filled with children my age. A piano player vigorously pounded out song after song. One of them was called "Roll, Roll Your Burdens Away." Once I had the words down, I threw back my head and sang those words from a heart filled with unchronicled burdens accumulated in my nine years of living.

> Roll, Roll Your Burdens Away
> Roll, Roll Your Burdens Away
> For Jesus Has Promised to Take Them All
> Roll, Roll Your Burdens Away.

After the church service on Saturdays, lots of people, including Uncle Clarence, Aunt Mae, Verneda and me would go on a picnic to some wonderful place. One Sabbath, as they called it, we went into the hills to find the mineral baths. Smelly steam rising from the water almost stopped me from going in, but my love of water and my desire to feel its warmth and its wetness, overcame my resistance. These outings became an experience of community, an experience of belonging.

Uncle Clarence took me to the pastor's house for Bible lessons. "Turn to Leviticus 11," the pastor said. "You see, Vernetta, in this chapter God tells us what animals are clean to eat and the ones that are not."

I had never heard that before! I remembered sitting on the counter in our café in Albert where Grandpa used to let me put my hand in a big jar and pull out a pickled pig's foot to eat. Now the pastor was telling me pigs aren't good for me to eat.

"Next let's turn to First Peter, chapter 3, verse 3." He began to read. "Your beauty should not come from outward adornment, such as braided hair and the wearing of gold jewelry and fine clothes. Instead, it should be that of your inner self, the unfading beauty of a gentle and quiet spirit, which is of great worth in God's sight."

"Do you understand?" he asked when he had finished reading.

"I guess so. It's better to be beautiful on the inside than the outside, and you shouldn't wear jewelry or braid your hair. I wonder why it's not okay to braid your hair. I like to braid my hair," I said, wondering what the pastor would think.

"Well, you can braid your hair. I think the women Peter knew braided expensive things into their braids and that's what he meant." I was satisfied.

Of the things we read, there were two that really caught my attention. "Let's read in Exodus next. Here God has given us the Ten Commandments, His principles of love to guide us in our daily living."

We carefully read each one and talked about it. I was especially interested in the one about the Sabbath. Planted right in the middle of those "principles of love to guide us in our daily living" was the statement that our Creator had created the world in six days and then rested from His labor on the seventh day. The seventh day of the week was the only day God Himself had sanctified and set aside as Holy. It was on this day we were to remember and worship our Creator.

"The seventh day has been preserved throughout the history of mankind by God himself," the pastor explained, "and Saturday is the seventh day."

"Wow, I've never heard anything like that!" I said to the pastor and Uncle Clarence. "I always go to Sunday school on Sunday." They didn't say much more about it, but it sure got me thinking.

"Let's turn to Matthew, chapter 24."

I was relieved to hear the pastor say, "We'll stop after we read and talk about it." As he read, I got scared at some parts but happy at other parts. I loved the part that said Jesus would come again and take to heaven those who believe in Him and love Him and follow in what He said. I had met Jesus in Sunday school class. I already loved Him, but I didn't know He would come back to take me to heaven until the pastor read it to me. My heart was happy to hear such good news. I was scared when he read the yucky stuff that would happen right before we saw Jesus coming in the clouds of heaven.

Several Sabbaths later, we were told on a Friday evening that tomorrow would be the day of Communion at the church service. My sister and I were expected to attend.

"What do they do at Communion," my sister asked Uncle Clarence.

"We celebrate the Last Supper in remembrance of Jesus."

After some probing, Verneda learned some things about the celebration she didn't like. "I don't want to go and have my feet washed," she told Uncle Clarence.

"Jesus washed the feet of his disciples and told us to do the same thing for each other," he explained. 'Tomorrow at the church, people will divide in pairs to wash each other's feet. You and Vernetta are goin' with us." End of discussion. Verneda and I went to bed.

When the next morning came, my sister said to Uncle Clarence and Aunt Mae, "I'm not goin'."

"Well, you are goin'," my uncle said.

Verneda crossed her arms, looked at him and said, "I'm not goin', and you can't make me."

Uncle Clarence rose to the challenge, "If you don't go, you can't stay in the house 'cause I'm gonna lock the door." She raised the ante, "Lock the door, I don't care but I'm not goin'."

The decision was made, my sister would not go to the ceremony and Uncle Clarence would lock her out of the house. The focus shifted to me. My loyalties lay with my sister.

"If she doesn't go, I'll stay home with her," I said softly to my uncle and aunt. They accepted my choice without answering. My angry sister and I sat on the front lawn, locked out of their home until they returned from church.

On Monday when we came down to have breakfast, Aunt Mae was cleaning raspberries in the sink. She was always gentle and soft spoken. "Would you girls like some raspberries?" she asked.

"I've never had fresh raspberries," I told her. Aunt Mae let me gorge myself.

"We're goin' into town right after breakfast. Would the two of you like to go with us?" Aunt Mae asked as she kept cleaning raspberries.

"I would!" I said, hoping for an adventure. But Verneda said she would rather stay home.

That night, when we were lying on our mattress looking up at the night sky we could see through the window above our heads, my sister whispered to me, "I took a ride on Uncle Clarence's motor bike today."

"You did!" I said in amazement.

"Yeah, I got it started real easy. But when I got on the road, I hit the gravel. Me and the bike flew into the ditch. The bike landed on me." Then she added the last part of her story, "I'm bleedin', like I got my period."

"We better tell Aunt Mae," I urged.

"Nah, they'd just tell me it was my fault for takin' the bike and then I'd get in trouble. I got the bike put back. I don't think anyone knows I took it."

"But you're bleedin'; we better tell her," I said with concern.

"I'd just get in trouble. Go to sleep now," she said as she rolled over with her back to me. She bled for three weeks but refused to tell anyone.

Aunt Mary and Uncle Herman had a little house in town too, so we got to visit on the weekends sometimes when she wasn't working. Once in a while we got to go see her at the large downtown cafe where she worked. Before coming to Idaho, the last time I had seen my Aunt Mary was in Larned about two years earlier. She took her place forever as my favorite aunt that late summer and fall of 1947.

At work Aunt Mary wore a waitress uniform with a sweet little handkerchief poking out of her top pocket. Other things sticking out of her uniform were her long skinny neck, equally skinny arms, and skinny legs, from which her nylons hung in folds. She wore a tiny starched-white apron around her waist and a funny little hat, that was hardly a hat but more like an elongated triangle, atop her netted, thin, lightly curled brown hair. Her little scarecrow figure, though she was a tall woman, was comparable to the sound of her voice. Out of her mouth came thin, narrow nasal tones. But I heard music when she spoke to me. Her beauty, perhaps invisible to others, encompassed me. I loved her.

I didn't love her because she bought me my first bicycle, or because she bought me a beautiful flannel nightgown, or because she bought me the delicate, silver Indian bracelet. I didn't even love her because she generously shared her tips with me that bulged from each hip pocket of her waitress uniform. She loved me first and I loved her back.

Verneda and I sat in a booth waiting for Aunt Mary to come. A song played on the jukebox. Aunt Mary came over to us and gave each of us a hello and a kiss on our cheek.

"I like that song, Aunt Mary," I said after she had given me my kiss.

She dug into her pocket. "Here's a dime. You can play it again if you want to."

"But I don't know what the name of it is," I said.

Aunt Mary showed me a little box on the end of our table. "See, each song is listed by name. The number next to the name is the one you choose if you want to hear the song. The one you like is "'Til The End of Time."

"Why do you like that song?" my sister asked. "It doesn't have any words."

"I like it because the piano is playing such beautiful music," I told her, putting in my dime to hear the song again.

When Aunt Mary got off work, the three of us were walking past a store where Verneda saw in the window a beautiful pair of white boots with wheels attached. "Shoe skates." she said in a soft voice as she stopped in front of the window. "Shoe skates!" she repeated excitedly to Aunt Mary and me. The three of us stood looking through the window at the white boots with shiny chrome wheels attached. "Can we go in to see 'em?" she asked.

"I need to be home in a few minutes," Aunt Mary began, then paused. "But if it doesn't take too long…" Verneda was already in the store before Aunt Mary could finish her sentence. When we left the store, my sister was overjoyed.

"What does 'layaway' mean?" I asked Aunt Mary.

"That means I couldn't give the man all the money at once. I gave him part of the money and when I give him the rest, then we get to bring the skates home."

Early in August, Verneda got her shoe skates. For the rest of August, my sister went to the local skating rink as often as Uncle Clarence and Aunt Mae would allow.

September came. We were enrolled in a large, sprawling brick school where it felt like the whole Twin Falls population of school-aged children attended. But that didn't last long. Going to a strange school in a strange town triggered something in Verneda.

"Aunt Mary, can I stay at your place this weekend? Just me," she asked. There wasn't much discussion and Verneda got what she wanted.

Sunday morning, I heard Uncle Clarence say, "She climbed out the window in the night to run off with some boy she met at the skating rink."

Aunt Mae said, "Poor Mary. Frantic when she found Verneda gone. Out in the night searchin' for her."

The discussion went to how helpless the aunts and uncles felt; what to do to control Verneda; and ended with a decision to send us to Uncle Herman's farm in Hagerman, Idaho, away from the skating rink, away from the friends she had made.

I didn't know where Hagerman was, and I hoped with all my heart it wasn't a long train ride away. I started thinking about my mom. "Aunt Mae, why did Mom send us here and do you know when she's comin' to get us?"

"Your momma's getting married to Norman and they are on their honeymoon," is the answer she gave me. I didn't know how Norm could be marrying my mom when he already had a wife and kids of his own, but I didn't ask.

"When's she comin; back to get us?"

"Don't know, honey."

I sat in the backseat of the car next to Aunt Mary as we headed from Twin Falls to Hagerman. She began stroking my arm, talking to me as we drove along. How splendid it was to be simultaneously soothed by her touch and comforted by her words. The landscape quickly turned to sage interrupted by an occasional farm. After a short trip, Uncle Herman turned the car onto a dirt driveway that went down into a small valley where a pleasant looking white house sat with soft hills rising around it.

A barn stood a few hundred feet from the house, straight ahead of us. "We have horses. When Clarence comes tomorrow, you can ride them," Aunt Mary said, trying to make the change a happy one for us.

Vernetta, Aunt Mary, Uncle Herman, Verneda

The huge horses frightened me, but I rode them anyway. "Watch out when ya turn 'em around; hold on tight," Uncle Clarence called as we rode slowly and peacefully away from the barn. But as soon as I turned my horse to go back, that horse almost ran out from under me as he headed full speed for the barn.

Someone enrolled us in the country school. Verneda and I walked from the house up the hill through the sage.
"Mmm," I said, "What's that smell"
"I don't know, and I don't care," she grumped. I knew we were in trouble.
"But it smells so good," I said as I picked a piece of sage to sniff at it. "That's it, that's the smell!" I shouted.
"Who cares," she said as we continued up the hill, across the highway and stopped to wait for the yellow school bus.
The next day on our walk to catch the school bus, I heard the song of a bird I once heard when I was a very little girl, years

ago in Twin Falls. I didn't know the name of the bird, but I knew the song. I was enraptured and tried to whistle it.

"Why don't you just shut up. You're drivin' me nuts."

Things got worse a few days later. The bell rang; recess was over. Verneda stood by the swings.

"Come on," I said to her.

"I'm not goin' in," she told me. I watched as the other children went inside.

"We'll get in trouble."

She kicked the dirt with her foot. "I'm not goin'."

I walked over and sat on one of the swings. The emptiness of the schoolyard held just my sister and me; her misery became mine.

When we got home, Aunt Mary was especially excited. "Your Mother called. They'll be here in a few days to take you to Salt Lake City with them." My sister got a lot happier.

Finally, toward mid-October, Mom and Norm drove up in a new car. Well, it was new to me, but it wasn't really new. It was a large, two-toned green Buick with an intriguing ornament that stood splendidly on the hood. I was eager to hug my mom when she got out of the car, but she was busy talking to Aunt Mary and Uncle Herman.

Chapter 20

Utah
October 1947 – May 1949

Autumn was well underway by the time we arrived in Salt Lake City, Utah in October of 1947. Our brand new eight-by-twenty-four-foot trailer was parked with two rows of trailers that sat facing each other in a community called Sugar House on the crest of a hill. Mom got out of the car first without saying much as she pulled open the door of the trailer, then the screen door. "Go on in," she told us.

A miniature scene with the scent of newness greeted eyes and nose. In front of the door stood a small table with two chairs. On the right was a very small sofa against the front-end wall of the trailer. Next to the front door on the left stood a strange object that I would become acquainted with as the cold of the Utah winter came. The trailer was divided into three playhouse-sized areas: the living room with its sofa and table; the kitchen defined by a tiny stove and sink; and a single bedroom across the back end of the trailer, which of course was Mom and Norm's space. I liked the crisp newness of the trailer but even more, I liked being where my mother was.

Mom pointed to a small sofa. "You kids'll sleep here; it folds down," she said without emotion or apology for its lack of privacy or its size. She moved to a narrow door. "Vernetta, this is where you can hang your clothes." I stared into the miniature space, not hearing the place my sister was told to put her clothes.

"Where's the bathroom," I asked.

"The trailer park has bathrooms and showers," Mom answered, going to the window of the trailer to show us where they were. In the morning, I saw a parade of people in bathrobes with towels over their arms, headed in that direction.

She took me down the hill to a school that was only a few blocks away on the same street as the trailer park. We sat in the Principal's Office as Mom gave her the information needed to enroll me. Then down the hall we went to the fifth grade I was assigned to. This was the third school I had attended for fifth grade. I felt shy and frightened and struggled to hold back tears when two girls came and offered to share pencils with me.

"You can collect leaves wherever you find them," the teacher said to the class after she seated me in the middle row. "Keep them in a notebook. We'll identify the name of tree they came from."

When school was out, I ran to the tree-filled-hollow behind the trailer park. It was a wooded area that flowed down the hill in the shape of an elongated bowl. It had a fragrance I couldn't identify but one that gave me deep pleasure. The colors of autumn were ripe. I had many beautiful and different leaves from which to choose. I selected quite a few. I picked up one with alternating rounded and indented shapes that made their way around the entire edge of the leaf. It was my favorite. I placed my leaf collection loosely between the pages of a simple-softcover-spiral notebook.

The teacher went around the room, carefully paying attention to each student's leaf collection. When my turn came, I held up my favorite leaf.

"That is an oak leaf from the oak tree," she told me sweetly.

"An oak leaf," I repeated to myself. After school ended, I took my notebook with my leaves carefully tucked between the pages and began my walk home. It had been raining all day and the gutters were filled with water. Somehow, I made a misstep, and my leaf notebook went flying from my hand and floated upon the water of the gutter. I yanked it up as quickly as I could but still it was soaked and many of my leaves were wet or were swept away.

When I got home, I didn't tell anyone about my leaf notebook or how awful I felt because I knew no one would be interested. I went back to the hollow to find more leaves, but I saw two boys running in my direction who frightened me, so I hurried out of the hollow without collecting more leaves.

Rain fell the next day. October was almost at an end. I sadly realized it was too late to collect more leaves. I'll get some in the spring, I told myself. I'll find different shapes and sizes and maybe even learn the name of the trees they're from. My love for trees and their leaves deepened beyond where it had started when I was a fourth grader, looking out Mrs. McVeigh's classroom window.

The very best part of moving back to Salt Lake was Maxine. She had last seen me when I was five years old in December of 1942. Now I was ten. Her son Dale, or Tudy as we called him, was taller than I was even though he was almost two years younger. Ray, her husband was a small, gentle man who always had a pleasant smile on his face. Of the three of them, Maxine was my favorite. Her words were always kind and softly spoken. One thing I really liked was that she didn't cuss and swear. I noticed that she and Tudy were the best of friends and when I came back to Salt Lake, she included me as her friend. She let me come to her home as often as I wanted, a warm safe place that reminded me of earlier days with her father, Grandpa Hoffman, when I lived with him.

Ray, Maxine and Tudy lived in a brick house, a short distance continuing up the hill from where our trailer was parked. The house seemed large to me. Tudy had his very own bedroom that was probably larger than the interior of our trailer.

"You're sure lucky, Tudy!"

"Why'm I so lucky?" he asked.

"'Cause you have a bathroom right next to your bedroom," I said.

Maxine let us skate in the basement. Tudy and I skated round and round the coal furnace that sat at the bottom of the stairs to the right. On one of our rounds, he suddenly stopped.

"Look," he said, as he pointed into a large round metal tub. "It's my turtle; he's asleep." Tudy explained that his turtle slept all through the winter months.

Maxine called to us, "I need to get back to the café, kids. Come on up."

Maxine and Mom had already gone into business together before Mom brought Verneda and me to Salt Lake City. They bought a little café out on WN Temple Street to serve their own home-cooked meals. It wasn't much, a small rectangular cinderblock building separated from the busy street by a gravel parking lot with views of sky and mountains on the other side of the street as you looked across a vacant field. Norm liked it I'm sure because when he came home from work, he stood behind the counter drinking all the beer he wanted.

The Café

One day in the middle of November, Mom said, "We're movin' the trailer out behind the café." That's one thing about a home on wheels. You can hitch it up and take it someplace else. I found myself wishing I could live in a brick house like Tudy, instead of a trailer Norm and Mom pulled around on wheels to move whenever they felt like it.

Norm pulled the trailer across town and parked it behind the café. He backed it over the weeds, maneuvered it around a bit and then I guess he was satisfied because he turned off the car then unhooked the trailer. It sat a few feet from the back door of the café, across a stretch of gravel.

I didn't know where we were going to shower or go to the bathroom, but Mom answered that question without my asking. "You can use the toilet in the café. When ya need ta wash yourself, you can use the cafe sink."

How in the world am I supposed to take a bath in that sink? I wanted to ask as we stood looking into the two large metal sinks where the café dishes were washed. Nevertheless, these sinks became bathtubs for Verneda and me, as long as the trailer was parked behind the café.

"You're goin' to a different school," Mom said as she enrolled me in the fourth new-school I had attended for fifth grade. Onequa grade school was a wonderful two-story brick building set in a quiet neighborhood surrounded by abundant open space. The inside was even more inviting than the outside because I liked my new fifth grade teacher and my new friends.

But I must admit there was one boy I tried to avoid at Onequa. His name was Leon. He had flaming red hair. I don't know if he helped his dad on the farm, but Leon wore checkered flannel shirts and overalls like my Uncle Kenneth who was a farmer. That was okay with me. He had a dumb look on his face, I thought. He even acted dumb. That was okay with me, too. But when he picked his nose, I watched him put his finger in his mouth to suck off the goober. That was definitely not okay with me. That's why I avoided him no matter how far out of my way I had to go.

Right before Christmas Mom said, "We're movin' the trailer back to Sugar House." I went back to the same school where I had collected leaves.

"We're movin' the trailer behind the café," Mom told us in February. I returned to Onequa school.

About two months later in April, I was told again, "We're gonna live in Sugar House."

I went alone to the Principal's Office at the school in Sugar House. "We've moved back, and I need to go to school here again," I told the principal.

She looked at me across the huge dark wooden desk where she sat. "Now Vernetta, is this going to be the last time?"

I shrugged my shoulders. "I don't know." If only I could disappear, I thought to myself, shrinking down in my chair, wishing to be out of sight of the principal and her disapproval of my going in and out of her school. Doesn't she know that the adults in my life are in control of these constant moves?

When Mom and Norm moved the trailer once again behind the café, I hoped we would never move back to Sugar House because I didn't want to face the principal or hear her say, You again, Vernetta! Sorry you can't come back this time.

My fifth-grade teacher at Onequa, unlike the principal at Sugar House, welcomed my return in her pleasant kind way. "For music class today, we'll practice singing some of our Christmas carols. Let's begin with 'O Come All Ye Faithful.'" She walked up and down the rows while we were singing. She stopped at my desk and told the class, "Vernetta has the best little alto voice I've ever heard." I was glad she liked my singing.

In class several weeks later, she announced to the students, "Jerry Bell and Vernetta Schreiber will each sing a solo for the class."

We all sang, drew and square-danced our way through the remaining school days of fifth grade, but especially and always we tried to avoid Leon who picked his nose and ate it.

School continued to be the safe haven it had become long ago in Jarbidge, Nevada, although in Salt Lake it wasn't as important as it had been in the past. The days of Mom's endless drunkenness had been left behind in Kansas along with my being left alone at night.

When my pregnant Mom was as ripe and as round as a summer watermelon in July 1948, Vernon Schreiber showed up in Salt Lake with that "goddamned Kae Hicks." I'm not sure how he found us. But Mom said, "Your Dad is comin' to see ya."

Verneda had known him and loved him and blamed Mom that he had left us, so she was excited he was coming. I didn't think much about the news, curious maybe, but to me he was a stranger, someone I had never met. However, I did get caught up in the excitement or rather, the inconvenience his coming caused my pregnant mother with his arrival.

Our trailer was parked at Sugar House when Vern came. I was glad for that. It was a much nicer place than behind the café. Grandma Schreiber, Vern's mother, came with them. Maybe she's the one that encouraged the visit; I'm not sure.

Vernetta with Vern

They didn't come into the trailer. We all stood outside on the gravel for a short time before Verneda and I left with Vern and Kae to go to Temple Square. We toured the great Mormon Tabernacle, listening to the man talk about how it was built, when it was built, and the remarkable acoustics. He separated himself from us by going to the other end of the Tabernacle, some distance away. He proceeded to hush the small group of tourists.

"Now, I want you to listen carefully for the sound when I drop this pin," he said to us. Silence filled the large, rounded shape of the elongated building. Then we heard it, a tiny sound the pin made when it dropped to the wooden floor.

"Let's take pictures by the fountain, Vern," Kae suggested just before they whisked us back to the trailer and were suddenly gone, the silence between us once again intact.

Not long after Vern left, the baby was born and named Glenda. What do we need with a baby in a bassinette that blocks our way from the living room to the kitchen? There isn't even enough room for Mom and Norm and Verneda and me, I complained to myself. Mom's last name isn't the same as mine anymore, I continued to grump to myself. I felt alone and yucky, like I didn't belong to their family or any family. Now they have a baby of their own with the same last name, I lamented. Mom belongs to a different family than my sister and me, I concluded, wallowing in self-inflicted agony.

Edna and baby Glenda

Verneda still had the same last name as I did but that didn't mean all was hunky-dory between us. She brought her friend Valerie home for a sleepover in September after Norm pulled the trailer from Sugar House and parked it behind the cafe for the remainder of the time we lived in Salt Lake.

"Valerie's gonna spend the night," Verneda told me.

I looked up at the gigantic Valerie. "Where's she gonna sleep?"

"On the couch with us."

"Not on my side." It was one of those rare times that I stood up for myself.

"There isn't enough room for her to sleep on my side."

"No, there isn't enough room for two so how do you think three of us can sleep on that little couch? I'm not sleeping in the crack between the wall and the sofa."

But Valerie did spend the night, sleeping mostly on Verneda's side of the couch. From her looks and her sounds, I guessed Verneda would make me disappear, if she could.

I'm sick and tired of your complaints, Vernetta," Mom told me. "I'm takin' you to a doctor."

My visit to the doctor came after several mysterious nightly episodes in the trailer.

"What in the hell is happenin' to that stove, it keeps goin' out," Norm complained. He was talking about the heater that sat to the left of the front door in its own little corner.

"So that's what that thing is, a heater," I said to myself the first time Norm struck a match to it.

At the bottom of the heater was a round hole about the size of a quart jar lid. Sometimes fire would spit out the round hole. "That stove frightens me, Mom," I told her.

"Ah that stove ain't gonna hurt ya," was her reply, which didn't help my fear at all. The stove sat a short distance from where I slept and when the fire came spitting out of the hole, I was afraid it would catch my bed on fire.

One morning Verneda said to me, "I come home last night, and you was standin' at the front door. You didn't say a word. You jist went to the stove, turned it off and went back to bed. You was like a zombie, jist turned it off and went back to bed.

"Well, that solves that mystery," Norm said when he heard the story.

Maybe that's why Mom decided it was time to take me to the doctor. The doctor directed a question to me. "Where do you sleep?"

"I sleep on a foldout sofa with my sist--" I was about to continue but Mom cut me off.

"Does Vernetta sleep on a foldout sofa with her sister?" the doctor asked.

"Yes, but it's only temporary."

Later the doctor asked me, "And what do you eat for breakfast?"

"Usually cold cereal," I answered.

Mom quickly added, with an edge to her voice, "Sometimes I fix eggs or biscuits and gravy." Mom was upset with me when we left the doctor's office.

"But I was just telling the truth," I blurted out; then realized I might be in trouble for talking back. It surprised me when Mom didn't say anything. She's sure a lot nicer than she used to be, I thought, and I'm so happy she isn't getting drunk any more.

Beyond having to take care of baby Glenda sometimes after school and in the evenings, my life was pleasant. I enjoyed freedom to play with my neighborhood friend Danny; to eat potato chips from the café kitchen whenever I wanted; to play the tilt machine that sat in the café; I even got to play our punchboard and win a tiny "Little Bo Peep" doll dressed in blue. I bought myself a Mickey Mouse watch. I wrote poetry. I completed a Bible correspondence course over a period of months and rejoiced in my accomplishment when my Certification of Completion came in the mail.

It also made me feel good to be chosen as one of the singers in sixth grade to represent our school at the Tabernacle in Temple Square where we would join children from other schools to present a concert.

"Mom, I got picked to sing at the Tabernacle," I told her. "Will you please come?"

"I don't know, Vernetta. I gotta work."

The time approached for the concert and miraculously, Mom went with me. I don't know if she went because I didn't have any other transportation or if she went because she wanted to go, but she was there and that's what counted. This was the first of my school events that she had ever attended.

When we arrived, masses of people were everywhere. I joined my group high up in a balcony overlooking the main floor. "Oh no," I said as I looked down at the main floor. "It's crowded with people." People had filled the seats and were standing around the perimeter.

"I'm worried about my mom," I told the girl standing next to me. I wanted her to have the best seat and I so much wanted her to be able to see me. It didn't work out that way, but the nicest part was, Mom wasn't mad. That made it all the more special. She didn't even bitch about the crowds.

One day I brought home a large black record I had spotted sitting on the top of a trash heap. I was ecstatic with the sounds I heard when I played it on our old Victrola. The label on the record read "Beautiful Ohio." I played it for anyone who would listen. I played it repeatedly for myself. Mom and Norm liked cowboy music, people who sang with twangy sounds and used words like "ain't" or "don't" where doesn't is supposed to go. Mom called some of her music "Cryin in your beer songs."

Humming one of the beautiful songs from my record, I skipped through the back door of the café surprised to see Mom. She was sitting on a stool, nursing baby Glenda, but that wasn't what surprised me. It was the sad expression on Mom's face as she looked down at baby Glenda. She was totally unaware that I was there.

I continued on to the kitchen, wondering why Mom was so sad when she was looking at the baby. I couldn't figure out the answer. I was too young to understand that returning to Salt Lake might have triggered memories in Mom, painful memories of Bud leaving her, memories of losing her baby, Buddy, Jr.

New Year's Eve of 1949 was the first time since we had left Larned, Kansas that I saw my mother drunk. She was in the back seat of our car, parked between the back of the café and our trailer. I wasn't sure why she had gotten drunk, maybe to celebrate the

New Year, I thought. But flopped out alone in the back seat didn't seem like much of a celebration to me. It was a reminder of how wonderful these past months had been without her getting drunk.

"She's gotten too big for that thing, Norm," Mom grumbled. "Kicked the end right out of the damn thing."

Each day the end of the bassinette opened more and more, the top rail separated from the weaving of the basket that revealed a larger and larger gap. Glenda looked like "giant baby" in the little white falling-apart bassinette. I never heard them talking about the decision to move back to Kansas but when Mom spoke of the bassinette - "No place to put a baby bed in this goddamned trailer" - the tones were ominous, as if the problem we faced was almost insurmountable. I knew something heavy hung over our heads. It was as if the growth of the baby determined when we would leave Utah, for it was after Glenda kicked the final pieces out of the end of her bassinette that Mom and Norm told us we would return to Kansas, toward the end of May 1949.

"Can I stay here to finish the school year?" my sister pleaded. "I can stay with Valerie, then come to Kansas after school's out."

Mom responded in a tone that allowed no room for negotiation. "No, you're comin' with me."

Verneda tried desperately to convince Mom to let her stay in Salt Lake. "Only a few weeks more so I can finish ninth grade," she begged. But Mom would have nothing to do with it.

My sister, caught in a power struggle, said angrily, "If you take me to Kansas, I'll quit school." That was where she stood her ground, actually believing that this position would get what she wanted. She hadn't counted on Mom's total indifference to the value of education. Mom herself had gone no further than the eighth grade and books were foreign territory to her.

"We're sleepin in this motel a couple of nights then we'll be goin'." The sound of Mom's voice was different. Maybe she's sad we're going, I thought. "You kids kin sleep on that mattress," she said, pointing to a bare mattress that lay on the floor.

The dilapidated motel sat further up on WN Temple, past our café, across the street from a small grocery where my friend Coy was a cashier for her mother. I went in to say goodbye.

"I'm sorry you have to go. Wish we could finish the sixth grade together," Coy said.

"Me too. I'll miss you," I said, then turned and left the store.

Since Mom wouldn't allow Verneda to stay in Salt Lake, she agreed to let Larue, a fifteen-year-old friend who smoked and drank, come to Kansas with us. Now there were four of us in the back seat: Verneda, Larue, Glenda and me.

Out the back window of the car, I saw a small, covered trailer hitched to us. I wonder what Mom and Norm did with our other trailer. But I didn't really care. By the time we left it, wherever we left it, I was glad to be rid of it. I felt sorry for the new people who would have to live without a bathroom.

Maxine waved goodbye to us from the doorway of the café. I sadly waved back, asking myself the question, why are we moving back to Kansas? I was only a kid, so no one bothered to explain it to me. Norm turned the nose of the car in the direction of Kansas. Kansas again.

Dale/Tudy, Grandpa, Vernetta

Verneda

Chapter 21

Kansas
June 1949 – August 1949

The Ross family thought nothing of landing on each other's doorstep, suitcases in hand for an indefinite stay. That's the way it was when we pulled up in front of Aunt Nettie's house in Hays, Kansas, only we didn't bring a suitcase, we brought a trailer stuffed with our things.

I got to sleep in the double bed with my six-year-old cousin Lisa, the one I stuck with a pin when she was a baby. Her ten-month-old sister Gena, who slept in a crib in Fritz and Nettie's room, was about the same age as Glenda. A mattress on the floor of a space between the living room and the kitchen, erroneously called the dining room, is where Mom and Norm slept. My sister and her friend Laru slept in the attic space, accessed through the bathroom ceiling. The household swelled to ten with our arrival. We filled every niche of the two-bedroom, one-bath house for which Fritz paid the rent.

Fritz was much older than Nettie. He seemed like an old man to me, an eleven-year-old, with a tiny patch of gray hair running around his bald head from one side to the other exactly like my grandpa. He even wore eyeglasses almost identical to Grandpa. Otherwise, there was no resemblance whatsoever. He was a "good Catholic." He was faithful in going to work. He spent his evenings lying on the floor next to the console radio listening to the ball game in summertime or literally "gone fishin'." He was good at staying out of everyone's way.

Nettie kept a meticulous house, when she was sober, with her primary complaint directed at the bathroom sink and the hair bits left by Fritz when he shaved. Nettie shared the same childhood home with the same parents as my mother, but she came away without the anger baggage my mom carried. Nettie was three years and five months younger than Mom, the youngest of all mom's brothers and sisters. It became obvious to me while living with Aunt Nettie that she was my mother's favorite sibling. They were a close-knit pair, often huddled together in private conversation talking and laughing or gone drinking somewhere.

Sunday morning after Aunt Nettie came home from church she told me, "Change the diapers on Glenda and Gena, Vernetta. Lisa, you go use the bathroom. We're gonna take a ride into the country."

"Yippee," Lisa and I shouted, then scurried in different directions to get ready. I ran out to her funny little old square car with Glenda in my arms, Nettie was ahead of me with Lisa and Gena.

"Why are you getting in the passenger seat?" I asked Aunt Nettie.

"Cause you're gonna drive."

"But I don't have a license and besides, I'm only eleven years old."

"Well hell, that don't make no difference. I'll give you drivin' lessons."

"I sure would like to have drivin' lessons, Aunt Nettie," I said as I jumped into the driver's seat.

Hays was small and surrounded by country, so it didn't take long to drive right out of the town into the country. I took a quick look at Aunt Nettie. She was sitting there with a bottle of whiskey sticking partly out of a brown bag. She'd say something to me, laugh, then tip that bottle up to guzzle its contents. Her drinking didn't bother me because I was happy driving on country roads up and down and all around for most of the day. Aunt Nettie was completely drunk by the time the car sputtered to a stop.

"Why did it stop going?" I asked her.

With slurred speech she said, "Hell, I don't know. Try startin' her up again." The car made a few noises, but nothing happened. Aunt Nettie leaned across me to check the gauges. "By God, we run out uh gas, I guess." I knew that wasn't good. Here we were miles from nowhere. I thought we were stranded. "Put that thing into neutral and let her coast on down ta that farmhouse."

"But I don't know how."

"Put yer foot in on the clutch, move the stick shift to the middle and off we go." Sure enough, the car inched forward until it started down the hill. I swung into the driveway of the farmhouse where luck was with us.

"We're outta gas and I need ta git my kids back home. Could you spare us some?" Aunt Nettie said in a sweet, if slurred, voice.

"Sure," the farmer said without hesitation. What I learned that day, besides my driving lessons, was that farmers always have tanks of gasoline on their property to run their farm equipment.

"Would you like to go to the drive-in movie tonight," Aunt Nettie asked a couple of weeks later.

"Sure, you know I love to go to the movies," I replied eagerly. Nettie drove us four kids to a place where she stopped.

"Okay, we're gonna git in that car over there." She pointed to a sleek, black car with a man leaning against it. When we all piled out and headed toward the black car, the man opened the back door.

"Git in, kids," he said as he looked around nervously. Then he whisked us off to the drive-in movie.

While Lisa and I sat in the back seat with Glenda and Gena, trying to watch the movie, Aunt Nettie and the man were kissing and squirming all over the place. It was my first time to experience her acting like that with a man that wasn't her husband. I didn't much like what was going on in the front seat and I decided I didn't like Aunt Nettie.

There were always rumors flying around the family about her having sex with Vern when Mom was married to him. Then there was the rumor that Fritz wasn't the man that fathered Lisa. I kept watching the movie, but I thought about those rumors, stuck in the backseat trying to ignore the gymnastics of Aunt Nettie and her married man.

Nettie and Mom were equal in height at five foot four inches, but Mom was more beautiful. Her shiny black hair, high cheekbones and deep brown eyes made the plainness of Aunt Nettie's features even plainer, I thought. I imagined it was Nettie who knew the heart of my mother better than anyone and any secrets she might have. Mom didn't ever say much to me, but she sure talked a lot to Aunt Nettie. Those two were close. When Mom would sit with the palm of her hand against the front of her face, covering her nose and mouth, appearing as if she were somewhere else, my guess is that Aunt Nettie knew what she was thinking, knew what secrets she kept quietly to herself. It was a place my mother went, to which I was never allowed access.

For reasons I didn't understand, Kansas brought out the worst in Mom. The person she was in Utah got left behind, like the trailer and the café. Nettie and Mom fueled each other's restlessness. The two of them started drinking together weekdays at a bar located out on the highway at the edge of town. Day after day, I paced the cracked, broken sidewalks while I took care of baby Glenda and Gena. As the forever hours crept by, I helplessly wondered, when will they come home?

Edna and Nettie

Not long after our arrival in Hays, Mom got a job tending bar. Now she had good reason to be at the bar in the evenings too. But then all hell broke loose when Mom took Verneda and Laru to the bar. She pulled down the bottle from the second shelf with the label "Gin" on it.

"What kind uh sodie pop do you gals like?' she asked the two girls.

"Do you have grapette?" Laru asked.

"Yeah, I like that kind too," my sister added. Mom mixed a drink of gin and grapette soda.

"Here, this'll give ya a buzz," Mom said as she handed the drink to the two fifteen-year-olds. Knowing Mom had added gin to their grapette, she and Laru drank down the first one as well as the second one Mom gave them.

Verneda stood up to go to the bathroom, but one foot didn't go in front of the other as she expected. The gin had taken its full effect. She staggered.

"I can't walk."

Mom laughed, along with others at the bar. "Do ya want another one?"

"Here," someone said as he took Verneda's arm, "let me take ya to the bathroom."

When Verneda came back Mom took her arm. "Come on, we're gonna take ya two to git something to eat."

They threw Verneda and Laru in the backseat of the car and sped off to a little café up the highway.

"I can't sit very good in this booth," Verneda complained. Mom and Norm laughed.

"Go on, eat your hamburger, you'll feel better."

"But I feel all numb," Verneda managed to say.

"You're chewin' on your bottom lip for Christ's sake," Mom said as she took away the hamburger.

"Git some coffee down her and then we'll git her home," Norm said with a laugh.

On the drive home to Nettie's, Verneda yelled from the backseat, "I'm gonna puke."

"Well roll the goddamned window down for Christ's sake. Don't puke in the car!" Mom yelled back at her. Verneda put her head out the window of the speeding car, vomit spewed from her mouth leaving splatters of puke streaks on the outside of the car.

I was asleep on the couch when the glaring overhead light woke me soon enough to see them pour into the living room. I opened my eyes, but I stayed ever so quiet; invisibility was the best choice under the circumstances.

"How do ya like bein' drunk? Feel good?" Mom taunted Verneda as they passed by me on the couch. I waited for all of them to get through the living room; then I could hear Mom yelling at my sister in the next room. I got out of bed and slipped into the small dark hallway that led to the dining room. Mom and Nettie were laughing as they dragged my drunk sister from the bare mattress on the floor to the toilet in the bathroom where she puked. The more she puked, the more Mom and Nettie seemed to enjoy it.

I returned to the couch, sorrowful to see Verneda drunk; hating to see how she was being treated. Emotions flooded my thoughts. A deep sense of shame, disgust, repulsion, sadness all whirled around inside me. I wanted to blame someone. Verneda and I were not close at this time because I didn't like her choices or the way she treated me; she didn't like who I was. I wanted to blame her, but I couldn't because in my heart, I knew this was my mother's doing.

"You goddamned kid, if you wanna drink, I'll let ya drink," Mom said to Verneda a few days later.

"No Mom, Laru and I ain't gonna drink. We don't wanna drink."

"You're a-comin' with me," Mom ordered. There was no choice. Verneda went to the bar.

"Gonna give ya something different this time," Mom told her as she placed a bottle of Miller's Highlife on the bar and slid it down to Verneda. Mom kept the bottles coming. "Let's see how many ya kin handle."

By the time the bottles stopped coming, Verneda had drunk eight full bottles of Miller's Highlife. The feeling of being drunk was familiar from the last time but the panic of not being able to walk was now experienced as a bothersome inconvenience.

"Ya gotta learn to handle your booze," Mom said to her as they zigzagged toward the car.

Suddenly Verneda shouted, "I'm gonna puke!" The vomit splashed on Mom.

"What the hell!" Mom yelled at her, "Git your ass in the car. I'm takin' you home."

Mom turned her attention to another vice for Verneda sometime in July of our first year back in Kansas of 1949.

I was sitting in Aunt Nettie's living room reading comic books, and Verneda and Laru were painting their toenails when Mom came through the front door.

"I know ya smoke. Here, have some cigarettes," Mom said as she threw the pack of Lucky Strikes at Verneda. "I'd rather you drink than smoke."

My sister protested, "Mom, I don't smoke!" Without another word, Mom walked right past her into the next room.

"Give 'em to me," Laru said, "I'll smoke 'em." Verneda pulled away with the package of Lucky Strikes.

"No. I'm gonna need 'em to practice with."

Fritz had gone fishin' so he wasn't sitting with Norm, Nettie, Verneda, Laru and me around the kitchen table a couple of weeks after Mom got them drunk on Miller's Highlife. Mom came raging into the kitchen.

"You was out to the bar, drinkin' and carousing!" she yelled at Verneda.

"No, Mom, I wasn't there. It wasn't me!" she wailed as she scrambled to avoid getting slapped. I don't know which infuriated Mom more, my sister's words or that her slap missed its mark, but Mom seemed more violently determined. She went after Verneda. Verneda tried to protect herself with words.

"It wasn't me, Mom. It was Laru." Maybe Mom hadn't noticed that Verneda and Laru dressed alike, were even mistaken as twins by some. Words didn't satisfy our enraged mother.

"You goddamned liar," Mom cussed at her, connecting this time with a slap across Verneda's face.

While Mom slapped and hit her, the rest of us sat dumfounded, frozen. We watched as Mom tore the wood slat from the kitchen blind and viciously hit Verneda across the face with the slat and then shoved Verneda so hard that she struck her head on the stove and fell to the kitchen floor. Immediately Mom pounced on Verneda and sat on her with an angry disfigured face.

"I'm gonna run away," my sister said defiantly.

"Oh yeah?" Mom jeered, "Ya can't, cause I'm sittin' on ya." The voice of my sister came back calm and decisive.

"Well you can't sit on me the rest of your life. When you get up, I'm leavin'."

The next morning, I heard Mom talking to Aunt Nettie, "They're gone. They ain't up there. Guess she meant what she said about runnin' away."

Days went by before we heard anything. "She's in Salt Lake City," Mom was saying to Aunt Nettie, but I stopped listening. I was thinking about my sister and how she wanted so much to stay there and finish school, but Mom wouldn't let her. Instead, she brought her to Kansas, got her drunk over and over, then viciously beat her. Now at least she's where she wants to be and safe from Mom, I thought.

The habit of going to the movies when I was a third and fourth grader in Larned came back to me after Verneda had run away. It was my own personal way of running away. "I guess I'm gonna go to the movie tonight," I told Aunt Nettie, since she was home and could take care of Glenda and Gena. I was too new in town to have friends and so I walked by myself that evening the three blocks down the hill and about another half block around the corner to the movie theater.

I looked up at the marquee to see that "San Francisco" was playing. The names Clark Gable and Jeanette MacDonald were in huge black letters against the lighted background of the marquee. Clark Gable wasn't my favorite actor because he reminded me too much of Mom's brother Russell. They each had rather a harsh manner of speech erupting from a mouth that had a sparse thin mustache unattractively dressing the upper lip. But I paid my ten cents, bought my popcorn then took a seat toward the back of the crowded theater.

I went to the movie not knowing one iota of what I was going to see the same as I had done in Larned. Although eleven and a half years old, I didn't know anything about earthquakes, and I had never heard of the April 1906 San Francisco earthquake that inspired this movie.

It started out with MacDonald singing some music I liked, along with a romance between the innocent MacDonald and the harsh experienced character played by Gable. Then it happened. On the screen a shaking started. Buildings collapsed onto people, burying them underneath the rubble. Gable saw an arm reach out from one pile of rubble and rushed to free the man but just as he was trying to help, the earth started shaking again. A large building front fell over the helpless man, completely burying him. Suddenly the ground split apart like a hungry gaping mouth, swallowing up the people who stood near it. Then as fire ravished the city, a wounded tattered Gable wandered the streets in search of Macdonald. Minutes later the movie ended with their reunion.

I stood to leave, but my legs buckled. I sat down as people passed over me to get to the aisle. I tried again. This time my aching, trembling legs tenuously supported my steps out of the theater and into the darkness for the walk home. The muscles of my legs held the terror of the movie, almost rendering my legs useless. When I finally reached Aunt Nettie's, everyone was asleep. There was no one to talk with about how terrified I was feeling.

In the morning, I heard Aunt Nettie and Mom talking in the living room, so I got up to tell them what had happened to me at the movie, but they were engrossed in conversation. Aunt Nettie was saying to Mom, "I was layin' on the couch, sick as a dog with a gallbladder attack, and that damned Fritz came and screwed me right there on the couch, then got up and went to bed."

"Hell, that's all men think of, screwin.' Remember when you and me was sleepin' and Poppa would come in?" Mom asked.

I backed up quietly before Aunt Nettie answered. I may have been a fairly informed eleven-year-old on the subject of sex, but I didn't want to hear more of what they were saying or even think about it. I returned to my bed until later, knowing they hadn't seen me. I didn't try again to talk with anyone about the movie. But the terror of it stayed buried in my mind, along with a distant curiosity about what Aunt Nettie might have said when she answered Mom's question about Grandpa.

Once in a while on a summer evening, I got to play kick-the-can with the neighborhood kids. I stayed out in the warm Kansas evening until the darkness of night put an end to our play.

While hiding from the one who was "it", I delighted in watching the rhythmic blinking of the lightning bugs. But after Verneda ran away, some evenings were not so pleasant.

When Fritz left to go fishing for the weekend, Aunt Nettie went to the bar with Mom, leaving me alone with Lisa, Gena and Glenda. Lisa and I got into bed after I put the babies to sleep, "Tell me a story, tell me a story, please," the little six-year-old pleaded. We lay in the bed hearing the wind groan and moan outside as it whipped around the corners of the house. The wind grew stronger. We saw the flash of light and then heard the rumble of thunder in the distance. I ran out to the front porch where I sat to scrutinize the lightning as it flashed across the sky.

"Now how did that text go?" I asked myself. I was desperate to remember it correctly as I watched for the next streak of lightning, "As the lightning comes from the east and flashes to the west, so will the coming of the Son of Man be?" I watched each flash as I tried to determine if it came from the east and was it flashing to the west because if it did, then I thought Jesus would be coming again. I also thought that if He came tonight, I wouldn't get to go with Him because I hadn't been baptized.

The Bible lessons the pastor had given me in Idaho, when we read Matthew, chapter twenty-four, told all about the second coming of Jesus. The pastor, Uncle Clarence and I didn't realize that my understanding of what some of the texts meant was incorrect and they probably didn't know that I was frightened by what a few of the texts said. Now, alone at night in the midst of a thunderstorm, I thought Jesus might come and I would be lost because I wasn't baptized.

I began to cry, "Did I remember the text right?" I asked myself. I wasn't sure which direction was east and which was west. As I sat sobbing on the porch midst the storm, Lisa came and sat beside me with words of comfort while she patted me on the back. "I'm gonna be baptized," I told my six-year-old cousin Lisa who had no idea what I was talking about. In that moment, I determined in my heart I would be baptized. When or how, I wasn't sure. Eventually, the two of us went back to bed and fell asleep.

I remember the comfort I felt during some of those severe thunderstorms when Fritz got up and walked through the house, looking out the windows as he made pleasant sounds or comments on the most recent flash of light or sound. But Fritz wasn't home when I needed him most.

Once again, I was alone with Lisa, Gena and Glenda. The storm this time seemed to settle right above our house. Great bolts of lightning struck at us in loud cracking sounds, one right after the other as they lighted up the room. The wind blew fiercely. Terrified I took the three children and ran to the neighbor's house.

"Can we come in," I asked the lady when she opened the door.

"Why of course. Get yourselves in here."

At first the fury of the storm continued to attack with light and sound then gradually it moved further and further away.

"I think you'll be okay now," the lady who took us in told me. "Why don't you take the children back home and put them to bed." I didn't want to go but I did as she asked.

The couch in the living room was my bed that night. The other three children were asleep, but I was still awake when Mom came home.

"Mom, there was a big thunderstorm. I got really scared and took the kids next door."

Mom looked at me with disgust. "Oh, you big scaredy cat." She was off on another of her belittling episodes. I pulled the covers up around me, pulled my knees up tight against my chest. It was up to me to comfort myself.

Chapter 22

Kansas
September 1949 – May 1950

Because we still lived with Aunt Nettie when September came, I walked to Hays Jr./Sr. High to begin seventh grade. For the first time in my school experience, I moved from one room to another with a different teacher for each subject. I particularly liked Mr. Sipes, my English teacher. He didn't frighten me the day he threatened another student, "If you don't stop talking," Mr. Sipes told him, "You will be required to write a five-hundred-word essay on Why a Bird Dog Doesn't Fly." Something about his dynamic teaching methods ignited my desire to study literature and poetry.

Verneda was lucky she didn't live with us. In mid-November, Mom and Norm moved from Aunt Nettie's into the basement of someone's house. We entered their back door, went down dark, steep stairs into a space that had a double bed. My bed was an army cot set up in the small kitchen. I heard Norm talking about centipedes. "Them bastards have got about a hundred legs. They like dark, damp basements like this one and they kin climb straight up a wall." Alone at night, trying to sleep, I worried about the centipedes coming. I never did see one, but they crawled around in my imagination after I got into bed.

A boy named Don Pratt invited me to go to the football game on a Friday night late in November.

"My Mom and I will come to pick you up."

I thought about where I lived and wished I could meet Don at the football game. "Okay," I agreed reluctantly and gave him my address.

I met his mom at the back door. She talked nicely to me as we walked through the back yard to get around to her parked car, but I could read on her face that I lived on the wrong side of the tracks. The house was entirely dark when they brought me home after the game.

"Goodbye," they said in chorus when I got out of the car. I watched them turn left and disappear around the corner. I wasn't surprised that Don Pratt didn't invite me out again.

After a short time, we moved a few blocks away, across the street from a grade school, into a small white house with a porch extending across the front of it.

"We'll have to share the bathroom with the people that live in the basement," Mom told me.

"Why?" I asked.

"Because this house has only one bathroom!"

The stairs from the basement came into our space between the living room and the kitchen with the bathroom at the top of the stairs. "Do they just come up these stairs and into our bathroom?"

"Yeah."

"But there isn't a door to lock. They can just come up here any time?" Mom didn't answer. No locks, I thought sadly.

Of course, Mom and Norm took the only bedroom, along with Glenda and her crib. I graduated from the army cot to a rollaway bed, but the kitchen was still my bedroom. The two large blindless windows in the kitchen stared at me in the stark blackness of night when the lights were turned on inside. At least I don't have to worry about centipedes, I reminded myself.

We still lived in the small white house across from the school when my runaway sister came back. "I have a new name," she told me when I first saw her again. "You can call me Terry."

"Well, I'll try to call you Terry, but it feels weird."

We were alone later that Saturday morning when I asked, "What happened to you? What did you do?"

"After the beatin' Mom gave me in the kitchen, I ran away. I told her I was gonna run away and I did. When they went to sleep that night, we come down the stairs and out the door. There were these two guys that worked at the service station. Their names were Oil Can and Augie. Laru and I used to go there, borrow their car, and go to the outdoor dance. We'd come back and leave them their car and walk on home. They were never our boyfriends; they were just two kids who'd let us use their car. So when we run away, we went back down to the service station and asked them if they could give us a ride out of town so we could start hitchhiking. Instead of them giving us a ride and dumpin' us off, we all four just kept on goin'.

"The one kid drove for a long time. He got sleepy and tired--that was before we got to Colorado--and I said, 'Well, I'll drive.' I didn't have a driver's license. He got in the back seat and went to sleep and the three of us was in the front seat. Well, I guess I fell asleep while I was drivin'. When I woke up, I slammed on the brakes and that car just rolled. It just rolled end over end before it stopped.

"We rocked it to get it back up on its wheels. Augie broke his thumb when it went through the back window, put a hole in the window. We had to kick out the front windshield to get out. So after we all got it back on its wheels and on the highway, we started into the Colorado Mountains. Oh, we stopped at different places.

"One kid sold his watch. We had eight dollars from what we had left from our paychecks to get gas. We sold the radio out of the car to the workers that were working along the road so we could get gas to go on. After the accident, it was cold. With no windshield, the cold air was comin' in and that car was rattlin' and knockin'. So we decided just to take the things out of the car Oil Can wanted. We took off the license plates and pushed the car off the road down a hill.

"We started hitchhikin'. An old couple picked us up. They took us right into Salt Lake City, Utah and let us off. So then I went to Valerie's house. The two kids, I left them at the Courthouse yard. I told 'em I'd meet 'em back down there 'cause we were goin' on to Twin Falls. That's what we were gonna do. We were gonna go on to Twin Falls. But they got picked up by the police and Valerie's Mom called and told my mom where we were. Mom said I could stay for a month."

"You're lucky to be alive. Amazing that no one was killed! I wish when Mom was beating you that I could have stopped her. I wanted to run away, too and if I did, I'd never come back!"

"Yeah, but I didn't have no money and no place to stay," she said.

Mom turned the care of baby Glenda over to Verneda during the day. I don't know what time Mom left, but when I came home from school, she wasn't there. Although Verneda wanted me to come right home when school was finished, I often stayed to take part in the afterschool tennis lessons, despite the guilt I felt.

A few days after Verneda told me about her runaway experience, I came home from school, and she was sitting on the couch crying.

"What's the matter? Why are you crying?"

Finally, she started telling me her story. "I had a friend drop me off at the bar because I needed to see Mom, but then I didn't have a ride home. Mom asked Joel, a guy who worked with her at the bar, 'Hey Joel, can ya drop Terry off at the house?' And he told her, 'Sure Edna, be glad to.' When he pulled up, he parked by the school. He slowly reached across the seat. I thought he was gonna touch my hand but then he jist suddenly grabbed it and twisted my arm behind my back. With his free hand, he unzipped his pants. I hit at him and screamed 'Let me go!' His erected cock stuck out through his unzipped fly. I screamed and screamed, 'No, No!' Without a word, he let go of my hand. I yanked on the door handle, kicked the door open with my foot and run for the house. Those people that lived downstairs, I run down to them. They told me to call Mom and tell her what happened."

I looked sadly at my sister as she sat crying on the couch. There wasn't much I could do to help. Hearing a car door slam, I looked out the window. "Mom's home," I said, imagining that she would help. Mom came through the door with an air of indifference.

"I asked Joel about it. He said he didn't do nothin."

"But Mom--"

"I don't wanna hear it! He said he didn't do *nothin*," Mom almost shouted, with an emphasis on "nothin," meaning end of conversation. She picked up something from the bedroom then promptly left.

"She didn't believe me." My sister sat vacant eyed on the sofa. Her almost inaudible words ricocheted across my mind escalating into a blur of noise.

Between Mom's indifference or her rage, Verneda probably favored Mom's indifference. Within weeks of

Verneda's return, I observed her successfully stand against Mom's raging. It was late Saturday morning. Verneda was in the bathroom getting ready to go out.

"Where in the hell do ya think you're goin?" Mom demanded.

"I'm gonna meet Donnie at the service station," Verneda answered.

Suddenly, for no obvious reason, Mom lunged at her, pinning her in the corner of the bathroom. Verneda wrestled herself free and grabbed Mom's arms. Mom cussed and threatened what she was going to do to Verneda, as she struggled trying to free herself. But Mom couldn't get loose to follow through on her threats.

"Now I'm gonna let ya go but if you dare hit me, I'm gonna hit you back," my sister warned. Mom said absolutely nothing. When Verneda let go of her arms, Mom walked out of the bathroom and exited straight out the front door.

Verneda slumped down on the sofa shaking and crying. "I never know why she's mad at me. What did I say or what did I do to make her mad at me? I have no idea why she whips on me. It's probably my mouth; sometimes I just snap back at her."

After a while, my sister wasn't around very much. There were many nights when she wouldn't come home at all. I don't know where she stayed.

Verneda never did go back to school. Her choice might have reflected a determined effort on her part to have control over what happened to her. For whatever reason, she couldn't calculate the consequences of her decision. Her days lacked structure or purpose. In spite of her intelligence, her survival instincts, her leadership qualities, and her strongly social personality, she had unknowingly sentenced herself to a punishing kind of isolation. The headaches she had struggled with since she was six or seven years old became her constant painful companion, sometimes making it impossible for her to function. Perhaps unresolved trauma associated with Buddy, Jr. was the cause of her debilitating headaches when she was put in charge of yet another of Mother's babies.

On one of the evenings, I was alone in October, I reached for the JC Penny Catalogue. "Fall 1949 Issue," I read. It was the only reading material in the house; the only entertainment I could find. Men modeled dress and work clothes in the first section, "Not interested," I said and turned the page to the women's section. "Nope, not for me." At last, I found the children's section. One girl, about my age, posed wearing a dress that became my heart's desire, especially after reading the description and checking the price. That doesn't seem like a lot of money, I said to myself.

The first chance I had I showed Mom the picture of the dress in the catalogue. She had stopped sewing dresses for me in Larned. "See this Mom, isn't it great?" As she looked at the picture I said, "Can I have it for my birthday?" My twelfth birthday was only a week away."

To my surprise she responded, "Yeah, I guess so."

It was an exciting time when the small brown package from JC Penny's came in the mail. I felt the stiff, coarse material on my fingers as I freed the dress from the paper. I had thought the fabric would feel smooth, soft and elegant. Although the cotton fabric was coarse, I liked the pleasant shades of brown; I liked the ruffles on each side of the checkered bodice. This doesn't match the description in the catalogue, I complained to myself. It wasn't as special as I had imagined from the description. I was disappointed but not aware that I could return it for a refund.

A school dance was announced for the first Saturday evening in December. My group of friends talked of their party dresses and their black patent leather shoes. I didn't have either.

"Mom," I began, "There's gonna be a school dance and I don't have a party dress."

"You got a new dress you can wear," she retorted.

"What new dress?"

"That one I bought ya for your birthday."

"But that was two months ago, and it isn't a party dress," I said softly, hoping not to get her mad at me.

"Well, ya ain't getting no new dress, that one's good enough. You can wear it to the dance."

Andrew was an eighth grader whose locker was in the same section as mine on the first floor. At first, he smiled at me when I was putting books into my locker. Then he started saying, "Hi," when he walked by me. I smiled back and said, "Hello." I was really surprised when he stopped to talk with me right before Thanksgiving break. Words seemed to flow smoothly from his mouth.

"I was wondering if you would like to go with me to the Christmas Dance next month."

I looked up into the face of this attractive eighth grader. For a moment or so, I stood looking into his brown eyes. "Well, I guess the dance is right before our Christmas break. Isn't it?" I asked.

"Yeah," he said. Should be lots of fun."

"Yeah, sounds fun. I'd like to go," I said.

"You wanna go with me?" he asked.

"Oh," I laughed. "That's what I meant. I'd like to go with you."

When he picked me up, I was dressed in my JC Penny's cotton brown dress, wearing my rubber soled oxford school shoes with laces neatly tied into bows. The school gym was dimly lighted with soft music playing as we entered. We passed by Bonnie in her pink taffeta dress and shiny black shoes. Then I saw my best friend Nicky in her blue chiffon that had sparkles on it. "Hi," I said and kept walking with Andrew to stand by the wall some distance away. I wanted to run out of the building away from my beautifully dressed friends or disappear into the brick wall I leaned against when Andrew interrupted my imaginary flight from misery.

"Do you want to dance?"

"Okay," I said as we moved away from the wall onto the gym floor. The soles of my rubber shoes kept catching on the floor instead of sliding.

"Sorry for my jerky dance steps."

"Doesn't bother me," Andrew reassured me. "Let's have a good time."

I left the dance with a smile on my heart. Even though I had worn my JC Penny's dress and my school oxfords, my friends still liked me. Mom never asked me anything about the dance.

Christmas Eve, Glenda and I were alone in the house. She was asleep in her crib. I was lying awake in the darkness on my rollaway bed in the kitchen, looking out at the stars through the bare window. Alone on Christmas Eve, I moaned, feeling sorry for myself. Mom's sister Mary often referred to this kind of thinking as "sittin' on the pity pot."

Eventually, sometime in the night, Mom and Norm came home. I sat straight up in bed when they flipped on the kitchen light. Norm walked past my bed and flipped on the bedroom light. As Mom staggered past the end of my bed after turning off the kitchen light I called to her, "Mom, it's Christmas Eve." She mumbled something but I couldn't understand what she said. I heard them in their bedroom muttering to each other but after the lights went out, it became quiet.

Once again Mom and Norm survived the long, tumultuous inebriation that came with the holidays. We had all made it safely through another Christmas and New Year's. The bareness of January, February and March finally began to yield to the promise of spring.

April brought with it another confirmation that my friends cared about me. This time, I learned that I was liked despite where I lived or what my mom did. It was my turn to have the sleepover at my house. My friends came--Nicky Shady, Mary Lou Powell, Bonnie Paxton, Virgie Binder--along with a couple of other girls. We had already had our sleepover in Bonnie's beautiful home that sat up on the hill. Her Mom had greeted each one of us with welcomes and smiles. She bustled around making us comfortable, feeding us goodies and snacks. The sleepover at Mary Lou's house was also especially nice in her pleasant home. Even though her mom had to be at work, the beds had been made for us and food was prepared. It wasn't Nicky's turn yet, but I had spent the night with her in her upstairs bedroom with its huge bed and the white frilly curtains at the window. Despite my embarrassment of where I lived, I wanted to take my turn for a sleepover.

"We'll sleep here in the living room," I told all of them on Saturday evening. We lifted the couch seat to see if there were any blankets in the storage area. The sight of dirt, dust balls and old feathers greeted us, but there were no blankets to use as padding against the hard floor.

"Oh well," Nicky said, "let's all put our sleeping bags here in the corner of the living room."

"Sorry," I apologized, "I wish we had carpet on the floor instead of linoleum."

"It'll be great," Mary Lou said as we maneuvered the bags around on the floor.

For a brief time, Mom was home doing something in the kitchen before she came into the living room. I was happy she had come in to meet my friends.

"This is my mom."

"Hello," she said and smiled at them as she and Norm moved toward the front door. "We won't be able to stay, but you girls have a good time."

They were away until late in the night and when we woke in the morning, they had already gone again. The house was empty.

I took my friends to the kitchen. "What would you like for breakfast? I can fix eggs." We stood gazing at the unappetizing grease laden metal grates of the gas stove.

One girl started, "I'm not very hungry."

"Me neither," chimed another.

"I hardly ever eat breakfast," said another. I was relieved I didn't have to cook breakfast.

Thank goodness Norm didn't have his Sunday morning ritual after the sleepover. The ritual happened in the kitchen at the table in the center of the room. As each man arrived, he placed his contribution of booze on the table, then the drinking, the smoking and the dirty jokes started and kept going for several hours.

One old man came regularly. Tufts of his white hair stuck out from the brown fedora hat he always wore, never even removing it inside the house. His glasses reminded me of the ones my grandfather wore, clear glass with no rim. I was in the living room this particular Sunday when he came from the kitchen toward me. Suddenly he grabbed me, holding me tightly. His face came into mine.

"Let me go," I demanded as I tried to push him away. My words were silenced by the force of his mouth on mine, his tongue thrusting to the back of my throat before he let me go. I watched him saunter back into the kitchen. I ran into the bathroom, slammed the door behind me, leaned over the toilet and tried to spit the disgusting feel of his tongue from my mouth.

"The Old Man"   Edna

It didn't come as a surprise that Mom didn't do anything about the old man. After all, this was only a kiss compared to near rape of my sister that Mom had ignored. I had learned by fourth grade that I couldn't count on her for much of anything. I always thought it was because she didn't like me. There were times I would brazenly show my disapproval of her actions either by the expression on my face or a few choice words that I let escape from my mouth. It was clear then why she didn't like me. But other times when she expressed her dislike, I was mystified.

"Start packin' your things; we're movin' on Sunday."

Each time I heard that we were moving, I got a hopeful expectation. I imagined the new place would be wonderful like my friend's homes. Lawn would cover the front and back yards; carpet would flow throughout the house. But best of all, I would have my very own bedroom with a real bed. When I learned that we were moving, I was excited.

We drove along one of the major streets in a shabby section of town. Norm slowed down, then made a left turn across the highway into a small driveway and parked in the carport. My heart sank. This can't be it, I said to myself. We walked to the front door of the duplex whose siding was red tarpaper meant to give the illusion of bricks, like the siding on the little red house we had left behind in Larned.

Maybe Mom and Norm thought their living conditions had been bettered. It was the first time since Mom had married Norm that I would have a bedroom of my own, except for those times when Verneda stayed with us. The one window in this small bedroom looked out through the carport to a view of the busy street that many evenings was to become my only companion. The living room was barely large enough for our sofa and chair, with a small, useless room attached to it and my bedroom. The least-used room in the house was the kitchen, except for Sunday where Norm maintained his Sunday ritual.

I disliked the kitchen, the back door that opened directly onto a paved alley, and the door in the bathroom that connected us to the owners of the place, two old people and their three large, ugly bulldogs whose tongues dripped saliva wherever they went. The lock on the door which insured our security, consisted of a small hook that fit loosely into a metal circle.

I went from room to room in search of carpet. No carpet, I concluded as I scuffed at the ugly linoleum covering the floor. This was a dingy, drab, miserable place rarely experienced by Mom and Norm except on Sunday morning when the bar was closed. The bar was really home to both of them, more so than where they paid rent to live.

I began missing a lot of school. I frequently called in sick with all kinds of made-up problems. "I can't come to school because I have the mumps." That time I stayed home for at least two weeks.

Mom let me run my own business. She never asked me, "Why didn't you go to school?" or "When are you going back to school?"

It didn't matter to me. I didn't care that she didn't care! I made my own decisions about school. I finally returned to school after my bout with the "mumps."

Mr. Massey, the Vice Principal at Hays Jr. High, called me into his office and referred to me by the new name I had given myself when I started seventh grade. "Mickey, you've missed a lot of school. I want you to come to see me every day. Would you do that for me?" He asked so nicely that I did just that. My attendance became regular for the remainder of seventh grade.

"What's that bed doing in there?" I asked Verneda as I pointed in the direction of the normally empty, useless room.

"How should I know? Ask Mom."

I didn't have to ask because that night we had company. It was Norm's two sons, the ones he left behind when he met my mother. I heard Mom say to Verneda, "Susan couldn't come; she's too little."

Later I asked my sister, "Who's Susan?"

"Don't you know nothin'?" she asked. "That's Norm's youngest kid."

It was a surprise to me when I peeked around my bedroom door to see two large boys lying there in the bed looking back at me.

"Hi," I said. "My name's Mickey."

"I'm Bobby," the dark headed boy said with a big grin on his face. The other bigger boy with brown hair didn't say anything so Bobby said, "This here is Harold. He's my big brother."

"Hi, Harold." He gave me a little nod.

"My real name is Robert," the dark-haired one said, "but everyone calls me Bobby."

"That's funny. My real name is Vernetta, but I like to be called Mickey. Where do you live?" I asked

"Larned."

"I used to live in Larned."

"I know," he told me. Bobby and I had lots of fun before he left on Sunday.

Robert/Bobby, Vernetta

Verneda was "too old" to pay much attention to a couple of boys from Larned, but she spent Saturday night with us. Later Sunday morning, just as she was in my bedroom getting dressed, Norm looked at her as he passed through the middle room.

"It pays to advertise," I heard him say.

It was surprising how he could strike a forceful blow with only a few well-chosen words. But my sister didn't let him know that he had the power to crush her spirit. Instead, she rallied. Her quick wit speedily returned a quip of her own. Match. The tension between the two of them, tension that had been there since he first came into our lives, got worse and worse. At the same time, tensions swelled and ebbed between Verneda and me.

"I earned enough money to buy myself a new bathing suit!" I told Verneda in late spring, picking up the shopping bag to show her.

"How'd ya git the money?" she asked.

"The landlady wanted me to mop her kitchen floor," I explained. "Boy did the place stink, and those bulldogs had made a mess all over the place with hair and junk to clean up. But I'm gonna clean it for her some more so I can buy me some new clothes for school."

"Let me see it," she said as she took the package from me and pulled my new bathing suit from the bag.

"Wow, it's pretty. Can I try it on?" she asked.

I took the suit from her, "No, you'll stretch it. You're bigger than me."

"I'm not gonna stretch it!" She went on and on about how selfish I was. She mimicked my words and voice, "I'm gonna stretch it." She sneered at me the way Mom did to her and kept chiding me about "don't stretch it." It was always hard to stand up for myself when it came to Mom and Verneda. Strange how each one seemed threatened if I asserted myself, as if I were to remain a passive nobody they could treat as they wished, staying within the bounds they had set for me, like a role I was forever destined to play in the drama of our lives.

But to some extent my sister still took ownership of me, even my unfulfilled Larned dream of taking piano lessons. On my way to my bedroom, I started to pass through the empty, useless room when I was suddenly startled by the presence of an enormous reddish-upright piano.

"Do you like it?" she asked me when she came home. "I know you always wanted to play the piano." She told how she had gotten it for me. The memory of my asking Mom if I could take piano lessons popped into my head.

"I didn't know you remembered," I said.

"I remembered you wanted to take piano lessons in Larned and Mom wouldn't let you. Now you can take lessons."

The two of us stood side-by-side, arms around each other, looking at the huge upright in a state of oneness we hadn't experienced in a long time. Unfortunately, the piano never became my friend. I never took lessons. I'm not sure why. The emptiness I felt no longer held my passion to play the piano. So the piano just sat.

I didn't see very much of Mom during seventh grade, but I especially wish I hadn't seen her that one upsetting Sunday. She was drunk, passed out on her bed. The man who wore the brown fedora hat, the one who had thrust his tongue down my throat, hovered over her, slobbering kisses all over her face as his hands wandered over her breasts. I turned away. Why didn't I yank his hat from his head! Why didn't I pull his glasses from his face!? Why didn't I push against him with all my might and scream at him, "Get away from my mother!!" Instead, I retreated to my room.

"We're gonna be movin' next week," Mom said for the umpteenth time.

"Where are we going?" I asked.

"You'll see," she said. "It's a house not too far away."

I had just finished seventh grade with plans for myself that summer. A move was not one of them. But anything would be better than here I told myself, most likely not realizing it was the aloneness I wanted to leave behind more than the place itself.

Chapter 23

Kansas
June 1950 – June 1951

To my surprise, the new house was better than the other three places we had lived.

"Look," I said, "a porch swing. It looks like a bench!" Nobody said anything. As soon as the car stopped, I jumped out and ran to the swing. Back and forth I went before I looked up. The chains on each side of the swing went straight up to the ceiling of the porch. Norm walked by about that time.

"How can the swing hang from the ceiling?" I asked.

"By bolts, ain't ya got eyes!" he said as he went into the house.

Norm had two ways of dealing with me: he treated me as if I didn't exist or chided me unkindly. I liked him best when he treated me as if I didn't exist.

The length of the long room we entered at the front door wasn't shortened much by the couch Mom put catty-cornered next to the entry. The room retained a certain emptiness all the time we lived there. The dark wood trim hung gloomily around the doors and windows. Linoleum, again," I thought, but at least there aren't any bulldogs! The two bedrooms were each off the long entry room.

"Yes. I get my own bedroom!" I said.

"Terry will sleep with you if she comes to spend the night," Mom reminded me.

"Wow, and we have our very own bathroom again!" I exclaimed.

Mom's sister Mary came from Dighton to visit us at our new place late in June. I thought she lived far away but Hays, Larned and Dighton sit on triangle points from each other, not many miles apart.

"Do you mind sleepin' on the couch, Mary?" Mom asked.

"You know me, I can sleep almost anywhere. Don't mind at all," she added.

I noticed Aunt Mary focused on her appearance. Her hair was perfectly prepared, for what I wasn't sure. She paid special attention to her nails, filing and polishing them, primarily red. But what I especially noticed about her was that she liked to talk. Oh, most of her conversation was about herself but the flow of words streaming from her was somehow comforting after living with Mom and Norm who did little more than grunt out a few sounds.

Shortly after her arrival, she came through our front door with a good-looking married traveling salesman. When I first saw him, I didn't know he was married, but Aunt Mary threw that fact into her stream of chatter. I remembered something I had heard her say when we stood in her living room in Dighton a year or so back. "Why hell," Aunt Mary had said of her husband, "High was bringin' men ta me ta sleep with em for money! Can you imagine?" Her voice went up an octave along with an emphasis on "imagine."

When I heard her tell Mom, I wondered, did she *sleep* with the men High brought home to her? My curiosity went no further but her story went to that place in my mind where other family sex stories idly linger. A fresh, personally experienced one was about to be added.

Floating into my bedroom that night were the mingled low tones of the salesman's voice and the cooing sounds Aunt Mary made followed by a rhythmic squeaking sound that filled the entire house. I was no dummy. I knew what Aunt Mary and the salesman were doing on our foldout couch. The conversation and laughter of the adults the next morning confirmed it.

"Thought you was gonna break the damn springs of the couch," Norm said with a snicker as he lit up his cigarette. It was at these events that happiness of a sort seemed to show up on their faces.

After the squeaking couch incident, I took the first step to put my summer plan into action. I wrote a simple letter to my other Aunt Mary, who had moved to Lamar, Colorado about three hundred and fifty miles away. It went something like this:

Dear Aunt Mary and Uncle Herman,

My Mom said I could come and visit you if you say its ok. I'd really like to come.

Can you let me know right away if I can come? I could ride the bus.

XXXXOOOXX   Vernetta

    In my letter I purposely didn't mention anything to Aunt Mary about my plan. I especially didn't breathe a word of it to Mom or Verneda. I knew better. If I got to go see Aunt Mary, I was determined to be baptized, a determination that had been planted in my heart the night of that terrifying thunderstorm. My resolve had only strengthened with the passage of time.
    "Git the damn phone," Mom called from the bedroom. I ran to the ringing phone.
    "Aunt Mary! Mom, it's Aunt Mary on the phone, she got my letter."
    When they finished talking Mom turned to me, "I guess you're gonna go visit your Aunt Mary and Uncle Herman."
    On the outside, I controlled my excitement, but on the inside, I jumped up and down yelling, "Yippee!"

    Their modest farm with house, barn and pastureland was about fifty miles from Lamar, Colorado. The first chance I had, I told my Aunt Mary, "I really want to be baptized."
    "Well, did you ask your mother?" she wanted to know.
    "No." I said casually but groaned inwardly. "I didn't ask because she probably doesn't care."
    "Then you better write a letter to ask her permission," Aunt Mary suggested. My heart sank until she added, "But of course we can go ahead and schedule it just in case she says yes."
    We scheduled my baptism for two Saturdays away. Aunt Mary and Uncle Herman still went to church on Saturday, just as we did when I stayed with them in Twin Falls.

"We're going to go to church tomorrow and Uncle Herman and I thought maybe you could sing a song for the service," Aunt Mary suggested on Friday. "You could sing that song I heard you singing the other day, 'In the Garden.'"

"I guess I could sing it. Do you want me to sing it by myself?" I asked.

"A lady will play the piano for you," she said.

Aunt Mary and Uncle Herman were sitting on the wooden pews looking at me as I stood by the piano to sing. They smiled sweetly at me. The pianist started playing, then she nodded to me, and I began to sing, "I come to the garden alone, while the dew is still on the roses." When I sang the word "roses," I looked at my aunt and uncle. He had his big old handkerchief out dabbing at his eyes. She had tiny tears rolling down her cheeks. I kept singing, but I wondered why they were crying.

"You drive," Uncle Herman said as he sat down in the passenger seat and handed me the car keys after church was over.

"But I don't have a driver's license," I said, repeating what I had told Aunt Nettie. I hadn't driven a car since running out of gas while driving the Kansas countryside with her and all the kids in the backseat.

"That's okay. I bet you're a good driver." I'm not sure what it was, adults letting me drive. Maybe because they had driven trucks and tractors on the farm when they were children, they thought nothing of asking a twelve-year-old to drive a car.

"Wow! I love to drive!" I said to Uncle Herman when the speedometer hit fifty.

"Um hum," he responded.

That afternoon I wrote the letter to Mom asking her if I could be baptized. "Put it in the mailbox and the mailman will pick it up," Aunt Mary told me, "or, we can mail it in town next week when I take you shopping for a new dress."

"A new dress?" I said in disbelief.

"Yes, if you're going to get baptized, I want you to have a new dress." Aunt Mary truly knew the way to my heart in more ways than one, but she hit dead center on that shopping spree.

"I think it's too big for you, sweetie," she said to me as I looked into the mirror at my reflection in the corduroy dress I had fallen in love with. She tugged at the belt.

"Your waist is up here but the waist of the dress is down there," she showed me.

"Please let me have it. I just love it," I said with emphasis on "love". She smiled and nodded yes.

Vernetta

The next day after we had bought my new dress and mailed my letter to Mom, Aunt Mary said, "Let's go horseback riding. I'll saddle up a horse and the two of us can ride it together."

"I'd love to, Aunt Mary. I can hold on to you!" I was especially excited to hold onto her because the last time I rode their horse by myself in Hagerman it scared me when it ran madly in the direction of the barn.

She got into the saddle then reached down to me. "Give me your hand. Put your foot in the stirrup and I'll pull you up."

"It worked." I said, settling onto the horse, behind her.

"Now hold on tight," she said over her shoulder. At first, we bounced up and down, a ride as bumpy as the rutted road we were on. "I'm gonna make her gallop," she said as she turned onto a field. We flew together out across the land, not a care in the world.

The pleasant days of being with her went quickly by until Friday, the day before I was to be baptized. "No letter from your mom yet," Aunt Mary said when she came back from the mailbox.

"It's been a long time since I wrote to her. She probably doesn't care if I get baptized," I said, shrugging my shoulders. "Can I get baptized anyway?"

"I don't want your mom mad at me, but we did send the letter a long time ago," she pondered out loud. "I think we'll go ahead."

"We have to go into Lamar for your baptism. It's not the church where you sang," Aunt Mary told me, "We'll go to church first and then down to the river."

"I'm gonna be baptized in a river?" I asked.

It was Aunt Mary's turn to say, "Um hum."

"It's gonna take us an hour to get there. May take us longer," Uncle Herman added. "Rain's comin' down pretty good." I sat in the back seat with Aunt Mary as we drove, watching the rain pelt against the car windows.

"Can you see good enough to keep going, Herman?" Aunt Mary asked.

"It's pretty bad but we can make it," he said with a confidence that was a comfort to me.

"There's the church. Pull in over there, Herman," she directed. Usually, Aunt Mary did the driving because he liked to be a passenger.

When church was over, the rain was still coming down hard. A small caravan of cars drove out of town to a place where the bank of the Arkansas River sloped gently down to the water's edge.

"Can't baptize you if this rain doesn't stop," the pastor said to me. He turned to the others, "Everybody wait in your cars and pray for it to stop raining."

Uncle Herman parked us under the trees. We watched the muddy brown waters of the churned-up river flow swiftly by as the rain continued to fall. Aunt Mary stroked my arm, soothing my anxious feelings.

"Let's get your clothes changed, so you'll be ready," she said as she started taking off my beloved new corduroy dress.

"I wish it would stop raining God, so I can be baptized," I said to Him and myself. We waited. Everyone waited. Then it happened. The rain stopped.

A few people gathered on the shore by the river as the pastor led me into the muddy water. He raised my arm up with his, as if reaching up to God Himself. "I baptize you in the name of God the Father, His Son Jesus and The Holy Ghost. Hold your nose, honey," he said, laying me back beneath the waters, totally immersed. When I came up out of the water the little group of people on the shore were singing, "Shall We Gather at the River." It sounded like heavenly angels singing the joy I felt because I was baptized at last.

Uncle Herman, Vernetta, Aunt Mary

"Why don't you go see if we have any mail," Aunt Mary suggested when we got home from Lamar. In the box was a letter addressed to me from Mom. It was okay with me that she finally wrote because now it didn't matter. I was already baptized and there wasn't any way for Mom to undo it. I waited to open it until Aunt Mary could read it with me.

      Dear Vernetta,
         I don't want you getting baptized until you're older.

You're only twelve. Maybe when you're sixteen. I need you to come back home.
Love,
Mom

    I was surprised she wanted me to wait, because she didn't seem to care about anything else I did. So why did she care if I got baptized, I wondered. I was relieved the letter was too late, because now I didn't think she could put the blame on me. I thought about what Mom wrote, "When you're sixteen." I'm almost thirteen and I know what I want; a few more years won't change that, I declared to myself. I didn't like the part telling me I had to go back home. But within a few days, I was on a Greyhound Bus back to Hays, Kansas.

    It was nighttime when the bus pulled into the stop at Hays. I looked around for Mom. Instead, I saw my other Aunt Mary who was Mom's sister, with two of her kids and Glenda.

"Where's Mom? Why didn't she come?" I asked.

"She's at work, so she asked me to pick you up and drop you off at the house."

"Oh, she's at the bar." I said, disappointed.

"Yeah," Aunt Mary answered. She paused long enough to let me out of the car, then drove off, leaving me with Glenda. The bare light bulb set high on the porch ceiling was little competition against the darkness that surrounded me later as I sat alone on the porch swing. Back and forth the swing and I went in rhythmic movement as I thought about my mother and me. One convincing thought wouldn't go away: Mom doesn't love me. She brought me home just so I could take care of Glenda.

"What are you doin' here?" I asked Verneda on Saturday morning when I came out of the bedroom.

"Mom wants me to help clean the house," she snapped at me.

    What's wrong with her? I wondered. I wanted to keep my Sabbath, which was Saturday, but I was required to clean the house Saturday mornings.

Verneda was in one of her "get little sister' moods. She started making fun of me because I had gotten baptized and because I didn't eat meat from pigs.

"Well, you eat *ham*burger don't you?"

There wasn't much use in exchanging words with her when she was like that, so I kept sweeping the stupid floor of the ugly long living room until I could get out of there. When we finished cleaning, Verneda yelled at me.

"I'm leavin and I ain't comin back!"

"Well, why are you yellin' at me?"

"You weren't here when Mom got mad at me, only this time she had help from Norm. He held me while she beat me with the phone," Verneda cried. "I'm leavin'!" She kept her word. She left and didn't live with us anymore.

Cleaning house with Verneda on Saturday wasn't the last or only time I would be taunted for my choices. On a weekend late in summer, Norm and Mom took Glenda and me the ninety miles to visit Lucky, Mom's old drinking friend, who still lived in Larned. By bedtime, Mom was high on booze. Shirley and I were lying end to end on a sleeping bag right next to the table where Lucky and Mom sat when it started.

"Goddamned kid got baptized, thinks she's so smart. Thinks she's too good to eat pork or ham," Mom told Lucky. Then she turned on me. "Ya outta be glad ya got anything to eat! You think you're so goddamned smart, got baptized."

She kept it up, pounding away on me as only a hateful drunk can. A sick emptiness swallowed my insides but left the rest of me there in isolation on the sleeping bag. Why is she so mean? I wondered, beginning to feel sorry for myself. She can't seem to hate me enough.

When we returned to Hays the next day, I called my best friend Nicky. We met at the swimming pool in the late afternoon with some of our other friends as we often did that summer. Nicky was round in her tummy with nice round breasts. In contrast, I was tall and skinny with a totally flat chest. We went up on the deck of the snack building.

"Take our picture," Nicky said to Virgie who had brought her camera. Nicky and I stood arm-in-arm, our wet permed hair half dried by the summer heat with our nose plugs hanging at the end of rubber strands like necklaces around our neck.

The swimming pool substituted for school in the summer months as my preferred place to be. Years before, in the Larned swimming pool, I had gotten the taste of satisfaction that came with accomplishment. I strived for that satisfaction when I signed up for swimming lessons at the Hays pool. By the time summer had come to a close, I had certificates that certified I had successfully completed two swimming courses. I ran my finger over one of the gold seals and read my name on the certificate. "That's me; I did it!" This affirming world was a universe away from life with Mom.

When school started, I went to the Vice Principal's Office to see Mr. Massey. "Do you know if there are any churches in Hays where the people meet on Saturdays?" I asked him.

"Why do you want to know that?"

"Well, that's my Sabbath and I want to attend church on that day."

"Check back with me tomorrow, I'll see what I can find out."

The next day I went back to see him, "No, Mickey, there aren't any churches in Hays that meet on Saturday. This town is almost one hundred percent Catholic, and they all attend church on Sunday. Sorry," he added.

"Thanks a lot," I said as I started to leave.

He called after me and told me with a smile on his face, "Mickey, you're kinda cute, just don't find it out for a few years."

"Are you going to the football game Friday night?" Nicky asked.

"I'm not sure, that's the beginning of my Sabbath. She seemed disappointed so I said, "I guess I'll see you there." I went to a couple more games on Friday evening then it happened on the next Friday. I was sitting on the bleachers enjoying the band and watching the game when I noticed the moon was looking strange. "Look at the moon; what's happening?" I asked Nicky.

"I don't know," she answered, unconcerned.

In Idaho, when Uncle Clarence and the pastor took me through Matthew twenty-four verse by verse, we read "and the moon will not give its light" and other frightening things that would happen right before the end of the world. Now here I sat watching a football game on Sabbath eve and surely the world was coming to an end because the light of the moon was slowly going out as something moved over it. I stood up abruptly. "I gotta go home." It was a terrifying night for me as I watched the moon almost disappear completely.

At school on Monday, I learned that there had been a total eclipse of the moon on Friday evening. I had never heard of such a thing, but the teacher explained it to us. I decided to pass on attending football games on Friday evenings. I didn't want to be at a football game on Sabbath when the world came to an end.

A boy that sat behind me in math entertained me with his recent knowledge. "Do you know how birds do it?" he asked smugly. But before I could answer that I didn't know, he shoved a book in my face and said, "See, the male bird sits on the female's back and that's how they do it."

"Oh," I said. As far as I was concerned, learning about birds was far superior to the agony of trying to learn math. I still wasn't able to make sense of math since my introduction to multiplication tables in second grade at the Albert country school. "If a train going 50 mph passed a train going the opposite direction at umpteen mph and the town was x miles away then what and how long..." Bubbles of confusion drowned my brain into a state of nonfunctioning. And yet, I felt lucky. I got a C in math.

But I didn't feel lucky when a big boil erupted on my arm. "Mom, look at this. It really hurts."

Mom stopped doing her nails and looked at the boil. "What do ya want me to do about it?" From the way she asked, I wasn't sure if she cared or didn't care.

"I don't know but it hurts," I said, trying to hold back tears.

"That thing is gonna drain. Leave it alone," she said and went back to doing her nails.

After the boil drained, I woke up with a swollen eye. "Mom, Mom," I ran into the kitchen from the bathroom to tell her, "My eye hurts and it's all swollen."

"Hell, ya always got somethin' wrong with ya! That ain't nothin but a damn stye. It won't kill ya."

No use asking Mom for help, I told myself. The boils and styes kept coming one after another. Wish I didn't have to go to school, I said to myself in the mirror, I look ugly, I feel ugly.

Moving made me feel ugly too, but like my boils and styes, I couldn't do anything about another move, and I didn't know why we were moving again. This was definitely a move in a downward direction into a big, old, brown-shingled building that held several apartments located closer to town but on the same street as the bulldog duplex.

"Where are we going, Mom," I asked as I followed her up some stairs into the building.

"We got a furnished one on the second floor," she said in monotones of gray.

I wondered to myself what she and Norm did with the furniture we used to have.

"This place ain't got no bathroom; you'll have to use this one here in the hall." She pointed in the direction of a door we passed. She opened an apartment door, about halfway down the dimly lighted hallway, where we stepped into a small, dark living room. Open to the living room and extending from it was an attached alcove featuring the double bed where Mom and Norm would sleep.

"This here's your bed," Mom indicated as she sat on a broken-down single bed in the living room, which served as a sofa by day. I tried not to show my disgust. I thought about Verneda and how lucky she was that she didn't have to live with us. I didn't see much of her, but I knew she spent most of her time with Donnie, her boyfriend who worked at a service station. Then Donnie decided to join the army and got stationed in California. Eventually, after a few weeks, Verneda went to California too.

The kitchen was the only other room in the house: not much to look at, but as usual it didn't matter because we hardly ever went in there. But on one rare occasion Mom cooked. Aunt Nettie was there by herself having dinner with us.

"I'm going into the living room," I said when I had finished before everyone else.

"We're gonna go out, you kin stay here with Glenda," Mom said to me when she came into the living room.

"But Mom, can't you stay home tonight?" I asked.

"Oh, you big ba--"

I interrupted her. "Are you going to the bar?"

She raised her voice. "None of your goddamned business where I go!"

By now, Aunt Nettie and Norm were in the room, one on each side of Mom with me sitting on my bed.

I opened my mouth. "You never stay home with me, you go off drinkin--" Suddenly Mom was all over me, hitting my head with her hands.

Give it to her, Edna!" Nettie said.

Mom slapped me hard on the face. "You goddamned kid! Think you can tell me what to do!"

"Shut up that damned smart mouth of hers, Edna!" Norm said.

After she finished beating on me, the three of them buddied up to go off to drink. Nettie went out the door first, then Norm, but Mom stayed long enough to say, "You git in there to that kitchen. If that ain't cleaned up when I git back, you're gonna be sorry."

The same old story, leave me with a dirty kitchen. Threaten me if I don't clean it.

We lived a few months in this old, brown-shingled building. Right before we moved again, Bonnie came to me. "It's your turn to have our Girl Scout meeting at your place."

"Well, I think we're getting ready to move."

"Everyone else has taken a turn. We could meet tomorrow before you move, maybe," Bonnie urged. I had found out that we weren't moving until the weekend.

"The girls can come for our meeting on Thursday, Bonnie," I said reluctantly. When my friends came for the meeting, I didn't tell them how uncomfortable I felt for them to see where I lived.

Later, I was glad that my turn happened at the old, brown-shingled building instead of the place we moved to next.

"Your family sure moves a lot," Nicky commented.

"Yeah, this will be move number seven since we came to Hays."

It was another big old house but this one was very public. It sat on a downtown corner of Hays on Main Street, right next to the movie theater. The side street ran straight up the hill to the Hays Jr/Sr. High school I attended. Many of the students left school, came down the hill and walked right past this house on their way home.

Probably many, many years ago this had been a stately home. But now it sat in a dilapidated condition, nothing more than a rundown old house surrounded by powdered dirt and a few dried weeds. Someone had divided the interior space into apartments. It was my misfortune to be counted as one of its tenants. A wish I'd made at other times of desperation came again: if only I had some magic dust to make me invisible, I thought as I stood across the street from the old, dilapidated house. I looked around, then quickly ran into the house, hoping no one I knew had seen me.

A sickening odor filled the entry, the stairs and the hallway. My thirteen-year-old nose and eyes assessed this as without question the very worst place I had ever lived. Our apartment was at the top of the stairs, consisting of two rooms and a triangular space too small for a closet but large enough for a chest of drawers.

This private space with an old chest of drawers became my very own coveted space in this two-room apartment where privacy didn't exist anywhere else. Besides the usual repulsive kitchen, the other room held a double bed and a sagging, tired couch that was probably home to millions of dust mites and bacteria that had been growing on it for eons. "You'll sleep here," Mom said as we stood looking at the couch.

"Do we have a bathroom of our own, Mom?" I asked carefully, in an effort to avoid a rebuke.

To my surprise, she answered nicely, almost apologetically, "No, it's down the hall on the left."

I went down the hall to my left and found the door open. The first thing I saw was the dirty black ring around the tub, which repulsed me, but seeing the remains of pubic hair here and there resulted in waves of nausea. I flew back to the apartment I totally detested from a bathroom that I wanted to dynamite. By nature, I am orderly and clean, and I prefer to bathe rather than shower. Each time I bathed in that loathsome room, I took the Bon Ami and scrubbed the hell out of that dirty bathtub as if preparing it for royalty.

One of the teachers talked to the eighth graders. "It is very important to take good care of your teeth," she said firmly. "You will want to see your dentist for a check-up at least once a year." She continued to give a graphic explanation of the undesirable results of not caring for our teeth.

Alerted to my need to go to a dentist, I decided to ask Mom if I could go but I avoided telling her the details the teacher taught because I didn't want to upset her. "Mom is there any chance I could go to the dentist. I've never been."

"Why are you askin' about seein' a dentist?"

"The teacher at school said it's a good idea," I said, stating it as simply and as briefly as possible. When she gave me her approval, I was ecstatic. "I get to go to the dentist!" Large cavities were found in my back molars and filled. "That was really nice of you to let me go to the dentist, Mom. At least now my teeth aren't going to fall out!" I tried to keep it light. She smiled.

"Here kid," Norm said one Sunday as he held out the keys to the car. "I want you to go get us some beer."

"But I don't have a driver's license," I reminded him without budging in the direction of the keys. He jangled the keys in front of my face.

"Hell, that don't make no difference."

"But they won't sell beer to me; I'm only thirteen."

"Sure they will. You go on down to the bar by the railroad tracks and tell 'em Norm wants some beer."

I took the keys, stuffed the money in my pocket and out the door I went. Good thing Aunt Nettie gave me driving lessons and Uncle Herman let me drive his car, I thought to myself as I headed down the stairs. Norm was right, they sold me beer and I took it home to him.

The next day at school, Mr. Massey came into our eighth-grade classroom, first period.

"Before the school year ends two weeks from now, the administration has decided to interview each eighth grader about your future plans." He told us the interviews would begin soon, smiled at us, then left.

At my interview they asked a bunch of questions, which I answered but promptly forgot, all except one. "Do you plan to go to college?" she asked.

I responded without hesitation, "No!" I thought I'd be lucky to get through high school, but I didn't tell her that. No one on Mom's side of the family had gone beyond eighth grade.

My own sister had quit school in the ninth grade so I felt I would do well just to make it through high school.

Another move rescued me from the dilapidated old apartment building in June, after I completed eighth grade. But this wasn't another move across town.

"I heard you and Norm talking about movin' to California, Mom. Are we gonna move to California?"

"Yeah, we're goin' to Long Beach. We'll stay with my brother Ralph 'til we kin git our own place."

"Where's Verneda staying?" I asked her.

"She's at Ralph's or Eva's in Santa Maria where Donnie is."

Verneda had been in California since March and that's most likely where Mom and Norm got their inspiration for this move. I didn't know if I should be happy or sad.

The news of another move was old news to me. I knew moving was as much a part of our lives as the drinking. But this move came with a bonus that made me happy. I no longer had to live in the old smelly house.

However, there was always sadness when the move meant I had to say goodbye to friends I loved. Saying goodbye to Nicky was the hardest goodbye of all. But a hopeful expectation countered my sadness: maybe life would be better in California. Hope sat on the perch of my heart once again.

Chapter 24

California
June 1951 – June 1955

    When I climbed into the back seat of our old black Chevy, I didn't know that it would be nearly impossible to get Norm to stop for anything, even my need to go to the bathroom. He drove us straight through to Long Beach, California. No good night's sleep in a comfy bed, no sightseeing along the way, and the reading of historical markers would never have entered his mind. Mom sometimes reached over to play with Norm's ear or rub his neck. She might say something to him, and he would say a word or two back. Most of the time, I sat looking at the back of their heads or sat in silence watching the scenery go by as Hays was left further and further behind.

    "Ya got yourself a nice place, Ralph," Mom told her brother when we arrived at his duplex in Long Beach.

    "Well hell, come on in. Della will show ya where things are. C'mon into the kitchen Norm, I'll get ya a beer." Ralph farted and laughed as Norm followed him into the kitchen.

    Della took Mom and me to see the bedroom where we would sleep. "We moved some beds into Billy's room,"

    It was the same but older Billy who had asked me to suck his penis years before in Larned.

    "Billy, Gene and Terry sleep in here too," Della explained. "Gene is my grown son from my first marriage. We put the army cot there for you, Vernetta," she indicated as she went on pointing at beds where the seven of us would sleep in this one bedroom.

    "I need to go to the bathroom, Aunt Della," I said with some urgency. She took a step out to the small hallway.

    "It's right there," she smiled, pointing to the bathroom only a few feet from the bedroom where we would sleep. I noticed another bedroom to the right on my way to the bathroom. Aunt Della saw me looking. "That's our room."

    "What kinda footage ya got, Ralph?" Norm asked.

"We got about eleven hundred square feet of livin space. Stay until ya git yer feet under ya," Ralph was saying to Norm when we all walked into the kitchen.

"Did ya buy the place, Ralph?" Mom asked.

"It kinda owns us." Ralph opened his mouth wide allowing a raucous belch to escape. "But yeah, we're buyin' it," Ralph seemed proud to say. "The other part of the duplex helps make the payment."

The next day Della drove Mom and me into downtown Long Beach. "Look at those funny trees. I guess they're trees. Are they trees, Aunt Della?"

"Them's palm trees," Della said.

"Almost as tall as a building," I said, gazing up the trunk of one palm. I thought of the poem we memorized for Mr. Sipes in eighth grade.

"I think that I shall never see a poem lovely as a tree.

A tree that looks at God all day and lifts her leafy arms to pray…"

The leafy arms of the palm look like giant green fans on top of its tall trunk. Aunt Della's voice interrupted my thought.

"Have you ever seen the ocean?" Della asked.

Mom and I both said "No."

"We'll drive through town and then we'll go see the ocean."

"You sound like a real tour guide, Aunt Della."

All the towns I had lived in were small before we came to Long Beach, except for Salt Lake City and it was dwarfed by the area and population of Long Beach, this beautiful city where the Pacific Coast ran along its Western boundary.

"Everything sparkles," I said as we drove along, past elegant shops on busy streets full of shoppers. There was something different about the way light danced here under the California sun.

"Get ready, we're gonna see the ocean!" Della announced with excitement in her voice. The street came to a dead end. Right there in front of us was the Pacific Ocean in deep colors of blue, running to meet the sky on the horizon far beyond where we gazed in awe. Della made a left turn, driving us through an unsurpassed experience of beauty along the Pacific Coast shoreline. Mom seemed carefree and happy as she talked with Della. "I'm glad we came to California, Mom."

Three months after sharing a bedroom with seven people, I heard Mom tell Della in early September, "We found us a little place up on Signal Hill."

"Can I see it?" I asked when I got a chance to talk to Mom.

"We're gonna go over there soon as Norm comes home from work," she said.

The demons that seemed to possess Mom when we lived in Kansas were quieted with our move to California. She became more like the person she was when we owned the café with Maxine in Salt Lake.

Much later in life I came to understand that Kansas held deep psychologically disturbing experiences for my mother. I'm sure that for her, any return to Kansas became a trigger into these associations, resulting in the escalation of her drinking and her anger. When we left Kansas and went to California, she became a more peaceful woman. She still drank but I rarely saw her drunk. The most dramatic difference I experienced was the absence of her raging anger.

I couldn't wait for us to have our own place, but I was a little anxious as Norm parked the car beside a small white house. When we opened the front door a surprise of new furniture greeted us in each of the rooms.

"We got all three rooms of furniture real cheap," Mom said. "Don't you think so Norm?"

"Yeah, it was a good deal," he answered, surprisingly cordial.

"You'll sleep on the sofa, Vernetta; it makes out into a bed." I didn't mind sleeping on the sofa because I had the living room to myself. I thought it would be a lot better than sleeping with my face to the wall on an army cot, trying to get some privacy, trying to sleep with the noise of six other people in the same room at Uncle Ralph's place.

"Ya gotta go through the bedroom to get to the bathroom," Mom said as she took me to see it. Passing through her bedroom, I enjoyed the experience of light pouring in through the windows of this fresh, clean space.
"I like how new it all smells, Mom. It's a lovely place to live."
The next week, Della picked me up to go shopping but Uncle Ralph was sitting in the passenger seat.
"You going shopping with us?" I asked him.
"Hell no," he said with a grin.
"I gotta drop Ralph off at home first," Della said.
As we were driving on one of the main streets going toward their house, Uncle Ralph suddenly leaned out the window and yelled at the people on the sidewalk. "Scatter, you sons-uh-bitches!" He looked at me and laughed. I gave him a faint smile rather than tell him how weird I thought he was.
"C'mon in," Della said to me when we got there.
She and Ralph went into the bedroom while I waited in the dining room right next to the kitchen, watching fish swim in their aquarium. I hadn't been there very long before Uncle Ralph stormed through the kitchen.
"Let 'em fuck shit!" he yelled.
In all the years I'd heard foul language, I'd never heard anything like that. Inexperienced and not quite fourteen years old, I stood there trying to imagine what he meant but this was one time my imagination failed me.

In early October, a week or two before my fourteenth birthday, a woman selling Bibles came to our door. It surprised me that Mom let her come in to show us the Bibles.
"This is one of our most beautiful Bibles," the woman remarked. I noticed the round gold medallion centered on the brown lid of the box, a profile of Jesus embossed on it. "The cover is made of leather," she continued, running her hand over

the relief of the gold grape vine pattern on the front of the Bible. She turned the pages.

"There are many pictures in it but please notice a special feature in the New Testament. The words of Jesus are printed in red ink, so they stand out from the remainder of the text which is printed in black."

"Oh Mom, could I have one of these for my birthday?" Mom resisted. The woman said something about payments.

"Please can you buy it?" I asked again.

"I guess I could give it to you for your birthday." She said to me then turned to the woman selling the Bibles, "I'd have to make payments."

"Here, I want you to sign it for me, Mom," I said after the woman had gone.

There was a special page in the front where I watched my mother write my name in the "Presented To" space, her name in the "Presented By" space, and the day of my birth followed by the year of her gift.

"Thank you so much, Mom! I'll treasure this forever."

I didn't make any connection between Mom buying me the Bible and the scowl Norm gave me the next morning as he passed me on the back-porch step where I sat reading. I guess he doesn't like me reading, maybe that's why he gave me that ugly look, I thought, somewhat wilted by his disapproving look.

In the fall, I started ninth grade at Franklin Junior High and somehow got signed up for "Office Practice." This meant that one hour a day I worked in the office of Donice Hamilton, an official School Administrator as well as a school Counselor. It wasn't long before she was calling herself my "school mom." She often had me come into her office to talk as friends do.

"What is your life like at home?" she asked one time.

"It's much better now that we live in California. Mom doesn't get drunk as often. I hate to see her drunk; it makes me feel bad."

I loved having Mrs. Hamilton as my school mom. She had style, she had education and she took a loving interest in me. That's the way school was for me, a place where I met people who became an important part of my life.

One day, Mrs. Hamilton took it upon herself to convince me that social drinking was possible and acceptable.

"But I don't even want to drink socially," I told her. "I don't want anything to do with alcohol."

"But Mickey, lots of people drink socially but don't become alcoholics."

"I've seen what drinking does to people, and I will never drink, not even socially."

I was glad I had decided a long time ago not to follow my mother's example of drinking, because my school mom was very persuasive. I must have convinced her because she never again approached me on the subject.

At the end of my first semester of ninth grade, she called me into her office. "Now Mickey, baby, you know that I graduated from UCLA. It's a big school but you can make it." She expounded on her goal for me, to attend UCLA. "But we need to get you started in Algebra," she continued. "I've talked to Mrs. Coffey, and she said she thought you could start the second semester of Algebra without having taken the first semester."

"But I've never been any good at math; I'm terrible at math--

She interrupted me. "Mrs. Coffey will help you. You're smart, you can do this."

My school mom enrolled me in the second semester of algebra. In all my subjects the first semester, I had earned A's, and I wanted to do the same for second semester, but I didn't see how I could get an A in algebra. But driven by my desire to honor my school Mom's belief in me and a desire to maintain my record, I tackled algebra and earned my much-desired A. It was boring to go to summer school just to earn the credit for first-semester algebra, but it was an easy A.

That was the same summer Ralph, Della and Billy took Mom, Norm and me to their favorite beach for the weekend. "Seal Beach is the real name of the place, but people call it Tin Can Beach," Ralph said.

"Hows come?" Norm asked.

"You'll see for yourself when we get there," a half-drunk Ralph said.

"Well, where in the hell is it?" Mom asked.

Della quickly answered, "Just south of Long Beach."

I was watching Ralph stuff an ice chest full of beer when I asked Della, "Where are we gonna sleep?"

"We got tents and sleeping bags," she said with a smile. "We'll sleep right on the beach!"

When we arrived at the beach, I looked out across sand littered with cans and discarded items left by campers. "Now I know why they call it Tin Can Beach," I told Billy, but as usual he didn't say a word.

I was wondering why Billy was so weird when the noise of the ocean caught my attention. I watched huge swells crash thunderously on the shore then subside into shallow quietness as the water came running toward my feet.

My drunk Uncle Ralph grabbed me by the hand. "Let's go catch a wave," he whooped, pulling me unwillingly into the water.

"But I don't want to," I protested. His laughter mocked me.

"We're gonna catch us a wave!" he yelled. "The goddamnest biggest wave you ever seen!"

A large wave crashed over us and smashed me down into the sand. I struggled to get my footing. Ralph had a strong grip on me when another wave crashed down on us.

"Let me go!" I screamed at him. Drunk and belligerent, he was impossible to reason with. Breaking away briefly, I tried to make it to the shore before another wave came. He grabbed at me, caught my arm. "Come on, ya sissy!"

I panicked as I fought to get away from him. Down I went into the bubbling water. Up I came. "Mom, Mom!" I yelled.

When the next wave hit, I was ripped away from Ralph. During the few moments when the water was calm and before another wave formed, I struggled to shore with all the strength I had left, leaving drunk Uncle Ralph not far behind. He managed to get back to shore right behind me, laughing and making crude comments.

"Why didn't someone help me?" I screamed at wide-eyed Billy. "Where's Mom?"

He pointed at the tent. "In there."

"Is she sleeping," I asked Della when I looked into the tent.

"I think she had a little too much to drink."

"Ralph nearly drowned me!" I cried to her.

"Well, honey, try to stay away from him when he's drunk and be careful when you go in the water. Them undercurrents can pull you right out to sea."

What? My insides screamed. Why didn't anyone tell me!

For the remainder of Saturday and Sunday, I stayed as far away from Ralph as possible and didn't stick even a toe into the water.

Billy, Ralph, Norm, Edna, Della

A few weeks later, Mom didn't mention that we were moving, again! Her sister Nettie and her two children were coming from Hays to live with us. We continued living on Signal Hill but in an old house with two bedrooms. Aunt Nettie came the same summer I took my algebra class. She got a job with Mom working in a nearby laundry while I took care of the children, cleaned, and did the ironing.

On first arriving in California, I could feel the freshness of a new start, but as time passed, old ruts returned. Lightness gave way to the familiar heaviness, which hung over us for reasons I didn't understand. There were those few times, after we came to Long Beach, when I had experienced Mom's rare sweetness. The anger that normally separated us had temporarily vanished. I loved her. She was my mother. But one evening her alienating and frightening ways returned as she was preparing dinner.

"What are we having?" I asked.

"Ribs."

"Beef ribs?"

"Yes," she said without hesitation. "They're beef ribs."

We all took our places around the table: Mom, Norm, Nettie, Lisa, Gena, Glenda and me. When the plate of ribs was passed, I took some. Broad grins came on Mom, Norm and Nettie's faces after I ate my ribs.

"What's so funny?" I asked.

The three of them laughed. "You just ate pork," Nettie said.

"Them was *pork* ribs," Mom said with great satisfaction in having tricked me. She knew I had decided before I was baptized not to eat pork.

Another of the old ruts showed up on a Saturday evening. Mom and Norm were both drunk, and a quickly escalating argument was underway. Fearful, I ran out the front door and across the street to watch from there, putting distance between this ugly scene and me.

Norm came out of the house, yelled something. then got in the car. Mom came running out the door screaming at him. She reached for the passenger door handle just as Norm put the car in reverse and hit the gas pedal. Mom hung onto the door handle, but Norm continued to tromp on the gas, dragging her along down the driveway and onto the main road.

"You're going to kill her," I shouted at Norm. Suddenly, the car stopped. Mom picked herself up and got in the car. They sped away.

The next morning, I approached Mom, emboldened by the experience of the night before. I said to her, "Last night was terrible. I thought you were going to be killed. I don't want to go through anything like that again. I'd like to go away to the Christian boarding school in Monterey Bay."

She had a hard time looking at me but said, "I don't want you to go." This came as a surprise to me. I didn't think my presence had much value for her, but I didn't question her motive. I repeated what I wanted and in return she said, "I don't want you to go."

Although I didn't get to leave home then, my time of living with Mom and Norm came to an end about a year later. I stayed for my last move with them to North Long Beach at the beginning of my sophomore year in high school.

When I started my junior year, I moved to live with my friend Patricia and her family in Lynwood within walking distance of the private school we both attended. Her brother Russell was off to college. His vacant room was offered to me. Mom was willing to pay five dollars a week for my food and Russell's room, which I knew wasn't nearly enough. I had two jobs myself, but what I earned from assisting the secretary to the principal helped pay my tuition. The other job I had of ironing once a week for Dr. Burdick didn't pay very much but it enabled me to purchase my clothes.

Laura, Patricia's mother, was a dedicated wife and parent, educated as a nurse but devoted to caring for her family and home while her husband, a medical doctor, spent long hours away. Laura kept the attractive home they had designed immaculate. A delicious breakfast, lunch and dinner were served on a predictable schedule. Patricia enjoyed a large room to herself with a walk-in closet overflowing with clothes. After school she played her violin, filling the house with music. I thought places such as this exist only in the movies.

I was grateful to live in the home of Dr. and Mrs. Hoxie, yet uncomfortable because I was haunted by feelings of being in the way, as I had been when living with my mother. For this reason, I sometimes left this bit of heaven to spend the weekend wherever Mom and Norm happened to live at the time. But during my junior and senior year of high school, I didn't see very much of Mom, unless I went to see her – a pattern that continued for the rest of our lives. I wanted her to come to meet Dr. and Mrs. Hoxie but for reasons she kept to herself, she didn't come.

Even though my mother didn't come to my school to hear me sing in our trio or share in my honor at being elected girls Vice President of our three-hundred-member student body, it didn't stop me from longing for her to experience my success. I especially wished she had come the day the essay prizes were awarded at a student assembly in the auditorium.

"Today the prizes for the essay contest will be awarded," announced Mr. Weeks the chemistry teacher. I sat forward on my seat.

"We will begin with the fourth-place prize," Mr. Weeks said, calling the person's name. I watched as the prize was delivered.

"Third place is awarded to…" announced Mr. Weeks, but it wasn't me. When he called the name for second place, I slumped in my seat, thinking that I hadn't won anything.

Then Mr. Weeks called the name of the first-place winner. "Would Vernetta Schreiber please come to receive first prize for her essay, "Alcohol Unveiled." Maybe it's just as well Mom didn't come. She probably wouldn't have liked the subject of my essay.

In June, I found myself once again wishing for the impossible. "I wish my mom would come to my graduation," I told my best friend, Marlene.

"Is she coming?" Marlene asked.

"I don't think so." A funny little thing came to mind that Grandpa had once said, "If wishes were horses, beggars could ride."

Mom didn't come to my high school graduation.

Chapter 25

California
June 1955 – June 1956

"You must pay the tuition you owe before we can release your transcripts," the accountant said.

"Could I pay part of it?" I asked, eager to have funds left for college.

"No, I'm sorry. You'll have to pay the entire sum before we can release your transcripts to college admissions."

"Well, I need my transcripts." I gave her almost all the money I had earned at my summer job.

Miss Willeta Carlsen, the college Registrar who hired me, asked with a hopeful expectation, "Is it possible for you to come to campus two weeks early, before classes begin?" Although her protruding teeth stretched her upper lip into a faint smile, her face appeared stern as her tall, thin body towered over me waiting for an answer.

"I can come early," I heard myself say as I nervously stood up, moving toward the door. Her unattractiveness lingered as I considered that my income from working for her wouldn't begin to pay all of my tuition.

Was it coincidence, my experience a few days after arriving early on the almost empty campus? As I was walking toward the main classroom building, my attention was drawn to a male student striding across the lawn at the bottom of the hill. No one else there but the two of us. Stopping some distance away on the upper side of the slope, I stood momentarily mesmerized, strongly attracted to him. But it wasn't until many weeks later that I saw him again.

In some ways, my transition from high school to college was similar to the frightening upheavals of change I experienced as a child. Aunt Mary might have said I was sitting on the pity-pot because of how I felt about being stuck on the first floor in a cavernous room decorated only by two empty twin beds sitting on a bare floor, away from the "in crowd" on the second floor whose rooms qualified as samples of how to decorate your college room on an unlimited budget. But I knew from past experience that if I made myself endure whatever discomforts this change threw at me, I could be successful.

"Mom, can I use the twin bedspreads for my dorm room?" I asked on the phone. "My room is empty and ugly, and I don't have any money to decorate."

"I suppose, but Glenda won't have any if you take 'em."

I changed the subject to my koala bear. "Do you know what happened to the koala bear Chuck gave me?"

"Haven't seen it," she said.

Chuck wasn't related to me but was the son of my Aunt Della. We had spent time together during the summer, but I stopped seeing him before college started. When Mom found out, she got that ugly look on her face and said sarcastically, "He ain't good enough for you!" My mother frequently threw this accusation at me, or told someone else in slightly different words, "She thinks she's too good…"

"So, you haven't seen the koala bear? I want it to put on my bed."

"I told ya I ain't seen it."

I decided to call Chuck. "I can't seem to find the koala bear you gave me."

"I have it," he said, "Your mom gave it to me. Said she took it off your bed when you weren't home."

"Oh," I said in dismay.

"Do you want it back?" he asked.

"You go ahead and keep it," I said before saying goodbye. I tried to understand Mom's behavior, but I couldn't come up with anything that might relieve the pain I felt at being betrayed yet another time.

With my heart set on being in the choir, I joined the other students waiting outside the music building to be auditioned. "How did it go?" I heard one of the students ask another.

"He's tough! You're expected to sight-sing."

I sat there anxiously wondering, what is sight-singing? After a long wait my name was called. A student led me into a choir room and seated herself at the piano. A formidable-looking man with white hair stood by the grand piano,

"Please sing the first verse only of this song," he directed.

Oh no, I said to myself, it's a song I don't know. The student began to play the accompaniment. When I opened my mouth to sing, pinched-thin sounds trickled into the room. Crying with my face to the dorm-room wall didn't really help when I learned that I hadn't gotten into the choir.

Finally, about one or two miserable weeks later, I told my roommate, "I've decided to leave campus."

"But why?" she asked.

"I don't have money to pay my tuition and besides things just aren't working out."

"Mom, can you come and get me?" I asked on the phone.

"Let me ask Norm. Hold on a minute. Yeah, Norm says it's about an hour's drive. We'll be there soon." I hung up thinking, she didn't ask me any questions.

"I wonder if you might be willing to talk with me before you leave campus,"

Mrs. Little, my adviser and English teacher, asked. I was more than willing.

"Why are you leaving campus?" She had a cool, reserved quality, unlike Mr. Sipe, Mrs. Craig, or Mrs. Smith, other English teachers I had experienced.

I explained my financial situation. "I've already called my mom and she is on her way."

"Do you mind if we pray together?" she asked.

When I left Mrs. Little, I can't say I floated down the hall with hopeful expectation, but my spirits had been lightened.

Mom scooted over to let me ride in front with her and Norm, probably the only time I ever rode in the front with them. No one asked me any questions. Not a word was said, just total silence in the long drive back to Long Beach.

Within a day or so, Pastor Watts from church came to see me. "If you'll return to college, the church will pay a portion of your tuition."

"It's my heart's desire, Pastor Watts, to return to college."

"If you return to college, you can be certain we will help with your tuition." Returning was not difficult or awkward since

I had been away only a few days. At the time, I didn't fully realize this decision was a crucial pivotal point in my life.

My work in the Registrar's Office included helping to prepare the "Dope Book," an illustrated booklet of each enrolled student, distributed to the student body. When I got my copy, I carefully looked at the photo of every male, circling a selected few, including the male student I had watched stride across the campus when I first arrived.

"Oh," I said out loud. "His name's David!" Later in the first semester, I saw him walking with William, a classmate of mine from high school. I wanted so much for him to see me, but he kept walking and talking to William, oblivious to others, which unfortunately included me.

But a surprise encounter awaited me in the gymnasium the morning of February seventh at the beginning of my second semester of college.

"We'll have a co-ed skating class over the next several weeks," the instructor announced to the women of Gladwyn Hall when we arrived. The room was already filled with men from Calkins Hall.

Suddenly the men's coach was giving us instructions. "Women, please form a circle and men, form a circle on the outside of them." Music began to play. "Men, please move forward to the next person when I blow this whistle." Each man advanced to the next woman at the sound of the whistle. When a new guy arrived at my side, I gave him my complete attention and asked myself, would I like to know this guy better? No one particularly interested me until a guy who skated forward and said, "Hi, I'm David." I looked up into his warm brown eyes and said, "I'm Vernetta."

"Yes, I know." I was surprised he knew my name, but I didn't tell him I had first seen him walking on an empty campus weeks ago. I didn't tell him I had circled his picture in the Dope Book.

"Where are you from?" I asked.

"Washington. I'm from a little town just north of the Columbia River."

"Oh, Washington; I've never been there. Is it beautiful?"

"Well, we went six weeks without seeing the sun last winter," he said smiling at me.

"I hardly ever see you on campus."

"That's because I live in the village. I'm planning to move into Calkins Hall this semester."

The whistle blew and David skated forward to the woman in front of me. I didn't pay a lot of attention to the next guy at my side; my attention was on David. I watched him glide along on his skates. Hmm, I thought. I like his tall, slender body and thick brown hair.

My dreamy state was interrupted by the next guy that skated forward. He was talking even before he reached me, continued to chatter until the whistle blew again. "What do you think? Co-ed skating! Unbelievable! Some of the guys think they add something to the cafeteria food to keep us guys uninterested in the females. Now here we are, together." I was glad to hear the whistle blow, but I was sorry to see David skate further and further away.

"I met David in skate class today. Remember, he's the guy in the Date Book. He's so good looking! And – he's tall!"

"Tell me more," my roommate said. I lowered my voice and said very seriously, "But his teeth look like they're wearing coats!" Silence prevailed for a moment and then we roared laughing.

"You'll see him again tomorrow, won't you?" she asked.

"Well, we have skate class again but I'm not sure if I'll get to skate with him. But at least I should see him."

The next day in skate class, I didn't see much of him, but later in the day, there was a knock on my dorm door. "Phone call for you in the lobby."

I spoke into the receiver with no idea who was calling. "Hello."

"Hi, it's David. How's it going?"

Something inside me danced up and down. "David? Oh, hi!"

"I wonder if you'd like to go to the program on campus tomorrow night."

Not knowing anything about the program, I said, "That'd be great!"

On Saturday evening, David eventually told me, "I feel really lucky you didn't already have a date. Dan told me I'd have to call at least two weeks in advance to get a date with you."

I didn't tell David until weeks later, "Dan is a very nice guy, but kind of short. He didn't really interest me. The three or four times he asked me for a date, I tried to be very polite in the way I said no. Good thing I was nice to him!" I jokingly told David. He understood.

On Valentine's Day, seven days after David and I met, he came to my dorm unannounced. "Didn't mean to surprise you, but I have to get to the bakery, and I wanted to give you this," he said, handing me a heart-shaped card.

"A Valentine!" I paused, then blurted out, "I have one for you too." He remained silent, looking at me with a soft smile, as if waiting for me to say more. "I made one for you but it's in my room." I managed to say.

He took a step closer. "Would you like to go to vespers tonight?"

"I'd like that very much."

"See you at seven then," he said, but lingered a moment before hurrying out the door.

On our walk back to my dorm after vespers one evening, he reached for my hand. A startled "Oh" almost escaped my lips as I felt his large hand encompass mine.

"Would you like to climb Two-Bit tomorrow?" he said.

"You mean that big hill that sits behind our dorms?"

"Yeah, I thought we could climb it in the afternoon after church." David paused beneath a tree to pull something down.

"What's that?"

"These are my cinnamon rolls." He grinned.

"That's a funny place to put those!" I teased.

"It was easier than running over to my dorm after I got off work. Didn't want to be late picking you up."

We sauntered to a stop near the front of my dorm where we stood for a moment silently looking at each other. What a sweet guy, so easygoing, I was thinking when just beyond David, I noticed Randy on the steps of my dorm with one of the girls. When we had dated in high school, I broke up with him for good. I had sized Randy up as a guy who would probably cause me a lot of heartache, maybe like Vern cheating on Mom.

David's voice broke through my thoughts. "So, would you like to climb Two-Bit tomorrow?"

"Yes, I'd really like to. I'd love to climb Two-Bit with you!"

He leaned toward me ever so slightly and gently squeezed my hand. "Tomorrow then, see you tomorrow."

Several dates later I asked David, "How much have you dated?"

"In high school I had a girlfriend my junior year, but she broke up with me. When I was a senior I dated a freshman, but I broke up with her. That's about it."

His dating history concerned me. I had a strong need to marry a man who wouldn't cheat on me. This strong need came from my experience during childhood where infidelity was the normal way of life and had significantly impacted my life several times. When I learned that David had dated only a couple of women, I found myself asking two questions.

How can a man who hasn't dated very much really know what he wants in a wife? How can he be counted on to be faithful? I thought I might actually be safer with David if he chose me from a number larger than two. If a guy dates enough to know what he wants in the woman he marries, then there's a good chance he'll be faithful. That's what I told myself and that's why I said what I did to David. "I don't really want to be with someone who hasn't dated enough to know what he wants. You go date some other girls and then if you're still interested, come back and see if I'm available." This was less of a risk for me than glibly moving forward in the relationship. My heart may have skipped a few beats with this intellectual decision, but I would not allow my emotions to guide me on this important issue.

I thought he understood, I thought it was settled, but the next morning, he was there to take me to breakfast. "I don't want to date anyone else."

About a week or so later in skate class the instructor said, "Please form a very large circle." When the music began, he called out, "David, Vernetta! Will you please come to the center. I'd like you to demonstrate the gliding technique we've been practicing."

With my body against his, with arms entwined, the rest of the class faded from sight as smoothly, effortlessly we moved as one--surrounded by music, lost in each other.

Some of the students on campus had their own cars but David couldn't afford a car. As a result, our time together was spent primarily on campus. We found pleasure in the simplest of things such as what we did one beautiful afternoon when we were both free. We walked hand in hand from the campus across a worn path through a pasture to reach a small sandwich shop where we sipped milk shakes, talked, and laughed together.

My love for David deepened during those special times when he shared stories of himself. With the accumulation of the stories he told of his childhood, came the understanding that, like my mother, his mother had been in charge of his life. But as he spoke of her, I got the impression that his mother was not only present and available, but kind and sober as well. I imagined that when and if she expressed anger, it would read as mild irritation compared to my own mother's volatile nature.

Listening to the stability David enjoyed as a child, I was transported to a mental image of boredom, compared to my life of instability. While I moved back and forth across the country, David had stayed put in the same little community until he left at age eighteen. But I assessed that during all those years, he had lived in financial poverty. It didn't occur to me that I too had lived in poverty, though of a different kind. At the time of our courtship, I didn't have the capacity to appreciate the importance of the differences between David and me and what that would come to mean in my life, and his.

But that was far from my awareness as I listened to his childhood stories over the course of weeks and months sitting in the parlor. I particularly remember his stories that moved me emotionally, for one reason or another.

"Beginning when I was around seven," he said, "my mother took me with her to the cherry orchards every year for ten years to pick cherries along with my brothers and sisters. When I got a little older, my mom and I had friendly competitions to see who could pick the most in the shortest amount of time."

I didn't think at the time of the companionship, the continuity and regularity this activity brought to David's life, or of the underlying sense of security and self-esteem that became his as a result. It didn't occur to me either that at the age of seven the training of the work ethic his mother instilled in him had begun. Instead, my shallow response was that of being stunned and appalled to learn his mother had started him working to earn money at such a young age.

"We picked everything." David smiled then told me a story that became one of my favorites. I think I favored it because I could see how good it made him feel about himself, and maybe his mother as well.

"The guy at the filbert place weighed the bags of filberts I'd picked. Then he told me, 'There's too much weight! You couldn't have picked that many filberts. You must have put some rocks in your bag.'"

"My Mom insisted that he empty my bags. 'There aren't any rocks in there,' Mom told him. 'Empty it out and you'll see.' She told the guy in a nice way there weren't any rocks, but she wasn't going to accept him accusing me," David said.

"You're very fortunate your mom stood up for you," I said. I don't really think he understood the importance of what I said because he hadn't experienced a mother like mine.

"Mom would wake me early in the morning to go pick. I'd tell her, 'It's still dark, Mom and it's raining.' "I didn't want to get out of bed when it was dark. Besides, I was sleepy. I had to go anyway. I didn't really have a choice. Mom would say, 'The sooner you get outta the bed the sooner you'll get to come home.' I remember picking green beans on one of those cold and wet days. Water ran down my arms as I picked."

David told me this without even a hint of self-pity. I found myself questioning his acceptance of her, his lack of resentment in the kind words he said. I sat there thinking it was cruel to make a child go out into the cold and wet to earn money.

David's mother Olga may not have consciously set out to teach David discipline or to train him to deny his feelings, but I thought she accomplished both by her approach. I had already seen how hard he worked and how disciplined he was in his bakery and cleaning jobs. By comparison, discipline of a positive kind was quite absent from my life with Mom and my sister.

David understood his training as it related to his feelings. "You might say of me that I was not trained to rely on my feelings to determine what I did." I probably sat there with my mouth open as I thought of what he said, basically that emotions aren't allowed to dictate which action to take.

Again, I found myself comparing Olga and my mother. Feelings seemed to dictate the choices my mother made. From my perspective, her choices didn't seem to be based on reason. Feelings had played a very important part in my own decisions. I might even have allowed my feelings to lead in major decisions. It took time for me to grasp how these important differences in our training might play out in our relationship.

Besides thinking it was cruel to take young David out in the cold and wet when it was dark, I questioned what Olga did with his earnings. She took all his earnings from when he started working at age seven through high school.

David said it this way. "The money I earned went to Mom to buy the things I needed. When I wanted to buy something, I think she let me have the money to do it if she approved. But she managed the money." The way he said it suggested his mother's way was fine with him.

Probably because of my youth and the perception altering nature of falling in love, I spent no time considering how this might affect us if we married. It never occurred to me that one day, I would assume Olga's role of taking charge of our income and, without questions from David, dispense it as I thought best. Nor did I ever consider how the significance of his relationship with his mother would impact my future relationship with him.

Further differences became apparent, especially about money. During my grade school years, money flowed into my hand from my mother's boyfriends. I spent it as I wished. When she married Norm, the money flow stopped. It was then that I decided I needed to earn my own money for the things I wanted. So, I did babysitting when I was younger and ironed clothes for others when in high school. I got a job as a typist when I was fifteen by lying about my age in the job interview. Fortunately, Mom didn't interfere with me. I earned my money, managed it, and spent it. I bought all my own clothes, took myself on a train trip to see Maxine in Utah when I was sixteen and paid some of my high school tuition.

Money, in the stories that follow, continues to be a theme in David's life. These stories also continue to reveal the kind of Mother Olga had been.

We compared our stories of going to the dentist. I thought his was definitely sad compared to mine. But he told it without any emotion, more as an accepted fact.

"I never went to the dentist other than to have my teeth pulled. Like when Mom couldn't stop the pain in my aching tooth, she'd take me to the dentist."

"How many of your teeth were pulled?" I asked, instead of focusing on my shock. But I was interested in the answer.

"I'm missing most of my back molars, upper and lower. My brother Les and I were playing with a gallon jug. I got hit in the face with it. That's how this front tooth got broken."

His broken front tooth and apparent lack of regular brushing became less important to me as I sat there looking at this precious man I had fallen in love with. My own story of asking my mother if I could go to the dentist when I was a seventh or eighth grader seemed unimportant by comparison. But I felt lucky that when Mom let me to go to the dentist, I didn't need to have any teeth pulled.

David and I lived at a time when doctors thought it best to remove the tonsils of children. I was surprised when I learned how young David was when Olga had his removed, but especially so when I learned that his tonsils didn't need to be removed. Coupled with the dentist story, it gave me further insight into Olga's attitude toward money and the priority it held in her thinking.

"Two for the price of one if my mom let the doctor take out my tonsils the same time as my brother Les. I was very young, three or four. There was nothing wrong with my tonsils," David said as a big grin rippled across his face, "but my mom couldn't resist 'two for the price of one.'"

Hmm, I thought to myself; his father Henry hasn't been mentioned once in any of his stories.

But Olga's action, or lack of it, that I experienced when David told me the milk-can story, was more startling to me than the dentist story or the tonsil removal story. It was unacceptable to me if lack of money was her motive for the choice she made when David hit his face on a milk can.

"When I was eleven and we lived on the farm, I was running, and I tripped over the handle of the milk cart and hit my face on the top of a ten-gallon milk can. I had a terrific nosebleed that took a long time to stop. Because the bleeding finally stopped, I wasn't taken to the doctor. Years later I found out I'd broken my nose, and as a result I have a deviated septum." David paused, then he kind of laughed when he said, "My mom was a band-aid person."

"What does that mean?" I asked.

"Don't see a doctor unless you absolutely have to. That was her attitude. That was because we were 'unrich.' I came by my cavalier attitude legitimately," David said of himself.

My mother would have taken me directly to a doctor, I told myself, as she did after I swallowed the key. Why is David so completely accepting of Olga's choices? I wondered.

"Where have you lived?" I asked David on one of our talks.

"We lived in about five different places in a small farming community when I was growing up. But three of those years, we moved fifteen miles up to the farm when I was in fifth or sixth grade. We always upgraded when we moved until finally, we moved into a house we had built ourselves. My Dad was a carpenter. I helped build the house, along with my brothers. What about you?" he asked.

"We moved a lot from state to state. Sometimes we moved to several different places within the same town over a short period of time," I said, without going into detail.

"You've seen a lot more than I have. I never went more than two hundred miles from home until I came to California. I can't remember our family ever going on a vacation," David said.

By the time he came to college, because of the work ethic his mother had taught him, David knew how to provide for himself financially. He worked in the college bakery on campus in the evening and late into the night. During the day, he collected clothes that needed to be cleaned from the men in the dorms. He had no shame about what he did when he took these clothes from the men who came from affluent families. His lack of shame perplexed me.

I would not be able to do what David could, without shame. Shame clung to my mom, my sister and me like warts on a toad. But David had self-confidence, a self-assurance that seemed to suggest he felt inferior to no one. Not only did he completely earn his own tuition, but he also had a surplus of money from working two jobs while attending classes. Much later, David and I would experience the downside of this well-learned work ethic. Work became his solution to most problems, despite the cost to himself, to us, to me. Work even prevailed as his source of pleasure.

David never used the word poverty to describe it, but poverty is the word I chose to describe his circumstances after several months of getting acquainted. He never acknowledged it to himself, however one time he referred to his family as 'unrich.'

The poverty he experienced was particularly obvious about seven months after I met him.

"When the soles of my shoes eventually got holes in them, my mother cut cardboard and put it on the inside of my shoes. There was a shortage of food. We never had any leftovers after dinner." He thought, then said, "I never felt poor. We had limited money, but we always had a roof over our heads. Had what we needed."

A comforting silence offered the benediction.

Chapter 26

California
June 1956 – June 1957

The summer days before my second year of college trickled slowly away. But endless, tedious days had nothing to do with my mother. No, I saw very little of her. It was the miles, the miles that separated David and me. He worked on campus at his bakery job and I in Long Beach typed away at my desk enclosed in a windowless room, thinking of him.

The first week of returning to the campus in the fall, I was brushing my teeth, oblivious to anything else, when I heard David's voice, "Good Morning!" I turned, looked out the window and there was David smiling at me. "How in the world can you be at my window, I'm on the second floor!"

"There's a ladder out here so I decided to come and surprise you!"

"That's a terrific surprise," I said through my laughter, "but if Miss Carlsen sees you, we're in trouble." Silence for a moment, then we laughed and laughed as he went back down the ladder.

Around November, long after the ladder event, Miss Carlsen called me into her office. "Shut the door, please," she instructed, staying seated. "Vernetta," she began, "Miss Hodkins and I are concerned about you and David. We see you walking around campus, and he has his arm around your waist. If you do that in public, what must you do in private!" I could hardly believe what I was hearing. She didn't know that David had waited months before he kissed me the first time. This "arm around the waist" was as intimate as we had gotten in private or in public. "I want to reassure you, Miss Carlsen, that we are innocent of any wrongdoing in private," I said in great seriousness with a solemn face that must have communicated my honest message. She allowed me to continue working in the Registrar's Office.

"Let's take a walk behind the dorms," David suggested after dinner one evening not long after my talk with Miss Carlsen. It was pleasant to follow the canal that flowed behind and beyond the back of the dorms. Twilight had not yet faded, and reflections of wispy clouds could be seen in the water. We walked near the men's dorm where rocks naturally formed a crude circle, "I've never been here before; what is it?" I asked.

"This is where the men of Calkins Hall come to have prayer together," he said. David and I had each talked about the importance of God in our lives within our first few dates. "I love the story of how you came to be here for college. Tell me again," I urged him.

"Originally, I wanted to stay in Washington to go to a local college to get started where it wouldn't be so expensive. Sometime in August Mel, a guy I had known in high school, wrote to me about coming down to California to go to college. I had no idea why he got in contact with me. We hadn't been in touch. I'd done stuff with him, but he was a year or two older than me. I didn't answer him, so he wrote again telling me to get myself down there. Finally, when he didn't hear anything from me, he called. "There's a nice family where you can stay. They'll give you room and board in exchange for helping them. You can also have a paying job with the man at the campus store. So, get off your duff and make a decision." I finally got the idea he had a place for me to stay and a job waiting. I had never been more than a hundred and eighty miles from home. It was unlike me, but I packed a bag and got on a bus to go to California. If it hadn't been for him, I wouldn't be here."

By now, twilight was beginning to give way to darkness. David put his arms around me as I sat in front of him. He spoke softly, lovingly, "I would like you to become my wife." His proposal came as a welcomed surprise. I was in love with David. There wasn't any question that I wanted to marry him.

"You know, I've never told you this before but when I was a junior in high school, we had a special devotional week. For some reason, the speaker's wife started talking to me in the hallway. After a while she said, 'Honey, it's not too early to start praying for the man you're going to marry someday.' I was impressed with her sincerity and started praying for the man I would marry."

"I think God brought us together," David said. "Would you like to go home with me at Christmas break to meet my family?" he asked. "I think we could catch a ride with Mel." The thought of going to Washington at Christmas break was an invitation to heaven, I thought. I imagined myself meeting the family I had always dreamed being a part of. I had visions that David and I would live in Washington, far, far away.

I dialed the number; it was ringing; finally, she said, "Hello."

"Mom, I'm engaged!"

"Oh", she said with a hint of interest in her tone. I chatted on as if speaking to someone who was an intimate part of my life; chatted on in spite of the many lessons when she taught me that she is not available emotionally.

"Yes, I'm engaged to marry David!" I repeated.

"Isn't that nice," she said in a somewhat affectionate tone." Silence followed.

"Well, bye for now. I'll talk to you soon," I said, hanging up the phone.

Several weeks later, David leaned over and said to me, "I have something I want to share with you after church."

When the final hymn had been sung and we were walking out I said, "What is it? You look so serious."

"We need to go someplace so we can talk. Let's go to the women's parlor. It'll be quiet there; everyone will be at lunch."

"What is it?" David handed me a letter, "It's from my mom: 'Son, I want to tell you…'

His mother Olga wrote him a letter to tell him that Henry, the man David grew up believing was his father, was not his father. She decided to disclose this truth after learning he had become engaged to me. With the news of his mother's infidelity, I couldn't escape feeling an incredible disappointment that I didn't want to acknowledge to myself or to David. "How are you with this, David?" I asked.

"Surprised, I guess, that Henry isn't my real father. I hope this doesn't change things between us," David said with concern. My love for David crowded out my disappointment for the moment. The full depth of my feelings remained temporarily repressed. "This doesn't change how I feel about you." We made our plans to go home to Washington for Christmas.

We turned onto the driveway of David's home and there was Henry, hooking the latch on the gate from the barn as he held a pail of fresh milk with the other hand. He waved at us, standing in the headlights of the car. Quite a small man, I thought, unlike David who was a bit more than six feet tall. David and I followed him into the house through the back door into the kitchen.

Olga came into the kitchen with a warm smile on her face. Except for her glasses, I was aware that her physical appearance somewhat resembled my mother's. She was about the same height, but her hair bore the most striking resemblance. Was it the fact that the color of her hair was dark like Mom's or was it the tight curls in a row that sat on the top of her head? I brushed the thought aside.

The meager surroundings of the kitchen came into focus: run down, worn kitchen countertops; linoleum floors with patterns worn almost completely away, with bare patches in places. A tired sofa sitting at the end of an almost empty living room held little beauty for the eye to savor. I sat down in a rocker next to the wood-burning stove while David and his mother had their reunion.

One at a time I was introduced to the last of Olga and Henry's children still living at home. Byron had straight thin hair, light brown in color. I observed that he seemed uncomfortable when he spoke. I couldn't determine if he was shy or simply awkward. Phyllis was a sweet, young grade-school girl eager to meet me. Blond-headed Jerry was quite young, but full of self-confidence like David.

Olga had a simplicity about her that was even less sophisticated in some ways than Mom. "Is there anything I can do to help?" I asked when she began to prepare our dinner. She didn't look at me but continued to scurry about the kitchen.

"You can set the table." There wasn't anything else for me to do when I finished setting the table, so I sat watching Olga.

It wasn't hard to start down the slow pathway to disliking Olga. It didn't begin with the grated carrots on the outside of a bread wrapper. Although I tried to deny the impact her infidelity had on my feelings toward her, I couldn't seem to outrun my denial.

Sitting there, watching Olga grate carrots, her confession of infidelity stormed into my thoughts uninvited. The man I'm engaged to is the product of adultery. I wanted to scream. This admission seemed to defile the innocent purity of our love. This link to my past threatened to couple itself grotesquely to my present. Revolting memories from my past sped darkly through my mind: Vern slept with Kae Hicks while married to my mother; Norm had sex with Mom while married, then left his wife and children for my mother; Ferd had sex with my mother over a period of years even though he was married. How I had longed to be free of people who behaved this way, I thought as I watched Olga. Now here it is, in my face again.

At nineteen, I had the dream that my own life would "rise above" what I loathed from my childhood. Perhaps not. Look dummy, I heard myself say, you wouldn't have David if Olga hadn't slept with the man at the furniture store and gotten pregnant. Henry got over it. So why don't you? I felt a hand on my shoulder.

"Dinner's ready," Henry said with a big grin on his face. "You look like you're lost in thought. Ready to eat?" I was relieved Henry interrupted my thoughts.

After dinner in the evening, David sat at the kitchen table across from Olga with me at the end. "You know that Vernetta and I are engaged to be married," he said to her. I waited for her response. Her eyes stayed on David.

She was a soft-spoken woman who put smiles in her voice for the serious parts she wanted to express but the words often came out of her mouth almost inaudibly and somewhat mumbled as she spoke. "You're not dry behind the ears yet, are you?"

David parleyed with a soft defensive comment. I sat back in my seat. What was it I hoped I would hear Olga say, this woman whose son I had fallen in love with? Olga directed her words to David. I wanted to be included. I sat expecting more of Olga than she apparently had to offer. The same mistake I had made with my mother. And probably Olga's passivity toward me was an additional connection to the pain of my mother's indifference. Clearly however, I knew that I detested her act of infidelity, just as I had my mother's.

I confronted myself with the reality that Olga could never be the mother I dreamed of gaining when I married her son. Eventually, I transferred from my mother to Olga all the anger I carried but could never put where it belonged, on my own mother. The understanding of what I had done became clear as time passed.

"David," I said to him after dinner, "Did you see your mother grate carrots on the outside of a bread wrapper from the grocery store?"

"Yes, that's the way she does it," he said.

"But what about germs?" I asked.

"I'm sure she doesn't think about it," David casually answered.

On Christmas Eve I met the rest of David's siblings. Manfred, the oldest, married with three children, had successfully completed college and was a Certified Public Accountant. Marilyn, two years older than Manfred, was married to Al, who some would label as a "loud-mouthed loser." She had one of those happy faces that must have been shaped from birth by smiles that Olga gave her, but she looked much older than her years. Les, wearing large tear shaped sunglasses with a cigarette pack rolled up in the sleeve of his tee shirt, showed up for a short time with his wife, Kate. He reminded me too much of my Uncle Ralph, Mom's brother, for us to become friends.

Olga handed Al a camera. "Could you take a picture of us?" She and Henry sat in the middle with the rest of their seven children surrounding them. Yes, I said to myself as Al was about to take the picture, David is taller than all the males and most definitely has a different head shape. Handsomer too!

"Did you and your mom talk about what she wrote you in the letter?" I asked David later.

"No, she didn't bring it up and neither did I."

Toward the end of spring, the last semester of our second year of college, an upper classman invited me to be on the committee that would prepare the Mother-Daughter Banquet. With great flourish, the event was announced to the female college students with the expectation that each would attend the banquet with her mother. What am I to do? I thought.

"Vernetta," Sharon said, "you'll be sitting with your mother at the top table with all the committee members and their mothers." Now, it seemed, matters had gotten worse. I didn't want to sit at the banquet next to an empty chair. I didn't want to say I couldn't be there, so I overcame my resistance and called my mother.

"Mom, we're having a banquet for mothers and daughters. If you don't come, I'll be sitting alone at the top table," I began on the phone to her. I'm not sure what else I said that finally convinced her to attend the banquet, but she came! A photographer went around taking pictures of each mother-daughter duo. Without knowing it, he had recorded a monumental moment in history when he took the picture of us, my mother attending my school function. I looked at the picture days later and thought, my mother is so beautiful.

Chapter 27

California to Texas
June 1957 – February 1962

Spring semester came to a close. "I don't want to move in with Mom and Norm," a loud voice protested. Well, we don't have any money to stay anywhere else until the wedding in August, I yelled back inaudibly to the voice in my head. But out of financial necessity, I lived with Mom and Norm until David and I got married.

"They need a bookkeeper at GMC where I work," Norm said. "You can ride to work with me," Norm offered after I got hired. "I gotta be there a half hour earlier than you, but you can sit in the truck 'til it's time for you to go to work." The two of us rode a half-hour each way, every day of the week, without saying a word.

When I came home from work a week after I started my new job, Mom was standing at the kitchen sink looking out the window. I started to pass through the kitchen when I saw it, a strange letter on top of the refrigerator.

"What's this?" I asked as I picked it up, recognizing her handwriting, intrigued by the special delivery stamps. But I was more intrigued by the stamped hand with a finger pointing to my mother's return address with the ominous message, Return to Sender. I waved the returned letter at her and asked again, "So what is this?"

"I was tryin to find Buddy, Jr." Mom said.

"Oh," I heard myself say. I put the letter back on top of the refrigerator, realizing I hadn't thought of Buddy, Jr. since grade school. Curious that she would be trying to find him after all these years, I said to myself without uttering a single word more to Mom as I left the kitchen. Although I quickly set aside the incident, I never entirely forgot about it.

"Mom," I cried out from the bathroom around mid-July, "I'm bleeding!" Mom came running into the bathroom, "What's the matter?"

"I'm bleeding. I passed a big glob of blood," I wailed. "I'm scared."

"You need to lie down. I'll call the doctor," she said calmly. It was the same doctor who had taken care of my strep throat when I was in high school.

"We'll need to do a gynecological exam," he told me after hearing my story.

"I've never had one," I anxiously responded.

An alarmed doctor looked at me after the exam, "You have scarring in your vagina." I saw the shock on his face and didn't know what to think or say. I'm not sure why I didn't ask him, I'm a virgin, how can that be? Maybe it was the look on his face. I froze in place. His words "scarring in your vagina" repeated themselves in my mind as I left his office, a mystery that at the time presented no solution.

Mother's softness made a rare appearance shortly before my wedding. "What a beautiful cameo pin you're wearing, Mom."

She began to unclasp it. "This used to belong to Aunt Emma." She removed it from her blouse and held it out to me. "Here, you can have it."

"Are you sure?" I asked, astonished by her generous offer.

"Yes, you can have it," she repeated.

I looked at the precious family heirloom I held in my hand. "It's so beautiful, Mom." She loves me, I told myself, even though I had never heard her say so.

The realization that I simply couldn't afford an elaborate wedding gown finally seeped into my reality.

"My friend Jessie's daughter just got married and she's willing to loan you her dress," Mom offered.

"When could I see it?" Mom brought the dress home. "It's too long and it doesn't have any sleeves!" I moaned as I stood wearing it in the living room.

"Well, I can sew some sleeves for it," she said without hesitation. "But I can't do anything about the length. Jessie told me not to touch the length. You'll have to wear it long."

Mom did just what she said she would, sewing two beautiful lace sleeves and then inserting them onto the bodice of the dress. There wasn't even a hint that they weren't part of the original gown. But the length caused me an agonizing ascent up the altar stairs toward the Pastor and David.

Our first home together was a small apartment within walking distance of the campus. "David, I really don't like to be alone at night when you're working at the bakery," I told him about six weeks into the fall semester. "Since you plan to be a chemistry major, doesn't it make more sense to work in the chemistry department?"

He thought about it. "Maybe, but I'd have to take quite a pay cut. I'd do it for you if you think it's worth it."

With my encouragement, David changed jobs. I was relieved that I wouldn't be alone at night. I thought life would be better if David worked during the day in the chemistry lab distributing items to lab students. I was wrong. I experienced raging insecurities. I was fearful that some young co-ed would steal my husband from me. I didn't understand that the act of marriage had triggered painful fears of abandonment originating from my childhood experiences. But I understood that I was in emotional pain.

David spent no time babying me. Reason was the weapon he wielded against my fear. It was a band-aid approach for a gaping wound that required major surgery. We had only a surface understanding of my problem.

A recession brought a change to our plans when the company I worked for closed its doors. We sat talking in our parked car before going into our apartment. "There aren't any jobs in this area, David. What shall we do?" I asked as I sat in the driver's seat and he in the passenger seat.

"I'm not sure. What do you want to do?"

"I was hoping you had some idea of what we should do," I said.

He sat looking at me sweetly, but nothing came out of his mouth. I was about to learn another important lesson. David deferred to me as the leader. Olga had been in charge of David's life until he left home. Now that we were married, I realized he wanted me to be in charge. It was implied through his behavior, not his words. Both literally and figuratively, I was in the driver's seat.

When I was a child, my mother seemed like a powerful woman. I decided that I too would be a powerful woman, but I wouldn't allow any man to treat me the way she claimed had Vern treated her. This was another decision I had made back in fourth grade. So, in some ways, it was easy for me to be the leader in my marriage. But sometimes I felt alone, like when I mostly ran my own life after about sixth grade.

Out of a job, I decided we would move to Long Beach, a town I knew well. I didn't know what else to do. We now lived in the same local area as Mom and Norm, Verneda, Ralph and Della and Nettie and Fritz, a gloomy situation. My feelings were compounded by a phone call within a few months of moving to Long Beach, "Your mother has been in an accident and has been seriously injured."

"Mom's in surgery," Verneda said when we got to the hospital.

"What happened?" I asked impatiently.

"She was at a bar with her girlfriend, drinking. The two of them left the bar with a couple of guys to go to a different bar, apparently bar hopping. Mom and her friend got in the back seat and the two men, drunk themselves, got in the front. Not very far down the road, the driver ran the car off the road into a culvert, crashing into a telephone pole." I was consumed with anger toward my mother. Memories of the old days flashed into my mind, of her dragged into the house by a stranger, so drunk she had passed out.

"What's her status?" I asked.

"She has a severe head injury; she has broken ribs and a punctured lung. We're not sure she's gonna make it."

After recovering from this distressing news, I asked, "What about her friend who was in the back seat with her?"

"Her friend was even more critically injured." A day or two later, the woman died.

I had consciously rejected Mom's lifestyle since I was a fourth grader and my rejection at times spilled over into a rejection of her. As a child, it was very difficult for me to see my only parent make the choices she did. It was painful to see her passed out drunk or to see a strange man fondling her or to see her injured because she was too drunk to take care of herself.

After she married Norm, the drinking was constant but somehow more regulated.

Why, I wondered, was she at the bar drinking without Norm? I didn't have the answer, and none was given. When I was a child, before my mother met Norm, I wanted to keep her safe, but I was never able to do it. All I could do was observe. Now I stood at her hospital bed feeling as helpless as when I was a child. I'm still just an observer of her drunken behavior, I said to myself.

"Maybe death will be the consequence this time," I said angrily to David.

"Maybe not. Let's wait and see," David said to comfort me.

"If she can make it through the next two or three days," the doctor said, "we have a high expectancy that she will survive."

On the third day, when I walked into Mom's room, she was supposedly conscious, her eyes set in a strange, traumatized wide-open gaze. Her forehead held a large number of stitches.

The doctor came in to speak with David and me. "She's had a pretty rough time of it, but she's going to make it." I felt relief that she would live but I wanted to be far, far away from the life of my drunken mother.

Despair enveloped me. Too inexperienced, I failed to recognize my deep state of depression as David drove us to church. Color had vanished into a haze of grey as I sat gazing at the trees and flowers out the window of the moving car. I didn't realize I needed the help of a professional. David extended kindness and understanding when I frequently called in sick, unable to work a day or two at a time. He was patient and available even when I pushed him away and isolated myself from a life that seemed intolerable, not only because of my relationship with my mother, but also because of the mediocre life that now trapped David and me.

Before my mother's near-fatal accident, I had become ill without a phone, alone in our apartment. I went knocking on doors of our apartment complex, but no was one home. Across the street was a small building identified itself as a medical facility. I made it to the front office where I abruptly fainted. When I awoke, much to my surprise, they had performed surgery without my permission. David and I had no medical insurance; he had dropped out of the university. David didn't complain. It wasn't David's way to complain about anything. His usual approach to life kicked in; he dropped out of school and got a job.

Now I felt David and I were headed nowhere. That's when I received the call that my mother was in the hospital and might not survive. That's when life went colorless for me. Throughout the entire ordeal, David expressed in words and action, "It'll be okay. Don't worry."

A letter dated June 1961 relieved the mediocrity of our lives and brought reverberating changes. "You are ordered to report to Ford Ord, California." David had been drafted into the army.

"In college I heard about the White Coat Project back on the East Coast," David told me after he read the letter.

"What's that?" I asked.

"A medical research project with mostly volunteers from the army who don't carry guns. They're classified as conscientious objectors. That's my classification."

"It suits me fine that you don't want to carry a gun and kill people!" I said, but I didn't give any thought to what took place in the research project. I was thinking instead of the separation I anticipated from David, the love of my life.

We packed and stored away our belongings. "Let's see if we can find you a place where you'll feel safe when you're alone at night," he said. He knew that it was frightening for me to be left alone at night, yet he didn't criticize or find fault. What a contrast it was to live with David, who never criticized or belittled me as my mother had. The dreaded time came. I drove with him to the Los Angeles Grand Central Station where we said our sorrowful goodbye, not knowing when we would see each other again.

In Fort Ord, at the end of six weeks, the sergeant gave instructions. "You will continue your six-month basic training at

San Antonio, Texas. You will travel by plane on a ticket that will be provided. You are strongly advised not to bring your spouses." While at Fort Ord, David met someone we had known in college who had already been through the process. Those who are inclined spiritually believe there are no coincidences. "Take your wife with you to San Antonio." he advised.

David called me, "Would you like to go to Texas with me?"

"Would I like to go to Texas?" I said in disbelief. "I would love to go to Texas with you!"

So instead of flying to Texas, David caught a flight into Los Angeles. "I have a little money left over from turning in my ticket for the flight to Texas," David told me, "But it isn't enough to get us there."

"Maybe we could borrow some from Mom," I suggested.

After my mother almost lost her life in the car accident, I saw improved changes in how she and Norm lived their lives. They had purchased a nice home in an upscale neighborhood, and they didn't seem to drink as much. It appeared that they were doing better financially.

"Mom, I want to go to Texas with David, but we need money. Could you afford to loan us some?"

She gave me a fairly quick response, "Well, I could loan you two hundred dollars, but I'll need it back as soon as you can."

"Your loan will make it possible for me to be with David," I said as I gave her a hug.

We hitched a small trailer packed with a few of our belongings to our equally small German made DKW. We went to say goodbye to my mother. All on her own initiative she said, "Stand by the car, I want to take your picture." It was a precious moment of love between the three of us as David and I left for Texas.

In San Antonio, I made some good choices and some very bad choices. There were so many military wives looking for jobs that I wasn't certain if I would find one, but after a couple of interviews I was hired as a bookkeeper in a small, beautiful hospital where I worked in the front office with windows looking out to a marvelous view. I also ate one free meal a day in the cafeteria. I was able to complete my bookkeeping by three o'clock in the afternoon each day with nothing to do but answer the phone until five o'clock. I quit because I was bored.

What was I thinking! Monthly army checks were so meager that my salary was an absolute necessity. I spent the remainder of my time in San Antonio working at a temporary agency, going from one drudge job to another. Along with this pathetic situation I had created for myself came illness.

I sat and sat for a very long time in a large, rather sterile room, waiting to see a doctor. At last, a stocky woman in white with a little cap perched on her head called my name from across the large room. "Yes," I said, standing up.

She promptly called out loudly, stretching and elongating the words as if they were rubber bands, "Did ya empty your bladder?"

Feeling publicly humiliated, I shyly nodded yes.

Eventually the doctor examined me then quietly said, "You're pregnant."

"Mom, I'm going to have a baby!" I called to tell her shortly after the doctor's confirmation.

"Well, how are you gonna make it? Do you have the money you borrowed?" she asked.

"I don't have a job right now, but I have a chance to work for a lady who breeds poodles. We'll pay you back as soon as we can." After a period of silence I said, "I'll give you a call soon, Mom. And don't worry about the money. You'll get it back."

The call to Mom motivated me to drive out to see about the kennel job. "I can let you stay here in the back room," the breeder told me. "You can help clean the kennels and feed the dogs then a little later, I'll show you how to groom them."

"Thank you for giving me a place to stay. I'm excited about learning how to groom the animals!"

Things went pretty well with the breeder until my morning sickness flared. "I'm sorry, I'm sick again this morning," I apologized to the breeder.

For several mornings I hadn't been able to work. The breeder took one look at me and said, "I'm sorry, but you can't stay here any longer. It's not working out." I quickly got my things together and piled them in the car.

I boldly drove to the army base because I was desperate to find David. Groups of squads were marching along the road where I parked. David had been ranked as an acting Corporal in charge of a platoon. As the squads continued marching in my direction, I saw David fall out and head on a run in my direction. Is it any wonder the army didn't want the men to bring their wives? I sat thinking as David got closer.

The minute he got into the car I burst into tears. "I don't have a place to live. That woman asked me to leave! I don't have a job and I keep having morning sickness."

David embraced me with kindness and reassurance. "We got our wish," he said. "I've been assigned to the White Coat Project. I'll be based at Ft. Dietrick in Maryland. We'll leave in two weeks. Until then, I think you can get a bedroom in the church conference building.

"How do you know about that?"

"One of the guys in my platoon mentioned it."

Two weeks later, we loaded our belongings into the back seat of our very unreliable DKW for the trip from Texas to Maryland.

"How many miles have we gone?" I wearily asked after traveling for hours.

"I guess about three-hundred-fifty so far."

"I wish we had some money so we could stay in a motel."

David pulled into a closed service station and parked us under a light. "We'll sleep here tonight. Can you climb up on those boxes in the back and get comfortable?"

"I'll try."

He helped me onto the boxes then kissed me goodnight. David has all the virtues of an angel and then some, I thought. I dozed off thinking, I'm fortunate and blessed to be married to this wonderful man.

Chapter 28

Maryland
February 1962 – June 1963

"We'll look for a place in Tacoma Park," David suggested. "The guys tell me it's a small community with a college and only about a half-hour from Ft. Dietrick."

"I like the idea of being near a college; maybe I can get a job there," I said.

When David came back from his first trip to Ft. Dietrick, I greeted him with, "I got a job at the college as assistant to the Secretary of the President. Pretty impressive, hmm? I can even walk to work."

David went to the base during the day. I went to work at the college, thankful that I no longer had morning sickness. About six weeks after we had arrived, I said to David, "It's getting harder and harder to go up and down the stairs at the college."

He got a concerned look on his face. "Sounds like you need to see the doctor."

"I'm going to Walter Reed Hospital next week to see a gynecologist."

"Please put your feet in the stirrups," the nurse instructed as I lay flat on my back on a narrow table. Soon a young doctor came in and sat on a stool at the end of the table, hidden by the sheet that covered my legs. I felt the "cold-metal duck-bill" slide into my vagina.

Suddenly, the head of the doctor popped up above the sheets. He looked at me, momentarily frozen, with a startled expression on his face. Then he dashed off without a word, leaving the uncomfortable cold-metal apparatus inside me. I called out to the nurse, "Get this thing out of me."

Astonished, she asked, "Where did the doctor go?"

"I don't know, but I want this thing out of me," I insisted.

The nurse left without removing the apparatus. In a short time, the young doctor returned, followed by an older doctor.

Both of them hovered down below the sheet where I couldn't see them, conferring softly with each other, then both stood up abruptly.

The older doctor approached, "I'm afraid your cervix is almost fully dilated. You will have to go into the hospital immediately." I started to move to sit up. "No, you must lie back down. I'm sorry, but you won't be able to get up. We don't want you to walk; the risk of losing the baby is too great."

With that, I was taken to the ward where eventually a cadre of physicians circled my bed with one as the spokesperson. "You'll be going into surgery tomorrow morning. You have what is medically called an incompetent cervix."

"What does that mean?" I asked him.

"It means that the cervix doesn't have the ability to hold the weight of the developing baby. Your cervix will be sutured, somewhat like a drawstring, with the hope that the membranes may be held in place to keep your baby where it belongs for as long as we can. In the meantime, blocks will be placed under the end of your bed to tilt you downward toward your head. The purpose is to get some help from gravity to get the membranes to go back where they need to be."

I lay there in utter dismay. I had come in for what I thought was a routine exam. I had no idea that there were women who had complications with their pregnancies.

"No one in our family has ever had any problem like this," Mom said when I called her.

"I'm on a hospital ward full of women who have some kind of complication with their pregnancy," I lamented. "Why me if no one else in the family has had problems?" I didn't wait for her to answer. "The end of my bed is raised up so high that I slant from my feet down to my head, and they told me I can't even get up to go to the bathroom. I'll have surgery tomorrow morning," I told her, totally bewildered.

Mom said very little in response. In desperate times, I still continued to reach out to her in spite of the sparse return for my efforts.

"You are going to be famous! A nameless face jokingly told me as I was coming out from the anesthetic. "We took pictures of your bulging membranes while you were in surgery.

They will appear in a leading medical journal." In a more serious tone, he said, "The suturing was successful, and you are a fortunate woman that you didn't lose your baby."

I didn't feel very fortunate. At that moment, I had no capacity to understand the significance of not losing my baby, the baby that became my precious daughter, Jennifer.

Within the first week after the suturing of my cervix, the nurse brought me a message. "Your husband, David is in the hospital."

"Oh my gosh! Is he okay?" I cried.

"Nothing serious to worry about. He has developed what is believed to be empathetic symptoms."

"I don't know what that means. What does that mean?" I anxiously asked the nurse.

"Well, your husband developed inflammation in his testicles shortly after you had your cervix sutured then confined to your bed. There may be a correlation," she said, then left abruptly.

I smiled to myself as I thought about dear David in the hospital with "empathetic symptoms."

Colonel Patow, a military medical doctor, became my friend. When I was given fifteen pills to take at one time, I asked him, "What are all these for?" He explained. I appealed to him, "Please, I need to go home. Let me go home."

He said sympathetically, "We don't want to send you home, because the temptation will be too great to start doing too much and you will lose the baby. Your regular due date is mid-July."

"But that's months away. I promise to lie on the couch all day and do nothing."

Colonel Patow finally gave in to my pleas two weeks later. "I am releasing you to go home, with the stipulation that you come back once a week for an examination," he said, showing a sense of genuine caring. I eagerly agreed to his conditions.

All went well until about the third week of April. "The membranes are starting to bulge; you'll have to go back into the hospital," the doctor declared at one of my weekly visits.

"But July is such a long time away," I moaned, dreading the confinement to my hospital bed until then. Back into the hospital I went.

May came and with each passing day, I became more agitated. On May eighth, I announced to a doctor, "I'm going home. I can't stay here any longer."

Fortunately, the determined doctor somehow managed to keep me in the hospital. The next day, my membrane burst and our first child, Jennifer, was born May ninth, almost eight weeks premature, weighing only three pounds three ounces. She was placed in an incubator. Milk flowed into my breasts, but I held no suckling baby in my arms.

"How do you feel," the doctor asked as he made rounds the day after I gave birth.

"My arms feel ten feet long and very empty," I honestly replied.

David and I peered through a glass window at the tiny form in an incubator. "That's our baby," I said. "I wish we could touch her." A loving nurse had placed a pink bow in our baby's soft sprinkling of brown hair. As Jennifer gained in ounces, the nurse was able to hold her during feedings, purposely placing her own pinky finger in the palm of our baby's hand where it was clasped by tiny fingers.

"We don't have enough money to pay the rent, David. I haven't been able to work for months and bills we owed before you got drafted are still unpaid. We have to do something." Silence hung over us. "What do you think about this drastic idea?" I asked him. "I could take our baby and go to California. Maybe I could get my job back with Dr. Pelton. And if Mom could take care of Jennifer, we wouldn't have to pay a babysitter.

David was reluctant but started thinking of our situation, "If you did that, I'd be willing to get extra jobs. We could pay off our old debts." Our plan all along had been for David to return to college after completing the military. We didn't see how that could be accomplished if we were still heavily in debt.

I lacked the wisdom and experience to realize that separating our family should never have been considered a solution. Sometimes it is difficult to comprehend the underlying motives that compel us toward action. It's possible, I'm sure, to think we know what motivates our action, but sometimes the true motive lies beyond our reach. Why, why would I consider living with Mom and Norm again? Maybe it was because their lives were more in order than they had ever been, and I felt desperate. Whatever the reason, David and I executed this terrible-awful idea. Our baby and I flew away from David, placing miles between us.

David rented an upstairs room in an older couple's home. During the day, he was on the army base at his position in a Medical Research Laboratory. He spent his evenings working at a service station. During the night, he worked at a hospital as an orderly on the night shift. I worked the front office for Dr. Pelton while Mom took care of Jennifer during the day. Mother still had a residue of sweetness that came after her near-fatal accident. She never complained about caring for my baby, but a bond of closeness between us remained elusive.

Norm usually had a scowl on his face when he looked at me. He probably didn't like my being there with my baby. I stayed as long as I could.

"I need to come back, David, this is too hard."

"But we haven't paid off all our debts," he responded.

"I know, but I need to be where you are," I told him, with no room for negotiation. Bills and money took their proper place. Jennifer and I flew back to Maryland.

The taxi dropped us off where David lived. I went into the unfamiliar surroundings where my husband had stayed during our separation of almost three months. I found myself feeling guilty for coming back before reaching our goal. Maybe that's why when I heard his footsteps on the stairs, I took Jennifer in my arms and went into the large walk-in closet. But I had the comfort of knowing I had made a good decision the moment I saw his face; heard his loving words, felt his warm embrace.

"Of course, I would love to work with you again," Lottie, the President's Secretary said, when I asked about returning as her part-time assistant. During the few morning hours I worked,

Jennifer was in the care of a sitter I liked. But mysteriously, even though things were going well, I began getting depressed on Sundays. On that day of the week, I functioned minimally, unable to understand the source of my depression.

Near the end of his two-year military service, David said, "I enjoy the medical research I do at Ft. Dietrick. I think I'd like medical research as a career."

"There's someone you might want to talk with," I suggested. "Do you remember being introduced to the babysitter's husband?" I asked David without waiting for an answer. "He's a medical researcher. You should talk with him." David liked the idea. "Maybe we could see him next week."

"So, you're a medical researcher," David said on meeting with the sitter's husband. "That's my career plan when I get out of the army and return to college."

I listened with interest for the medical researcher's response. "Well, if you really want to do medical research, I strongly recommend you get an M.D. instead of a Ph.D. I have a Ph.D. but I'm limited. I can't work with patients, but an M.D. degree would allow you to work with patients."

This information became another pivotal point in our lives. Some might call it luck that the babysitter's husband was a medical researcher, the very career David had fixed his sights on. Others might call it Divine Guidance.

"What do you think?" I asked David later.

"It makes sense what he said." David hesitated, then added, "If I have an M.D., I won't be limited in what I can do. I think it would be wiser to pursue an M.D."

I had every confidence in David's ability. Shortly after we were married, he had taken a combination of intelligence and interest tests. "You have the IQ to succeed in almost any career of your choosing," the psychologist had reported.

It was time to make a choice of where David would get his undergraduate degree. "I want to stay in Maryland instead of going back to California. I don't want to live close to my relatives," I said, with little clarity on why I absolutely did not want to return to California.

"We can't afford school in Maryland because I'm not a resident," David reminded me. With all my heart I wanted to stay in the East, but when it came time for David to make application to a university, for financial reasons I agreed to return to California.

"It's very important to choose one of the top schools in the West for your pre-med requirements, that's my opinion, but I don't want to go back to Southern California."

David asked, "What do you think of going to the University of California at Berkeley? It's in Northern California."

"That seems like a good choice. At least it's not in Southern California," I happily responded.

Depression continued to smother me on Sundays as the threat of returning to California loomed closer. Why Sundays, I asked myself. Maybe there's a connection to Norm's Sunday drinking parties. But something inside me wasn't satisfied with this shallow answer.

Chapter 29

California
June 1963 – June 1965

A different world opened to us when we moved into the leftover World War II army barracks, which served as the UC Berkeley married student housing. The large two-story wooden barracks faced each other across a wide expanse of lawn interrupted in the middle by a wide concrete walkway flanked by clotheslines. A sandbox, for the children who poured out of the buildings each morning, sat at one end of the barracks.

The sight that greeted my eyes after I had climbed the steep straight stairs to our apartment in student housing, after traveling all night without sleep, hit me like a bad dream. "I'll get some sleep, then deal with it," I said to David as I fell onto the uncomfortable sofa upholstered in beige vinyl. The appeal of the apartment was still zero when I awoke. "I guess we're lucky we don't have to use an outhouse," I mumbled.

A few weeks later we moved to the opposite end of the same building to an apartment on the first floor surrounded by an expanse of lawn. Through the living room window was the view of a tree whose low-growing, long-graceful branches set against the background of an open field, gave me a satisfaction hard to describe. I found myself thinking as I stood looking out the window, I'm glad I try not to accept what I don't like, but instead, make an effort to change things for the better. Otherwise, I'd still be in that upstairs apartment.

Our meager existence from army days stretched into our Berkeley beginnings. In our talks about David going back to school, we didn't discuss how we would make it financially, but I think there was a silent assumption that I would work full-time to support us. One-year-old baby Jennifer would be left in the care of another. But on our way back to California, our stop in Topeka, Kansas to visit the Burdicks had an unknown impact on our assumption.

"I'm a psychiatrist at the Menninger Clinic," Dr. Burdick, the doctor I had ironed for in high school said. "Would you like to see the clinic?" he asked.

"Of course, we would love to see this famous clinic!" I said. After we had visited the clinic, our conversation turned to his wife and children. "Jean has her own clinic. Do you remember, Vernetta, that she is a Speech Therapist?"

"Yes, I do remember. Does she work full-time?"

His answer surprised me. "She does."

"But who takes care of the children?" I wanted to know

"Oh, we have a dependable woman who does that."

"I'm surprised. I thought a woman should take care of her own children."

His answer was somewhat of a zinger. "If that's the way you feel, then you need to stay home and take care of your children," he responded. It was a friendly exchange but one that remained in my thoughts and motivated the action I eventually took.

Within days of arriving in Berkeley, I was on a job search. What better place to apply than to the university itself, I thought. My resume apparently impressed the interviewers because I was immediately hired as Secretary to the Treasurer for the University of California Regents at Berkeley, located on the top floor of a building across the street from the campus. David enrolled in two summer classes, and I went to my new job.

For several weeks, David drove me to work with baby Jennifer between us in her car seat; I kissed them both goodbye, then off to work I'd go. One morning, I found it especially difficult to kiss my little baby goodbye. At lunchtime, I went off by myself to think about our situation. When I married David, our plan had been for me to complete my undergraduate degree two years after he had completed his, but six years later neither of us had a degree. I could be looking at years of supporting us without getting to raise our child, I thought. I remembered the many stories I had heard in college of women who worked to support their husbands through professional degree programs only to be dumped once the husband established his career. The prospect repulsed me, but I was unaware of any conscious connection to Vern and how he had dumped my mother. Instead, I thought of my conversation with Dr. Burdick and the desire I had to raise my own child.

A delightful silver-haired woman, whose office was in sight of my desk, had befriended me. When I returned from lunch, she was sitting at her desk holding a compact in one hand and a lipstick in the other.

"May I talk with you?" I asked.

"I'd love to talk with you. Sit and tell me what's on your mind."

I shared some of my thought with her about longing to be able to take care of my baby.

Our talk concluded with her saying, "There's an opening at the Lawrence Radiation Laboratory. Maybe your husband could look into the possibility of working there."

The time came to disclose my decision to David. "If you want to become a doctor, you'll have to find a way to support us because I've decided I want to be home to take care of Jennifer. I don't want to work for the next nine years to put you through medical school."

I watched the color fade from David's face, but I went on, "I've learned there's an opening on campus at the Lawrence Radiation Laboratory."

David quickly rallied and got the position. "They call it the "Rad Lab," David explained.

"What will your job be?" I asked.

"I'll be using an SMP, that's a Scanning Measuring Projector, to measure on film the trajectories of particles created in the hydrogen bubble chamber by the Bevatron particle accelerator. I'll also have a chance to learn machine language programming." I found the excitement in David's voice comforting.

"Sounds very complicated! Do you know what hours you'll be working?"

"I can go in at four and work until my first class," he answered.

"Four in the morning? That's incredible, but we'll make it work somehow."

"Gary and Eugenia are coming over tonight to play Trivia, David. Are you up to it?"

"That's fine. I can catch a nap later this afternoon." Playing board games with Gary, a doctoral candidate in physics and Eugenia, his wife who had a degree in history became routine. Their three boys and Jennifer played together daily with Natalie, daughter of our friends Mal, a post-grad architect and Sylvia, his wife, who was a teacher.

David was able to carry enough hours at the Rad Lab to support us while maintaining stellar grades. But he wasn't the only one dancing with excitement about grades. "I got straight A's this quarter! "Can you believe it? I got the top A in physiology." Life was sweet: during the day I was home with Jennifer; in the evening I worked toward an Associate of Arts degree.

"I guess we'll go down to see Mom on Christmas break," I suggested to David. "I haven't seen her for months and she never calls. Do you want to go?"

"Might be nice to get away," he said.

We arrived in Orange County at the house where Mom and Norm still lived when David and I had left for Texas.

"I like your tree, Mom," I told her when I walked into the living room.

"Git that slider opened, will ya, so the dog can come in."

"Where do you want me to put our stuff?" David asked her when he came in with suitcases and clothes on hangers.

"That front bedroom's fine," Mom answered, but to me, it seemed she wasn't truly present.

After I put things away, I went into the living room to sit with Mom. "Are you still working as a cook at the bar?"

She sat on the couch picking at something on her face. "I jist go over to help out now and then."

Finally, I said, "Do you still have a cat?"

"No, it run off. I don't know what happened to that cat." Mom's gaze seemed fixed on something in the back yard.

"Well, I have some packages I need to wrap. I'd better go do that," I said as a graceful way to exit the awkwardness of the moment.

David was lying on the bed when I came in. "You know, even though I'm physically here with Mom, I might as well be miles away."

"It's wonderful to be home," I exclaimed excitedly to David, after Christmas was over and we returned to Berkeley. "Home to friends and classes!"

As I prepared lunch, the radio announcer that followed Paul Harvey said, "And now for one of your favorites." The music of "Where Have All the Flowers Gone" filled the little kitchen. My thoughts drifted as I listened. David in medical school will challenge me. I pondered the reality of my awareness. Insecurity all wrapped up in anxiety has been my monstrous shadow since I got married, but I'm not going to hold David back for the sake of my own comfort, I told myself. I lingered on the wisdom of that thought, underestimating the difficulties that lay ahead for both of us.

"Do you have a particular medical school in mind?" I asked David when it came time to make application.

"There's a medical school in San Francisco."

We had lived across the bay from San Francisco for almost two years and each time we crossed the bridge to go there, I had experienced uneasiness. "I have a terrible fear of earthquakes. Remember I saw the movie 'San Francisco' when I was a seventh grader? There's no way I can live in San Francisco!"

"Then we'll apply somewhere else," David quickly offered.

"What other options do we have?"

"We can't afford to go out of state, so we'll have to stay in California. There's a medical school in Los Angeles. We could apply there," he suggested.

As usual, David and I were about to make another important life decision without the benefit of parental wisdom or mentors. It would be a decision based on finances, based on my fear of an earthquake I had seen in a movie, based on ignorance regarding fault lines in the Los Angeles basin.

"I've decided to apply to UCLA," David concluded. "The tuition is less expensive and at the interview I was told there are scholarships and other financial aid available to students." I wasn't surprised when we received his acceptance letter; I wasn't surprised when a dread filled my heart at the thought of returning to Southern California.

The realization that we would be moving to Los Angeles put me on a roller-coaster ride of depression into thoughts of suicide. I took scissors and randomly cut at my long straight hair, not understanding my feelings or my actions. I experienced myself as a helpless victim. If we move to Southern California, there would be no distance between me and whatever it was that the deepest parts of myself desperately wanted to avoid. I, in my twenties, did not understand why I cut my hair, or why suicide presented itself after we'd made the decision to return to where I would be near my mother and my sister.

Hints, answers to our whys, trickle into our conscious mind, threaten us with what we can only remember through a fog. What weapons do we have to defend ourselves against such obscurity, against deeply hidden assaults from the past? We stumble along in the present, battling the unknown that has happened to us, sometimes turning against ourselves in acts of violence. Without the fragments of memory linked together into a full picture of our past, we remain helpless victims. We continue, in the present, to experience mystifying explosive upheavals that are triggers to our unremembered past, which we mistakenly place on a present cause.

"The trailer is all packed and ready to go," David said.

"It's sad to leave," I told him. "These have been the happiest two years of my life. You have your bachelor's degree and at least I have an Associate of Arts degree. We've made lifelong friends. But Gary and Eugenia won't be here much longer, and neither will Mal and Sylvia, so even if we stayed, our friends would be gone."

"That's right, they'll leave soon, so keep that thought then you won't feel bad about leaving," David encouraged. I took one last look around the humble apartment that had been our happy home. "Time to say goodbye," David said. "Eugenia, Gary and the boys are waiting by our car." A few hugs and kisses later, David drove us away from student housing.

When we passed the exit to the university, my memory of my first walk on the UC Berkeley campus came to mind. "She's not wearing a bra!" I remembered saying to Sylvia as I watched a woman in a close-fitting garment approach us with her breasts restlessly unrestrained.

"It's a symbol of the women's liberation movement," Sylvia told me. "We better get used to it." We left Berkeley in the middle of that bra-burning era and the free-speech movement, about to enter the world of chaos in Los Angeles with Watts riots and the dry Southern California hills ablaze with summer fire.

"I'm going to let the guard rail slow us down," an alarmed David blurted out, "The brakes are almost shot. I thought this route would have less hills." We barely arrived in our sick little DKW that had towed a six-foot-by-twelve-foot trailer, a trailer much larger than the car, a trailer filled with our belongings, towed up and down the demanding terrain between Berkeley and Los Angeles. Our DKW came to its demise on that trip. The transmission was taxed beyond its capacity; the brakes were almost obliterated. At the time, I didn't know it was a perfect metaphor of what would face us over the next several years, a load almost too much for us to pull.

Chapter 30

California
July 1965 – February 1966

The DKW rolled to a stop in front of two rows of single-story apartments. "It's certainly more modern than Berkeley housing," I commented to David.

"Here's the one with our number," David called to me after finding our apartment.

"I wonder why that door is open," I said, when I noticed the front door opposite ours was wide open. "It's nice and spacious, David, but our little bit of furniture is going to get lost in it."

David was overlooking out the dining room window. "There are plenty of kids for Jennifer to play with."

I looked out the window at the narrow courtyard. It was filled with children running, screaming, playing. "The noise level is awful. Why is that?" I asked.

"The stucco buildings are so close, the sounds bounce off of them," he explained.

When I went into the kitchen, I noticed the back door immediately across from our back door was wide open, the same as the front door. As I stood looking out the back door, a woman came from the open door. "Hello, I'm Diane," she said. A boy came charging out from behind her, running into the backyard, "That's Darren, he's four."

"We've moved from Berkeley; David will start medical school soon."

"Oh, my husband is a resident in gynecology at UCLA. We should get together," she suggested before she went back inside.

I wandered through the rest of the apartment. "The windows only have views of buildings and more buildings," I whined. It wasn't long before I admitted to David, "I'm not very fond of living here. There's no privacy with Diane leaving her doors open. There's lots of noise and too many people. But I like living in this part of Los Angeles," I said to encourage David after the onslaught of my negativity. "I didn't know UCLA was situated in Westwood Village right next to Beverly Hills. I like that a lot."

The depression that had begun in the last days of being in Berkeley continued to cling to me in Los Angeles. Despite being an undergraduate student myself at UCLA, I couldn't seem to rise above the darkness that enveloped me. I was depressed to the core of my soul. In this state I sat alone one night at our dining room table, my hair rolled to my scalp in plastic curlers.

"I hate you!" an internal voice screamed at me. "I hate you and I hate this place!" I sat as if defeated by an angry foe. Hesitating, conflicted, I reached for the scissors. A dialogue started in my mind.

"Don't do this," a soft voice encouraged.

"Go ahead! Who cares," a hateful voice said.

"But I don't want to," the soft voice protested meekly.

I held the scissors in one hand while with the other I felt the curler to find the space between it and my scalp. Holding onto the lowest curler on the back of my head I placed the hair coming from my scalp between the blades of the scissors.

"No, No," the soft voice called out.

"Go on, do it!" the hateful voice demanded.

A swirl of conflicting emotions extinguished my ability to reason. The first cut was the most difficult. I hesitantly snipped at my hair where the curler met my scalp.

"What are you doing?" the soft voice cried.

It was impossible to hesitate in spite of the terror I felt. I reached for the next curler. I heard the crunch of the scissors on my hair as the second curler fell loose onto my hand. The attack continued until all the curlers with my hair wrapped around each one lay there on the dining room table in front of me.

As if in a trance, I simply got up from the table and walked to the bedroom where I slipped between the covers next to a sleeping David.

It took some time the next morning before David said, "What happened to your hair!" Visible things were frequently slow to register with him, if at all.

"I was depressed last night and cut off my hair."

David stood quietly looking at me. A deep surge of remorse went through me as I looked at him, knowing that he was a stressed-out freshman medical student in survival mode, taking it one day at a time.

He asked with concern, "What can I do?"

I glibly answered, "Nothing, unless you want to get me out of Los Angeles." It wasn't meant as a joke, but feeble little sounds of laughter from each of us lightened the moment.

"We'll get through this," he said as he hugged me, "I have to get to campus. We'll talk this evening."

After David left, I went to look at myself in the bathroom mirror. Hmm, I thought, this is the second time I've cut my hair, but this is the worst. Why in the world did I do that to myself, I wondered in bewilderment. My mind repeated the simple answer I had given David. I was depressed. I had no understanding yet of my past history and its impact on my self-destructive behavior.

Later when my neighbor Diane saw me leaving my apartment she casually remarked, "I had my hair cut that way once, very short."

I almost laughed. What a lovely person she is, I thought as I smiled and thanked her. "I'm off to my classes," I told her.

Somehow, I got the courage to go on campus to attend my classes. A male student was coming toward me. It was just the two of us on the long, empty sidewalk. As he got close to me, he started laughing and pointed at my hair. He probably thinks I'm trying to make a fashion statement, I surmised, smiling at him when we passed. I contemplated buying a wig, but I didn't act on the thought. I simply endured the embarrassment.

By the time Verneda and Gene came for their first and only visit, my hair was no longer an embarrassment but had grown to a respectable length. I was glad I hadn't told her about cutting my hair. No surprise that I didn't tell her; we weren't that close. There wasn't much to talk about after dinner and maybe that's the reason the two of them spread out on the living room carpet to sleep for almost two hours before they woke up and went home.

After they left, I found myself thinking of my attempts to visit Verneda during our first few months at UCLA. The last time we went, the living room had been filled with people, the same as on previous visits. People streamed in and out of her place, some sitting around the kitchen table, drinking; her four children looking as if they had to fend for themselves. I found the chaotic disorder emotionally exhausting, an atmosphere that inspired my "get-me-out-of-here" behavior.

No doubt about it, I told myself, she has gotten into a dark place. Her situation troubles me, but I don't know what to do, I thought helplessly. I'm overwhelmed fighting my own demons, no wonder I don't go to see her anymore. I detest living close to her and Mom. A surge of nausea came with the thought.

Mom and Verneda and me, the three of us; that's the family of my childhood, I thought, then realized I hadn't included Buddy, Jr. in my number of three. The ringing of the telephone penetrated my concentrated thought. I picked up the receiver but before I could say hello, I heard, "Hello! Hello Vernetta?"

"Yes," I said, recognizing Gene's voice.

"Your sister's in the hospital."

"Verneda's in the hospital? Has she had an accident?"

"Nothin like that," Gene answered. "She's supposed to get out tomorrow. Well, she's gonna get out if we don't sign for her to go to the Norwalk Mental Facility," he added.

"Gene, you're confusing me. Start at the beginning. What's going on?"

"Terry drove her car to a remote place and put one of them built-in vacuum cleaner hoses in the tail pipe then stuck it in the car window. She was gonna kill herself. Would have too if a cop hadn't found her almost right away. They told her it only takes five minutes to turn her brain to mush. The cops took her to the County Mental Health Ward for seventy-two hours observation. They told us she needs help, and we should sign to have her admitted. But we don't wanna do that."

"Who's 'we,' Gene?" I asked.

"Mom and me," he answered.

"Oh, you and Aunt Della are deciding?"

"Yeah. The doctor told us we have to sign some sort of release if we don't send her to Norwalk. He don't want to be responsible if she harms herself."

"You said you decided not to admit her, right?"

"Yeah, we don't wanna do that, but we don't want her hurtin' herself either. She told us she's not gonna kill herself and she just wants to go home."

"Is Aunt Della able to be with her until we're sure she is no longer a threat to herself?"

"That's what we was thinkin' we'll do," Gene said.

"You have a good plan, Gene. Stick with it. Take her home but keep an eye on her. Call me when you get her home, I want to come and see her."

I sat in a stupor after I hung up the phone. Gene's words played again in my mind, "She was gonna kill herself." Our closeness isn't much more than a slender thread, I thought, not a strong bond at all, but her suicide attempt really troubles me. Why don't we have a closer connection, I asked myself?

As I contemplated the question, random thoughts came into my mind about my relationship with my sister.

Verneda was my keeper, perhaps more of a mother to me than Mom. This first thought had never occurred to me before and if I had known then what I learned later about the details of my past, my thought would have been affirmed as true. But the support for my thought was sketchy at the time: Mom put her in charge of me for that long train ride when she was only five. And it was Verneda who saved my life when we were alone, and the little shack caught fire. She bought me a piano when I was in the seventh grade because she remembered I didn't get to take lessons when Mom had said no years before.

Larned memories came to mind. Mom almost beat her to death after we got back from the park. She had left the house after Mom told her not to leave me alone. That's when she turned on me, blaming me for her beating rather than taking the blame herself for disobeying Mom. Yeah, her resentment of Mom making her responsible for me has caused serious problems in our relationship.

Maybe that's why later, we were arguing, and I told her, "I wish you were dead."

"You wish I was dead!" she screamed back at me, "Well you can kill me if you want to. Go on, you stupid *thumb sucker*! Get that tube of rat poison from the kitchen. You can kill me with that."

"I'm not gonna do it, *pimples*!" I declared.

"No; go get the rat poison. Tell you what, you can get me a glass of milk and put the poison in it," she taunted.

"No! Leave me alone," I yelled at her.

She pushed me, "Go on, sissy! Get the poison!"

"You leave me alone," I cried.

She pushed me again, "Get me a glass of milk, you big baby."

I remember how I ran from her to the kitchen where I poured a glass full of milk, then took the tube of rat poison and squeezed some black stuff out of it. With the round black piece of rat poison floating on the milk, I delivered it to my sister.

"You were gonna kill me; you really want to kill me," she screamed.

Reflecting on the incident, I was glad that Jerry and Pat got involved after watching the whole scene and brought it to a peaceful conclusion. I kind of smiled at my memory of this exchange between Verneda and me and the black piece of poison floating visibly on top of the milk. No way would she drink the milk. However, as I remembered the scene, I realized that the underlying reason for the argument was serious.

We weren't close because as I got older, I became more outspoken about my choices that differed from what she wanted. Verneda was strong willed and always expected me to give in to her, like when she invited Valerie to sleep on that stupid narrow sofa with us, I reflected. And then there was the ugly scene, when she wanted to try on my new bathing suit, and I didn't want her to because I thought she would stretch it.

Other reasons came to mind that held memories almost too painful to recall: the many times I watched Mom mistreat her: getting her drunk when she was only twelve, at least twice when she was fifteen; terrible beatings, especially the one in Aunt's Nettie's kitchen that caused Verneda to run away. Yes, I said to myself, those times must have been the start of separating myself from her emotionally because it was too hard to stay close. Then I remembered that it was hard for me to see her drop out of school and waste away. I blamed Mom because she had insisted that Verneda move with us to Kansas when we left Utah.

Thoughts quickly followed to when I skipped school in my sophomore year to stay with her when she was eighteen. She was still a messy housekeeper; she was still plagued with terrible headaches that had started when we lived in Jarbidge, and she had a reoccurring dream that had haunted her since she was a child. She stayed up late watching television most nights, sleeping until around mid-morning the next day. I helped take care of her baby when I was there, but often Aunt Della would come to change diapers and help out until Verneda was out of bed.

Late one night she came to me and said, "Let's go clothesline stealing."

"What's that," I asked, but thought I knew what she meant.

"You'll see." I followed her into the alley that ran behind the rows of duplexes. She went into a backyard that had clothes pinned to the line, "Here," she said as she handed me an article of clothing over the fence, "Take this."

I continued along the alley carrying the clothes she had taken from her neighbors' clotheslines. I found no fun in it, I felt troubled.

During this same time when I skipped school, we were sitting at the kitchen table while she smoked her cigarettes and drank her coffee when out of the blue she said, "Let's color your hair to match mine! Your color is such a mousy brown."

The answer didn't require any thought on my part. "No! I don't want bleached hair. I like my hair color." I managed to dodge the suggestion even though she kept pushing the idea.

Staying with my sister was the closest I ever came to quitting school, I reflected. I would have dropped out for sure if I had allowed her to bleach my hair. I'm sure glad I finally decided after skipping for two weeks, that I would rather face the stress of school than hide out at my sister's. That was a close call, I realized after I reflected on the experience.

I felt quite tender toward her as I recalled that she was the only family member present at my high school graduation. I remembered the beautiful maple Lane Cedar Chest with the spinning wheel relief she gave me as a gift, a gift she couldn't afford. She was there for me when no one else was.

I sat staring out the window anxiously thinking about her suicide attempt, waiting to learn that she was home.

Chapter 31

California
March 1966 – November 1966

The drive to see my sister in the early afternoon following Gene's call was excruciating as I considered the simultaneous threat to ourselves each one of us had experienced. I, so depressed, attacked myself by cutting off my hair. She, more seriously, connected a hose to the exhaust to kill herself.

She was sitting on the couch drinking a cup of coffee when I walked in the door. I kissed her on the forehead, "Worried about you," I said softly.

"I'm gonna be just fine," she said, but the cool almost angry delivery didn't convince me.

"I'm sure you will be because you're a survivor." My response was almost as artificial as hers. "Tell me what happened."

"No, I don't wanna talk about it. Not now anyway."

Aunt Della came out of the bedroom with George and Tammy, my sister's two youngest. George started jumping on the couch, "Mommy's home! Mommy's home!"

"Do you want more coffee, Mommy?" Little Tammy asked.

"Are you staying today and tonight?" I asked Aunt Della.

"Yeah, I'll be here to help out with the kids." In a short while, Janet and Debbie, my sister's two oldest, then Gene, were all in the living room too.

Verneda lit up a cigarette. "Janet, can you make me a sandwich?" Janet almost ran for the kitchen. I wasn't sure if she and Debbie knew that their mother had tried to kill herself, but I sat quietly, knowing it was their father or grandmother who would have made that decision, to tell them or not. I went to Verneda and hugged her the best I could as she remained seated. Heaviness filled the awkward passing of time.

"I need to go now. And I know you are going be just fine. But call me; I'm here for you." Her flat affect left me with concern I tried to conceal when I left. I'd probably look and act like that too if I'd been on a mental ward for seventy-two hours, I thought on the drive home.

It wasn't easy to continue with my classes but as I strolled from the UCLA parking lot toward Schoenberg Hall, I didn't think of my sister. Instead, I thought of Mrs. Hamilton, my ninth-grade school counselor who called herself my school Mom. She would have been happy to know her wish for me had come true, I sighed. I'm a UCLA student. Sadly, I remembered that she had died in an auto accident years earlier.

The song I was prepared to sing in Barbara Patton's voice class started playing in my mind, *The Lord is My Light*. There were about ten of us in the small room with a raised platform at one end where the grand piano sat. Mrs. Patton, a formidable presence, took her place at the piano to accompany the first soloist. Eagerly I waited my turn because I loved to sing. I wasn't nervous nor did I feel inhibited by Mrs. Patton or the other members of the class. After a few weeks, Mrs. Patton approached me. "Vernetta, you have a fine instrument. Would you consider studying privately with me? You've sung alto primarily, but I think you're a mezzo-soprano. I could help develop your higher tones."

In the course of our working together Mrs. Patton said to me, "I'm a paid soloist for a very large congregation in Beverly Hills where Robert Young, the actor, is also a member. "Oh," I said, impressed. I've seen him in movies and on television."

"Vernetta, I would like you to sing in my place two weeks from Sunday. Would you be willing?"

Without hesitation, I said, "Yes, I would like that very much." Two weeks later, I stepped behind the podium and looked out at the hundreds of people sitting in silence as the piano played my introduction. I wonder if Robert Young is here today, I found myself thinking. My stomach sent little twinges up to my throat as I started to sing the first phrase.

After church I overheard Mrs. Patton say to her husband, "…not even the same voice. It didn't sound like the same voice," she repeated in disgust. "Let's get out of here." My nervousness had apparently affected the sound of my voice.

I've greatly disappointed her, probably even embarrassed her, I imagined. Wilting under this belief, not countered by any words of comfort from Mrs. Patton herself, I left the church devastated. Although I was unaware of it at the time, it was at that moment that Mrs. Patton became a critical rejecting mother figure. My ensuing voice lessons with her went from difficult to impossible. Singing was never the same for me after that experience.

Toward the end of the first quarter at UCLA, I began troubling myself over the question, "Should we have another child?" I could easily answer the question for myself, "No!" But I wasn't the only one involved. There was David to consider and our little daughter Jennifer, who was almost four.

"David" I said, "do you think we should have another child?" I posed this question to him shortly after he had established himself as third in his medical class; after he had proven to himself that he belonged at UCLA with classmates from Yale and Harvard. His answer was vague and ambiguous.

I thought of Jennifer; it's not fair to her to be an only child. Then I thought of myself. It's not fair to me to get pregnant, because I would have to deal with the consequences of my incompetent cervix. I wallowed in uncertainty and indecision. It was in this state that I became pregnant.

I continued to attend classes at UCLA but into the third month of my pregnancy the doctor said, "We will need to suture your cervix. You will have to severely limit your activities."

"Is it possible for me to continue taking classes," I asked.

A discussion followed about my walking up and down hills to get to class, climbing stairs to get into classroom buildings. "I'm afraid you won't be able to attend classes," was his response. "The risk is too great."

Resolve melted into flat resignation. I met my French teacher in the hallway outside the classroom door. "I will have to drop out of class," I told her, briefly explaining why. In her heavy French accent she said, "Oh I am so sorry, you are my very best student." I hadn't thought of myself as her best student; I almost never thought of myself as the best at anything I attempted. For a moment, my state of resignation received a challenging blow.

The Medical Center at UCLA is very large, including the medical school, outpatient clinics, research facilities and the hospital where the medical residents, as well as medical students, observe and participate in patient care. When it came time for my cervix to be sutured, I was admitted to the UCLA hospital.

At least five students circled the end of the table where I lay with each foot in a stirrup with the usual sheet draped over my legs, forming a tent under which the doctor worked, and the students observed. I had been given an anesthetic that affected me from the waist down, but I was wide-awake.

During the procedure, the stark white face of one of the male students suddenly appeared above the sheets, his eyes studied me as if searching my demeanor for signs of pain or discomfort. He disappeared as suddenly as he had appeared. He repeated this action at least two more times during the entire process. I surmised that he couldn't believe I felt nothing.

The sofa and I got well acquainted from then into the summer months. "At least I'm not in the hospital with an elevated end to my bed," I thankfully acknowledged to others and myself. We ventured out for a short camping trip to Tuolumne Meadows in Yosemite. A price was exacted. Shortly after we returned home, I woke in the middle of the night not feeling well. I moved onto the sofa in the living room so that I wouldn't disturb exhausted David. A flood of water gushed out of me. I put a towel under me, which was immediately soaking wet.

Frightened, I tried to wake David, "David, I think my water broke. David!" No response. "David," I said again. He woke slightly, "I think my water broke." But exhausted, he returned to a deep sleep. I went back to the sofa and waited for morning. For sure, I'm going to lose this baby, I thought.

David took me to the hospital early in the morning.

"Your water has broken, and the sutures must be cut," said the doctor after examining me. "There is too much pressure from the membranes." Hormones amplified my emotions.

"But it's only the end of July. My baby isn't due until the end of October," I wailed to the doctor as tears filled my eyes.

Waiting on the hospital ward, not knowing what was to happen next, I overheard the nurses talking about their concerns for me regarding the eventual "dry birth" of my baby. My anxiety increased. Two days passed before our second child, Elizabeth, was born three months premature.

"How much does she weigh, David?" I anxiously asked.

"They won't be able to weigh her until later. They put her in the incubator immediately." Later he came to tell me, "She weighs one pound fifteen ounces. As a medical student I'll be allowed access to the premature nursery, but I'll have to go through scrub down and wear special clothes." I felt comforted knowing that David could be close to our baby.

"The baby is having periods of apnea," the doctor reported.

"What does that mean?" I asked.

"Apnea means the baby stops breathing for a period of time." If he said anything else to me, I didn't hear it because my mind went on overload.

I left my room to look at her through a large glass window where her tiny, naked, little body lay in an incubator, connected to tubes and assorted instruments with no promise that she would live. This was as close as I could get for the entire three months she was in the hospital. I wrapped an invisible sheathing of guilt about me, unaware of the harsh judgment I had rendered against myself.

During this frightening time, my mother called me.

"Why in the hell haven't you been to see us," she said angrily.

I couldn't believe what I was hearing. Somehow, I managed to respond, "Mom, you know Elizabeth's in the hospital and may not make it."

But my mother was unable to enter my world of vulnerability and neediness with tenderness and understanding. I could have said to her, why haven't you come to see *me*? You could be a support at this time of our not knowing if our baby, your grandchild, would live or die. But I didn't say that. Instead, I listened until her angry words resolved into "goodbye."

On hanging up the receiver, I decided to confront this problem with my mother in person. David and I drove to Los Alamitos where she and Norm lived in a modest house. They sat at the kitchen table drinking beer. I had never in my life stood up to my mother. She had always been able to talk to me any way she wanted, and I always took it silently, unlike my sister. If I stood up to her in any slight way, as I had in Hays, she became aggressive and mean, and sometimes hit me. For the first time in my life, I raged at her. I stood and she sat as I let loose a verbal torrent.

"Our baby is in the hospital. I don't know if she's going to live or die, and you call and cuss me out because I haven't been to see *you*! Why didn't you come to see me? No, no, *you* never come to see *me*."

The sound of my voice began to escalate. "Not even *once* have you been to see me. But I keep coming to see you!" Then a voice from within me spoken by someone I didn't know shouted angrily at her, "I hate you. I've *always* hated you! I'm not your little girl anymore! You can't shut me up in a closet!"

When I heard these angry words flow from my mouth, I suddenly became a stupefied observer, stupefied by what someone within me had said: "I hate you…shut up in a closet." I may have been perplexed by what I had just yelled at her, but I left with the intention of never going back.

The next morning the phone rang. "Please make up with Mom," Verneda cried to me on the phone.

"No, I meant what I said. I'm tired of her anger," I said.

She continued crying, "Please don't do this." She continued to plead, and I continued to resist for several more phone calls. As usual, my mother made no effort to contact me, no effort to approach me for an understanding of behavior that was so unlike me.

"Okay, I'll go see Mom!" I finally told my pleading sister. "I'm going back for you, not for Mom and not for me."

I went to see my mother. I babbled on about being upset because I wasn't sure if my baby was going to live, then concluded with, "I'm sorry for the things I said." She was quiet and receptive, I thought. "I'll call you when Elizabeth is able to come home from the hospital. Maybe you could be there when we bring her home," I suggested.

"That'd be nice," Mom answered.

"I called Mom yesterday to tell her Elizabeth comes home today."

"Is she coming?" David asked.

"I guess not. She wasn't at the house before we left, and I haven't heard from her."

David, Jennifer and I gathered outside the premature nursery, waiting excitedly. Elizabeth had lived in her incubator for two months and had been in the nursery an additional month. "This is the day she gets to come home with us," I told four-year-old Jennifer.

"Your baby weighs slightly over five pounds," the nurse said as she walked toward us. She handed me our tiny, precious, pink baby, who had no apparent problems despite a three-month-premature delivery. As I looked at our beautiful baby, a prayer of thanks went from my heart to God who had blessed us with two children. My thoughts went to the women on the hospital ward when I was at Walter Reed. Many of them with similar problems to mine were unable to become mothers, I reminded myself as I held our baby in my arms.

"Think about the timing," David said on the drive home.

"The timing?" I asked.

"Jennifer was born while I was in the military, so we didn't have to pay for hospital costs. Elizabeth was born while I'm in medical school, so we don't have to pay for hospital costs. Otherwise, we'd probably be in debt the rest of our lives. Do you realize the total incubator time for the two of them was three months and two weeks?"

"No, my mind doesn't work that way. But I do know that they were born in the best places for their chance of survival."

"God has excellent timing," David said.

Chapter 32

California
November 1966 - February 1971

My dissatisfaction with student housing started me on a search to live elsewhere just before David started his third year of medical school.

I called my friend Earla. "Earla, I made up a list of things I want in a place. Will you present this at your prayer group on my behalf?"

I continued my search, which ended at a For Rent sign in front of an attractive white duplex five minutes from campus. The landlady opened the front door to an inviting space, almost exactly what I wanted. I say almost because I found that it had only one bedroom. "I'll take it," I said to my smiling future-landlady.

Earla and I went over my list as we talked on the phone. "Must be near the university; must be affordable; must have a yard; a laundry room; a place where I feel safe alone at night...," Earla continued to read the list to me. I laughed when she had finished reading.

"The blunder is mine," I said. "I didn't tell God how many bedrooms I wanted." Every item that I had written on the list was satisfied. If it had been a two-bedroom duplex, the rent would have been too much. We gave the bedroom to the children.

The transition to our new home coincided with David's shift in focus at medical school from the theoretical knowledge learned the first two years to the practical application of that knowledge beginning in the third year. Third-year students see patients in the clinic as well as taking responsibility for patients on the hospital ward.

"I'll see you tomorrow night," David told me when he kissed me goodbye before the sun had even risen.

"That's such a long time," I moaned.

"Thirty-six hours with no sleep," he said. "I'll call you when I get a chance."

When David returned to us after thirty-six sleepless hours at the hospital, he was in an exhausted, almost unreachable zone. The next morning, he was somewhat refreshed when he said, "I'll be home as soon as clinic is over today, somewhere around six."

"At least we can have a nice evening together," I said, with a shadow of hope in my voice.

I soon learned that this would be the routine for our lives until David completed his medical training: thirty-six hours away with no sleep; home exhausted in a zombie state for one evening; almost normal by the third evening. Quite often we had relief from this routine because David came home for lunch every opportunity he had.

It fell to each of us at different times to encourage one another. David had an inner strength that even medical school challenged. In those times when he told me, "I want to stop," I comforted him, and we kept going. For me, old issues of being alone at night continued to haunt me.

"Once you go into that enormous brick building, you're swallowed up!" I bitched to David. "I have no way of communicating with you! I feel abandoned, lost. It's just the two kids, the dog and me," I cried. It was David's turn to comfort me in a day before beepers or cell phones.

But on one of those long times when he was away from home, I took my frustration out on the tile surrounding the bath. I yanked back the shower curtain, took my first releasing-frustration missile in hand, drew it back then propelled it at the tile: crash, splash, splatter went the first egg, followed by the remaining eleven. Unfortunately, I was left with a messy aftermath, but I felt better.

"I've found my second love, pediatrics," David announced when he came home for lunch at the beginning of his fourth year of medical school. "I had planned to go into medical research, but I've changed my mind. I want to be a pediatrician." David rarely expressed himself so dramatically or definitively. I knew without a doubt he would be a pediatrician.

The summer of David's graduation from medical school - unattended by my mother or my sister - and before he started his

Pediatric Residency, we went to visit my mother. Standing by the car after our visit she announced, "We're gonna move back to Kansas."

Remembering her pattern of complaining about her circumstance as if it had mysteriously descended on her, as if she had no part in consequences that followed decisions she had made, I said, "If you're not happy about your choice to live in Kansas, please don't complain to me."

I had found a new voice in the way I spoke to her. I said goodbye to her still under the illusion that it was she, not Norm, who had made the decision to move to Kansas. As we drove away, the picture of her standing there stayed in my mind.

"She seemed vulnerable," I later lamented, thinking of what I had said to her. When it comes to my mother, I'm still the needy, disappointed, sometimes angry little girl who wants her to love me in the way I need her to love me, I cried to myself. What if I had sensed vulnerability or neediness in her when I said goodbye? Would I have been able to comfort her? Probably not, I said to myself, because she doesn't seem open to emotional or physical closeness, at least, not with me. I dismissed these hurtful thoughts. My life without her moved forward with very little contact between us. It would be ten years before I would see her again.

The first year of David's Pediatric Residency at UCLA was even more difficult than the previous two years. Residency took a deep emotional cut across my being. Fortunately, David learned that medical students and their families have access to mental health specialists. It was arranged for me to talk once a week with a Beverly Hills psychiatrist who volunteered to meet with UCLA medical students and their families. He was trained in the classical Freudian method except he didn't have the advantage of a couch in the sterile office where we met. He sat behind a metal desk while I sat in a straight-backed chair beside it.

He mostly met my outpouring with silence. I felt as if my words fell into a great void without even so much as an echo. There was almost no deviation from this format. Week after week, I left as empty as I had come. Non-verbal people, I began to realize, irritate me, even frustrate me. I began to connect the origin of this dislike to my own mother's silence, her lack of conversation, her lack of response.

"There must be a better way for you to complete your residency, David. What options do we have besides UCLA?" I asked. Do you think Loma Linda might have a better, less demanding schedule?"

"We can consider it for my second and third year of residency. At least I wouldn't be swallowed up by the hospital building," David teased. "I think it's rather small, like the community it serves. Loma Linda might be what we're looking for."

"This is a pleasant setting," I said, driving into Loma Linda, set against a backdrop of mountains and orange groves. After the interview, David said, "The residents take call from home. They don't have to spend the night at the hospital. There are a total of three pediatric residents, so call is one night in three."

"It sounds like good news," I said taking in the pleasant surroundings. "What do you think?"

"This will probably work better for us," he said.

Our arrival in Loma Linda came at the end of four challenging years of medical school and one even more challenging year of residency. I was emotionally depleted, longing for respite from the stresses of the last five years.

David had been in his new residency about three weeks when I went to the Pediatric Ward to see him. I hadn't met the other two residents yet. I looked through the glass window of a double swinging door where I saw the top of a woman's head. She was bent over with the front of her blouse hanging open with a view of her ample bosom. This was my introduction to one of the pediatric residents. The other pediatric resident I learned was also female, but I never met her. I only heard her voice on the phone when she called to talk with David.

Monstrous insecurities raised their heads. I seethed in helplessness that became anger that I turned upon myself. I parked the car in the garage, closed the door, and left the motor running. Then I climbed into the back seat waiting for the sweet relief that permanent sleep could bring.

A pleasant sleepiness came over me as I felt myself settling, drifting toward the inevitable. Suddenly a voice within me yelled, "Get me outta here!" As if propelled from someone other than myself, I threw open the car door and went into the house to wait for Jennifer to come home from school.

A week of deep depression followed. I was unable to attend the two classes I was taking at the university but withdrew to my bed where I stayed, oblivious of David, my children, or the world about me.

My return was slow. I eventually functioned enough to carry my share, which was still everything except the medical residency itself. Loma Linda was not the safe harbor I had longed for. David taking call from home had its own sharp edge. One minute he was there; the next minute a phone call came, and he was gone for an unknown amount of time. One night, about three quarters of the way through David's second year of residency, I sat awake in bed waiting for his return.

Around 3:00 A.M. he came into the bedroom. I said very calmly to him,

"If you want to practice pediatrics, we'll have to find a way to do it that is comfortable for me."

"For me too," my dear, exhausted David said.

"What about that large medical group we learned about" I asked him.

"Let's check into that, soon," he said, slipping into bed.

Chapter 33

California
March 1971 – September 1974

"I have an appointment for an interview with a member of the medical group we talked about," David said a few days later. "I want you to come with me."

"Why do you want me there?"

"Because this will impact both our lives. I want you involved in the decision."

"I appreciate your thoughtfulness. But isn't it rather unusual to bring your wife along for a job interview?" I can't remember David's answer, probably something humorous in harmony with his "keep it light" approach to life.

"This would be a nice place to work," I said, admiring the building we approached for the interview.

"We are looking for people like you," the doctor said, not long after the interview had begun. "We would be willing to hire you even though you have not yet completed your residency and are not board certified." He went on to explain the benefits. The offer he made exceeded our expectations. "When can you start?" he asked.

David looked at me, I smiled a "yes" to him.

"I could begin in July when I complete my commitment to Loma Linda."

Four months before David began his medical practice, I went shopping for a home. This doesn't make sense to be shopping for a home, I told myself, but I continued looking at real estate. What's driving me to search for a home to buy? After all we don't have the down payment. My self-talk yielded little in the way of answers but did nothing to curtail my activity of looking at real estate.

"This home has been available for about a year," the realtor said. "The builder is in a position to offer a very good price." The two story, beige stucco house jutted out of the barren earth on which it sat. The dry brown earth that rose up behind it barely supported the weeds. "You have a half-acre here," the realtor continued.

"Does that include the high banks in the front and back?" I asked.

"Yes, it does. But remember that the bank in front gives you privacy from the road."

Stepping inside, he continued to put a positive spin on this new home, one of the last houses to sell in the development. "This home has a generous twenty-five hundred square feet, and we'll give you a carpet allowance," he offered cheerfully as we stepped on the concrete floors in the living and dining rooms. "You'll be able to have the carpet of your choice." I didn't say anything, so he continued, "The location is very good, close to the Country Club if you and your husband like to golf."

"It's in a desirable part of town," I said. We had looked at a few other homes, but I thought this one had the most promise. "I'd like to show this to my husband."

Two days later, after David had been through the home, we entered escrow.

I awoke terrified by the shaking of our bed early one morning a few weeks after entering escrow. "David, it's an earthquake!"

"We're okay," David calmly assured me. "We're on the fringe by the feel of it."

The shaking stopped but my nervousness continued into the morning when I turned on the television. "Look David, pictures of damage from the earthquake!"

We watched as pictures of a crumpled apartment came on the screen. The announcer reported, "The epicenter of this quake is in the Northridge area. One survivor was pulled from the rubble of this apartment building whose first floor was completely crushed by the collapsing building, burying sleeping people beneath it."

"Like I saw in the San Francisco movie," I said to David in a daze. Uneasiness haunted me throughout the day after we had seen the rock facing from the fireplace scattered over the floor of the home we planned to buy. In the evening I announced to David, "I need to get out of this house deal."

I tried to explain my newfound insight to David, which went beyond the fear the earthquake had awakened in me. "When you got hired, my anxiety got triggered by the anticipated change. I started looking at houses to buy. I think I was searching for security. But what we don't need now is the burden of a big unlandscaped house. We don't have the money for a down payment and I don't want to borrow it." My conviction poured out of me in an avalanche of anxiety.

David listened and then simply said, "We're supposed to sign papers tomorrow. I don't want to back out now. It's too late."

The next day when David drove us to the realtor to sign the final papers, I felt helplessly angry but still tried to convince him to back out of signing. He pulled into the parking lot; we stood by the back bumper of the car continuing to discuss my need not to sign. David, who has more integrity than anyone I know, said in soft gentle tones, "We've made a commitment and it's too late to back out."

"But it isn't too late. We haven't signed the final papers! Escrow can't close until the final papers are signed. Escrows fail before closure for various reasons. I know what I'm talking about from working at a mortgage company!" I almost yelled at him.

But David stood firm. I, in the role of victim, went in and begrudgingly signed the papers.

"What we truly need in our lives now is comfort and relief from the stress of medical school," I said in the most pleasant voice I could muster after we signed. "We don't need a big house that will pile on more stress!"

There was no money to have the house professionally landscaped. There was no money to furnish it. There was no money to paint away the white-stark interior; it was like living inside a giant eggshell. We were captives to its emptiness inside and its bareness outside.

We put the house on the market a few months after we had moved in, but no one made an offer. David said to me, "I'm able to sign on for more clinic hours which means a larger paycheck. I'd like to do that, so we have funds for what we need."

This was one of those times I thought of Olga and her training; work is the solution no matter how many hours of your life you sell. My response was silence. The robe of victim hung in my mind's closet in many colors. But I didn't yet know that about myself.

David is a unit almost complete in himself, independent of needing or even wanting assistance from others. He thrives on challenge, especially if it is related in any way to my happiness. When he was home, even if it was night, he was outside scraping and digging in the parched-desert landscape of our property, preparing it for water systems, for plants and grass; or building walkways or walls or fences.

One evening when I was especially needy for us to be together, I went out to talk with him as he worked by the light of an old pickup we had purchased. "Could you please stop working now?" We talked a short time there in the headlights before he went back to work. I walked away, empty. He didn't know that work, his gift of love, had by-passed my lonely heart.

While David worked excessive hours in his medical practice and then spent the remainder of his free time with the parched earth that surrounded our house, I decided to return to college to complete a bachelor's degree. Already six years had passed since I earned an A.A. degree.

"Elizabeth is six and she can start first grade. With both girls in school during the day, I can finish a degree. The only affordable school available to me is San Bernardino State College," I told David after I had discovered the cost to attend the University of Redlands. "You remember how I always promoted the importance of going to a top university? Well, San Bernardino State is not a prestigious college."

"You don't need prestigious, do you?" he asked.

"It would be nice!" I admitted.

Winter Quarter I enrolled as a music major with trepidation bolstered by musicianship studies at UCLA with my beloved German teacher, Mrs. Front; piano lessons I had taken over the years; and musicians who had declared my singing voice as "exceptional."

"I need to correct myself for belittling this college, David. Arthur Wenk, a new faculty member, has a doctorate from

Cornell University. He'll teach the piano concerto course I've decided to take. Betty Jackson is a Rhodes Scholar as well as a brilliantly talented performer herself, I'm told. She is going to be my vocal teacher. Add those to Ed White, the English professor from Harvard that I had the first quarter when I was an English major and voilà, you have some high-powered scholars at this humble college."

"I had another one of those episodes last night," I cried to David a week later, on Saturday morning, "and I still feel very depressed. Those scenes from my childhood in Larned keep playing in my mind like bad old movies with no turn-off switch. It always seems to happen just before my period. My thoughts and feelings are painful."

"Tell me again what those are," David said.

"It's the same old stuff I've told you before. I go into a deeply depressed emotional state where I believe no one could possibly love me. I'm unlovable. I'm worthless. I'm in the way. I don't belong."

"You know I love you," David reminded me.

"Yes, but during these episodes, I don't *feel* like anyone could possibly love me, even you. It's hard to believe I'm loved; I'm valued. You know how I live with the underlying fear that someone will take you away from me! I choose not to even have a woman as my best friend because it isn't 'safe.' Didn't I hear repeatedly that "goddamned Kae Hicks" had taken Vern? Haven't I seen married men grab at the breast or crotch of a woman not their wife? Mom was sleeping with Norm when he was still married! My own mother took Norm away from his wife and three children!"

Words continued to erupt from the depths of my fears. "Whenever I come to see you at your office, I get giant butterflies just walking to the door of the building because I'm afraid I'll see a female smile a little too much at you, to put it in terms of the ridiculous. My underlying belief is that others can and will take from me who and what is 'mine,', that which I love and need. It's difficult to come to your office because I'm so anxious!" David tried to comfort me, but my needs exceeded his abilities.

My pain level reached an intolerable intensity. I bought a Smith & Wesson revolver. During one of my despairing episodes, I carefully loaded a bullet into each chamber of the cylinder until it was full, clicked the cylinder into place, removed the safety and held the gun to my head with my finger on the trigger. The debate inside my mind raged for and against squeezing the trigger.

I lowered the gun in favor of not killing myself in this moment. "I'll try again another time," I told myself. Over a course of weeks, I repeated this scenario until I decided to share with my friend Marc what I had been attempting. He talked with me soothingly until eventually he said, "I'll go with you to the gun shop if you want to sell the gun. I think that would be a good thing to do." And so that's what we did.

I felt driven to seek help. "I know a good therapist," Art Wenk, who had become my friend and accompanist at noon concerts, said when I disclosed my situation to him. "He's an instructor in the Psychology Department here at CSCSB but he has a private practice. My wife and I worked with him when we were having problems. I think you'll like him."

"I'm graduating in June; will he still see me even though I'm no longer a student?" I asked Art.

"That isn't a problem because his practice is totally separate from his connection with the campus," Art assured.

A very tall man answered the door of the modest home when I knocked. "Hello, I'm Mac," he introduced himself with a pleasing sound to his voice I thought. "Are you Vernetta?" he asked.

"Yes, we have an appointment." I followed him to the end of a hallway where we entered a room with books, a desk and chairs. His calm, relaxed manner eased the tension I experienced as I sat looking at his brown beard with matching brown hair, hanging a bit below his ears. A hint of hippie, I imagined.

Words flowed out of me, not as if I were meeting with a stranger for the first time, but more like I was with a friend I could trust with my life. "I'm afraid I'm going to kill myself. Images from a town in Kansas where I lived when I was in grade school run like old films in my mind with thoughts and feelings so painful, I think of suicide as my only escape." In a personable, conversational manner, Mac asked me to share the images. Then he asked me to repeat the painful thoughts. "I'm in the way; nobody loves me or wants me because I'm unlovable; I don't belong anyplace; I'm just a worthless nothing." I began to cry. Mac handed me a box of Kleenex served up with words of encouragement.

When I had recovered, he said, "Would you mind trying something with me? It's a therapy technique based on the work of Fritz Perls."

"I guess so," I answered timidly. Mac moved two chairs beside each other.

"You sit in this chair, facing the other chair. Imagine that you are the one who wants to commit suicide and then talk to the part of you who wants to live. Imagine that the part of you who wants to live is sitting in the empty chair. Let's start with "Suicide" and her argument in favor of your killing yourself."

At first it was difficult to talk to an empty chair, but I made a successful effort because Mac told me, "Good. Now I want you to move to the opposite chair where you now become the Vernetta who wants to live. You are going to tell "Suicide" why you disagree with her. Give her your reasons for wanting to live and why you will not kill yourself."

I was able to talk to empty chairs as if a real person were sitting there listening to my arguments. The hour went by quickly.

"I can see you next week at the same time if this works for you," Mac kindly offered.

"Yes, I would like to see you next week and the time is good for me." An ember of hope lifted my spirits when I left Mac.

Later in the summer, after I had been seeing Mac for several weeks, the television was on in the background while I tidied the family room. Suddenly something caught my attention.

"Harry Harlow, in his research into the subject of affection, has successfully demonstrated that nature fully intends a helpless baby to be well connected to a protector. Babies need their mothers; babies are born to need."

I was drawn to watch the program about the findings of Harlow in his research with baby monkeys.

"You know," Dr. Harlow said as he leaned toward the interviewer, "the dominant position had been held that babies didn't love their mothers or need them, that the relationship was based only on being fed. But I was smitten with the idea that mother love is a crucial part of a child's development, a concept that had been dismissed by psychologists as unimportant."

In his laboratory at the beginning of his early studies, about sixty baby monkeys were taken from their mothers six to twelve hours after birth and isolated in separate cages to protect them from disease. The monkeys gained weight, looked good and had no illness. "However," Harlow said, "I observed troubling behaviors in these monkeys: they would sit and rock, stare into space, and suck their thumbs."

"Suck their thumbs," I echoed. A whisper of words escaped my lips, "I sucked my thumb for the first eight years of my life."

"How could the monkeys look so healthy and yet be so completely unhealthy in their behavior?" Harlow asked himself. In spite of the current dominant position, this important question led Dr. Harlow to design a study directed at answering the question: Could it be that mother's love is crucial to a child's development?

Dr. Harlow began to share further details of the study he designed and implemented.
"Through trial and error, we arrived at the decision to build two surrogate mother monkeys. Cloth mother was our first surrogate. She was made from a block of wood -covered with sponge rubber and sheathed in tan cotton terrycloth. A light bulb was placed behind her back to radiate heat. She had a round head with a smiling face and a cylindrical body.

"Wire mother was metallic all the way through, with a cylindrical wire body but also warmed by a light bulb. She was perfect for the baby monkey to climb but she had no cuddly angles to her.

"We took eight babies and placed them in separate cages, which contained a cloth mother and a wire mother. In four of the cages, cloth mother held the bottle of milk, but wire mother had no milk. In the other four cages, wire mother held the bottle of milk, but cloth mother had no milk," Harlow paused.

The interviewer inserted the important question, "What were your findings?"

"Cloth mothers were magnets for the baby monkeys. All the monkeys spent the majority of their time with cloth mother. The monkeys, whose wire mother held the milk, hurried back to cloth mother after feeding."

"When a little monkey is frightened, does he look to his mother?" the interviewer asked.

"Yes," Harlow said, "When very young monkeys, who could barely walk, were frightened by a noisy toy, some of them ran to the cloth mother, clung to her with both hands, burrowing their faces into her cloth body."

"I understand you have brought film clips for us to see?" the interviewer said.

After I watched the film for several minutes, the haunting face of a frightened baby monkey clinging to a wire mother came on my television screen.

"My God," I exclaimed, stunned by what I saw that resonated within me, "that's exactly how I experienced my mother." The little monkey seemed to cling desperately to the wire mother, the hard non-responsive mother. "I know how you feel, little frightened monkey," I acknowledged to myself, almost bewildered by how strongly I identified with this little monkey.

The scientist was saying something about the wire mother's "lack of soothing strokes or cooing sounds" but his voice faded away as my experience of identifying with this little baby monkey engulfed me.

Chapter 34

California
October 1974 – March 1981

My mother. She was seldom in my thoughts until I sat stunned, identifying with a baby monkey clinging to a relatively useless wire mother. Now I was once again thinking about her. "My relationship with Mom perplexes me," I confided in Mac at our next session. "I keep wondering when I'll learn to stop wanting her to love me. I feel like Mom hasn't even liked me since forever. She used to yell at me, 'You're just like the Schreibers!' She hated them, or at least Vern, so I knew she hated me but I'm not sure why."

"Maybe it wasn't you she hated," Mac suggested.

I didn't stop to think about what he said until it came into my thoughts later. Instead, I continued purging old mother material that had infested my mind for years. "Sometimes when my sister or I got sick, she'd say, 'What do you want me to do, shit medicine?'" I began to cry. "How can an ill child look into the angry face of her mother expressing such vileness and feel loved and wanted?" Mac sat quietly, allowing me the precious time I needed for grief to mend the pain.

"I can still hear her words, 'You goddamned kids can't do anything right! If I want it done right, gotta do it myself.' No matter how we tried to do it right, we could never please her. We always failed her standard of perfection for us."

"How did that make you feel?" Mac asked.

"I always tried harder because I wanted so much for her to love me. I thought if I could get it right, she would love me."

"And did you get it right?" he asked.

"No! I couldn't seem to get it right and I don't think my sister did either. Mom always found fault with something, like a wastepaper basket we forgot to empty when we were supposed to clean the house. She didn't even say anything about the good stuff we had done. Sometimes she'd yell, 'You goddamned kids, the older you get the worse you get. I hope you have twelve just like you!' But stupid me, I just kept on trying to please her." I reached for a Kleenex to dry my face and blow my nose. We sat in silence. "It's hard for me to accept my feelings toward her," I finally said.

"What are your feelings toward her?" he posed.

"Ambivalent? Maybe that describes it best," I answered. Mac tried to facilitate my feelings, but we butted against a dead end. Before I changed the subject I told him, "She's been in Kansas quite a few years and there is very little communication between us, or my sister for that matter. I kind of like it that way," I admitted, then changed the subject. "I'm thinking of getting a graduate degree in counseling, Mac."

With no time left in the session for discussion Mac simply told me, "I think you'd be a very good counselor, Vernetta."

Just before I returned to the university to earn a master's degree, I had my last session with Mac. "The old films that used to run in my mind have finally faded away, Mac. I haven't had to deal with thoughts of suicide since we first started working together. Even though I'm going to stop our therapy sessions for now, it would be comforting to know that I can return if I need help with something. Other issues are not fully resolved, like my insecurity," I admitted.

Mac looked at me kindly, speaking in his gentle tone of voice as usual. "It may be very good for you to take a break from therapy. You've accomplished a great deal. You return when and if you want; I'll be here."

After I completed the first year toward a master's degree, David and I talked about the need for him to become board certified.

"I've been thinking about what I might do. A large portion of my practice deals with behavioral problems between parents and children. Child psychiatry seems like a good choice."

About a year later, David became board certified in pediatrics and I completed a master's degree.

Norm's son Robert called me about the time Jennifer and Elizabeth had finished the school year. "I'll be going back to Larned to visit my sister Susan this summer."

"Does she still live on a farm?" I asked.

"Yes, just outside Larned."

"Is there any chance Jennifer and Elizabeth could go with you? I'd like for them to experience Larned, maybe even swim in the giant pool I swam in and loved when I was a child. But I would very much like them to have the experience of being on a farm!"

Robert was still single in his late thirties, "They'd be good company. You know I drive straight through," he warned.

"Yeah, but they'll be safe with you, a policeman." We laughed.

"Susan and I are takin' all the kids and goin' over to Garden City to visit Dad and Edna," Robert said on the phone after they had been in Kansas a few days. "Susan's got two girls almost fifteen, same as Jennifer, and another daughter almost eleven, same as Elizabeth. They'll all be goin' with us," Robert said.

"Oh," I said surprised. "I didn't even think of the possibility you'd be seeing my mother." I wondered what it would be like for my mother to meet her grandchildren. When they returned home, I asked Jennifer, "How was it to visit your grandmother?"

"Well, the adults stayed in the house while they had us go out and play in the fifth wheel. I didn't really see very much of your mom," Jennifer said.

In November Al Avilla, the seventy-two-year-old organist who accompanied me on Sundays where I was the paid soloist, invited me to put together a Christmas program at the Veterans Hospital. I decided to use scenes from the musical "Mary Had a Little Lamb." At her grade school, Elizabeth had participated in this delightful musical of the stable animals telling the story of Jesus' birth.

"Let's invite those two talented brothers that were in your school production to help us," I suggested to Elizabeth.

"I'll see them at school tomorrow. I can ask them."

"Will you please get their phone number so I can talk with their mother," I asked her.

It was settled. The two boys and Elizabeth would perform musical numbers as well as selected dialogue. Elizabeth would play one solo on her cello, and I had a vocal solo.

We were quite well rehearsed and near our performance date when I heard a knock on our front door late in the afternoon. "Wonder who that is? Are you expecting anyone, David?" I called to him as I made my way to the front door. When I opened it, there stood my mother with Norm at her side holding a brown paper bag.

"What a wonderful surprise!" I threw my arms around Mom. Ten years had passed since I said goodbye to her in Los Alamitos. "We didn't know you were in California; didn't know you were coming!" I hugged her again. "So, you drove all the way from Kansas, Norm!" I exclaimed as I hugged him.

"Yeah, drove almost straight through."

"Well Norm, you sure haven't changed! Once you get on the road you just keep on goin' 'til you get there!" Norm managed a faint smile. "We don't have to stand in the entry. Let's go into the family room. Norm, can I get you an ashtray?" I offered as he sat down, even though David and I didn't smoke.

"You probably ain't got any," he answered gruffly.

"I'm sure I've got something that will work," I told him as I went to the kitchen, leaving them sitting in the family room.

"Here you go," I said, handing him a shallow dish. "Sorry I don't have any beer, Norm, but at least you can smoke!" I teased, producing a snicker from Norm and a silly grin on his face. Cigarettes and beer, these were the two necessary ingredients to keep Norm happy.

"Give me that bag, Norm," Mom directed. She opened the bag and took from it a stiffly stuffed cloth Santa Claus.

"Wow!" I said when I saw the Santa, "He looks like the one we had when I was five!"

"It ain't the same one from Albert I won off the punchboard. Somebody give him to me in my secondhand store," she explained. Almost void of emotion, she added, "I sewed new clothes for him." She held the Santa out to me, "I want you to have him."

"The clothes are wonderful, Mom," I told her, enthralled as I ran my hand over the red satin fabric trimmed in white, marveling at her sewing skills. "Are you sure you want to give him to me and not Verneda?"

"I want you to have him."

When I took the Santa from her, the beautiful clothes Mom had sewed proved a welcomed distraction from the distasteful expression on the Santa's painted face. "This is such a loving gift, Mom. It will always remind me of the Santa in Albert that I liked so much."

Norm lit a cigarette. "Did you see much traffic on the trip or run into any snow?" David asked.

"Not much this time uh year," Norm responded with one statement to cover both questions. Silence settled on each one of us. Fortunately, Elizabeth came down from upstairs.

"Don't we have to go pretty soon?" she asked after saying hello to Mom and Norm.

"Thanks for reminding me, Elizabeth." I turned to Mom, "We're doing a Christmas program at the VA. We're in need of some animal hats to help create our characters of a cow and a sheep. You sew so well, do you think you could help sew them for us, Mom?" Mom had a rather blank expression on her face when she shook her head ever so slightly in the direction of 'no.' I let it drop.

"Elizabeth and I need to be at a rehearsal in about twenty-minutes. Would the two of you like to come and watch?" I invited.

Mom looked at Norm, "I don't know, what do you think Norm?"

Norm immediately shook his head, "Nah, I don't wanna go, but you can if you want."

"What is it?" Mom asked me.

"I'm directing a short Christmas story with music. Elizabeth has a part in it. I think you'll enjoy it, Mom. We won't be gone very long. I think you'll like it," I pleaded somewhat.

"I guess so," she said with hesitation. Much to my surprise, she was willing to leave Norm and come with me.

"We'll take you out for Mexican food and a beer when we get back, Norm," I called to him as we went out the door.

When we got to the chapel of the Veterans Hospital, I introduced my mother to Al and the children. "Take your places, everyone, and we'll run the entire program to see what still needs work," I directed.

Mom was attentive and actually seemed to enjoy watching the children. Amazing, I thought, my very own mother is sitting here watching the rehearsal of our little production.

"The children did especially well, don't you think, Mom?" I asked her when it was finished.

"They did good," Mom said with a smile.

"You boys did very well this evening. Elizabeth, you played your cello beautifully. I think we're ready. The audience is going to love you," I told them.

Al interrupted me, "We haven't practiced your solo yet!"

"Thanks, Al! I almost forgot. We'd better do that right now."

When my solo ended mother looked at me and said sweetly, "My, you have a nice voice." In that happy moment of receiving from her what I remembered to be my first compliment, I unknowingly became incredibly vulnerable to her. The self-protection I had fashioned beginning in childhood, evaporated.

How I loved my mother that day! She and I snuggled together in the back seat of our VW bus while David, with Norm beside him, drove us to the restaurant for dinner. The scowl on Norm's face as he looked at me in the rear-view mirror with cold intensity in his eyes sparked the realization that perhaps he was jealous. Maybe he has always been jealous, maybe even possessive, I mused. How can that be? I asked myself. I lost Mom to Norm years ago when I was nine years old. He is the center of her world. I dismissed the thought.

After we returned home after dinner, Mom said with a sincerity I believed, "You'll be the first one we visit the next time we come." My heart danced. David and I stood waving goodbye to them as I held her words of love in my heart, and the assurance she would come to see me on her next trip.

But two years later, when they came back to California, I wasn't the first one they visited. In fact, they didn't visit me at all. I didn't even know she was in California until my sister, Verneda called. "Yeah, they drove right through your area on the way to Orange County. They should've stopped but they didn't," she commented, perhaps mystified herself.

"How long have they been in California?" I asked.

"About two weeks. They stayed a short time with me. They're visiting Nettie's son now. I'll have her call you when they get back," she said.

Several days passed and I still hadn't heard from Mom, so I called my sister.

"Do you know where they are?" I asked.

After an uncomfortable pause she answered, "They're here; they just got back."

"Can you get Mom on the phone?"

"I thought you were going to come and see me," I whined to Mom when she came to the phone, adding a surprising and perplexing remark that shot straight out of my mouth. I heard myself say, "This is just like when I was a little girl." There was an immediate click.

I stood for a moment listening to the echoing sound of the dial tone, still holding the receiver to my ear. Tears fell on the phone as I put the receiver back on its cradle. I slumped dumfounded into the armless upholstered chair. Why? I sobbed. Why didn't she come to see me? They drove right past me. Why didn't she call? Why did she hang up on me? No comforting answers came to my relief. I was still under the illusion that it was Mom who was in charge, not Norm.

Like a coat for warmth, I unconsciously covered my anguish with a thick layer of anger, which unknowingly enabled me to escape my feelings of helplessness. An energy accompanying my anger drove me into action. I ran to the closet where the Santa Claus sat that mom had given me when I saw her last. I yanked off the clothes. Then I attacked his cloth body. Through a tear in the cloth, I began pulling out straw stuffing from his stomach, then his chest and finally his arms and legs. Straw stuffing lay scattered all around me. I detested his face, which turned out to be a simple mask stitched to a cloth-covered head. Off came the mask. I gathered it all together, the clothes, the empty cloth body, the ugly mask face and lastly, the scattered straw stuffing. I threw it all in a large brown paper bag. I went to the garage and crammed it into the trashcan.

Mom returned to Kansas without calling me back, without coming to see me. I made an appointment with Mac to process my pain and anger.

Chapter 35

California
June 1983 – March 1986

The following two years nurtured a nagging need. It may have come from working with an older gentleman who directed me in several roles I performed in theatre, a man who reminded me of my grandpa. Maybe the need came as a result of my sessions with Mac.

"I want very much to take a trip to Larned. I haven't been back since I left at age nine. I have an irresistible need to go there. I feel it would somehow benefit me to go back. Will you come with me?" I asked David.

"I understand what you're saying, but I think I should stay home to watch over the business and the girls," David said. "Would it work for you to go while I stay home? I'll support you from this end."

We had purchased an ice cream-sandwich parlor from an older couple, who needed to retire because of illness. We remodeled it and renamed it The Playhouse. Our teen-aged children both worked there selling sandwiches and candy and serving ice cream. We paid a young man to manage it for us, but we were losing money daily. I understood David's desire to stay home.

"We can take a vacation together in August, but while you're gone, I'll keep an eye on the shop," David suggested. "Do you think John would be interested in going with you?"

"It won't be the same as going with you," I answered in disappointment, "But I'll call John. The trip will take about a week, maybe." It was fortunate for us that John, a young college student and family friend, was available, because I was determined, almost compelled to go to Larned.

With me at the wheel of my old green Dodge, John and I crossed the border into Kansas. "I moved with my grandparents, Mom, and sister from Albert to Larned right before I started second grade," I told him. "They bought a little house not far from the downtown area. That was my home for three years. We'll for sure go to see it. I'm curious to find out how far I walked to get home after I went to the movies at The Electric Theater."

"The Electric Theater is where I saw every movie that came to town, usually twice. I hope we can find it. There were lots of times I went there alone at night and then walked home by myself. Boy, was I scared to walk home alone after I'd seen a movie like the Wolfman or Frankenstein!"

"How old were you?" John asked.

"That was when I was in the third and fourth grade, so either eight or nine years old."

"Pretty young for your mom to send you to movies alone at night," John said.

"Well, I went to the movies instead of staying home alone. Mom liked to go to the bars at night, so she gave me money to go to the movies." I changed the subject, "Another place I want to see is my school. It was up on the hill and over about a block. I loved that school. We slid down the hill on our sleds right next to it when it snowed."

My thoughts turned to my dearest friend of second, third and fourth grades. "Steve Fox was my friend. We played together after school. He's the one who took me to his piano teacher about lessons. His Mom was going to let me practice at their house. I wonder what happened to him. Sure wish I could see him on this trip."

"Did you get to take piano lessons?" John asked.

"My Mom said no, but after I got married when I was about twenty, I rented a piano and took lessons and later, when David was at UCLA, I took lessons."

"Good for you," John said. I was surprised at how involved he seemed to be in my journey, my history.

"I never played very well really, never got beyond the level of mediocrity."

My mind wandered off in a different direction. "One other really important place I want to go is to the cemetery to find the graves of my grandparents."

"Oh, your grandparents are buried in Larned?"

"Yeah, they both died when I was in grade school. My grandma died unexpectedly near the end of my second grade. She was almost fifty-four and my grandpa died near the end of my fourth grade. That's when all our furniture was put out on the front lawn to be auctioned and the house was sold. Funny, I didn't remember the furniture on the lawn until my sister told me. Mom moved us to an ugly little house over on the other side of town."

John and I drove on in silence. As the miles between us and Larned dwindled, I felt elated. I was surprised that no deep-dark forebodings nudged at me. Suddenly, as I drove on Route 56, the road took a turn and there we were, right on the downtown streets of Larned. "There weren't any signs. I had no idea we were so close!" I sat silently experiencing the impact. Larned is real! Larned isn't just an imaginary town that exists within the limits of my mind.

"These brick streets are great!" John exclaimed, jarring me out of my emotional reflection.

"I always loved them myself and how I love seeing them again! Look," I pointed to the corner of Main Street and Fourth Street. "That's the corner where I turned when I walked home from the Electric Theater after the movie! It crosses an alley that was pretty scary to me at night."

"Don't you want to go see where you lived?" John asked when I didn't make a left turn.

"Let's see some of the downtown first. I need to calm down a bit before we see the house. It all seems so real and unreal at the same time! I'm in Larned!"

We continued driving a short distance on Main Street. "The Electric Theater was right here, I think." I pulled over and parked. "I'm going into the store to see if someone can tell me the location of the theater. This store might actually have been the theater."

"It's the building next to us," the store clerk explained without hesitation. "If you go out and look up on the store fronts you'll see where the sockets are imbedded in the brick. That's where the lights used to go for the theater. Yes, that's where the theater used to be," he said, flavored with a bit of nostalgia I thought.

I explained it to John who was waiting for me on the sidewalk. We walked out far enough from the buildings so that we could see the storefronts, "There they are!" I said, pointing at the sockets on the face of the building, "That's the building where the Electric Theater used to be! Can you take some pictures of it for me?" John, an excellent photographer, had purposely brought his camera to make a pictorial record of this important trip.

Electric Theater

I continued driving down Main Street. "There's Walgreen Drugs! Amazing it's still there where I remembered it. Some things don't change. Elizabeth Wiggins' father owned it. She was a grade behind me, wore her long red hair in pigtails."

"Looks like this is the end of Main Street," John said.

"It's time to go see the house. I can't wait any longer." I turned us around. We backtracked on Main Street, past the building where the Electric Theater had been, to Fourth Street and made a right turn. "There's that alley," I almost whispered to myself. "I can't believe it; you can almost see our house from here!" I exclaimed as I took in the short distance of the two blocks from Main Street to the corner of Fourth and Santa Fe Streets where the house was located.

"There it is!" I said in awe, in this almost sacred moment. I pulled up and stopped across the street from it. I couldn't budge. We sat silently, looking at the house. I remembered almost every detail of the exterior perfectly. I quietly realized as I looked at it.

"Do you want me to take pictures?" John asked.

"Let's wait a bit." Emotionally flooded, I sat experiencing a house that held so many of my memories and so much of my past life, a house I hadn't seen for thirty-six years.

"What I want now is to get inside that house. I've got to see it," I said, as I got out of the car.

"I'll wait," John wisely understood that he needed to stay in the car.

My adult feet walked on the sidewalk where I had walked as a child, then up the two steps onto the small front porch. The exterior of the house is well kept, I thought as I stood waiting hopefully at the door after I had knocked.

"My name is Vernetta," I began as I looked at the kind face of the neat, elderly woman who opened the door.

"Yes, I'm Mrs. Jenkins." Her kind manner gave me courage.

"I lived in this house as a child. I've traveled from California to revisit Larned. It would mean so much to me if I could see the inside of your home." There was no reluctance on her part. She opened the storm door and invited me in.

"Would you feel comfortable if my friend also came in with me?" I asked, pointing to the car where John waited.

"You're welcome to have him join us," she said.

This house and its rooms had lived in my mind since I had left it thirty-six years ago. Now I was actually here, compelled to come. My experience was a transforming one as I stood just inside the front door of the house where I had withstood life-crushing trauma as a child. In real time, not in memory, I now stood just inside the front door.

"Oh," I said, pausing to catch my breath, "I always loved these beautiful French doors." I stopped for a moment, unable to resist running my hand over the bevel of the glass. "They are still here, just as they were so many years ago." We walked past the doors into the bedroom. I tried to discreetly show John the area I had made into a cozy, private prayer corner behind the right French door.

Looking around the room, I told John, "This is mostly where my sister and I slept." He got a curious look on his face. I knew he didn't understand my comment, but I refrained from further explanation.

I walked back into the living room and noticed that Mrs. Jenkins had her TV sitting where the fake fireplace had once been. "You keep such a clean home, and everything is so neatly organized." I was thankful it wasn't in a state of chaos and disorder as in the past. I moved into the dining room area. "Is the furnace still there?" I asked as I pointed to a place in the floor where an area rug lay.

"No, that was removed a long time ago," she said.

My grandparents' bedroom, as well as the bathroom, had been off the dining room. I peered into the bathroom then looked up to see that the silly window between the bathroom and kitchen was still there. I went into the kitchen. Yes, that's how I remember it, I said to myself as I walked through it and out onto the back screened porch. I thought about how I had sat on a coffee can on this porch years ago capturing little "goat turds" in search of a swallowed key but decided not to say anything to John.

Flashes of familiar memories came to me as I went from place to place. "It's exactly as I remember it," I said. "There were times when this house lived like a nightmare in my mind, something that wasn't real, didn't truly exist. But here we are. It's real, not imaginary." Probably I can trust that the memory pictures I have of other places and people are also true, I silently assured myself.

"John, take my picture," I urged as we stepped out on the front porch after we had said goodbye to Mrs. Jenkins. "My sister and I used to sit on this porch when we were children. I'm going to send her a picture of me sitting on this porch and put a title under it: 'Nee-nee, we're all grown up.'"

"You might want to put the date on it too," John added.
"Good idea," I said, "I think today is July 1."

John answered, "July 1, 1983. Might want to write that in your notes." Since starting therapy with Mac, I had made notes of our sessions. It helped me capture what otherwise might have been lost. For the same reason, I continued my note making in Larned.

It became wonderfully clear to me as I sat on the front porch while John took my picture: I am not a child anymore. On many occasions during a therapy session as I re-experienced an event from my Larned childhood, my pain was debilitating. "Repeat after me," Mac often said during such times, "I am not a child." The experience I had on the porch of the Larned house was a visceral experience, not an intellectual experience, not a parroting of what Mac said, but a real gut level experience. "I am not a child."

After John took a picture of me sitting on the porch, I asked him, "Did you hear Mrs. Jenkins say that I was lucky the house is still here?"

"Yeah, I guess you're really lucky, or blessed," he added.

"Blessed," I think. "I noticed that a few of the houses down the block closer to town have been replaced with businesses. I'm so thankful the house is still here. I didn't realize it would mean so much to physically experience it as an adult."

John took more pictures of the house from the front and then we went to the side yard that ran parallel to Santa Fe Street. "The trees have gotten so big," I said. "It was somewhere by one of these trees that I had my sparrow graveyard." John smiled at me in an understanding way, I thought. "And," I continued as I pointed to the street, "that's where I learned how to ride a bicycle when my sister gave me a shove and told me to pedal. I was halfway down the block before I realized she wasn't holding onto me."

John laughingly said, "I think most of us have had a similar experience."

"Let's drive up the hill to my school."

"Do you know where it is?"

"Yes," I said pointing at the abrupt uphill portion of Fourth Street. "We continue on Fourth away from town, up that hill a couple of blocks, then we turn right and then we go about another block, and it will be sitting across the street on the corner."

"I'm impressed," John said. "After all the years you remember where it is!"

As we made our right turn, I pointed across the street mid-block. "Over there is I where I looked up into one of those trees and accidentally swallowed a little key I had in my mouth! Had to be x-rayed."

"That's a funny thing to remember," he said.

"Yeah," I agreed, but still kept quiet about the little goat turds.

A school was on the corner where I thought it would be, but the building was different. A strange new building sat where my school had once been. I didn't spend long looking at the new school because I wanted to keep the remembrance of the one I had attended.

"Let's leave the car parked and walk down Fifth Street," I suggested. "This is the street that was closed down for our winter sledding. We had so much fun. No fear. Look how steep it is. I'd be afraid to sled down it now." John quietly indulged me as I enthusiastically told him, "Here is where Steve Fox used to live!" We stood looking at the rather tired worn house. "Across the street is where his piano teacher lived."

My first day in Larned came to an end. I reflected on my inability to determine, before coming, the significance of retracing my childhood footsteps. For reasons I didn't understand, Larned, like Jarbidge, had implanted itself in my mind unlike any of the many states and places I had lived by the time I was thirteen. I pondered how deeply satisfying it was to see physical evidence of the Electric Theater's existence imbedded in the face of the building where it once thrived. However, I felt very glad that the theater itself was no longer there. The thought came to me that it was like a metaphor of my life. Like the Electric Theater, traces of where I once lived as a child are still here, but I am no longer a child. I am no longer a victim to the dark happenings over which I had no control.

It was the morning of our second day in Larned when John asked, "What are we going to see today?"

"I'd like to go to the cemetery but I'm not sure where it is. Let's stop by City Hall; I saw it yesterday when we drove down Main Street." The building sat with a large expanse of lawn surrounding it. Beautiful, I thought, it's a hot summer day but things are so green. A gentle breeze cooled me as I walked up the front steps of City Hall.

"They gave me a map, John. Looks like the cemetery is on the hill near my old school." It was a short drive to the cemetery, which sat at the top of a gentle hill overlooking farmland on the side away from town. "What a surprise! It's bigger than I thought it would be. But let's drive back and forth to see if we can find the headstone." We drove and we drove.

"Maybe we will have more luck if we get out and walk," he suggested.

"Doesn't look like there is anyone around to help us," I complained after we had walked and walked. "I guess we'll have to go back to City Hall." After I had found the right department, a woman gave me a piece of paper with precise directions.

"There it is John! Stop the car!" I hurried to the huge gray-granite headstone with the large, engraved letters ROSS. "That's my grandpa and his date of birth. Almost exactly one hundred years ago!"

"Did he die March 26, 1947?" John asked as he read the date from the headstone.

"Yes. And that's my grandmother's grave next to his. She died March 15, 1945."

"Look at what else it says. 'She is not dead just away,'" John read. Emotions overtook me.

"I'll wait in the car," John said, walking away.

I sat down on my grandmother's grave and wept quietly.

When I got back to the car, I started to say, "I'm sorry," but John interrupted me.

"You don't have to apologize." We left the gravesite and as we started to turn left to go back to town, I saw a familiar set of buildings at the bottom of the hill to the right.

"I think I know what those buildings are; let's go over there."

The buildings turned out to be the Larned State Hospital. We drove past the yards where people were confined behind tall wire fences. "When I was in grade school, they called this place the Nut House. Let's get out of here," I said to John, not remembering at the time that I had once lived there with my grandparents long before I lived with them in the house Mrs. Jenkins now occupied.

"I'd love to see the swimming pool where I spent my summers. I think I can find it if we go back to Santa Fe Street that runs past the side of my old house." John and I drove in the direction I suggested and without any problem, located the enormous pool I swam in as a child. "I can't believe it's still here! It's huge! You know how they say that things look bigger to you when you're a kid but when you see it as an adult it looks smaller? Well, this still looks huge to me!"

John began taking pictures from all angles. "Did I ever have fun here as a kid! I spent all my summer days here swimming and eating candy." I looked at the expanse of concrete surrounding the pool. Probably the same concrete I lay on to warm myself when I got out of the pool, I said to myself. "If only we had brought our swimming suits," I called to him.

"It's a beautiful pool," he said when he had finished taking pictures.

When we left, we drove past the park next to it. "Oh, that's the park, the park where my sister was."

"What about it?" he asked.

"My mother was angry with my sister, and we came and found her here. Mom beat her." We drove silently back to town.

That evening, I called information. "Do you have a number for Steve Fox?"

"I have a Steve and Karen Fox listed in Great Bend," came the reply.

"Please give me that number." Nervously, I dialed the number and waited.

"Hello," a man's voice answered.

"Would you be the same Steve Fox that once lived on Fifth Street in Larned?" I asked.

"Yes, my parents had a home on Fifth Street," he said.

I explained who I was and that I was in town briefly, "Would it be possible for us to meet?"

"My wife and I could meet with you for dinner tomorrow evening, if you're available."

"Yes, I am available and would be happy to drive to Great Bend." I felt like shouting, I can't wait to see you again, but I managed to control my excitement. After I hung up the phone, I thought about my childhood friend Steve and the good times we had shared together. I felt as if he had been a part of me all these years. It was as if I *needed* to find him, not simply that I wanted to find him. Someone lost but now found.

There were still places I wanted to see before dinner that evening with Steve and his wife. "I want to see the First Christian Church," I said on our last day in Larned. "It's located on the other side of town." It wasn't difficult to find. We pulled to the curb and stopped by the elegant old brick building on the corner. We sat looking at it for a moment. "This is the church where I met Jesus." I paused. John didn't say anything. "It still looks very nice and just as I remembered it."

"Do you want to go in?" he asked.

"I guess I could go to the front door to see if it's open." When I got to the door it was locked and no one seemed to be there. I turned away disappointed.

First Christian Church, July 1983   Pastor Bob Weitzeil, 1992

"The last place I want to see is the little red house my mom moved us to after my grandpa died."

"Let me guess; you know how to get there," he said with a smile on his face.

"I think so. We'll go back to Main Street. I'll have to feel my way after that." When we crossed the railroad tracks, I said, "I think we need to make a right turn here." We went down one street then up another. "There it is! Unbelievable!" I exclaimed as I pointed at the little house on the corner, still wearing its red tar shingles. "Who can believe it's still here?"

While John took a picture, I noticed that there was grass surrounding the house instead of weeds, the outhouse was gone, and a small addition extended from the side of the house. Probably the new bathroom I thought, realizing I had no emotional baggage attached to the memory of this little house.

When we drove back through town, I was impressed again with how clean and orderly it looked. "The downtown is well kept and fresh looking, as is the rest of the town. I'm surprised," I heard myself say.

"Why is that surprising?"

"Well," I began, "My view of the town came through the eyes of a child whose life was cluttered with alcoholics and disorder the last two years I lived here, after my grandmother died. When I lost her, things changed drastically at home, Grandpa, Mom, Verneda and I entered a very dark period. I'm sure a lot of my problems can be linked to the time I lived here after her death. But it's surprised me that I've felt very happy as we've walked and driven around, retracing where I had been as a child. I realize now there was much here that I loved."

"Do you mind if I go without you to dinner?" I asked John when evening came, and it was time for me to meet Steve and his wife.

"Not at all. I know this is between you and Steve. My presence might shift the focus." I was relieved that he wasn't offended with my need to be alone with Steve and his wife.

Even though thirty-six years had passed since I had seen his face, I recognized Steve immediately when I entered the café. There wasn't anything awkward about our reunion. In a sense, we were not strangers, but simply friends who had been out of touch, since fourth grade! Steve still had his curly brown hair and a pleasant, relaxed face. He and I were almost equal in height, five feet six inches.

We talked of grade school experiences and our mutual friends. "It was very difficult for me to leave my friends behind after my grandpa died and we moved," I told them.

Steve said that the life of his family had seen its own hardships before they moved into the house on Fifth Street. Toward the end of dinner, Steve said, "Would you like to come to our home? I have a picture I think you'd be interested in seeing."

I gladly accepted his invitation. It was a mystery why I needed to contact Steve, my grade school friend of three years. But the sense of loss I had been carrying all through the years since leaving Larned now felt as if it had melted away.

"Your home is lovely," I said, but not surprised to see his was a lovely home.

"Both of us work at the hospital," Steve said. "Karen is a nurse and I'm a physical therapist. Excuse me," Steve explained, "I want to get that picture." He was back in a few minutes. "Here it is." He handed me a picture of our fourth-grade class along with the third graders and our teacher, Mrs. McVeigh. "Which one is you?" he asked.

"That's me in the back row, standing next to Phyllis," I said pointing to the picture.

"Yes, when you called, I got the picture out to see if I could find you. That's the one I thought was you," he said, somewhat pleased then added, "Phyllis is with the FBI."

"I didn't know what happened to Phyllis, but she was my friend," I commented.

Steve talked about Michael.

"I remember him, a nice guy. But do you know what happened to Mrs. McVeigh?" I asked.

Steve didn't have any information on the teacher who had taught us for both third and fourth grades. When our evening together ended, they drove me back to my car. "I'll mail you a copy of the picture I showed you," are the last words I remember him saying to me.

"Are you ready?" I asked John the next morning. "I think we can make it home in time to celebrate the fourth."

"Sure! Let's make it happen."

Photo Steve Fox sent. Vernetta second from left last row. Steve first from left second row

Chapter 36

California
July 1983 – September 1987

The end of July came and brought with it freedom from the financial drain of our ice cream shop when escrow closed. But I wasn't free from whatever it was that drove me to continually seek higher education.

"I'm so tired of you remodeling this house," I complained to David. "I wouldn't mind getting away while you finish it. If I get accepted to the M.F.A. program in acting this fall, do you think we can make it work? Elizabeth is a junior in high school. It isn't crucial that I be around for her."

"Are you sure you want to jump into something like that now?" David asked with concern.

"Yes; I love theatre and I'd like to give it a try if I get accepted." David had never stood in my way; instead, he had always assumed the supporting role in making my dreams come true. "The letter of acceptance came today."

"What have you decided?" David asked.

"I'd like to go. You'll be busy completing the remodeling when you aren't at work. I don't see much of you anyway."

David looked tired but assured me, "If this is what you really want, we can make it happen.

"An apartment on campus would be nice. You could come and stay with me a couple of nights a week. I'd come home on the weekends."

When fall came, I had an apartment on campus. "The auditions for the musical 'Follies' are next week," the instructor of our acting class announced. Believing there was a possibility to land the lead female role, I prepared my audition song but wound up in a minor role.

"An assistant to Bob Fosse will choreograph the musical numbers," the director announced.

"I've never had any dancing lessons," I told the tall brunette standing next to me.

"There will be at least two tap numbers. If you don't have them, you'll need taps on your character shoes," the director said.

"Now I'm really in trouble," I said to myself.

The third time the choreographer met with the cast he told us, "This number will call for each of you to have an umbrella. Take one from the stack at the front of the stage. You'll open it on my cue."

"At least I think my feet know what they're doing now," I joked with the guy next to me. "All I have to do is add an umbrella!"

The choreographer gave the cue to open our umbrellas, but no matter what I tried, the umbrella would not open. Why he didn't yell at me, "Hey you, get your umbrella open!" I'm not sure.

After the rehearsal, I approached the director. "May I take this umbrella home to practice opening it?" He looked perplexed, then motioned for me to give him my umbrella. I watched him struggle to open it.

"This one has a problem. Better get a different one."

Elizabeth and David came to see the production. "I feel abandoned," Elizabeth cried. Her emotion-filled words provoked a visceral response in me. Without intending it, she had linked me to my own deep feelings of abandonment, not yet healed in therapy, but more, she ignited my desire to be there for her when she needed me, unlike my mother who failed me time after time. I came to my senses and moved back home at the end of the fall quarter.

With the coming of summer, I once again joined a summer repertoire company that performed on warm summer evenings on an outdoor stage set among graceful eucalyptus trees. It was a fun time that summer, singing in 'Act' and playing the role of an old lady in 'Arsenic' who innocently poisoned unsuspecting guests.

A senior Theatre Arts Major at the University of Redlands approached me in March of 1986, "Is there any chance you'd direct me in a one-act play to meet my performance requirement?" he asked. "I saw the one-act from 'Belle of Amherst' you directed for Vicki. It was great."

"Do you have any idea which play you'd like to do?" I asked.

"I have no idea."

"There's a one-act I like very much, 'The Loveliest Afternoon of the Year.' It's a zany play. We might be able to do it around the small pond of the President's old home," I suggested.

It was at the end of this successful production in mid-spring 1986 that I felt an undeniable urge to see my mother after seven years of silent separation. I drove to Lake Elsinore where I found her in a fifth wheel.

Edna and Vernetta   Edna, Vernetta, Norm

Several months later she was diagnosed with cancer. In time, Mom offered me the gift of pictures from her past. Our progress in looking at pictures had stopped when she came to one of Buddy, Jr.

"July 27, 1941 is when they took him from me," she said with sadness in her voice. I sat amazed, realizing that she had carried this photo of Buddy, Jr. since leaving Jarbidge, Nevada forty-six years ago. Strange, how the unresolved issues of the past remain in cluttered layers of our mind, waiting for resolution.

"They took him away from you July 27, 1941?" I asked, surprised that she knew the exact date. "What happened? Who took him away and why?"

She began telling me her story. "Bud and I went somewheres but we left the baby with his sister, Vi, to take care of. I don't know where you kids was. I come back in a few days to pick him up but Vi come out of the house and said, 'Come on Edna, let's go for a ride.' So, I went with her. She was drivin' and talking to me. 'You've got your two little girls to take care of and this baby is sick. Why don't you let me take care of him for you. You've got your hands full already.'

'Are you talking about keeping him for a few more days 'til he gets well?' I asked her.

'I'm talking about him staying with Roy, me and Gary. You can come see him whenever you want. Come on, Edna, it's the best thing for the baby. He's sick. How you gonna take care of him? You don't have any money.'

'I can see him anytime I want?' I asked.

'You can see him any time you want.'

"So, I let her take him."

I wanted to say to her, but you told us since we were children that Buddy, Jr. was taken from you and that when you went to get him, she threatened to have you thrown in jail. She threatened to take Verneda and me away from you. Why did you tell us that story? Why didn't you tell us the truth?

Instead of seeking answers to my questions, I put my arm around her as we sat side by side on the sofa. "Mom, Verneda made you a promise she would look for him when she turned eighteen, but she hasn't able to do that for a lot of reasons. Would you like me to see if I can find him?" Immediately after offering to find Buddy, Jr., I realized what an impossible task faced me. How could I possibly find a single lost person in this vast country?

Mom indicated in a quiet way that she would like me to see if I could find him. "I'll do my best." My words of comfort belied my trepidation.

"When I saw my mother today, we were looking at her old pictures and came across the one of Buddy, Jr. She seemed so distraught, I found myself offering to find him for her. How in the world am I going to do that?" I said to David when he came home from work.

"Does she expect that you'll start looking for him right away?"

"No, I didn't say when I'd start."

"Well, I don't see how you could possibly start looking for him now unless your search is by phone. We've just listed the house. The market is hot, so it shouldn't take long to sell. Most likely we'll be moving in a short while. Didn't you say you found a little house you want me to see? One that we may want to buy and remodel to suit us?"

"Yes, it's a modest little house close to downtown." Simply sharing my concerns with David and his reminding me of major events in our own life, let me to set aside an immediate effort to find Buddy, Jr.

Friday evening, Jennifer, now a senior in medical school, and Elizabeth, a student at the university, came home for dinner. "After the talk we had with the two of you about letting go of our family home of seventeen years, we listed the house with a realtor yesterday. We've already had a few people coming to see it."

"I think that makes so much sense. This is a large 'empty nest' to maintain," Jennifer assured.

"Change like this is a challenge for me," I told them, "But I'm eager to make the change.

After an unexpectedly quick closing of escrow, David and I moved into an apartment. Soon afterward, escrow closed on the modest home we purchased, and remodeling began. The change of selling our home, living in an apartment, and going through the process of a remodel jolted what stability I had managed to maintain since interacting so closely with my mother and her life. Now I experienced myself once again as a woman without roots, just as I had experienced myself when I was a child who was repeatedly moved from place to place.

I suffered with deep feelings of loss related to what my life had been before I began seeing my mother again. But the deepest loss I suffered was the loss of myself, my identity. I had periods when I temporarily lost my ability to function as an adult. Instead, for a brief time, a helpless-needy child, victim-of-circumstances, dominated my thinking.

Sometimes, I identified the world of Mom and Norm as my own. My past history with them got jumbled up with my current life. Feelings I dealt with were a mixture of the two: past and present. I identified their quality of life as my quality of life. This was true in the past, but I had to work hard to remind myself, "It is not true now, in the present."

But when I visited them in their fifth wheel, there were reminders of how I once had lived. It wasn't just their limited living space that I disliked, reminding me of the cramped space I detested in the small trailer where five of us had lived. I disliked the stark absence of beauty and comfort. I disliked the empty stares on Mom and Norm's faces that came from the boredom of doing nothing all day except sitting, smoking, looking out the window waiting, waiting for late afternoon to begin the daily ritual of drinking. I disliked breathing second-hand smoke from Norm's cigarettes. I disliked the junk sitting around here and there that silently screamed from its ugliness: poverty, ignorance, despair.

In leaving, I disliked walking past the dilapidated old-green-metal chair where Norm sat outside to smoke and beside it, the box filled with empty beer cans. All of this represented a lifestyle that repulsed me, a lifestyle I had no desire to identify as even a peripheral part of my life.

Although I didn't fully understand my motives for going, I continued seeing them regularly despite my personal struggles and their inability to discern that I too was a person with challenges in my life. I routinely drove from Redlands to Lake Elsinore, picked them up, and then drove them to Sun City for doctor visits where I interacted with the doctor on their behalf.

It was hard for them to deal with the doctor on issues relating to my mother's cancer and its treatment. I found it difficult to watch my normally stoic mother grimace in pain as she sat with a needle in her arm receiving chemotherapy. It was painful to be part of this process, not knowing when she might die. It absolutely dumbfounded me that I loved her despite how she had treated my sister and me in the past. But I wept when I thought of her death.

Chapter 37

California
March 1988 – June 1988

"Mac, I need to return to therapy," I said when I called him at the beginning of March. "I need help with this destructive anger I'm experiencing. I also need to talk with you about my mother's impending death."

Almost before I sat down in Mac's office, a stream of words flowed from me. "Jennifer has been accepted to a pediatric residency at Dartmouth to begin in July, three-thousand miles away. I only have myself to blame for the separation. She's heard me talk longingly about New England throughout her childhood. Not only that, but we paid for her to travel to New England, with Elizabeth as her companion, to explore residency possibilities. You probably remember that Jennifer and I are very close emotionally. The consequences of losing her to the East Coast for three years along with daily facing issues relating to my mother are probably the causes of my anger."

"Are you still using the technique of bioenergetics?" I asked but continued before he had a chance to answer. "I remember you had me wear a swimming suit then asked me to hit a pillow with a tennis racket to intentionally release anger. Do you recall my telling you, 'But I'm not angry, Mac. This isn't working. I don't feel angry,' but I hit the pillow anyway? Well today I'd be very good at that exercise because I feel so angry."

"I sometimes use bioenergetics, but I have found that hypnotherapy is quite effective in helping clients," Mac said. For this session and the next two sessions, we started with Mac suggesting that I was falling into a deep sleep. However, it seemed to me that I wasn't truly hypnotized.

At the beginning of our fourth session, I said, "I would rather not continue with the 'deep sleep' suggestion; let's see what happens without it." From that point forward and beyond, a strange phenomenon occurred.

There wasn't anything out of the ordinary for almost the entire portion of our session on March twenty-ninth, but toward the end of the session, I suddenly became an observer of myself as I heard a voice coming from me that I didn't consider my own, the content of which I couldn't recall when I shifted back to my normal self. "What was that Mac?"

"You shifted into a violent, angry, black, evil persona who talks like a witch," he said in his observation of my experience.

"I don't remember what I said but it didn't seem like my voice. The experience perplexes me."

"Don't be concerned. We'll meet next week and see if this was a one-time occurrence."

The next week passed without any unusual incident, but our following session on April twelfth was anything but usual. The session began normally but then I once again became an observer of myself. I shifted into a sobbing child whose voice cried out in pain, "Leave me alone! Leave me alone!"

I quickly turned into a cruel, vulgar, but blunt-speaking fragment who literally took me out of my chair and stood pointing at where I had sat, saying angrily, "Shut up that bawlin' you damn big bawl baby." It was her first appearance. I called her "Angry Mother."

Another immediate shift followed as I observed myself become a "Laughing Drunk," present only a moment, just long enough for me to laughingly tell Mac in slurred words, "I'm the toast and you're buttering me." I was amazed at how drunk I felt while in this empty-headed, laughing fragment, who made only one subsequent appearance, never to be heard from again.

Another abrupt shift introduced me to "Black Monster," who didn't speak in decipherable words, but uttered growling, frightening sounds. She was a terrifying fragment that shifted into a "Young Child," crying out for help to get away from the "Black Monster."

Undirected by Mac or by myself, I had shifted from one persona to another, in that session and in future sessions, until a number of what Mac called, "personality fragments" had appeared. Each had its own voice, its own emotion, and its own nebulous agenda, although at the very beginning of this experience, it was apparent that some of these fragments had no agenda as well as no lasting presence. I found it helpful to give each personality fragment an identifying name.

At our following session, Mac handed me an article with the title of "Multiple Personality." "This may give you some understanding of what's happening to you," he began, "but in my opinion, you are not a multiple personality. You don't have periods of blacking out then not remembering what happened, nor do you find clothes in your closet you didn't buy or wake up in a strange environment and wonder how you got there. I believe your fragmentation is a result of the trauma you've suffered. This fragmentation of the personality is one way a person's psyche deals with overwhelming trauma. It's a defense mechanism to cope with trauma."

Fleeting personality fragments emerged in our April nineteenth session. The most urgent fragment screamed, "I want to get away from Southern California. If I can get away from here, I can get away from my mother." Immediately I shifted into "Young Child," who sucked her thumb just as I had done as a child.

Before the session ended Mac exclaimed, "You have tremendous pain caused by your mother! She was really *mean* to you." He rarely gave me directives, but this day he told me, "I think it is best that you never have your mother live with you," then added, "and probably best for her, too."

During our May fourth session, I flowed from "Angry Mother" to "Laughing Drunk" into a frightening darkness. I described my experience to Mac after it had passed. "I felt like I was alone in whirling blackness on the inside of something like a black balloon with people on the outside pushing or making indentations on the wall of the balloon."

I continued describing my experience to Mac. "After indentations had come toward me on the wall of the balloon, I felt myself rise above the whirling blackness. I was 'up and out' of the whirling darkness of the balloon, looking down on it. Then suddenly I shifted into an evil, growling demon of darkness hissing out sounds. My hands were clenched, making fists when I came out of this fragment. The horror of this experience is overwhelming to me," I sobbed. "I felt so frightened, and I had a feeling of never being able to 'get out,' but I don't know what that means, not being able to 'get out.'"

"Did your mother ever shut you up somewhere? Mac asked.

"I don't know."

After I thought for a moment I said, "My Mom had an anger that could easily escalate into rage, a rage she directed physically at my sister or me."

In the May fifth session, my body stiffened when for the first time "Pride" made her entrance. "I'm the one who got us up and out of the whirling darkness yesterday," she claimed. An unexpected, rather sudden, shift occurred and "Frozen One" emerged for the first time. I experienced an inability to move my hands and arms, and then my whole body felt frozen. I could hardly speak.

Mac asked "Frozen One" several questions, but she didn't seem to have many answers. "How old are you?" he asked.

"I'm not sure. I think I'm very old."

"When were you born?" he probed.

A long span of silence passed before she finally said, "I have *a very hard time* thinking."

On May tenth "Pride" disclosed her role. "I defend against feeling pain, and I lift you up and out of terrible circumstances." But then Pride once again shifted into crying, tearful "Frozen One": "Nobody ever knew that I carried all this pain." Immediately on hearing this, I became very nauseous. I threw up and my legs ached as they had when I was a child.

Mac learned not to ask questions of these personality fragments because if he did, they would dissipate. Instead, he vocally comforted me, when necessary, until each fragment that needed to be heard had been heard and I could return to my normal state before leaving his office.

"I think I have a new insight," I told Mac at the beginning of our next session. "My life effort has gone into getting out of the Garbage Pail. That's my new awareness; I've structured my life around getting out of the Garbage Pail."

"Tell me what that means to you," he suggested.

"I've tried to get out of the Garbage Pail by being clean and neat as a person as well as making my environment neat and clean; by having a home in the most prestigious neighborhood; by driving a nice car; by earning the highest college degree offered; by belonging and contributing to the community; by having roots and becoming a lasting part of something. But the realization struck me that no matter how many 'prestigious homes' I have, no matter how many degrees I accumulate, regardless of driving a Cadillac, this effort to climb out of the Garbage Pail will never rid me of my mental garbage."

"What would happen if you accepted that as true?"

"Maybe if I accepted it, the frantic climb could cease," I mused. We sat silently for a long of time. "But you know, I think if I cease the climb, then I'm faced with worse monsters."

"Like what?"

"Like beliefs about myself that I've experienced during the dark times when I wanted to commit suicide. That I have no self-worth; that I'm an inferior nobody, a nothing; that I'm in the way; that nobody wants me. When I feel the pain that goes with these beliefs, I want to die."

"Maybe these toxic beliefs are the heart of the garbage you want to get out of your life," he suggested, setting in motion a new direction for my thinking.

"Mac, I've mentioned before that I'll be in New England for about two months, and that this will be my last session until I return. Jennifer graduates from medical school and has invited me to go with her."

"What will you do there?" he asked.

"I'll help get her established, but I think the main reason is to help ease the pain of separation for both of us." Mac didn't fill the silence when I stopped talking so I continued. "In the past few weeks, I've shifted into what you call 'personality fragments' or sometimes we call them 'different states of being,' but the experience is so confounding. Will you please help me make sense of what you've observed?"

Mac sat quietly for a few moments before he responded. "Why don't you tell me what your understanding is of what you've experienced."

"I should know by now that you want me to figure things out," I teased. "Let me start with Black Monster. She is so frightening, like a demon of darkness. I've thought about her, that she might be the way I experienced my mother when I was too young and frightened to understand her angry words. Instead, I heard them as angry sounds of hissing and growling."

"Doesn't Black Monster usually shift into a frightened, crying Child?"

"Sometimes, but sometimes a crying Child shifts into Black Monster or Angry Mother. Angry Mother is frightening but not as frightening as Black Monster. Angry Mother threatens to harm me or get rid of me, like my real mother did. She's also crude and swears like my real mother. I think she is the mother I experienced when I was a child. This reminds me, Mac. Do you remember my mother threatened to cut off my thumb if I didn't stop sucking it?" Mac nodded. "Well, I've had the experience two times when I was in such a state of self-hatred that I felt an urge to cut off my fingers. Almost a self-elaboration on what my mother threatened."

It was a relief to hear Mac offer a possible understanding. "The personality incorporates facets of the caregivers. These carry on some of the personality characteristics of the role models that have been in your life. Several mother fragments have emerged. A part of your personality is the mother fragment I label 'Persecutor.' She is the one who hates you, the one who wants to kill you."

"I'm not sure if I understand what you're explaining. But I do understand that I seem to have a lot of undesirable mother types inside of me!" I said with the intention of adding a bit of humor.

"Black Monster, Angry mother, Persecutor, Laughing Drunk all represent mother fragments in your personality," he said.

"What to do with them!" I said, somewhat overwhelmed.

"We can explore this when you return from New England, if you like."

"Yes, I'd like that. But I'm trying to remember what you said about the Angry Child fragment. I have a theory that maybe Angry Child emerged to escape the helpless victim state of Sobbing Child."

"It might be helpful to remember that these personality fragments have within them unresolved past traumatic events of pain and fear. As a child, you were very frightened, helpless, alone, often abandoned." He paused for a moment then asked me, "Weren't you frequently left in the care of your older sister?"

"Yes, I was," I confirmed.

"Children can be very cruel to the younger ones left in their care."

"That never occurred to me," I told him. "Some of what I experience may have been caused by my sister, not just my mother? You know, I remember something my sister said to me about children that gave me cold chills. She said, 'They won't stop making noise. I want to beat them to death. I feel rage.'"

"It's very likely she mistreated you when you were children."

To avoid the frightening images that started coming into my mind, I changed the subject. "I think there are only two fragments left, Pride and Frozen One."

"Tell me what you understand of these two."

"I would rather you tell me," I said.

Fortunately, Mac offered his understanding, "I think Pride is able to protect you from shallow pain caused from your losses of people and places."

"I experience this personality fragment as the one who chooses not to feel. She keeps people at a distance, declaring, 'I don't need anyone.' But she had or maybe still has the important role of 'lifting me up and above' loathsome circumstances of people and environments." I reflected momentarily, then told Mac, "You're right. She made the pain of leaving people I loved, when we moved so many times, as inconsequential by choosing not to feel."

"What about Frozen One?" Mac asked.

"I'll have to think about that. I don't know very much about her. She talks very little when she comes, and she doesn't come that often. Mac, before we stop our sessions for most of the summer, I want to say that while the last two months have been unsettling because of these personality fragments that have emerged, the experience is also an encouraging one, in spite of the craziness that comes with it!"

"This is the pathway to mental health. People who don't deal with issues of this kind can literally go crazy later in life."

"Then it's worthwhile to experience this while I'm young! By the way, I think I told you, I'll be making a search to find Buddy, Jr. sometime during the summer when I'm traveling. If it weren't for that, I'd have a hard time leaving Mom. Well, *part* of me would have a hard time." Mac and I smiled at each other.

Chapter 38

California – New Hampshire – Utah – Idaho – Nevada – Oregon
July 1988 – September 1988

When I visited my mother the week before I was to leave for the East Coast, I finally had the courage to bring up the subject of her lost son. "Mom, it's not quite a year ago since I told you I'd look for Buddy, Jr., and you've never brought it up or asked me anything. Jennifer graduates from medical school in June. You know she wants me to go with her to New Hampshire. I'll stay most of the summer while she gets started in her residency. I'm thinking that maybe on the return trip home I could begin my search."

I thought her eyes began to sparkle as she told me, "I didn't know when you was gonna look for him."

"I don't know if I can find him, but I'm going to try," I assured her. It was a great concern for me that she might get too hopeful only to be terribly disappointed if I didn't succeed. Although anxious with the potential prospect of defeat, I vigorously took on the task of finding Buddy, Jr. for my mother.

"I need all the information you have on Buddy, Jr. What was the name of his father?"

"We called him Bud, but his real name was Verlin Everett Johnson," she said.

"And what are the names of the people who took him?"

"That was Bud's sister Vi and her husband Roy. Their last name was Lee.

Vi and Roy Lee

They had a child of their own. They was a lot older than me."

Gary Lee   Vi Lee, baby Buddy Jr./Larry

"Where did they live when they took the baby?"

"Roy was a mail carrier into Jarbidge, but they lived in Twin Falls," Mom said.

"Where was the baby born?"

"Between Wakeene and Twin Falls on a farm at Bud's brother's house."

"That would be Idaho?"

"Yes."

"Do you remember the brother's name?"

"Dewey. Dewey and Grace Johnson of Twin Falls," Mom said without hesitation.

"Was the baby born February 11, 1941?"

"Yes, that's when he was born."

"I need to make a list of the towns you've mentioned. What were they?" I asked.

I wrote down the names of Gooding, Twin Falls, Wendell and Jerome. "These are all in Idaho?"

She nodded yes.

"Then of course Jarbidge, Nevada," I said as I wrote that down.

She couldn't think of anything else to tell me but then remembered, "I give Terry some things. You might want to see them."

At my sister's house in Garden Grove the next day Verneda told me, "I have some stuff in a bottom drawer Mom gave me. I think it's still there." I followed her into the bedroom as she continued talking. "You know I tried to make some calls to try to find him but didn't have any luck." She pulled open the bottom drawer and brought out a few things. "Here's a picture of Bud with his Navy buddies." She handed me a rolled-up picture of a few hundred men standing in rows on a navy ship.

That didn't seem like much help, but I took it.

"Here's an old newspaper article," Verneda said, holding out a yellowed piece of newsprint. At the top of the paper it read, Boise, Idaho, Tuesday April 28, 1942. I took it and immediately recognized Bud from among the fourteen men individually pictured. I read the caption under the photo, "Fourteen men, five of whom are married, were enlisted by the Boise recruiting station Monday for service in the U.S. Navy. They reported at Salt Lake City Tuesday to complete their recruitment." I read the names of the men in the photo but stopped when I came to Bud's formal name, Verlin Everett Johnston of Gooding.

"Oh," I remarked in surprise, "His name is spelled with a 't' Johnston! Not Johnson. This is a big help. Is there anything else?" I asked.

"That's it. I don't have anything else," she said as she closed the drawer. "Do you know how you're gonna try to find him?"

"I'm not sure. I need to give it a lot of thought. I'm leaving with Jennifer in a few days to go to New Hampshire. I'll have to think about it to see what I can come up with. Isn't it amazing that Mom kept these things for so many years?"

"When Mom got drunk, she used to cry to me about Buddy, Jr." my sister shared with me again. "She'd cry and say, 'You find him for me. When you get eighteen. You find him.'

When I turned eighteen, I didn't know how to find him. Then every February eleven she'd be drunk and call me and say, 'You know what day this is? It's Buddy, Jr.'s birthday.' Every February eleven she'd do that." She spoke in blended tones of pain and anger. "A few times, when I got drunk, I'd make some calls to try to find him, but never could," she remarked somewhat wistfully.

"I'm not sure where I was when she got drunk and cried to you. I didn't know for many years that she'd asked you to find him. Mom never talked with me about Buddy, Jr. The first and only time he came up was when I found that letter on her refrigerator, right before I got married. But I guess it's no surprise Mom didn't talk to me about him; we hardly ever talked about much of anything. Sorry you've carried this burden all these years," I said, in an effort to comfort her.

"Mom didn't talk with me!" Verneda said. "We *never* had conversations, especially about personal things."

"I'm really surprised! I thought Mom talked to you but not to me," I said.

"Mom didn't talk to either one of us. Children were not people. They were not human. Kids are just there, just there." Her generalizations became more painfully personal, as one thought triggered another. "Don't say anything; don't have an opinion; don't ask anything. If you did have an opinion, you'd get hurt for it, slapped. If I said I didn't like it, I'd get hit. You couldn't say 'no' to her. Mom would take hold of my arm and dig her fingernails into it when she got mad at me."

She paused. I waited. Then she said in soft, earnest tones, "I always wanted her to love me, to approve of me. She never told me she loved me except once. It was before she got real sick."

Going to New Hampshire with Jennifer for the summer helped to appease the concern I experienced in knowing that eventually a distance of thousands of miles would separate us for at least three years. David and Elizabeth stayed in Redlands supporting each other, with a plan to join us in New Hampshire late in summer. Jennifer settled into her residency while I decorated the two-bedroom army barracks she had rented through Dartmouth Student Housing.

In the early days of our arrival in New Hampshire, James, a man in her same residency program, seemed magnetically attracted to her. The two of them spent any free time together they could manage in the crazy world of residency where residents spent one-hundred-ten to one-hundred-twenty hours each week at the hospital.

Jennifer faced being on call every three to four days, which meant arriving at the hospital at seven AM one morning and not leaving until the following day at five PM, with little to no sleep during this entire time. The consequences of extreme sleep deprivation she suffered, that all the residents suffered, made no sense to me, considering these residents in their sleep-deprived state were sometimes responsible for life and death situations.

By contrast, my quiet time in a beautiful setting away from intense therapy, away from dealing directly with Mom's illness, allowed a deep personal restoration. At the end of each satisfying day, of either sculling on the Connecticut River, shopping in quaint downtown Hanover, going to the outdoor Farmer's Market in Vermont, or listening to French tapes in the language lab, I watched old movies on the American Movie Classics channel.

When I first started watching these old movies, I hadn't considered the value of seeing as an adult what I had experienced and seen as a child. It became apparent after only a short time. The realization dawned on me that I had identified with strong female actresses and some of the roles they played. These women had given me a view of myself beyond the cultureless, crude, unpredictable, drunken environment I had experienced in Larned. These women had been models for my higher aspirations, my inspiration to be more, become more, have more. The world of books could have provided this same contrast but there were no books in the world of my childhood.

David and Elizabeth drove together across the country, arriving at Hanover in early August. The four of us relished our experience of being together in New England. Sometime during the first week of September, I asked David "When does your vacation end?"

"I have until October first."

"I'm still thinking that we can search for Buddy, Jr. on our return trip. Are you up for that?"

"Whatever you want to do is fine with me," he answered in his usual pleasant manner.

"I'm going out today to buy a small spiral notebook, want to go with me?"

"You go, I think I'll stay here and read."

After purchasing my notebook, I stopped at Occom Pond to make a few notes. This beauty is breathtaking, I thought as I sat down on a bench, my attention captured by the reflection of trees on the still surface of the pond. Better get to it, I reluctantly told myself. At the top of the first page I wrote, Brainstorm Plan to find Buddy, Jr. Under that I decided to write, Baby's new name: Larry Gene Lee. Adoptive mother: Violet "Vi" Lee, sister of the baby's father. Adoptive father: Roy Lee.

I paused to think and found myself once again gazing at the pond. What was that? I wondered; something has sent a ripple scurrying across the surface. Never mind the pond, I told myself, how can we find Buddy, Jr.? What are some ways to get information? I wrote the ideas in my notebook: Birth certificate; Service Record; Social Security numbers; Salvation Army or other Missing Persons groups. The U.S. Navy Department might have records on the father. When I return to the house, I'll get the address for the processing center Bud went through in Salt Lake City back in April of 1942. We'll go there personally. No point trying to get my answers by telephone, I thought.

What other information do I have? I pondered. Oh yes. I wrote down: Vi and Roy lived in Twin Falls at the time of the adoption. I remembered that Mom had said. "He was a mail carrier out of Twin Falls." I stood to look once more at the pond before returning home. A little prayer rose from my heart, "Please Father, help me find Buddy, Jr. for my mother."

On the next day, September eight, I took out my notebook and made a list of the towns Mom had given me. Hmm, I thought, I can call information in each town to see if they have a listing for Verlin Everett Johnston, the Father of Buddy, Jr. But each response was, "No Listing."

"No listing," I said with an empty lost feeling as I hung up the phone on my last call. I thought of my mother and her lost child. What kind of pain has she suffered? I wondered; pain from willingly giving up her own baby.

It had been a dream of mine for numberless years to see the fall colors of New England, but around the middle of September I started to feel this urgency to leave for home.

"But you'll miss the fall colors," Jennifer said with a tone of disappointment, bewildered that my dream would not come true.

"The urge to leave is weightier than my dream. Something is telling me it is time to leave," I said as I hugged my daughter.

James stood next to Jennifer on the sidewalk outside the Medical Center at Dartmouth. It was time for David and me to say goodbye to our beloved daughter. As we drove away, it gave me some measure of comfort to see the two of them standing there, side by side. "At least, she's not alone," I said to David, "and she's coming home for Christmas."

My thoughts eventually turned from the sorrow of leaving Jennifer to the task ahead of us. "We'll start our search in Salt Lake City." I told David, "That's where Bud reported after he had enlisted at Boise, The United States Government Navy Department of Military Entrance Processing."

"Are you serious? Is that really the name of it?"

"Quite a formidable name, don't you think? But they might have some information I need."

Chapter 39

Utah - Idaho - Nevada
September 1988

"The records are only kept here for two years," the officer of the Navy Department said as he sat behind his desk playing with a pencil, "and then sent to D.C. while the person is on active duty. After that, the records are sent to St. Louis, Missouri for permanent record. But in 1960, most of the records were burned. Sorry we can't help you. Not long ago, I tried to make a search for someone I had hoped to find." Then he added this bit of discouragement, "but I was never successful."

In Salt Lake City, I had tasted briefly of failure and hated the thought of returning home with bad news. My expectations of locating my mother's lost son were low when we checked into the Residence Inn at Boise. I telephoned my sister right away. "Tomorrow, we're going on to Twin Falls to make a search there. I would love for you to come and do this with me," I told her. "You could catch a flight into Boise, and we could go together from here."

Verneda wasn't sure what she wanted to do. "Can you call me in the morning?" she asked, "That'll give me tonight to sleep on it." What was my reason for inviting her to come? I felt sensitive to what I thought her needs might be after so many tumultuous years of hearing from Mom about Buddy, Jr.

"Have you decided to join me in the search?" I asked Verneda the next morning when I called.

"No," she replied, "You go ahead. I'm not coming." No further explanation was forthcoming, and I didn't search for the reason behind her decision.

"The list I made of what to do when we get to Twin Falls gives me some comfort. At least I'm pointed in the direction of actions to take," I said to David. I had tried to plan ahead. I knew my emotions might not allow too much thinking once I was in Twin Falls with "what to do now" staring me in the face.

"This town holds a lot of my history!" I exclaimed as we drove into Twin Falls. "It's the town of my birth. It's the town where my sister saved my life from the fire. It's the town where

Mom sent us after my grandpa died. Now here we are to make a search for Buddy, Jr."

"What do you want to do first," David asked.

"Let's drive downtown to see if we can find the phone company. I want to get a phone book." No luck. The phone company is miles away, we learned. "Well, let's check into a motel. I can at least look at their phone book for Twin Falls. What time is it?" I asked David.

"It's almost four o'clock."

After we checked into the motel, I almost gave into my tiredness, willing to delay my efforts until morning. But the thought that followed countered that urge. No, people will be home this evening from work, and I'll have more success, I told myself.

"Here's the phone book," David said.

I looked at the loving face of my dear husband. "You are my darling. Always there ready to give just what I need," I said as I kissed him and took the book.

In Southern California, a telephone book is inches high and pounds heavy. "This book is so thin," I said in surprise, but then realized that Twin Falls is a small town in a sparsely populated state. I leafed through the white pages. The name Twin Falls appeared at the top of the pages, then the name at the top changed to Gooding, then Wendell, then Jerome and much to my surprise, the last town named was Jarbidge, Nevada.

"David, I don't believe it. Every town that I intended to search is listed in this *one* directory! Even Jarbidge!" It was a strange experience to hold this thin little directory in my hand with the contents containing everything I needed for my plan. The towns in this directory were the ones Mom had listed as places where she had been with Bud, places where his sisters and brothers had lived.

"I'm going to find a copy center and make copies of the listings for Johnston and Lee in each of these towns. Do you want to go with me?"

"No, I'd rather stay here," my tired husband said.

"I don't blame you. You really look comfortable stretched out on that bed. Wish I could join you. I'll be back soon." I resisted opening the directory to look for any of the names I hoped to find there. Instead, I found a copy center and copied all the Johnstons and all the Lees in each separate town. I had originally thought to copy only all the Johnstons in each town, but a little voice said, "Copy *both* names in each town."

On returning to the motel, I counted the number of Johnstons and Lees in each town to get an idea of how many calls I might potentially be making. There was a total of 17 Johnstons and a total of 44 Lees. I studied all the names to see if I could find a listing for Roy and Violet Lee or Verlin Everett "Bud" Johnston or perhaps even Larry Gene Lee. But there were no listings for any of them anywhere. Well, there was one Roy Lee listed but I had called him before I left California and found that he was not the Roy Lee I wanted to find. The rest of the names were simply unknowns.

My mother had given me the impression that the people who adopted the baby might not want to be found. I took this into account in my approach to finding Buddy, Jr. I'm sure I was divinely inspired with the decision I made not to inquire for Larry Gene Lee when I made my calls. I also decided not to ask for Bud. Instead, I said something like, "I'm in the area and wanted to locate some of my family. I wonder if you might be related to Roy and Violet Lee or know them."

"I think I'll start by calling all that Johnstons and then the Lees, in Twin Falls," I said to David. I also decided to make a note of each number I reached and what I learned. The first number I called was Al H. Johnston. "The number you've reached is no longer in service." I called the rest of the Johnstons, a total of seven, and came up with nothing.

I turned to the Lee column. The first one was another disconnect. I mumbled something to myself about two disconnects. I punched the numbers in for the second call, a listing for Berry Lee. A woman answered. "I'm trying to locate some relatives of mine and wonder if you know Roy and Violet Lee."

"Maybe you should talk to my husband," she said.

The silence finally ended when a man answered. I asked him the heavy question, "Are you related to Roy and Violet Lee, or do you know them?"

He quickly responded, "Yes, I know Roy. Roy is my uncle." I couldn't believe, dared not believe what I wanted to believe. I remembered the Roy Lee in the phone book I had called before leaving California, so I tried to clarify which Roy Lee he was related to.

"Do they have two sons?"

"Why yes, they do. I think both boys are adopted."

My mind raced away, almost out of control. I dare not get too excited or seem too anxious, I warned myself, or I'll scare him away.

"Victor died," I heard him say.

But who was Victor? I thought. Right at this minute, I really didn't care who Victor was.

Fortunately, he continued. "Oh yes, my brother Don Lee, visited Roy and Vi just last year and he could probably give you more information. His number is 549-0545. You know," he added, "Roy Lee's son Earnest Lee lives in Twin. You could probably talk to him."

I immediately located the number for Earnest Lee, amazed to learn that he was right here in Twin Falls. I called him before calling Don Lee because I thought that since he was Roy's son, he probably knew everything I needed. But there was no answer.

"Hello, I'd like to speak with Don Lee," I said to the man who had answered the phone.

"I'm Don Lee," he said. I thought of my good fortune to find him at home.

"I just talked to your brother Berry about Roy and Violet Lee. He said you had recently visited them and gave me your number. Could you tell me where they live?"

"They live in Lakeview, Oregon," he replied in a friendly way. "They're both doing well and seemed healthy when I was there last summer. Roy is 76 and Violet is 70. They may not be in Lakeview now because they go to Arizona for the winter."

"They have two sons, don't they?" I asked cautiously.

"Yes, they do. One of them was there when I visited." In spite of the physical sensations I was experiencing, I tried to be calm and casual as I attempted to learn which son was there when he visited.

"Well, it might have been Earnest," his voice trailed off momentarily. "No, I believe his name was Larry." Then he said emphatically, "Yes, it was Larry because I have a son with the same name."

At the sound of the name "Larry," and the fact that I was on the edge of finding Buddy, Jr. for my mother, in numbed disbelief, I dared to ask, "Do you know where he lives?"

"Lives in the area of Newport. He's a paving contractor."

On hanging up, I nervously punched numbers onto the telephone keypad to reach the operator. Information took the name Larry Lee and in exchange gave me the number. I pressed the keys of the phone for the precious number that could connect me, connect me to my mother's lost son, to a brother given away so many years ago. I was weak, nervous, excited. Did it ring three or four times? I didn't know.

A sweet woman's voice said, "Hello."

"May I please speak with Larry Gene," I asked.

"I don't expect him until around 8:30," she said.

"What time do you have now," I asked.

"I'm in Idaho and its 7:30."

"It's 6:30 here," she said.

"Oh, a time zone difference of one hour." Two whole hours before I could call back, I thought.

"Could you give me your name?" she asked. I told her my name, spelling both my first and last. I imagined her carefully writing it down. "Can I tell him what this is about?" she queried.

"I don't mean to be secretive, but I would like to talk with Larry first and then he can tell you. What's your name?" I asked her. "Sherry," the almost childlike voice said.

David and I couldn't believe it. We had arrived in Twin Falls at 4 o'clock in the afternoon and by 7:30 PM of September 21, 1988, Buddy, Jr. aka Larry Gene Lee had been located. The lost had been found. I offered a silent prayer, "Thank you Heavenly Father for allowing me to be a part of your Divine Process, for prompting me in what to do. I'm especially grateful that I can tell my mother that her son has been found."

I touched the keypad with the last number, waiting to hear my sister's voice, waiting to tell her the wonderful news.

"Guess what," I said.

In a breathless sort of way she answered, "What?" almost as if she already knew what I was going to tell her.

"I found Buddy, Jr." She was full of questions. I shared what I knew with her.

"But I have to wait for another couple of hours before he'll be home. Then I'll talk with him."

I assumed that since her eighteenth birthday, my sister had carried a tremendous burden during the following thirty-six years of her unfulfilled promise to find Buddy, Jr. Now at age 54, I imagined she would be unbelievably relieved that he had been located. I also thought that she would consider it an extreme privilege to be the one to tell Mom. With this in mind, I said to her, "Would you like to be the one to tell Mom Buddy, Jr. has been found?"

Of course, I would have been ecstatic to tell Mom myself that I had found her son, but it was now my sister's good fortune to tell her. I was very much at peace with my decision.

"David," I said after I hung up the phone, "What can we do with the two hours? I must do something."

"Let's get something to eat," he suggested. "We haven't eaten for hours." We sat at the Sodbuster's Café in Twin. I finished my salad then watched David eat.

"Let's see if we can find Uncle Clarence and Aunt Mae's cinderblock house where Verneda and I lived after Grandpa died." It was night but David humored me by driving around Twin looking for Jackson Street in the dark. No luck: we couldn't find it.

We returned to the motel and watched television. I purposely made myself wait an extra half hour before I called. I couldn't stand the thought of calling too soon only to find he wasn't home yet. Finally, the wait was over. A young man answered the phone, "Dad, it's for you." He called out.

"Hello."

"Hello," I said, "Is this Larry Lee?"

"Yes."

"Were you born on February 11, 1940, or 1941?"

"Yes, I was born February 11, 1941, in Jerome, Idaho.

"Well, I'm your sister. I don't know if this is good news for you or not. You do know that you're adopted, don't you? Your cousin knows so I thought you would too," I said rather awkwardly.

"Yes, I know, and I've always wondered but I didn't have any way to find out. My mom was upset with the way Gary went about trying to locate who his parents are, and I didn't want to cause trouble. We did go to the Court House to try to learn," he said. "Do you know who my father is?" he asked.

I couldn't believe he hadn't been given his father's identity because he had been raised by his father's sister. Dumbfounded, I floundered as I started to tell him, "Verlin Ev--" but before I could answer, he said, "Uncle Bud." "Hmmm" sounds were all that I heard from him for a few moments. "Uncle Bud, well, he was my hero when I was a little boy. He had two ships shot out from under him."

It was my strong desire to find Bud as well as Larry, so I asked, "Is he alive?"

His response surprised me. "I don't know. I've lost track of him." I had a sinking feeling. I really wanted to find Bud. A brief exchange followed with the two of us agreeing that we would like to meet, "We could be there either Saturday the 24th or Sunday the 25th.

After talking with Larry, I felt haunted by the thought that it would have been easy for anyone to find him years ago. And yet, no one had found him. Remember, I told myself, it was Divine Guidance that made it possible for you to locate him.

I tried again, after talking with Larry, to reach Earnest Lee, Roy's son. This time he answered.

"Earnest, Berry Lee told me that you're Roy's son. I'm in Twin and would love to visit with you if you're available. I used to live in Jarbidge. You might have been there the same time we were."

"Sure," he said without hesitation. "Stop by my place in the morning. That'd be great."

It was our good fortune that Earnest was a pleasant person who spoke freely of the past.

"My sister and I lived in Jarbidge with our mom in 1940 and 1941," I said

"I remember two little toe-headed girls in Jarbidge. I think I went to school with one of you."

"That would have been my sister, Verneda. She was a first grader in the fall of 1940."

"I was in the 5th grade that year," he said. "I went to school in Jarbidge 1st through 7th grades." Suddenly, he said, "Did you know you have a brother?"

"Oh, you know about my brother?" I asked.

"Yeah. I remember Bud and Edna. I remember Edna getting pregnant. Then the next thing I knew, Vi and Roy had a new baby. Roy is my father. He was married before Violet. She is my stepmother. I lived with my mother and George Urdahl, her new husband, in Jarbidge. Violet was real mean to me when I was a boy." He talked about how he wasn't able to be around his dad very much because of Vi. I listened carefully to his comments about Vi, storing it as information learned about the people who had raised Buddy, Jr.

"You know that Vi's brother Al Johnston used to live in Twin, but he just moved down near Bakersfield to Oildale, California to live close to one of his sons.

I couldn't believe what he was saying. "Al Johnston? I think he's the first one I called last night," I said as I pulled out my spiral notebook. "Yes, here it is, Al H. Johnston."

"Al Johnston is Vi and Bud's oldest brother. He and Blanche moved down to Oildale a short while ago," Earnest said, not realizing my shock.

The very first person I called could have linked me to Roy and Vi if he hadn't moved, I mistakenly thought. "Unbelievable," I said to Earnest. Later, I realized how fortunate it was not to be linked first with Roy and Vi before I had found Larry.

"Do you know where Bud is?" I asked hopefully.

"No, but I know where Dewey and Grace are."

"Who are Dewey and Grace?" I asked him.

"Bud and Dewey are brothers, and I think they were close. Dewey lives over in Graham, Oregon. I don't have an address, but would you like his number?"

"Sure. That would be great," I said appreciatively, not knowing what I would do with it. For a moment I thought to ask him for Roy and Vi's number and address in Lakeview, but I quickly dismissed the thought because I didn't need them; I had already found Larry.

Earnest continued to share important information. "Yeah, Bud was married. They lived around Los Angeles. He left her with a bunch of kids." His comment about Bud left me mildly curious to know more about the father of Buddy, Jr.

While Earnest talked of his boyhood in Jarbidge, my thoughts drifted momentarily. We had played on the same streets of Jarbidge when we were children. He knew my mother and remembered her pregnancy and the baby. Now, so many years later, we were meeting briefly once again.

"So, you're goin to Jarbidge today?" Earnest asked.

"Yes, I hope to find the little house we lived in. If it's still there," I told him.

"Oh, it's still there. You go through the middle of town and cross Bear Creek up about a block on the right-hand side of the street. Ask George Urdahl where it is. He's lived in Jarbidge since he was a boy. He's 83 years old. Lives with my mother Hazel, in a big grey house kitty-corner from your little white house. Do you know how to get to Jarbidge from here?" Earnest asked.

"I've looked at it on the map," David said. "We're going to go out through Rogerson."

"Yeah, that's the way to go," Earnest said. "You're about 2 ½ hours' drive from Twin to Jarbidge. When are you going to see Larry?" he asked.

"We'll get to see him on Saturday; only two more days," I said.

"I knew all these years who Larry Lee's parents were. I didn't dare tell because of Violet's anger," Earnest said, as if this was a secret he hadn't shared with anyone.

When Earnest and I stood together in front of his house while David took our picture, I didn't know that I would never see him again. I sent him a copy of the picture along with a thank-you note but after that I never heard from him. I heard about him from others but never had the opportunity to meet with him again. It is doubtful that he realized the importance of what he was willing to share with me. What he may have considered insignificant, I received as balm to further heal my Jarbidge wounds.

1988 on the way to Jarbidge

Getting to Jarbidge was a wildly fascinating trip. But I was extremely excited because I was on my way to see the other most important town in my life. I had already returned to Larned, and soon I would be in Jarbidge. It had puzzled me over the years, why of all the places I had lived, these two towns stood out from the rest.

"Stop, David. I want you to take my picture by that sign," I said as we made the turn at Rogerson onto the road to Jarbidge. The mileage marker read: 7 Salmon Falls; 17 Cedar Cr Reservoir; 64 Jarbidge, Nevada. I stood by the sign with a finger on the mileage indicator to Jarbidge.

"Got it!" David said as he took the picture.

We drove for a time across the flat terrain of the high desert surrounded by mountains in the far distance. "Where in the world can a town be? There's nothing out here," I said. Eventually we began a gentle descent into what became an expansive deep canyon. We came to a single building with a gas pump in front of it. David stopped to fill up.

"Getting closer," was his report when he got back into the car. A flowing river appeared parallel to us on the dirt road. We traveled with it, straight into the little town of Jarbidge, which sat cradled by small rolling hills backed by craggy, more ominously shaped hills. We drove for only a block or two, past a small café and another store or two, then past tiny houses of various shapes and sizes lining each side of the street. Unlike my experience of Larned, Jarbidge looked much smaller than I had remembered it when I had been there at three and four years of age.

"The main part of the town is only a couple of blocks long" I said in amazement. "And look, that river runs the length of the town behind the row of houses on the opposite side of where I think our house is. That must have been the river that flooded the town and frightened Verneda and me when we were left alone."

"Earnest said to look for a large grey house. That's where his stepfather George lives," David said. I was eager to find the house where we had lived.

When we connected with eighty-three-year-old George, who had lived in Jarbidge since he was a boy, I told him, "I lived here when I was a child. My mother's name was Edna, she went with Bud Johnston."

"I remember Bud," he said, "but I don't remember your mother Edna very well."

"We lived in a small white house," I told George as I recalled the picture of Mom hanging clothes outside beside it. "I think it's the one across the street from you and down a little," I said.

"Yes, that would be it," George said in his relaxed easy-going manner. "Some people from California bought that last summer. Nothing about it has changed really," he added as we walked toward it.

When we approached, I felt a bit startled. The small window on the opposite side of the house, from where the picture of Mom hanging clothes had been taken, was exactly where I had remembered it. I began to describe the physical layout of the interior of the house to George when we stopped and stood looking at it from the front. After I finished George said, "Oh yes, they were all built like that in those days."

Although I've frequently had confirmation that my memory is remarkable, I was surprised to learn that I had accurately recalled the interior of this little house I had left at age four and hadn't seen for forty-seven years.

"The house is locked up; you won't be able to get in," George said. Getting to see the inside of the house wasn't important to me for some reason. I stood on the front porch while David took my picture.

The hill behind the house that my sister and I had climbed as children was much steeper than I recalled. Fences impeded our access, but David found a way to climb up to the ridge and wave at me after he had taken a picture from that vantage point.

"Where is the school?" I inquired. George pointed up the road past his house. To my delight, it was up the road from our house in the direction I had remembered, and it was about five houses away. No wonder, I thought to myself, I could walk there by myself when I was only three years old.

I tried to locate the building where my sister and I had gone when the flood frightened us. "One of those buildings burned down," George said. "Another was turned into a home."

My mind momentarily turned to thoughts of my mother. Where was she when she left us alone and frightened? I wondered. She and Bud must have left town to go drinking somewhere else, but Jarbidge is miles from any other town! It seems she was often gone for a long time I thought as George talked with David.

When we headed back down the dirt road of Jarbidge, we stopped at a pay phone mounted on the porch post of the café. "Mom, I said excitedly when she answered, "Did Verneda tell you?"

"Yes," she said in a somewhat strange voice. "They found him."

I couldn't believe what I heard. "*They* found him Mom?" I said into the phone, "*I* found him."

"Oh," she said without excitement or appreciation. "You found him." Incredible, I thought, feeling disappointed with her response. "I'll see him in two days. I'll call you then," I said, before saying goodbye.

"She didn't even ask me any questions!" I told David when I returned to the car.

"What were you expecting?" he asked.

"I'm not sure. It was a disappointing conversation." I didn't know until I returned home that she was quite ill when we talked.

As we drove away from Jarbidge something eerie began happening. "David, my body feels strange. My chest hurts. My arms ache. I'm having a weird physical experience. This may sound crazy, but it feels like Frozen One is thawing out!"

"What do you mean?" David asked. I sat thinking, but I continued to experience what felt like a "thawing out".

"Well, finding Buddy, Jr. then immediately visiting Jarbidge is probably what triggered this body response. What feels like Frozen One thawing is probably my body releasing years of tension. No way did I anticipate that finding him would make a difference to me personally because I haven't thought about him most of my life! Does any of this make sense to you?" I asked.

"You've had body memories in Mac's office and with Mac's help we understand that dynamic. This certainly seems like a body memory, different from the other ones, but yes, it makes sense," David suggested.

Sometimes in the struggle to make sense of my life and my experiences, undeniable truth emerges. An undeniable truth emerged as we drove away from Jarbidge that sunny day in September 1988: I had accessed the frozen wilderness of myself where at age four I had stuffed my feelings of fear and pain when my baby brother suddenly disappeared. That beautiful day in Jarbidge I had discovered the answer to Mac's question. I finally knew when Frozen One was born and why.

Chapter 40

Oregon - California
September 1988

"Can you believe the beauty of this area, David?"

"We'll be there once we're across the bridge," David said, and by the sound of his voice the sight was speaking to him as well.

"The design of this bridge is truly inspired; the beauty of it is breathtaking; it looks new," I said as it carried us over the bay. "Unbelievable, we're almost there," I said, totally enchanted by a view of the bay lined with evergreen forests silhouetted against a blue-sky abounding in voluminous clouds of white and grey.

"It looks like a pristine little coast town!" I observed as we passed through part of it.

"This scenery is spectacular," David commented as he continued driving south up a hill, still within view of the ocean.

"Yes, it's spectacular," I agreed, totally absorbed in the rhythm of gentle waves lapping at the curved shoreline.

David made a left turn off the highway, easily finding the address Larry had given us. "Here it is," he said, pulling our Seville into their driveway.

"This is where my brother lives. I hope I remember to call him Larry and not Buddy, Jr. I can hardly breathe, David, I'm so excited. I'll always remember this day, Saturday the twenty-fourth of September 1988."

A modest but attractive home faced us. It was hard for me not to jump out of the car and go racing to the door, but I controlled myself. Instead, David and I walked together.

A teenager opened the door, "Hello, I'm Paul."

As he was inviting us in, a small rather slender woman with dark, curly hair greeted us, "Hi, I'm Sherry," she said with a friendly smile. I looked around. "He's outside in the back," Sherry said. "He didn't know what to do with himself, so I sent him out there."

Paul led us out the sliding back door, down the steps to the end of a long sidewalk where a man, leaning over with his head under the hood of a truck, was working on the engine. "Dad," Paul called.

When Larry stood up and we met face to face, I silently gasped in surprise. I was looking into the face of my mother! It was unsettling at first, but I threw my arms around him and said, "You're my brother." I looked at him for a moment then hugged him again saying, "and I'm your sister."

"And I'm not much taller than you," he said with a nervous laugh. "I'm kinda dirty," he said as he stepped back with a grin on his face. "Let me get cleaned up, then I'll be right in." Sherry took us back into the house. Larry, whose brown eyes, and cheekbones reminded me of my mother, came into the house and sat in a recliner.

"You have curly hair! Is it naturally curly?" I asked.

"Yeah, it's always been curly," he said of his brown hair. I didn't mention that his biological mother also has naturally curly hair. "Sherry cuts it for me." I said something about how talented she must be.

"We was really surprised to get your call," Larry said.

"I knew something was up when you called," Sherry added.

"I wonder what gave me away," I laughed. "Was it that I asked for Larry Gene, instead of just Larry?"

"Sherry and I had gone to the courthouse to see if we could find out something about who adopted me, but we couldn't get any information," Larry said.

Again, Sherry added to what he had said. "The records was sealed." The door opened and a dark-haired man in his twenties came through the back door. "This is our son, Rory," Sherry said. He didn't say much but sat quietly in a chair next to Larry.

"When I was about ten, Mom stood me between her knees and told me I was adopted, but that's all she ever told me. Well, she did tell me I was real sick when they got me, and the doctor said I probably would've died."

"I've never heard that you were sick when you were a baby. All I know is that you were our baby for almost half a year and then we didn't have you anymore." When I said this to Larry, I started to cry. "I got to go with Mom when she gave birth to you," I sobbed. "My sister took care of us because Mom was gone a lot." I was surprised at how I cried from an open heart in front of these perfect strangers. But I didn't feel that they were strangers. This was my brother. "What was your life like?" I managed to ask.

"Mom and Dad was good people. I grew up in Lakeview. Had a horse of my own. Dad taught me how to work on engines."

"You were better off than being with us then," I told him. "We moved around a lot. Mom liked to drink."

"I always wondered why I was given away, why my parents didn't want me," Larry confided.

"Bud and Mom weren't married. He was a lot younger than she was and probably not ready to get married. Mom always told us that you were taken from her. Vi threatened to have Verneda and me taken from her too by proving my mom was an unfit mother," I said, trying my best to explain my understanding of why Vi was the one who got to raise him.

"It's strange to find out that my mother is really my aunt, and that my uncle is my father, and my brother Gary is my cousin." Larry said somewhat jokingly.

I looked at Rory and said without thinking, "And your grandmother isn't really your grandmother."

"She is my *real* grandma," Rory said.

"Of course, she's your real grandmother," I apologized to Rory, choosing not to push the issue, although I knew that Vi was truly Rory's great aunt, not his real grandmother. I turned my attention back to Larry. "Do you wonder why your mother didn't tell you that her brother is your father?"

"I don't know. Uncle Bud stopped comin' around when I was a boy. But he was my hero, had ships shot out from under him when he was in the navy," Larry said.

"Would you like to go to church with us tomorrow?" Sherry asked. "You'll have a chance to meet our daughter, Tammy."

I looked at David, who gave a little nod. "We'd love to!" I answered.

On Sunday when we attended church with them, a lovely dark-haired woman entered the back of the church. She looks a lot like my mother, I thought, but at the same time wondered if this was Larry's daughter. About that time Sherry gave the beautiful woman a wave and she came our way with her two young daughters.

Over lunch, Larry explained how they used to visit the coast when they lived in Lakeview. "One summer when we was visiting, I saw a road crew pavin' and workin' on the highway. 'Gee, I'd like to be over here doin' that,' I told Sherry. It was time for me to get out of Lakeview, so we decided to move over here. I got a job workin' with a paver. Then he retired and I bought the business from him this year. My Mom and Dad are still in Lakeview. They came over once to see if they wanted to live here but it rained all the time they were here, so they didn't move," Larry said in a monotone.

"Would you like to see some pictures?" Sherry asked, holding a box in her hands.

"That would be fun. Pictures of your family?" I asked.

"A few of Larry when he was younger too," she answered. As we looked at random pictures loosely stored in the box, I learned more about Larry and his family history by the comments made as we sorted through pictures from his past.

Larry with grandchildren and Vernetta

Monday morning came and it was time for us to leave Larry and Sherry. "We'll try to get down to California real soon," Larry said, maybe as an encouragement to me because of what I said earlier.

"That will be great, Larry. Mom will be so anxious to see you. She has almost lived past the time doctors said she would." I repeated myself from what I had said earlier, hoping he'd understand the urgency of his need to come soon.

When we had been on the road only a short time I asked David, "Where is Lakeview from here?"

"It's east of here and south; close to the California border. We went through there that summer we went up to Pendleton."

"I can't believe it. You mean we went through the very town where Larry was living?" I waited for a moment, wondering if I dared ask David to give me my heart's desire. "Could we go to Lakeview before we go home? I want to see if we can find Roy and Vi. I'd love to talk to Vi," I said, aware of how many miles we had already covered since leaving Jennifer in New Hampshire.

"We can do that," David said in his usual kind way, "if it's important to you."

"Thank you Lord for David!" I said out loud. Was there ever a time when he stood in the way of what I wanted to do? I found myself thinking. Ah yes, the purchase of the Palo Alto house. But I couldn't remember another single time.

Larry had given me Roy and Vi's mailing address. I thought I could get their residence address through that. When we arrived at Lakeview, we went to the post office. "I have a post office box number for Roy and Violet Lee. I wonder if you could give me their home address," I asked the postal clerk.

"I can't give out that information" the man said. "Sorry."

Before returning miles away to Southern California, I wanted so much to meet the woman who for years I had believed snatched the baby from my mother. Reluctantly I said to David, "Looks like I'll have to call Larry."

I lucked out; he was home. "Larry, this will probably be a surprise to you, but David and I are over here in Lakeview. Would it be all right with you for us to go and see Roy and Vi?"

"I guess so. Don't really make no difference to me, I suppose," Larry said.

"I'm not going to say anything to Vi that I found you. I think you should be the one to tell her. I really want to meet her for my own reasons. I hope to talk with her and maybe she'll tell me her side of the story. What do you think?"

It was a delicate situation. In our talks, Larry had told me enough about his relationship with Vi for me to conclude that the past fell into the realm of an unspoken subject between them. I considered that it might even be a forbidden subject.

"I don't know if she'll talk to you."

"Do you think it's worth a try?" I asked, trying to allow him to make the decision. I didn't want to upset or alienate him by pushing my needs and wants.

He repeated himself, "She might not talk to you, but you can try. They live about five miles from town. They've got a mobile home that sits on some acreage out there in the country." Precise directions followed.

David parked us on a gravel driveway. "This is the place," he said.

A man and a woman sat on the back porch, separated from me at some distance by a split rail fence and a row of shrubs. I got out of the car and walked to the fence that went around the yard. I disliked the distance that separated me from them, but I wasn't familiar with the property, otherwise I would have managed a closer encounter.

I reminded myself that I needed to protect my new relationship with Larry. I must not do or say anything that would get back to him in a way that might prevent him from making the trip to see my mother. This decision greatly changed how I chose to relate to Vi. If she had known that I had already found Larry, she might have related differently to me as well, but I had given that to Larry to share with her at his own choosing.

"I'm not sure if I have the right place. Are you Vi?" I asked after we had exchanged greetings and she stood looking at me from the porch.

"Yes, I'm Vi," she responded.

"I'm Vernetta. You knew me when I was a little girl. I'd love to talk with you."

"I'd rather not," she said. I was surprised by her quick negative response.

"I had hoped you'd talk with me. I've had a hard life and I thought you might help me learn more about myself."

"Yourself!" she exclaimed. I thought she sounded somewhat astonished at what she'd heard, quite different from what she was probably expecting.

"Yes, about some of the things that happened to me," I explained further

"What is your name?" she asked.

"Vernetta. You probably recognize my name. Do you remember me?

"No, I don't. What is your last name?"

"Schreiber."

When she heard the name Schreiber, she turned and said something to Roy and then turned back to me. "I'm sorry you've had a hard life." She paused, and her voice softened. "But I have a past to take care of too." Her soft words ricocheted off my thoughts yielding an interpretation she probably didn't intend.

"Well, life is much better now. I think I almost have it together and I have a wonderful husband," I heard myself say.

"I want to wish you the best," she said in a dismissive tone.

"Thank you. I'm glad I at least got to see you."

Did she wonder why I wasn't more forceful, more persistent in my desire to talk with her? She didn't know that I probably would have climbed over that fence and marched right onto her patio if I hadn't already found Larry. Let her be for now, I thought. I don't want to alienate Larry.

"The content of that conversation was strange," I told David when I got back in the car. "Some of the stuff I said didn't even sound like me! Or make sense! But I was trying to appeal to her curiosity as well as any thread of kindness she might have."

"You did good," David said as he reached for my hand.

"At least I feel good about keeping the agreement I made with myself. I didn't tell her I'd found Larry." I drove away thankful that I needed nothing from Vi to help me locate my mother's son, my brother.

My encounter with Vi gave birth to a passion: I wanted to learn everything I could about her, this woman who had persuaded my mother to give up her baby. By this time in my life, I had learned that information is powerful. It holds the potential of clarifying the truth. It dispels the vague imaginings of the mind. Yes, I experienced a passion to know her but when I returned home, my passion had to be pushed aside for more pressing priorities.

Our route home took us past Bakersfield, which sits next to Interstate 5 north of the Grapevine that takes one down into the Los Angeles basin. An hour or so before we got to the Bakersfield area, I said to David, "Al Johnston, Bud and Vi's brother, lives in Oildale, just before we get to Bakersfield. Let's call him. Maybe he'll talk with me."

"What if he is like his sister Vi and won't talk to you?" David asked.

"It's possible that he'll be like Vi but I'm willing to take the chance."

"Who did you say your mother is?" Al asked me when I talked with him on the phone.

"I'm Edna's daughter. We used to live in Jarbidge," I repeated.

"Oh, Edna. Sure, sure. I knew Edna in Jarbidge."

"We're on our way home from Twin Falls and we'd love to stop by and see you," I suggested.

"Oh sure, you come on ahead," Al agreed, then gave me directions.

Fortunately, Al was friendly and loved to talk. His wife Blanche was friendly as well. "So you're Edna's girl. I remember you when you was little," Al said with a smile, then added, "Edna was a mighty fine person."

"Yes she was," Blanche chimed in.

I may have been a bit surprised by their comments but certainly I was pleased how they regarded my mother.

"My mother is dying of cancer but hopes to be reunited with Buddy, Jr. So, we went to Twin to make a search."

"Did you find Laddy?" Al asked. "That's what we used to call him."

I wasn't going to tell them I'd found Larry unless I was asked directly. I hesitated and then said, "Yes, we found him."

"Where does he live?" Al asked.

I couldn't believe that he didn't know where Larry lived. "He owns a paving company over on the coast," I told Al and Blanche.

After I had given them an abbreviated version of finding Larry, Al said, "So Vi never told Laddy about his past and who his parents are! That sure surprises me. We sure would have told him if he ever asked us. It's his right to know."

"Larry and I agreed that it's his place to tell Roy and Vi that I found him, so please don't say anything to her about it if you talk with her," I urged.

"Oh no," Blanche and Al both said almost at the same time. "We won't say anything. We don't keep close touch," Al said. "Yeah, there are only four of us left--Dewey, Vi and Bud and me--but we don't talk much to each other."

He began to talk freely about Jarbidge. "There was about a hundred to a hundred-and-fifty single miners in Jarbidge at that time and twenty married miners. It was a rough town. No place for a single woman and two little girls. People would go to the dance with one partner and go home with another. Edna was at a dance there in Jarbidge with ole Red Getchel. Bud cut in on 'em and then went home with Edna and never left. About a year later, Edna got pregnant and had a baby," Al said as he paused for breath. "I think Red is the one who brought her to Jarbidge from Twin. That Bud, he was a heavy drinker and a rounder."

Al was about to continue, but I interrupted. "I don't know what a rounder is, Al."

"He likes the women, makes the rounds," Al informed me with a smile on his face. "Ole Bud would find out which miner was working that night and then he'd go sleep with the wife." He paused momentarily, "Yeah, he and Edna used to go to the bars and leave the baby in the back seat of the car. Violet didn't like that and got real mad. Probably why she took the baby." I sat enthralled as I listened to Al provide stories of when Mom lived in Jarbidge.

"Do you know where Bud is?" I asked, still hopeful to find him.

"Bud was in Carbondale, Colorado fifteen years ago but moved a few years back. Let's call him," Al said eagerly.

"O my gosh, you know where Bud is! Larry said he'd lost track of him, didn't know where he was."

"Well," Al said, pausing for a moment before enthusiastically repeating, "We can call him right now."

"Oh no, I'm not ready to talk to him just yet.".

"Are you sure? We could call him right now," Al offered again.

"It would really be nice to have his number so I could call him later." Al gave me the number. "You know, Al, when I was in Twin Falls looking for Larry, I called your number, but it was a disconnect."

"Yeah," he said. "We left Twin not very long ago."

"I was surprised when Earnest told me the number belonged to you, Bud's brother. I was so happy when he gave me your phone number here."

Al began to talk about his family history. "My father was a musician and an engineer," he told us proudly. "He died in 1920, the year Bud was born. Bud was the last one of six of us kids. I was the oldest son and tried to keep things together for mother by getting jobs and giving her the money after our dad died. The three youngest kids were Dewey, Vi and Bud. Dewey and Bud kind of stuck together over the years and Vi watched out for Bud." Al talked a little about a run-in he and Bud had had years ago. "Haven't seen him for years; he's kinda held it against me. But we talk now and again," he reflected, then changed the subject. "So you found Laddy. We'd talk to Vi and ask about him, but she never says where he is or what he's doing."

Al and Blanche both said, "Come again any time." It was the last thing they said before we drove away.

"You know, David, when Earnest told me that the first number I dialed was Bud's brother, I felt disappointed because I thought I could have found Larry with the very first call. But Al didn't even know where Larry was or what he does until we told him."

Some think that truth can harm, I mused to myself. Vi is probably one who believes that the truth would harm Larry or harm her relationship with him. Some believe that truth can free us. I wanted to believe that the truth I shared with Larry had freed him. He had said himself that he wondered who his parents were, and why they had given him away. He had asked himself, "Why didn't they want me?" The truth answered these haunting questions for him. Perhaps provided a foundation his life has lacked, I thought.

Chapter 41

California
October 1988

The dry Southern California landscape awakened me to the realization we were almost home. I had been away for three months and now I felt this urgent desire to see my mother, especially to share news of Larry with her.

"Mom, I want to pick you up and take you to lunch today," I proposed enthusiastically the day after returning home.

"That'd be nice," came her usual response.

When I stepped through the door of the fifth wheel, her arms went around me. She held me as she had never done before. She said nothing, not even a word or question about Larry, but she gave me a precious hug. It was her way of thanking me for finding her son.

"Ready to go to lunch, Mom?" I asked.

"We can go, if you want," she said.

We sat in a booth next to a window as we ate our Taco Bell tostados. I talked to her about visiting with Larry. She wasn't riveted to the edge of her seat listening intently, as I had imagined but seemed distracted and only mildly interested. I stopped talking. We ate in silence for a few moments until her words caught me by surprise.

"Norm didn't know I had a son. I didn't tell him until a few years ago." She had been married to Norm for forty-one years but had only recently told him of Buddy, Jr. My relationship with her hadn't included intimacy of this nature. Because I was still relating to her as a dominated child who was not allowed to intrude on her privacy, I didn't ask the question I wanted to, why did you wait so long to tell him? Instead, I simply asked, "And how is Norm now that he knows about Larry? And how is Norm now that he knows about Buddy, Jr. we all know now as Larry?"

"It don't bother him. He's okay with it." came her brief reply.

Questions came uninvited as I watched Mom eat, questions I asked myself like why did she keep her son a secret from Norm, the one I imagined is closest to her? Are there other secrets she might still be holding close to her heart? Shaking off these provoking questions, I asked Mom, "Would you like to see some pictures of Larry and his family?" She smiled faintly, nodding her head.

I took the pictures from the brown envelope. Mom looked at the first one with some measure of interest but as I tried to share the treasure I had brought her, she became restless and wanted to return home. Disappointment was my silent response. I was perplexed that her anxiety to return home overshadowed seeing the pictures of her son and hearing the stories about him that I wanted to tell her.

"She can't remember how to wash her hair," Norm complained after we returned from lunch.

"What do you mean?" I asked him. Mom sat next to me on the couch listening. I looked at her and tried to make a little joke.

"She gits in the shower but doesn't know what to do." I heard desperation in his voice. I sat bewildered for a moment by this new information about Mom. But then I took the brown envelope that held the pictures Larry had given me. "Here, Mom, I want you to write your name for me," I said as I handed her a pen.

She didn't hesitate to begin with a nicely formed script capital E. The small "d" that followed was acceptable, the "n" after it looked even better. The last letter "a" was also nicely formed. I tried to keep it light.

"You did good, Mom. Look at that, "Edna." You haven't forgotten how to write your name. Now we just need to help you remember how to wash your hair." The tension eased. "Norm let's make an appointment with her doctor to see what he thinks. We need answers from him." Norm agreed.

I changed the subject to Larry. "He wants to come to see you, Mom but he doesn't know when he can get down here. He bought a paving business this year. He'll come just as soon as he can get a break from that," I told her reassuringly, wishing I could end the uncertainty of when he would come. "Are you okay with that, Mom? He'll come when he can."

"We'll have to wait," she said quietly.

Thoughts of my mother filled my mind on the drive home. She still seems strong, I told myself, but now shows loss of memory. Two years since she was diagnosed with cancer, I calculated. The thought of her eventual death reminded me of a recent conversation with Norm.

"We're gonna be buried right here in the Lake Elsinore Cemetery," he stated with certainty.

"Do you have the plots yet?" I asked.

"Not yet," he replied.

"Well, it'll be hard enough to deal with Mom's death. We don't want to deal with choosing a plot then!" I exclaimed and he agreed.

"Why don't we go when you come out next week to take us to the doctor," he suggested.

"Sounds good to me. How about you, Mom? What do you think?"

"Whatever the two of you thinks best," she answered.

At least we can buy the plots before Mom dies. There's comfort in that I told myself as I pulled into my driveway.

The next week before we went to select plots, we took Mom to see her doctor specifically about her memory loss. I shared with him the incidents Norm had described.

"The disease may have gotten into her brain. I'd like to run some tests but that will need to be done on her next visit," the doctor explained. We were given an appointment for the following week. We left feeling as helpless as when we had come.

"I'll drive us to the cemetery," Norm told me when we got back to Lake Elsinore. I reluctantly climbed into the back seat of his car. Immediately I became the frightened child who didn't want to be any part of buying grave plots, a frightened child who didn't want to sit looking at the backs of Norm's and

Mom's heads. Fortunately, the drive was short. I emerged from the back seat as an adult able to face the task at hand.

Two days after we had selected the plots, the phone rang. "Have you been sick or something?" Mom asked. I was surprised to hear her voice because she almost never called.

"No, why do you ask that?" I asked.

"Well, I haven't heard from you for so long I thought maybe you were sick. I oughta spank your butt," she threatened.

"Mom, it's only been two days since I came to see you!"

"I'm concerned about Mom's memory loss, David, but I don't know what to do. We saw the doctor today and the results from the tests were inconclusive. There's no definitive answer for her loss of memory. Look, I made a list of the things she's forgotten: her cataract surgery; her chemotherapy treatment; her hospitalization of two days which she thought had been five days; her scolding of Glenda."

"Her cancer is probably an important contributing factor," David suggested.

"Do you think the pills she's taking could cause memory loss?"

"Did you ask her doctor?"

"No, I didn't think of it then," I groaned. "The other day Mom called to scold me for not coming to see her and I had just been there!"

The next morning, I woke with such concern for my mother that I drove to see her even though I was tired. When I arrived at Lake Elsinore, I found Mom and Norm sitting on the porch watching the cat play. I sat with them. Norm smoked. Mom swatted at flying insects.

This trip was unnecessary! I hate being here!" an internal voice yelled at me.

On that visit, I experienced Norm's perspective of my many trips on their behalf: "You have more time than Glenda."

He thinks I have nothing valuable to do with my time, I told myself. He has no idea that I have made them the priority in my life. It occurred to me that if I took less responsibility, perhaps Glenda and Verneda might get involved. I'm not the only one who can help them, I told myself. They have two other daughters.

As I watched Norm smoke and Mom swat at insects, another possibility struck me: I'm over attending to my mother. Why am I doing that? I asked myself. Because I still need her to love me, I wondered? A familiar thought came to mind when I looked at her. For some reason, I have a need to take care of her, to protect her. But from what? I sat there, tired, and perplexed, with more questions than answers.

Chapter 42

California
October 1988

In early November, I felt as if the dams of hell had broken loose inside me. I reflected on what might be the cause: Frozen One began to thaw in Jarbidge; I searched for, found, and met Larry; I left my daughter at Dartmouth; I do nothing but relate to Mom and Norm. That's pretty overwhelming, I told myself. But I probably feel like I want to die because I may be taking care of Mom if the doctor says Norm needs surgery. I imagined the worst, that I might have to care for one or both of them indefinitely. I'll have to manage my anxiety a few more days, until I see Mac.

"Your appointment with Mac must be cancelled today. There has been a death in his family. He will see you next week at the regular time," the voice said. I hung up the receiver and slumped into a chair. Suicidal thoughts comforted me. Instead of fighting it, I followed Mac's advice from many sessions ago. "Allow yourself to go into the experience to learn what you can from it, instead of trying to block the feelings," he had instructed me.

The following Tuesday, I recounted the incident to Mac in our session. "I experienced myself as suicidal last Tuesday and Friday. It was as if a part of me intended to deal effectively with any objections to dying. I found it hard to resist getting into my car and asphyxiating myself with carbon monoxide.

"What would that accomplish?" Mac probed.

"Relief from Pain with a capital 'P'. I'm afraid someday I'll get into my car, and I won't come out."

"Your life is in peril. I need to see you twice a week. I can help you deal with your pain."

On the weekend prior to my next appointment with Mac, David drove through the countryside on our way to a favorite restaurant in Oak Glen. While we paused at a stop sign, I looked across to a nearby hillside where I saw a male donkey, with his enormously long penis, attempting to mount a female donkey. I had a deeply profound revulsion, which left me feeling ill.

At my next session with Mac, my body began to tremble as I talked. With the trembling came the remembrance of the donkey on the hillside. I started telling the story to Mac, but when I said, "I saw a donkey with this incredible erection," the trembling in my body took complete control. The center of my body just below my waistline felt as if my intestines were being twisted and twisted. At the same time, I felt that something was pushing down and against my middle area; my jaw shuddered rhythmically. Saliva poured out of my mouth along with strange vocal sounds, no words, only sounds. I remember I felt deformed; my left arm flopped as if spastic. Then all activity suddenly ceased. For a moment I was calm and clear, but then fear along with trembling that resembled "cold chills" came over me followed by crying. I became, I thought, the small child of Jarbidge. I remembered this young crying child from an earlier therapy session. It was unsettling to have such a profound body experience, my very first.

"What is your understanding of what happened to you last week?" Mac asked at our next session.
"I think I was sexually molested as a very young girl. The size of the erection on the donkey tapped that memory."
"I have the same hypothesis," Mac said.
"I'm thinking it might have happened in Jarbidge, Nevada. Lots of drunken miners knew my sister and I were left alone. It could also have happened in Larned. Mom had a lot of drunken parties with men coming and going. Both these towns have always stood out from the other places I lived."
"You have been a very abused child," he said. "Do you recall the article I gave you to read after the fragmented ego states started coming out in session?" Mac asked.
"The one on Multiple Personality?" I questioned.
"Yes, that's the one. Multiples tend to be highly intelligent, perceptive, and sensitive. I see these qualities in you. While we've determined that the label of multiple personality is not correct for you, I believe your fragmented ego states are a result of dissociation. Would you be interested in listening to Pia Mellody on a cassette tape discussing dissociation and the kind of

body experience you've had? I think it will give you a better understanding of what you're going through."

I eagerly took the offered tape. Although Mac had left his teaching position at the university to become a full-time therapist, he continued to be a teacher in our therapy sessions. This approach helped me tremendously. I listened to the tape very carefully, then listened again to make detailed notes:

"Children whose major caregivers unintentionally inflict harm on them revert to different defense mechanisms." Of the six methods listed, I identified strongly with the defense mechanisms of "forgetting." I reviewed them:

The automatic forgetting of material too painful to remember.

The conscious forgetting of experiences too painful to remember.

The dissociating from the experience.

"Of the three types of forgetting, dissociated memories are the hardest to retrieve. Dissociation is a very, very, very special process," the voice on the tape said. I wrote it down. "The abuse is so overwhelming, so profound, the child believes she is going to die. This defense is usually reserved for profound sexual abuse. The child splits off from the experience and goes away to a different place. One place the child can go is to the ceiling, where she becomes an unfeeling observer of what is happening to her. The most severe place the child goes, because she believes she is going to die, is to a black hole or black tunnel. In this place, the child can no longer see, smell, or hear. In this defense, the data is no longer available. She is *gone* from herself. If the child uses dissociation a lot as her means of survival, she can be without any history or have long periods of no memory."

The next thing I heard on the tape made a tremendous impression on me, "The body seems never to forget in spite of the mind forgetting." I thought in amazement: the body itself has a memory! The speaker on the tape called it *body memory* and described it as "a sudden, overwhelming unusual experience happening in your body that has no explanation. Body memory occurs when the body is trying to surrender memories that have been stored in the unconscious mind as a result of the process of dissociation. Age regression can occur as the body memory begins to surface, that is, the person regresses to the age when the memory happened."

Never before had I been exposed to the idea that memory was anything but consciously stored information that could be recalled. Regarding body memory, my experience preceded my knowledge of its existence. I didn't need to be convinced that body memory is real. My experience underscored its truth.

Pia Mellody described a second type of memory called "feeling memory, which is a sudden, overwhelming feeling experience. Four different feeling realities are usually involved: Anger, Fear, Pain, Shame." I was surprised to learn that feelings of worthlessness are associated with shame.

Many times, I had experienced what I called an "emotional flooding." My feelings drowned my thoughts like rising waters, flooding my mind with an inability to think. I had no way of knowing that I was experiencing a feeling memory until I heard it described on the tape. "Body and feeling memories start coming up in someone who has dissociated a lot. Body and feeling memories are two experiences one can use to retrieve personal history, forgotten memories difficult to retrieve."

"Why is it important to retrieve my history? I wondered. Then the voice on the tape supplied the answer. "Important in the process of healing is to get your history straight. Write and talk about your history: 'This is what happened to me…' Include the feelings that go with what happened. Do this without defending, without minimizing, without denying, without deluding yourself. The process of getting your history straight is not about blaming others. Therefore, allow the account of your history to be free of judgment against yourself or others. Avoid comparing your history with the history of others." Years earlier I had heard similar words of wisdom on the importance of getting my history straight as part of my healing process. I had already begun trying to organize the chaos of my personal history.

"David, the information on this tape is tremendously enlightening. I feel more hopeful now, maybe courageous even in facing whatever comes next."

"We're a team, we can do it together," he assured me.

"I wouldn't want to go through this without you, I couldn't. I don't think we could do this without Mac. I think he is a superior therapist. I'm fortunate that Art told me about him."

"Aren't you forgetting someone?" David smiled.

"Hmm. Who have I forgotten?" David pointed a finger upward.

"God? I didn't mean to leave Him out! Without Him, I couldn't go through any of this!"

I didn't know at the time of my first body memory that more would follow. The information on the tape relieved me from the fear of the unknown, but not the terror of the body memories themselves. At least now I understood what was happening to me. Mac and I worked to put the dissociated pieces of myself together, and to shine light into the dark recesses where trauma memories too painful to remember were tucked away, waiting to become known.

Chapter 43

California
November 1988 – January 1989

On November sixteen, Larry responded to my lengthy letter of October twenty-second. As I took his letter from the envelope, I was intrigued: he uses the same kind of paper as Mom, I mused, as I looked at the small piece of paper with its large spaces divided by inked lines.

Dearest Sis,
Sorry about late letter. I'm not much of a writer. I can't put into words how I felt when I read your letter. It really touched me. We had a hard time keeping tears down.

Not sure when we will be able to come down. Maybe after New Years, hope it's not too late.
Boy the pictures were really great.

Thanks for Bud's address not sure what I'm going to do.
My work has slowed down. Sure glad.
Well better close if I am ever to get this in mail.
  Love much – Larry

I folded the letter safely away, not understanding the delay in his coming. I had considered the possibility that he wouldn't even come when almost a month passed before he responded. But his letter renewed my hope. He will come, I told myself, eventually.

"Mom, Larry can't come until January or later," I said on my next visit. Despite her bout with memory loss, she hadn't seemed to forget that she was waiting to see the son she had last seen forty-seven years ago.

A few days after I read Larry's letter to my sister, she called. "My house needs some stuff done before Larry comes, but I don't have the money," she began. "I thought of refinancing it." She hesitated, then said: "I don't want to go to the bank alone."

"I'll go with you," I offered.

When I got there, she was nervous, "I'm not good at this kind of thing."

"Don't worry. I've had a lot of bank dealings related to real estate. We'll get through it together."

After the loan officer explained the process, Verneda turned to me and said, "I'd like to apply for the loan, but I don't have the two-hundred and fifty-dollar application fee. Could you lend me the money?"

"David and I can lend you the money, but we'll need to get it back. We spent thousands getting Jennifer to New England then setting her up in an apartment," I explained.

"You'll get your money back. If the loan doesn't go through, they'll refund your money and I'll give it to you. If it does go through, I can pay you back from that," she assured me.

"I don't qualify for the loan by myself. I'm getting the application fee back from the bank," she said to me six weeks later. I offered to help her in other ways, but she didn't respond. By the first of November, she had a new plan. "Can I borrow the two-hundred and fifty-dollars the bank gave back to me?"

"For how long?" I asked.

"Oh, about 40 years," she said flippantly.

"I'll talk with David about it and get back to you." Obviously, she wasn't concerned about what I said when we lent you the money, I thought. I didn't confront her but listened as she kept talking.

"I'm going up to see our dad, he's gonna give me a car." She hit a soft spot.

"I've tried to tell you before that I never knew Vern as a father. I don't consider him my dad," I said emphatically.

"Well," she continued, "I'm gonna see him and stay awhile then drive my car home.

"How are you getting to San Francisco?" I asked.

"On the train."

The morning she was to leave, I called her. "David and I have decided give you the two-hundred and fifty dollars as our Christmas gift."

"Oh, thanks," she said. "I'm so glad you called. This is scary. I'm shaking."

"Well, be sure to call me so I know how you're getting along," I urged her.

Four days passed; I heard nothing from her. I got Vern's number from her daughter. "Operator, I want to make a person-to-person call." I heard the number ringing. "Hello," Vern answered, then Verneda came on the phone.

"Haven't heard from you. How is it going for you?" I asked.

"Fine," was her first word, followed by something about the car Vern had given her. Then she asked, "Do you want to talk to Dad?"

"No. I was concerned for you and wanted to know that everything is going well."

When I hung up, I felt hurt. Why didn't she call me? Why can't she respect my position with Vern and not impose her agenda on me? I had not healed enough to separate myself from my sister and appreciate her condition.

Verneda returned home safely in the used car Vern had bought for her. "On Saturday I drove out to see George in Anaheim Hills to show him my new car," she said when I called her. "I'm gonna go to Lake Elsinore to show it to Mom and Norm." She didn't offer to drive to Redlands to show it to me. Seeing the car didn't matter to me; I cared more about how she was relating to me.

"I've just been talking to our dad..." she started but I didn't let her finish.

I couldn't believe she said, "our dad." With a firm voice and words chosen to try once again to make my point I said to her, "You knew Vern as your dad, but I never knew him. I never called anyone Dad or Daddy. He didn't live with us after I was born. I never had a father. When I think of my family, it is **Mom** and **you** and **me**." I was so focused on my own need for her to hear me that I didn't once consider why it was so important to her that I think of Vern as my dad, my father.

At first Verneda cried when I confronted her with the truth, then she got angry. I thought she was going to hang up on me. Purposely, I softened my voice as I tried to comfort her when I said, "I know you remember him as your father and you love him, but I never knew him as my father."

We managed to end the conversation civilly. But when she called in the future, I was no longer as emotionally available or as helpful as I had been. I sent her a Christmas card, but I didn't hear from her. I was determined, however, to keep the channels between us open until Larry came.

Unfortunately, I was unable to consider what my finding Larry might have awakened in her. This probably motivated her behavior. I never thought about how it might make her feel that I was able to do what she wasn't. She may have resented me for being the one to find him. Our drunken mother had placed on her the burden of finding Larry, repeatedly reinforcing it over the years of her youth. I mistakenly thought she would feel grateful to me for relieving her of that burden, but she expressed no such feelings. I hadn't thought either of how she felt about baby Buddy, Jr., who had vanished from her life when she was seven, now coming back as an adult named Larry. I hadn't thought about it because I was too swallowed up in my own effort to survive.

New Year's came and with its passing, Larry and Sherry finally arrived in Southern California. "There they are," I said in excited anticipation as I looked out my kitchen window. I watched them slowly make the U-turn by our home at the end of the cul-de-sac, but incredibly, they kept going. "But they're not stopping!" I called to David.

I ran out of the house, calling to them, "Wait! Wait!" The motor home came to a stop. Sherry leaned out of the window on her side, "I didn't bring your phone number and wrote down the wrong number for your address."

"But you're here now," I said, my heart filled with joy. "Come in and let's have something to drink before we go to see Mom."

After a bit of small talk, I said to them, "I haven't told Mom or Verneda you might come today just in case you didn't make it. I'm trying to think what would be best for Mom. She had a small stroke in November, and she has been quite sick lately from her last chemo treatment. It might be best for her if we just go without calling first. What do you think, Larry?"

Larry looked at Sherry, "What do you think?" he asked.

"Might be a good idea just to go on out so she doesn't get anxious waiting for us," Sherry answered.

"And I haven't called Verneda. We could call her now or wait until we get out there," I said.

"Let's keep it simple," Sherry suggested as she looked at Larry.

"All right, we can call Verneda after we get out there," I agreed, thinking that this might unintentionally fuel the already existing tension between Verneda and me.

"Mom, look who's here," I said as I came into the fifth wheel with Larry right behind me, "It's Larry!" As she remained seated on the sofa, her face displayed an array of changing emotions while her eyes stayed fixed on Larry. He went to her and for a moment embraced her. No gush of emotion, no flowing tears came from my mother.

"Norm, this is Larry," I said. The two shook hands.

"Here," Norm indicated, "Have a seat." He got out two folding chairs that he placed across from the sofa where Larry and Sherry sat. Norm talked to Larry about truck engines. Mom was silent as she continued to focus on Larry. Then without a word, she got up from the sofa, crossed over to him, and kissed his cheek. Her face touched his as she whispered something to him. Then she walked past him and into her bathroom.

I sat there dully trying to imagine what Mom or Larry's needs might be. My mind drifted to what I imagined my needs might be in this situation as Norm and Larry continued talking about engines. If I were my mom, I would want time alone with my son to talk about whatever my heart had waited so long to tell him. If I were Larry, I would want my mom to myself to ask all the unanswered questions I had carried for so long. I don't know what Mom or Larry's needs were because none were expressed.

I got up from the sofa. "I'm going to call Verneda," I said as I reached for the phone. In less than an hour, she arrived to meet the brother she had last seen when she was seven. Instead of words spoken in tenderness after saying "Hello" to Larry, she grumpily said to him, "You have *another* sister, you know!" She turned to me with a hateful look and a tone of voice to match. "Did you call Glenda?"

Oh, I thought to myself, she's *really* angry. "No, I didn't call Glenda. Glenda can meet Larry later. She wasn't in Jarbidge with us," I retorted without emotion. In our growing up years Verneda was always the one in control. Now I could see that she didn't like not being in control of Larry's visit, as shown by her anger and antagonism toward me. I felt anxious.

In a short while, the tension eased when Sherry stood up and suggested, "Why don't you all sit next to your mom, and I'll take your picture." Larry sat next to Mom on the sofa with Verneda on her other side and I sat on the floor at Mom's feet.

"Take one more," someone requested.

Verneda, Larry, Edna
Vernetta

"Would you like to go to lunch with us?" I asked Mom and Norm.

"You go on," Mom said. "I'm a little tired."

"We'll come back after lunch," I told her and kissed her good-bye.

In the café booth, Larry and I sat on one side with Sherry and Verneda on the other. "You know, Larry," I began as I pointed to Verneda, "She's the one who took care of us in

Jarbidge when you were a baby, and I was about four." Larry nodded slightly. Verneda talked about Jarbidge.

"When are you going back," she asked him after the topic of Jarbidge had been exhausted.

"Probably leave tomorrow," Larry told her.

"Wish you could come to my place and meet my family," she said.

"Maybe next time," he said, "when I can bring my kids for you to meet."

I noticed her disappointment. "They aren't going back until tomorrow. Do you want to come to our place tonight with some of your family?" I asked Verneda.

She brightened up a bit, "Yeah, maybe we can do that." In the almost twenty years I had lived in Redlands, I couldn't remember even once that she had come to visit me. It was I who always went to her.

After lunch, we went back to spend more time with Mom but in my opinion, nothing happened. Maybe more happened than I thought but sitting on the porch watching Norm smoke falls into the category of nothing as far as I'm concerned.

I wasn't sure what Mom was thinking or what she wished would happen, but she did nothing and said very little. Had she imagined anything about this meeting with Larry? I wondered. We just sat there. Mom pleasantly responded to anything Sherry said, but emptiness hovered over us as we sat.

"We'll try to get down this way again," Larry told Mom when we got ready to leave. "I'll bring some of my family with me next time."

"Oh," Mom said, "That'd be nice."

On the way home I told Larry, "I'm grateful for your being kind to Mom. If only you knew how special it was that she came to you with a kiss. I was deeply moved by her expression of love for you."

Larry and Sherry nodded but didn't say much. A deeper exchange would have been greatly satisfying but neither one spoke to fill the vacant pause.

Eventually, words of relief from my heart filled the emptiness. "The chapter is finally closed now that you've come to see her. It probably marks the end of her longing after you. She's seen you and held you at last. Maybe now she can be at peace. It's a great gift you've given her. And my sister? She's finally free from the promise she made to find you."

Verneda arrived with two of her daughters and one young grandson in the early evening. We filled the living room with laughter and conversation. The next morning, strong winds blew so hard that it was reported that semi-trucks were being blown over by the Santa Ana winds coming through the Cajon Pass.

"It isn't safe for us to leave in this wind. Is it okay if we stay until it lets up?" Larry asked.

"Sure. That'd be great!"

"Did they leave?" my sister asked when she called later that morning.

"No, they aren't able to leave because of the strong winds," I explained. "They may be able to leave later today."

David and I took them on our usual morning walk in the Redlands hills. Later I gave them a tour of our small but lovely town.

When we got back home, the phone rang. It was Mom. "Verneda said they're still there. Why are they at your place?"

I explained to Mom about the wind, and we talked briefly about how she was doing. "I'll call to let you know when they leave," I told her.

"Would you like to look at some pictures?" I asked Larry and Sherry. They said yes but I thought it lacked heart. About that time, the phone rang.

"Have they gone yet or are they still there?" Verneda demanded.

"They're still here."

"They should be spending the time with Mom!" she complained, with an edge to her voice that I knew well.

"That would be nice, but Larry said it's too dangerous to drive the motor home in these high winds. I wish he could drive over to spend the day with Mom, but the winds are so strong he can't leave the area."

I guess she doesn't believe we're having dangerously strong winds, I thought. And why does she keep calling? I wondered. She acts as if I've done something wrong. She was in a huff when she said good-bye. Anxiety filled me to the brim.

"Looks like I'm in trouble with my sister," I said to Larry and Sherry.

"Oh?" Larry said.

"Yeah, she thinks you should be with Mom instead of with me," I said as I handed him a picture of Mom when she was younger. "I want you to see what she looked like when she was a beautiful young woman," I told him.

"Yes, she was pretty," he said briefly. I handed him more pictures, but I sensed he wasn't really interested.

"If there are pictures you'd like copies of, I'll get them for you." He made no indication that he had a desire for even one of them. I put the pictures away.

"We're gonna go take a rest in the motor home," Larry said.

"I'll fix us a salad and some lasagna while you rest."

I was nervously putting together the lasagna when the phone rang. My sister was on the phone again, even more irritated that Larry was still at my house. It was as if big sister was telling me, "You are breaking the rules by having him at your house." I allowed her badgering to make me miserable.

My sister didn't seem able to understand that Larry couldn't drive his motor home out of our area because of the danger. He couldn't drive to Lake Elsinore even if he wanted to. By the time Larry and his wife left the next morning, I was as wilted as the salad from dinner the night before.

Important information, that I lacked at the time, might have given me an understanding of my sister's behavior. Many years later, I learned that the lifestyle we choose can enhance or negatively impact our ability to reason. Apparently, the frontal lobe of the brain is the control center of our judgment, reasoning, intellect and will. These important functions of our brain can be compromised by the use of marijuana as well as alcohol, caffeine, nicotine, and drugs. All of these were in my sister's system at one time or another in different combinations over a period of many years. Maybe that's why she couldn't understand the reason Larry was still with me.

Chapter 44

California
January 1989

After listening intently as I related the details about Larry's visit, Mac said, "Larry's visit reawakened the relationship dynamics that once existed between you and your sister."

"You mean Larry with me instead of her violated old unspoken relationship rules?" I asked. Mac nodded.

"Well, I *felt* like I was breaking rules, but I didn't understand why. Something was making me very anxious," I said.

"You took up the same role you had with her when you were a child. She probably sees herself as the dominant one in your relationship," Mac added.

Old relationship dynamics; I hadn't thought of that. That helps explain why my sister was so upset when Larry was with me. I didn't understand her animosity and I didn't understand why it made me feel so anxious. I left the session grateful to Mac for the insight he gave me.

The next morning, I called Verneda, determined to get past the tension between us. Experience had taught me that it was better to face an uncomfortable situation than pretend that it didn't exist.

"We're in a crisis. We need to talk," I told her. It was my indirect way of saying, I'm willing to work things out if possible but I feel like shutting you out of my life.

"We're in a crisis?" she snarled back. "You mean *you're* in a crisis!"

"I'm trying to tell you that we need to deal with the tension between us."

"You're the one that's tense. You feel guilty because you kept Larry to yourself," she sneered.

"That's not the way it is," I said softly. "Mac says we've fallen into our old ways of relating."

"What do you mean fallen into old ways of relating?" she asked somewhat more calmly.

"When Larry came and stayed with me it upset you," I began.

"It didn't upset me!" she claimed loudly before I could say anything else.

"Well, I'm trying to explain, but I guess this isn't working."

"Whose fault is that?" she snapped back angrily then hung up on me.

Just like Mom. Hang up on me and maybe I'll disappear, I muttered as I put the phone back on the receiver. I didn't call her back. I hope she doesn't call Mom to vent her anger, I thought. Mom's so sick. Verneda didn't call me back.

I took no further action in her direction. Instead, I went to the university campus to pick up a class schedule. This led me to a discovery, a method to help knit together the remaining separated conflicted fragments of myself. I shared my discovery with Mac in a session two days after my sister had hung up on me.

"Mac, I've come up with a way to work with the personality fragments that still remain to be integrated."

"What would that be?" he asked with interest.

"The Gestalt Method of 'chair conversations': I've expanded it to a larger number of chairs, and I call it a 'committee meeting.'"

"Go on," Mac encouraged.

"Even though I function now from mostly my core personality, I continue to experience myself as split into parts, not as many as there used to be, but each part seems to want or need something different."

"Would you like to tell me about your committee meeting?"

"I decided to have a 'committee meeting' where each fragmented ego state has her own chair where she sits to express her desires, wants, and needs to the other committee members."

"Have you had a committee meeting yet?" he inquired.

"Yes, I have!" I said eagerly. "Yesterday I had a conflict I tried to resolve: Take classes at the university this quarter vs. Take no classes at the university this quarter."

"Tell me how it went," Mac said.

"I sat in a chair and waited patiently. A confident mature voice said decisively, 'I want to take two classes: the Dickens and the Shakespeare courses.' I gave her the name of English Lit. When she finished, another voice started to express a conflicting desire, so I moved to a different chair.

In a soft voice she said, 'I would like to take the Children's Literature course.' She wasn't pushy in her request but seemed gentle, with almost a spiritual aura. I gave her the name of Children's Lit. Right after Children's Lit had expressed her desire, I experienced fear and so I moved to a new chair.

As I heard myself speak in a childlike voice, it struck me that this is a frightened child. She was crying and saying, 'I can't go to school late.' She talked of being frightened to go late to the classes we were thinking of taking and cried, 'Please don't make me.' I gave her the name of Frightened Child.

Frightened Child gave way to one who energetically jumped out of the chair, went, and stood by my desk. I gave her the name of Desk Person. 'Fuck School!' she yelled crudely. I became a shocked observer of myself. I never use language like that because it repulses me. I was mystified for a time until later I thought, that's the way my sister talks and feels. This seemed like my sister in me, expressing her hatred for school! I love school. Desk Person flipped into the attitude, 'I don't want to think about it.' This trait also typified my sister's approach to life."

I stopped talking. Mac sat quietly as if waiting for me to continue. "What do you think?" I asked him.

"You've taken a major step toward integration. Quite creative of you," Mac began. "We've talked before about how a personality can take on characteristics or traits of close family members. You may be accurate in your conclusion about Desk Person. I encourage you to continue this process. It seems to be working for you. Keep me in the loop."

"It's hard to keep track of what each one said so next time, I'm going to record the meeting. Also, I thought I'd keep the names I gave them at this first meeting. The names are rather silly, I suppose, but at least it's a way of identifying each one."

"Naming each one is important because they present as individuals with separate needs. Identification by name helps to separate the characteristics of each. It is important to facilitate communication between each one. Conflicts between them will be resolved. In this way, integration will eventually be achieved." Mac's affirmation not only encouraged me, but I also became more self-accepting in this strange experience of myself.

Within days, I called a committee meeting for the second time, recorder in hand. Larry's visit had thrown me into an emotional turmoil, especially regarding my sister. The internal chaos pushed at me relentlessly. I wanted release from the torment of the pain I felt. After the meeting, I transcribed the recording:

Neutral: We need to make a decision regarding cutting Verneda and Mom out of our life. If we hold onto Mom, she'll keep us connected to Verneda.

Desk Person: I want you guys to leave me alone. I'm sick and tired of your agendas. I want you to just bug off. I don't want to think about it.

Children's Lit: I think the ideal thing to do is to try to keep the door open. Seems to me that's the healthiest thing.

Eng Lit: (firm voice, almost angry, but very determined)
We have tried keeping the door open and it doesn't work. You see what happened to you. They keep interfering in our lives, and we can't get anywhere except just deal with mother and deal with Verneda. Keeping the door open does not work. I want to cut them out. I want the phone number changed. I want them out of my life. I'm sick and tired of wasting time. We have lost almost two years.

Children's Lit: I don't feel that we've wasted our time. I feel we've been able to heal a lot. I mean it seems like we were going in all kinds of directions before and so many of us weren't wanting to go in a direction one of us would choose. What we've been doing is going out and visiting mother, we've been in therapy, and I think we've learned a whole bunch about ourselves. I think a lot of healing has taken place. If you cut them off, I think it's going to hurt all of us. I think we're going to feel really bad. We'll be the bad guy again.

Frightened Child: I'm scared. I want to take care of my mommy. I feel real bad if you do this. (crying) I'm frightened. (She began sobbing intensely. I felt very sick.) I'm sick. I'm so sick. (I began to have deep, repeated dry heaves as if vomiting. Massive amounts of saliva kept filling my mouth.)

Neutral: I don't know who is telling you, Frightened Child, but someone said, "You always feel frightened." Who said that? I think it is Desk Person.

Desk Person (disgust, repulsion) I'm sick of you **aaalwaaaaays** being frightened and scared. It doesn't make any difference what we try to do, you are always scaaaaared, you're always friiiigh**Tened.** You want to hide.

Neutral: I don't feel that we're going to accomplish anything by being unkind to each other. You meet things head on by saying "fuck you." She's a frightened child. She's been badly damaged. She has good reason to be frightened. I think you need to be more understanding of her. I can appreciate your impatience, but I would like for you to be more understanding.

Neutral paused. During that pause, I had a very important realization, one of those "Ah Ha!" moments. My mother and my sister showed rejection, contempt, and disgust when as a child I expressed feelings of need or fear or sadness or hurt.

Neutral: One of you is saying that we need to cut these people out of our lives, another is saying let's keep the door open. English Lit said, "We tried to keep the door open and look what happened to us when Larry came." I agree with you, it was very painful. The Child took over and we simply weren't able to function very well.

Neutral continued: When I said, we need movement in our lives, I meant that we need something going besides seeing Mom and besides focusing on Verneda. My position would be somewhat supporting of the one that says, "Let's keep the door open." At the same time, let's try to find a way to get movement going and see if that works.

English Lit held to her position that she wanted them out of our life. Children's Lit reminded her that "Those people who mistreated us are still not well and we are much better off than they are. There won't be close contact anymore, not since Larry's come." Frightened Child sobbed as she expressed her need to be loved by Larry, that the two of them could be family and she wouldn't be alone. Neutral reminded her "We do have David, Jennifer, Lizzie and Marc who love you."

Someone said, mournfully, "Nobody's been able to give me what I need. I'm an empty pit longing after parents who will never love me. I *needed* parents that love me! I need parents who care about me! But that's not going to happen because they've *never* been there for me. I *know* Mom never loved me. Vern wasn't even in the picture. I don't care what the rest of you want. I checked out a long time ago. I say let em all go to hell. I hate their guts. I hate their guts."

"Mac," I said at my next session, "I had another committee meeting. I'm in agony about my sister. I figure the only way I can get rid of the pain is to get her out of my life. But that means Mom needs to go too because I'll keep hearing about Verneda from her and vise-versa. Mom seems to be doing well. She's lived longer than the doctor expected. As long as Norm is with her, I think she'll be fine."

"There are other ways we can deal with the pain. As much as possible, it will be better to work through this instead of shutting these people out of your life," Mac suggested. Mac had made it clear that the decision was up to me. I already favored the idea of keeping the door open, despite the strong temptation to walk away.

"A sobbing child who needs to take care of mother spoke up at the meeting. It upset me," I told him.

"Let's see if we can talk with her," Mac suggested.

I sat relaxed in my chair, head down. We didn't have to wait long. "I want to take care of my Mommy. I feel bad when I see her hurt, like when she got drunk, fell against a stove, and burned her arm real bad. I want to take care of her."

"What needs to happen so you can take care of her?" Mac asked.

"I need to get these people away from my Mommy," the child said. I knew she was talking about the many men who came and went in our lives. I knew she was talking about the drinking people who surrounded her.

Each time the child made a statement, Mac asked the same question. "And then what needs to happen next?"

"I will put my arms around my Mommy and hug her." There was a pause and sadness came into her voice as she cried softly, "But she pushes me away and I know she doesn't love me."

"And then what needs to happen next?"

The child is crying as she says, "I need a Mommy and a Daddy who will love me and want me."

"Can the Mommy and the Daddy comfort the child who is feeling so bad?" Mac asked.

"There is no Mommy and Daddy to comfort me," the child said as if to set Mac straight. "I want to run away," the child sobbed.

"And then what needs to happen next?"

"I'll run away to school. My teacher loves me, and my friends are there," the hopeful child answered.

"And then what needs to happen next?"

"I need to grow up so I can take care of myself."

"And then what needs to happen next?"

"I need to earn a lot of money, so I won't need anyone."

"And then what needs to happen next?"

"Nothing needs to happen next," the child said quietly.

Does one need time or distance to perceive what is too close for a clear perception? It was months or years later that I was able to comprehend what the child had given me that day in Mac's office toward an understanding of my own behaviors.

During the painful period of dealing with my mother, dying of cancer, and addressing the difficult relationship I had with my sister, I felt a need to take classes. I was literally "running away to school" to escape the painful reality I felt regarding them. They triggered the childhood pain of my dissociated, fragmented self. Additionally, by badgering myself to prepare for a career and to generate income, I was trying, unconsciously, to satisfy the need of the child who said, "I need to earn a lot of money, so I won't need anyone."

One morning a week later, toward the end of January, I felt an urgent need to get dressed and to get out of the house. I can't stay here feeling like this, I said to myself. "Mary Ann cleans today. I drove the few blocks to Marc's. Marc came into our lives around 1974 when John, the one who went on my first return trip to Larned, invited him to join our Bible study group and attend church with us. During the early months of our becoming acquainted, Marc made no effort to hide the grief he had suffered at the loss of his beloved who had returned to Italy when her visa expired. Small in stature and pleasantly relaxed in manner, Marc brought an intellectual richness to our lives. Despite my dislike of him in the beginning, and an age difference of fifteen years, a slender thread of friendship developed into an enduring relationship.

"I'm surprised you're still here," I said when I found Marc home.

"Getting a little late start today," he acknowledged, smiling at me.

"I'm not feeling very verbal," I told him.

"Unusual for you!" he teased. We both laughed. "What's happening?" he asked encouragingly.

"Well, I feel this 'noise' in my mind, multiple undecipherable sounds all mixed together, creating a feeling of pressure like I'm about to explode. I don't know how else to describe it. I think what's happening was triggered by a card I got from Larry yesterday."

Marc's comforting tones relaxed me, and I began giving way to the "noise." An experience of being swallowed by a frightening darkness overcame me. The "noise" in my mind released itself as sounds pouring from my throat. Undecipherable images appeared in the deepening darkness. I sprang from the couch to avoid the "trip" I felt coming. I ran into the bathroom but there was no escaping it. Fearfully I called to Marc as I collapsed in the hallway, "Help me."

Marc held me as strange, repeated sounds came out of me. I had no awareness of how long we sat on the hallway floor. Eventually, I got up with the intention of walking into the bathroom to get a Kleenex, but my legs gave out and I tumbled to the floor. "Here, let me help you," Marc said gently as he assisted me to the sofa. "I'll get you a blanket." As he covered me, he comforted me with these words, "Remember, I'm only a block away. Call me; I can be home in an instant." The rest of the day, my brain felt as if someone had also covered it with a blanket. I sought refuge in sleep and television.

In the early evening, I was able to review my notes taken from listening to Pia Melody: "The child splits off from the experience and goes away to a different place. The most severe place the child goes, because she believes she is going to die, is to a black hole or black tunnel." At Marc's I had felt swallowed by a frightening darkness. Reviewing Pia gave me an understanding of my disturbing experience. I held tenaciously to this understanding as a lifeline to sanity and healing.

Chapter 45

California
February 1989

"Mac, please help me understand what rules from childhood I'm still living by between me, Mom and Verneda."

"What rules are you aware of?" he asked.

"I know a couple of things. I get uncomfortable when I start to feel happy. When I was happy, my mother didn't like it. I think Mom felt threatened when I was happy. My 'Happy One' went away." Intermittent muscle contractions in my torso made it difficult to talk, but I continued to search for 'rules' that still had power over me.

"Something I think is closely related to the 'Happy One' is what I call the 'Ceiling on my Success.' I mostly rise to mediocrity in what I do. I never seem to get past the 'beginning' stage into the 'advanced' stage of anything."

At this point, the muscle contractions were beginning to feel unmanageable. They began as if the center of my torso had received repeated shocks causing strong contractions that shot from my navel to my vaginal area. I heard myself make mournful, wailing noises. Then came blackness. It deepened until I experienced a state similar to losing consciousness when I was given ether in the second grade.

"Hold onto me," Mac said.

I held onto him but the frightening darkness, the contractions, didn't go away.

"Tighter," Mac urged.

I squeezed my muscles as tightly as I could, and the experience melted away. But it was a brief respite.

The muscle contractions returned, this time without the blackness. It was a strange body trip: muscles tightened and contracted sending my body into what felt like a non-breathing writhing state. From this condition, I experienced myself emerge as a small, cold, naked Child.

Mac put a blanket around me.

"Bad" was there. I don't think I felt I was bad, but maybe the situation was bad. As I cried, wrapped in the blanket, I heard someone in my mind demand, "Don't get 'snot' on that blanket!"

Suddenly I was taken over by an Angry Persona who got up and moved over to the couch, away from the small cold Child. "Shut up!" she demanded of the Child. "I hate your snot-nosed sniveling!" She went on to say in a most nasty way, "I could kill…" She hated the Child. This Angry Persona came suddenly and was quickly replaced by another persona.

I'm unable to name this persona because I remain uncertain who she was. She was genuine, gentle, concerned. She walked as she talked, "We used to be able to control… but it is your fault, Mac, that it is no longer working," she accused gently.

When this persona left me, I was sitting on the sofa in a panic. My eyes were unable to focus correctly, unable to see the room in proper perspective. Although I had never been drunk in my life, a drunken persona appeared. I don't remember what she said. I reminded myself to yield to the process. I reminded myself that whatever happened to me in the past cannot hurt me now; I need not be afraid. I returned to the person I usually am.

"Mac, am I going crazy?"

"This is the reverse of going crazy. This experience is not one that leads to craziness but heals one of the craziness already in the life," he said in the most comforting way.

At the very beginning of our session the following week, a young Child appeared. She sat with her fingers in her mouth. She couldn't look at Mac. Instead, she looked at objects away from him or turned the back of her head to him. She began sobbing, "My Mom puts curls in Nee Nee's hair; I don't get curls."

Another Persona displaced the young Child, charged out of the chair, rushed behind Mac's chair, pointed back to where the young Child had sat, and then screamed in a contemptuous chilling voice, "I hate you; I hate you!" When the episode passed, Mac told me reflectively, "The Child that came today is in terrible pain."

Three days later, David and I went for our usual morning walk. "I feel so grumpy and irritable," I admitted to him. We walked and talked. It helped some but by the time he left for work, and I had bathed and straightened the house, I felt disturbed. Maybe it has to do with Mom, I thought. I had been talking to her regularly and had been driving to see them about once a week. It isn't that I've let her down, I told myself. I was flooded with feelings. Unfortunately, I had forgotten what I learned from the Pia Mellody tape about feeling memory. My agitation and upset increased. I felt totally alone. I decided to go with it rather than resist.

I pulled back the bedspread and lay on the bed, allowing myself to feel my feelings. When the painful experience of aloneness continued, I left a message for Mac to call me; then I called David. I thought it would help to connect with the one I knew loved me unconditionally. I cried into the phone to David. He tried to comfort me, but he couldn't come home. I paged Marc but he didn't respond. I called my sleep-deprived daughter in New Hampshire. We talked and I cried on the phone.

This was a relentless pain, which still held me in its grip despite my calls to my husband and my daughter. I paged Marc again. With a blanket wrapped around me, I wandered from the study to the bedroom crying. The phone rang but I let the answering machine pick it up. I heard Marc say, "I'm on my way over."

When Marc came, I sank down in a comfortable chair wrapped in the blanket. He listened and watched as I drifted between a very young Child and an Adult. The phone rang. Despite my condition I was able to get to the study to answer. As I hoped, it was Mac. As I talked with him, a body memory started coming and I was unable to speak. "Let me speak with Marc," I heard him say.

I stumbled back into the bedroom. As I fell into the chair, my back arched itself painfully, my head went back as if being forced into this uncomfortable position. I had a frightening sensation and I thought I was going to die. "I can't breathe!" I called out desperately to Marc. My back stayed stubbornly arched and I could hardly breathe.

I felt Marc touch my arm. "You're in no danger. Mac said that you had actually lived through this experience at some time earlier in your life." His words comforted me as this frightening body experience continued.

Even though I had my eyes closed, I saw something as if it were placed in front of my eyes. It was blackness with little breaks of light in it. Then I heard myself screaming. When my screaming stopped, I was very cold and crying. The body memory had ended.

Marc held my hand, "Your scream was that of someone in mortal danger." He added, "When you were in your Child, you talked about your sister being mean to you."

Some of my body memory experiences resemble dreams in that one can speculate on their meaning but when trying to exact a specific interpretation, it's like trying to capture a cloud. However, it makes me wonder if there is a connection between this body memory and how Verneda treated me, left in her care when a baby and young child, considering what she said when we were adults: "Children. They won't stop making noise. I want to beat them to death. I feel rage."

I remembered my sister telling me, "I pinched my children, but they don't remember I did it." She was surprised they didn't remember. I have no way of knowing what else she might have done to her children. I have no certainty of what she might have done to me when I was in her care.

What I do know is how I treated my own children. I didn't replicate my mother's behavior. Never, ever did I slap or hit them, nor was I ever tempted to harm them in any way. I rarely experienced anger toward my children but when it came, it was anger expressed by non-degrading, loud verbiage that quickly evaporated.

In the fourth grade, I had made the decision I didn't want to be like my mother. That decision has permeated every aspect of my life although not through an effort to be different, but rather I experienced myself as naturally different from my mother.

As they were growing up, I reminded myself that my children were only *temporarily* children; they would be adults for the majority of their lives. From this point of view, I raised them with the hope that we would become close friends. My hope has been realized.

Chapter 46

California
Late February 1989

Early the next morning, I said to David, " I need to see my sister."

"After yesterday, do you think you're up to it?" he asked.

"It's amazing, but I feel clear and very motivated to make contact with her. I need to meet with her in person to see if we can get through this." Once David was convinced that I was fine, he gave me his blessing. I was out of the house by seven-thirty and in my sister's living room by eight forty-five. I was surprised to find her sleeping on the couch. I touched her stomach.

She woke immediately. When she saw it was me, she abruptly sat up, put on her pants, picked up her cigarettes, then walked to the dining room table where she put down the cup of coffee her daughter Debby handed her.

Excusing herself she said, "I've gotta go to the bathroom." When she came back, she said pleasantly, "Hello, how are you?"

At first, I said, "I'm fine." But then I said, "Well, let me change that to I'm all right."

I sat down at the dining room table across from her. "I came because I didn't want years to go by like it had when Mom hung up on me. "And," I continued, "I don't think we finished our conversation."

"I listened quietly on the phone when you talked," she said, "but when it came my turn, you interrupted me and said I sounded like big sister. I wasn't angry." She paused for a minute, took a sip of her coffee then continued coldly, "Well, maybe I was angry." Silence was my loud response.

"You didn't find Larry by yourself," she said, then paused to take a drag from her cigarette. Smoke and angry words came from her mouth, "You're mean and vindictive."

This hateful accusation riled me. On impulse, I picked up her coffee cup with the intention of throwing coffee on her, but I quickly sat the cup back down, splashing coffee onto the table.

This enraged her. She jumped up and moved behind the chair across from me screaming, "Get out of my house!"

"I'm not leaving" I said calmly.

This irritated her even more. "You need to be in control," she accused me. "You're controlled on the outside but angry on the inside." Then she screamed out the zinger, "I hate you and I have always hated you!"

"Why do you hate me?" I asked. She seemed confused by my question. "I have been nice to you." She scoffed at me. "I gave you money so you could go see your dad," I reminded her.

"Yeah, you've given me a lot of money," she jeered.

"I wrote you a loving letter from New Hampshire." When I mentioned my letter, she opened the sliding door next to where she was standing and ran into the backyard.

Verneda's daughter Debby came in from the kitchen and said to me, "You've upset my mom because you told her you didn't want to see her anymore and hung up on her."

"That's not the way it was, Debby. Your Mom hung up on me and this is between my sister and me," I said as I exited the house to find her.

She was leaning against a little shed with her arms crossed, her head against her arms, sobbing. I approached her and tried to hold her. She pulled away, saying, "Leave me alone."

She moved over to a little bench against the house, sat down and took control of herself. I listened while she talked, primarily about pain with a capitol 'P.' "You've caused me pain since you was three years old!" she exclaimed.

"Since I was three years old?" I repeated. She continued before I could understand what I had done to her at age three. "I loaned you one of my dresses once and then when you got three new ones and I wanted to borrow one, you wouldn't let me." She went on to blame me for losing her job.

"Once you called me at work. I couldn't function so they sent me home," she declared. I said nothing to her but recalled how she hated her job and had deliberately missed many days of work hoping to be fired. The blame was misplaced. I knew I wasn't responsible for the loss of her job.

She mimicked me as saying to her, "We don't have anything in common."

"Must have been years ago if I said that. I don't remember it," I responded cautiously. She admitted that it had been years ago. We truly didn't have very much in common other than the past we shared. The choices we had made took the course of our lives in wildly different directions.

"I'm so sorry for any pain or hurt I've caused you. I'm very sorry. I would never intentionally hurt you or cause you pain," I told her, a truth spoken from my heart.

As she continued her recitation, with so much hatred toward me, it was hard to stay and listen. "You think you found Larry! You didn't do it alone. You needed the things Mom had given me, things I had kept for forty-five years," she declared, stressing "forty-five years."

Forty- five years, I thought, of carrying the burden of a promise to mother to find Buddy, Jr. My mind stopped recording the ugly things she said in scorning my gift to her and to Mom in locating Larry. She refused to give me any credit for finding Larry. She portrayed me as smug and self-righteous about being the one to find him. Her accusations hurt. I listened in disbelief. I had felt very humble about being able to locate Larry and eagerly gave the credit to God, not myself. I could never have done it by myself. She made no mention that I had invited her to come to Twin Falls to share with me in the search for him, and that she had declined the invitation.

"You talked on the phone about competition between us," she said angrily.

"Mac suggested we might have fallen into our childhood roles of competing with each other over Larry," I said.

She said hatefully, "You give Mac the responsibility for what you said. Hell, you been in therapy most of your life." Then out of the blue she said, "I've never been jealous of you." I was dumbfounded. Where did that come from? I asked myself.

She mocked the way I talk. She nastily mimicked what I had said on the phone, "We're in a crisis and we need to talk." "*You*, are in a crisis," she had thrown at me, "not *we*." She had been unable to comprehend what I meant. I thought that if I were to eliminate her from my life, it would significantly impact her, so I wanted to see if we could work through what I called a crisis.

Once again, she mocked the way I had said, "We're in a crisis and we need to talk." "Who in the hell talks like that?" she jeered.

I could have said, "Educated people." But instead, I told her, "I've always offended you and Mom just by being who I am. I am just me."

"I'm just me," she echoed disparagingly. "You think you're better than me." I kept quiet. She continued, "You've ruined *everything*! I was full of joy about Larry and then you called me about being in a crisis. You ruined everything."

Her "full of joy" statement caught me by surprise, because this was the first time she had revealed any feelings about Larry being found. I didn't ask her to elaborate on how I had "ruined everything." I tried to remain calm during her monologue. I could hear and feel her intense hatred for me. I could feel her excruciating pain. I realized I was a large part of her problem and right then, I couldn't be part of her solution, even though I wanted to.

"I guess this isn't going to work," I said to her as I stood up. "I'll be leaving now, and you won't have to ever see me again." She followed me into the dining room. As we stood there for an instant, I looked at her and said, "I hope things go well for you."

"Yeah, sure you do. Who the hell believes that?"

"I love you. I drove all the way from Redlands to see you."

"Well now you can drive all the way back to Redlands," she said chillingly.

It was difficult to leave my sister in so much pain. I was mystified and didn't know what else to do. Why does she hate me so much? I asked myself. I left not ever again wanting to be available as the target for her anger and hatred.

That Saturday morning of February 25, 1989, when I left my sister, I got on the freeway with the intention of returning home. But when I saw the exit that would take me to Lake Elsinore, I took it. An emotional decision, not an intellectual decision, drove me straight to Mom and Norm.

"What are you doing here so early on a Saturday morning?" Norm asked.

"I have something very serious to talk with you about," I answered as I sat down by Mom on the sofa across from Norm.

"I'm on my way home from talking to Verneda. She hung up on me not long ago and I went to try to make it right. She's angry and hateful. I don't want to deal with her anymore."

"Why I can't imagine," Mom said. "What on earth?"

Norm took a long drag on his cigarette, sat there looking at me and said nothing.

"I don't want you to talk to me about Verneda and don't talk to her about me or I'm not going to be able to come to see you any longer."

"I don't want you to stop coming out," Norm immediately said with such sincerity I believed him.

Mom joined in, "If you're here and she comes she can just keep going."

"We don't want to get involved in it," Norm said.

"I agree. That's your best choice."

They assured me they could give me what I wanted, but Mom was upset. Before I left, she started kind of taking my side.

"Now Mom, you don't have all the facts. I think it's a good idea not to get involved. I hope Verneda keeps coming out to do things for you."

"Gettin' our porch and house cleaned was the first thing she ever done for us," Norm said.

"I hope she keeps doing things for you," I told him. I leaned over to give Mom a kiss goodbye, thanked Norm and out the door I went.

Had I thought about it for even a few minutes before I took that Lake Elsinore exit to go to see Mom and Norm, I would have driven straight home. Why involve them? I would have asked myself, knowing it wouldn't do any good for them or for me. But with emotion in the driver's seat, I hadn't made a rational decision.

Chapter 47

California
Late February 1989 – May 1989

"I'm very pleased you went to see Verneda," Mac said quietly at my next therapy session. He continued, "The anger she expressed toward you is most likely a projection of *everything* onto you. She may not be able to relate to you any other way."

"I don't want to give her a chance to vent her anger on me again. I thought she would be so relieved that she didn't have to carry the burden of finding Larry. Instead, she is so resentful toward me.

The subject turned to Larry and an urgent need I felt. "Mac, I want to go to Oregon to see him." Immediately on saying I wanted to see Larry, repeated muscle contractions sent jolts of vibrations through my body. "Oh no," I groaned, "here it comes."

As if a drawstring were pulling me into position, my back arched, and my head hung painfully backward while my body continued to jerk with contractions. I heard myself scream. Words coated in fear dribbled slowly out of my mouth: "I can't breathe," I tried to cry out to Mac.

"I'm here. You're safe," he assured me.

The physical experience eventually melted away; the contractions ceased.

"It's the same as I experienced on Friday, just four days ago, Mac." His soothing words of encouragement followed me as I left his office where I returned to a world dominated by my mother, her illness, and the estrangement from my sister.

After I left Mac's office, I didn't fully understand why I still felt the need to see Larry. However, I was aware that I longed to reverse the many years of separation that had come between us. With no other apparent agenda, I took an immediate trip to see him. Driving north along the California coast, I felt wonderfully free from concerns about Mom and Verneda. When I arrived in Oregon, Larry and Sherry welcomed me as if we had been close friends for years. On returning home I told David, "We had a great time getting better acquainted."

On our way to visit Mom, I told David, "I've decided not to say anything to Mom and Norm about going to see Larry. That trip was for me."

Not long after we arrived, Norm started talking with David about Mom's illness. Sometime during their discussion, Mom turned to me. She had a peaceful tone and a pleasant look on her face as she unexpectedly talked about the past. "I was just thinking about you kids the other day. Verneda couldn't have been more than four or five, just a little thing. I left her to take care of you. I had to leave at about eight and didn't get back until four o'clock. She'd do the dishes and try to take care of things. She was the cutest little thing."

I was almost too stunned to respond when I learned that my mother had left my extremely young sister to care for me, a baby, all day long. I managed to say to her, "It must have been hard for you to leave us and go to work all day."

"Sometimes I'd come home for lunch and check on you. Things were always all right," she said with a sweet smile.

I put on a nice dress the morning of May second for my dental appointment, even though I knew I had an appointment with Mac shortly afterwards. I should be wearing "working clothes," I told myself as I walked to the door of Mac's office. I heard myself say, "But I don't want to work today. I don't want to deal with therapy today." It is a necessity, more than a luxury, to follow my heart's desire whenever possible, but at the time I was unable to give way to my own desire. Instead, I dutifully entered Mac's office.

Eventually Mac and I overcame my resistance to working. My body began to jerk with muscle contractions. Unfortunately, I can't remember the order of events that led to the appearance of a rational suicidal persona who spoke through the turmoil of my moving body. The forgotten events that preceded her appearance may be crucial to understanding what provoked her resolve. She presented as calm, wise, and mature when she said, "I'm resolved to commit suicide because it all seems empty. Nothing is worthwhile."

The following events unfolded like a wild strange dream that makes no sense. I became a small child enclosed in a small dark space. "I must be very quiet," the small child said. "I can't make any noise." I began "throwing up." I went through the physical sensation of vomiting. Mac pushed a wastebasket strategically near. The dry vomiting led to a trembling in my hands. My head shook. "Nobody loves me," I cried in a young child's voice.

As the intensity of the pain increased, another persona emerged who jumped up, threw the wastepaper basket across the room, and yelled, "No, I'm not going to feel that!" She cussed at Mac then fell into a crumpled heap in the chair.

Mac reached out his hand to me, "I want you to shake hands with me that you won't commit suicide until we can talk next week."

I gave it some thought then said to him, "I'm not willing or able to do that."

"I'm gravely concerned for your life. Are you willing to see me this evening at nine?"

When I returned at nine, the body contractions started again. "I don't like this, Mac! Pain of this intensity is private, for my eyes only." What did Mac say that made me willing to allow him once again to witness my agony? I don't remember.

"I need you to shake hands with me that you agree not to commit suicide," he urged once again.

"I can't do that right now, Mac," I repeated as before. I tried to talk it out with him. "I need to be in control during this emotional recall experience. I tried to take care of myself as a child and isn't it natural I would try to take care of myself now as the adult re-experiencing the pain? Also, control is something I had very little of as a child. Adults were always the ones setting up situations. I used whatever emotional or physical means I had at the time to try to take care of myself, to be in control. So why would I give control to you? Don't you see, Mac, suicide hovers over me like a protective wing, a promise of relief from pain. I must hold onto the right to take care of myself, even if it means killing myself to deal with this dreadful situation.

Suddenly, I blurted out a torrent of words to Mac. "My Mom's dying of cancer, I don't know when. I gave up everything two years ago. I don't do theatre, I don't sing. I don't do anything but deal with my garbage in therapy and have these strange body experiences. My daughter is 3,000 miles away and I don't know if she'll come back. I deal with the fear of losing her to this scary guy she's dating that wants to keep her to himself. People who know him tell her he's an angry person. Then there's Larry. Finding him thawed me out. Now I have all these feelings and memories to deal with besides the fact that my sister and I aren't speaking."

Mac was pleasant. He understood but he wasn't happy with my decision not to shake hands; still he was wise. He allowed me the freedom to pass through my crisis without his interference, which in turn made me stronger and closer to forsaking suicide as my solution to pain.

Chapter 48

California
May 1989 – July 1989

With the passing of days came relief from pain. I even accepted my decision not to leave my mother to go to New Hampshire for the summer; Elizabeth would go in my place. The only thing that disturbed my peace was a phone call from Norm around the end of May.

"What are you doin' today?" he asked.

"Why?" I said, "Do you need something?"

"I wanted to let you know Verneda's comin' and she's bringin your **father**." He laughed. "Yeah, **your father's** comin'," he said again, emphasizing "your father" and laughing as he said it. Silently I listened as he goaded me about my father, a point of contention between Verneda and me that she had shared with Norm, I thought. I remained quiet until his laughter turned to silence.

"What time are they coming?" I asked, without revealing the disgust I felt toward Norm because once again he had violated our agreement not to talk to me about Verneda.

"I don't know," he laughed again.

"Why did you call to tell me this?" I asked in a cool firm tone.

"I don't know." Then he laughingly said, "I knew you wouldn't come."

I was silent.

He changed the subject, "The cat's bringin' somethin in."

Riled up emotionally after talking with Norm, I wanted to take action. What do I want to do? I asked myself. I fell into an old rut: Be free of them, done with them! Change my phone number! Stop going to see them! This imaginary fantasy to escape by running away filled me with hope. I wanted to run but I reminded myself of a poster I had seen in Mac's office: "The Best Way Out is Through." With renewed resolve I told myself, I'm not going to run away. I'll stay open and available to them.

I went to sit in the comfy green chair that faced our garden with its blooming jacaranda trees. The purple blooms against lacy green leaves distracted me momentarily from the question, "Should I go see Vern and Verneda today at Mom's?"

I gazed into the garden as I thought of when I had seen Vern in my lifetime. We met for the first time in Salt Lake City the summer before my sixth grade; I visited him at Thanksgiving when I was a ninth grader; Aunt Mary and Uncle Herman took David and me to see him shortly after we were engaged. I really didn't get to know him on those short visits, I admitted to myself. I recalled visiting him and Mae about once a month when I had the opportunity to become acquainted with him during the two years we lived in Berkeley, with no resulting bond of connection. It was an unemotional decision I made not to go to Lake Elsinore to see Vern, like trying on a dress and then simply returning it to the rack. But someday, I told myself, I want to hear his side of the mom and Vern story.

"I'm gonna have prostate surgery," Norm began. "Can you take care of mother?"

"Yes, you can count on me. Do you know when?"

"July twelfth, I go into the hospital," he answered.

"I guess that's not quite two weeks away. Plenty of time to plan ahead," I said, more to comfort myself than him.

During the seven days that followed Norm asking me to take care of Mom, blackness like night came and went. Daily I fell onto my bed as if drugged, where sleep held me comfortably hour after hour. My body, devoid of energy and drive, moved heavily through the house when I awoke. The truth of my reality, that I was surrounded with love, safety, and beauty, was illusive.

On the eighth day I struggled to gain insight into my condition, which I knew had been provoked by the anticipation of taking care of my mother. I searched for answers in my fragmented self, eventually arriving at a conclusion: Frightened Child is afraid of being alone with Mom! Frightened Child's needs are being overridden, not only by the Adult who wants to help Mom and Norm, but by Little Child who loves mother and *wants* to take care of her. With this insight, my symptoms gradually subsided, but the day I started taking care of Mom, a sharp-edged residue of anxiety accompanied me.

"Be sure to take mother's nightgown and her pillow when you go to Redlands tonight," Norm told me.

"I'm getting in back. It'll be too hard for you to get outta the back," Norm told Mom when he got into the back seat of my El Dorado.

I glanced at Mom as I drove us to the hospital. Her jaw was tight, and her lips stretched thin. Wow, Mom is angry about something, probably doesn't want to go to my house, I guessed. But I was relieved that her anger seemed to vanish when she became involved in the admitting process.

Norm was signing the final papers when a nurse from surgery came to the doorway. "I'll take you when you've finished, to prep you for surgery." The four of us walked down the hall until the nurse stopped suddenly and opened the door to a room. "You come with me," she ordered Norm as she whisked him into the room, then abruptly closed the door in our faces after a dismissive nod in our direction.

"Mom," I suggested, "Let's go back to your place to wait." I took her hand, but as we started down the hall, I realized Mom and Norm had been separated without any warning.

"Mom, you didn't have a chance to say goodbye to Norm."

She glared at me and in a cold voice declared, "It's *not* goodbye." How had she misunderstood my intention? Of course, this was not a final farewell, as her response seemed to suggest.

"My mother didn't have a chance to say goodbye to her husband," I told the nurse when I found her. "Could she please see him?" She took us past cubicles filled with patients on gurneys.

"You have thirty seconds," the nurse announced with the tone of a drill sergeant as we arrived at the cubicle where a red-faced, disgruntled Norm lay on a gurney. Mom kissed him repeatedly, saying tender things to him in soft tones.

"Surgery is supposed to be at eleven thirty. I gotta wait a long time!" he told me as I kissed his forehead.

"Hang in there. We'll see you later. I'm taking Mom home for a while."

The rhythmic swelling and subsiding of magnified little stresses continued throughout the long day, persisting until we were almost ready to leave for Redlands.

"We need to get the cat before we go," Mom told me. "We'll lock him in the trailer."

"Do you know where he is?" I asked.

"Sometimes he's on the porch. Or he goes down to the neighbors a couple of trailers away."

"I'll look for the cat while you change your clothes, Mom."

I found the cat three trailers down, lying in the grass close to a little black kitten. I called "kitty-cat" and began walking towards him. He moved away and under a trailer. When I saw him come out the other side, I tried to move quickly in his direction. He increased his pace and slipped under a plywood porch. I lost him.

"I found him, Mom, but he wouldn't come."

"Let's go see if we can find him," she suggested. Arm in arm we walked on the slope behind the trailers calling, "kitty-cat" "kitty-cat." But kitty-cat didn't come.

"Mom, you're exhausted. We've been looking for almost an hour. Let's go back. We'll figure something out." I took her back to the fifth wheel and just as we stepped onto the porch, the cat leaped onto it from a different direction and rubbed against Mom's leg. She put the cat inside. I pulled the door shut.

"What a relief," I told her as I placed the key in the lock expecting it to turn. "I can't get the door to lock, Mom," I complained.

"No; you have to latch it from inside. The key don't work."

"Well, if I open the door the cat might get out!"

"Go ask Jerry to come after we're gone. He can lock it," Mom said. After a trip to the neighbor's, we were free at last to leave for Redlands.

"You can sit here at the end of the table," I suggested early the next morning as I sat a plate with pancakes and grapes in front of her.

"Git those things offa there!" she ordered, pointing to the grapes. I obliged. I went into the kitchen and threw the grapes away.

"I don't eat this much food!" she complained when I returned.

"Eat what you want Mom; leave the rest," I told her.

She started eating the pancake. "Hmm, this is good," she said as I sat there wondering why she was so grumpy.

About an hour and a half later, we were on the freeway somewhere near Corona when Mom suddenly started talking. "That sister of yours is out to get Norm," Mom exclaimed in tones of anger mingled with fear.

I had heard her say these exact words on Sunday: "Oh, that sister of yours. She's out to get him," she said, poking the air with her finger. "I could tell you some things." I had gone home on Sunday thinking that Mom meant Verneda was maliciously "out to get" Norm. But mother's intention became clear as we drove through Corona.

"What makes you think Verneda wants to get involved with Norm?"

Mom ignored me. "She's nothing but a pig, a slut! I didn't think anything of it for a long time. They used to talk on the phone. I always tried to go with him, but then Norm went over to her place a couple of times without me. That fellow that used to be our neighbor went."

I recalled Norm and Verneda's early relationship, which amounted to a hateful animosity. I didn't believe that Verneda had any interest in becoming involved with Norm. I felt positive there was no justification for Mom's fear. Something Verneda said to me a few years ago came to mind. "Mom told me when I was still pretty young that she was afraid I'd grow up and take Bud away from her." Mom's fear about losing her man to Verneda had been around a long time, I thought as I puzzled over the question, "What has caused Mom to fear losing Norm to

418

Verneda?" How can I help Mom without expressing my own disbelief? I asked myself.

Mom interrupted my thought. "They talk on the phone. They laughed and joked about the tomato plants and were carrying on over the phone."

"I remember Norm saying he bought Verneda some tomato plants."

"Yeah, and they carry on over the phone! She calls but I don't want to have *nothin'* to do with her. She knows that I'm at your place so she can come and see Norm when I'm not there. She might have been there this morning."

Here it was at long last, the reason she didn't want to leave Lake Elsinore to come to Redlands, the reason for her anger of yesterday and her irritability of this morning. Mom was afraid Verneda would come to see Norm, would make advances in his direction, would take him away from her. Mother had decided that if she could stay in her own place at Lake Elsinore, Verneda would not come to see Norm.

I tried to comfort her, "Mom, she has a job. Even if she didn't, she can't get to the hospital before nine because it's an hour's drive and she hates getting up early. But I'll check with the nurse to see if Norm has had any visitors since yesterday afternoon." I retreated for a time into silence, driving and thinking.

"I wish we were coming to take him home," Mom said as we arrived at the hospital.

"It's Thursday, Mom. He won't be coming home until Saturday," I reminded her as she sat down in the wheelchair, my way of transporting her to conserve her energy. Eagerness and anticipation gave her countenance a younger happy look. As I brought the wheelchair to a stop outside Norm's room, Mom instantly rushed to his side. Kisses and more kisses were exchanged between the two of them.

Mom was so tired by the time we returned to the fifth wheel at noon, she needed rest more than food. "Why don't you take a little nap and I'll go get us some lunch." Fortunately, she took my suggestion.

"Look who's here, Mom; 'kitty-cat!' I said when she woke from her nap. "I've been stepping over and around him since we got back. Are you hungry? I bought us tuna sandwiches and salads for lunch."

"That sounds good," she said, smiling at me.

She can be a sweet woman, I thought. I'm glad to be here for her. She has strength and courage in spite of her illness. Then I remembered yesterday when several times her energy suddenly plummeted, and she went into a frightening state of collapse. "Help her so she doesn't go through that again today," I asked God silently.

"I'll go up and change my clothes; then we can go see Norm."

When Mom returned, she handed me some folded clothes. "Here's some clothes you can put in the car. I want to take them when we go back to Redlands tonight to wear tomorrow." She surprised me when she made the choice to return to Redlands instead of staying the night in Lake Elsinore as I had offered.

"We'll go straight to Redlands after you visit Norm at the hospital. Shall we leave kitty-cat in the fifth wheel?"

"Yeah, he can stay in," she confirmed.

I leaned over to stroke him for the umpteenth time. "I feel sorry that we have to shut him up alone in the trailer."

"He'll be all right," she said.

I picked up kitty-cat and held him when Mom went outside. I turned the lock on the door handle, put the cat back inside and closed the door. "That was a lot easier than yesterday! I said to Mom with a sigh of relief.

"I don't feel very good," Mom told me the next morning.

"Maybe you'll feel better after you eat breakfast," I said, then hugged her and kissed her.

"I'll feel better when Norm gits out of the hospital," she answered.

We drove to the hospital in silence for a while then she started talking again about Norm and Verneda.

"If I die first, Norm will get together with Verneda."

420

"But Mom, Norm loves you so much. I don't think he wants anyone but you."

"He might not go after her, but she'll come after him," she stated helplessly. She continued talking about her concerns, but I felt totally inadequate with no solution to suggest.

Walking from the car to where I had left Mom in front of the hospital, I realized I was exhausted. Only three hours of sleep from eleven until two-thirty and only one more hour of sleep between six and seven. No wonder I feel tired! I told myself.

I wheeled Mom into the elevator. Enclosed inside, I experienced my old anxiety of being trapped in an elevator. How I wish we could take the stairs, I said to myself as I watched the floor indicator. I heard the comforting "ding" as the elevator came to a stop and the doors opened.

"I wanna go home," Norm said, the minute we came into the room.

"What does the doctor say?" I asked.

"Says I can't go home 'til tomorrow."

"I'm going back to the fifth wheel to do a little work," I told him. "Call me when Mom needs to come home and I'll get her.

"What are you gonna do?" he asked.

"None of your business," I said jokingly as I gave him a tiny goodbye kiss, hoping Mom wouldn't think I was "out to get Norm."

I worked as fast as I could to clean the inside of the trailer and then tackled the outside. I was in the midst of sweeping the artificial turf on the deck when the telephone rang. "Mother will be ready to go home by the time you get here," Norm said.

Chapter 49

California
July 1989

"I wanna have my nap here on the sofa. I'm too tired to eat lunch now," Mom said as she lay down after I brought her home from the hospital. I went up to her bed thinking I could rest as well. I was pleasantly drifting toward sleep when I felt something bite me. I changed positions but again something bit me. I searched for the biting vermin but found nothing. After several more times of being bitten, I extracted myself from the infested bed and went to the kitchen to prepare lunch.

When Mom woke from her nap, she looked at me across our lunch plates and said wearily, "I don't know if I can make that drive today."

"I guess you didn't see me put your pillow and nightgown in the car this morning, Mom. We won't be returning to Redlands tonight. We're going to stay right here. I'm tired too and the traffic is terrible on Friday nights. Neither of us has the energy to make the trip." Her eyes expressed tenderness and sweetness. A faint smile of relief softened her weariness.

"I hope we can go back to the hospital now," Mom said later in the afternoon.

"If you're up to it, we can go anytime."

"I want to change my clothes first." With vigor she went up the three steps. I was surprised she could go up to her bedroom, rummage through clothes that were folded or hanging from an old upside-down towel bar, and then come back in a different, attractive polyester top and pants. "I'm ready," she said as she passed by me, filling the room with the fragrance of her perfume.

How lovely, I thought. Age hasn't changed her desire to be attractive to the man she loves. As we turned the last corner on our approach to the hospital I reminded her, "The next time we come, Norm will be going home with us."

"I'll be glad when I have him home," she again repeated what she had said each time we arrived at the hospital.

"Norm, I want to get your Beef Stew recipe," I said shortly after we arrived. "You know I'm a vegetarian, so I don't even know what kind of meat to buy!" We both laughed as he told me where to buy the meat, what kind to buy and step-by-step directions. "Mom and I will stop at the store on our way home." I left the room to call David.

"Honey, we won't be coming back to Redlands tonight. Mom is too weak to make the trip and I'm very tired. Do you want to come out here?

"Well, there's not enough floor space to put sleeping bags in the fifth wheel," David said.

"Maybe we could sleep on the porch in sleeping bags. No, that won't work, too many spiders!"

We both knew in our hearts we wouldn't be together that night, but he said to me, "I'll think about it. Call me back in 20 minutes." When I called him back, I knew the answer before he told me, "I'll stay in Redlands and go with Marc to hear Desmond Ford speak this evening."

Just as I finished talking with David, Norm and Mom came around the corner. "Norm, Mom looks so ill it's frightening!"

"Better get her to the cafeteria for some dinner," Norm said with concern. "Food usually helps her feel better."

"We'll come and say goodbye before we leave," I told him as I wheeled Mom away to the cafeteria.

"I'm going to park you here at the end of the table while I get your food," I explained. She didn't respond. It distressed me to experience her this way. I quickly got some potato salad from the salad bar, a sliced tomato, and a cup of chicken noodle soup. When I got back to the table, she was slightly bent over, moaning softly. I placed the food in front of her. She picked up her fork and pushed the salad around a little. She hardly had the energy for the bite or two of salad she ate.

"Mom, this soup will be good for you. Do you want me to feed it to you?"

"No, I think I can feed myself." She managed to eat the soup.

"Do you want to go back and say goodbye to Norm?"

"YES," she almost shouted at me, "I'll say goodbye even if I DIE."

"It's too difficult to get Mom and the wheelchair into your room, Norm," I told him when we returned. "She still isn't feeling well." He walked across the room to where she sat in the hall. With tear-filled eyes he looked at me before he bent to kiss her. In all my life, I've never seen Norm in tears, I realized. If only Mom could experience Norm's love for her as I have just now, she would never be insecure about losing him to someone else, I thought.

When we got to the car, I helped Mom into the passenger seat. "Rest, Mom. I'll have you home soon," I promised as I reclined her seat, terribly worried about her condition. How had she suddenly become so gravely ill, I wondered. No way will we be able to stop at the grocery store to buy the beef.

"Mom, you wait in the car," I told her when we arrived at the fifth wheel. "I'm going to put kitty-cat in the bathroom, so he doesn't get away from us." By the time I had finished with the cat, Mom was out of the car and almost to the porch.

"I want to go to bed," she almost whispered.

We got her into her nightgown and as I tucked her into bed I said, "I need to go to the store to buy the beef to make stew for you and Norm tomorrow. It's eight o'clock. Will you be all right if I leave you alone for about thirty minutes?" She assured me she would.

I unplugged the phone in the bedroom, put the cat in the living room, and closed the sliding door that separated the bedroom from the rest of the fifth wheel. Mom should be fine for a short while, I told myself as I went out the door. But when I returned, I saw a light on in the living room that had been off when I left. What could be wrong?

Entering the fifth wheel, I noticed the sliding door was hanging off its track at a strange angle, partially opened. I managed to get past it into the bedroom where Mom was sitting on the end of the bed, moaning.

"What happened?" I asked. Her answer didn't make much sense. I tried again, "Mom what woke you?"

"The phone rang," she groaned.

"Who called?" I asked, surprised that the phone ringing in the living room had awakened her.

"I think Glenda called. Then Norm called," she added. I had been gone only a few minutes and both of them had called!

"Let's get you back into bed," I urged.

While I was in the living room talking on the phone with Norm, and then Glenda, Mom came down and lay on the sofa.

"Turn on the TV," she requested when I completed my calls.

"The subject of our program this evening," the gentleman on the television announced, "is about people who claim to have been helped by angels." Just what I need, the help of angels, I thought to myself.

It was about nine o'clock when Mom decided to go back to bed. "Where are you gonna sleep?" she asked.

"I'll sleep on the couch, or I'll sleep upstairs with you."

"The sheets are clean. Nobody's slept in the bed." She repeated what she had told me several times earlier in the day, "Nobody's slept in the bed." I was moved by her look and the tone in her voice as she repeated that the sheets were fresh. The decision to sleep with my mother wasn't an easy one. The bugs that had munched on me in the afternoon were fresh in my memory. I reluctantly joined her, hoping that both of us could sleep peacefully through the night, then wake refreshed in the morning to bring Norm home.

The nightlight in the bedroom cast a beacon of brightness into the small space. I unplugged it then settled in on my side of the bed. Problem solved, I imagined. But light poured through the open windows from neighboring porch lights because the drapes had been opened in hopes of catching a cooling breeze. My weary body wanted to dismiss the need for cool air and darkness. As I adjusted my position in the bed, mother rose, looked around then settled back down.

I was just beginning to drift into sweet sleep when I heard the cat charge up the stairs. I felt him jump onto the end of the bed on Mom's side. From there, he leaped onto her nightstand, zoomed across the top of the bed, and then jumped down. For the second time, Mom rose and then lay back down. Quiet returned. The cat repeated his routine one more time. He jumped onto the bed, leaped onto the nightstand, and zoomed across the top of the bed before he jumped down. A momentary quietness returned until the cat gently propelled himself onto the end of the bed and began to preen himself. Suddenly Mom sat bolt upright in bed. "You goddamned cat!" she yelled as she grabbed his tail. "Get the hell offa this bed!" she screamed, throwing him into the air off the end of the bed. As he flew through the air, his front claws dug into my ankle and foot. Unbelievable! I said to myself.

A short time later, the cat jumped back onto the bed. Mom got up and I followed her. "Let's shut that son-of-a-bitch in the living room," Mom growled, yanking at the sliding door to re-hang it.

"Go to bed, Mom. You've got to get your rest. I'll take care of this." The task of re-hanging the door tapped into my sense of helplessness when challenged with anything remotely mechanical. But it was urgent to get that door re-hung. I tried and tried until finally it hung precariously from the track. I went back to bed thinking our problem was solved for the night.

Sleep was gently carrying me away when I was awakened by a loud sound. The cat was attacking the precariously hung door. It sounded as if he was throwing his whole body against it. On his third attack, I got up. Mother was still not asleep, and I was going to see that she got her rest no matter what!

I reached into a cabinet over the bed where Norm said the sheets were kept. I pulled out something that I hoped was a sheet and down the stairs I went. When I opened the precariously hung door, it fell partially off the track. I tried to pull it shut but it touched at the top only, leaving a wide-open gap at the bottom. I moved the trashcan over to plug the hole, but it wasn't tall enough. The cat could jump onto the trashcan and then right into the bedroom. So I held the cat while I awkwardly placed the sheet on the love seat. I lay down, holding the cat to my breast. His ears went back, and his tail was in motion: "swish, swish" from side to side. I stroked him. It took over an hour to sooth him.

When I began to fall asleep, I felt him slip away. I whispered loudly, "Kitty-cat" "Kitty-cat". I couldn't see him. He must not go back and disturb Mom I thought desperately. Then I heard him crunching the dry food that Norm kept in one corner of the living room. Whew! At least he didn't go back to Mom. A Bible text ran like ticker tape across my mind. I can do all things through Christ who strengthens me.

I continued my cat vigil. He briefly came back to me before jumping down again. This time he scratched around in the kitty litter box at the end of the love seat. The air filled with the smell of cat shit. I had two windows open, one behind the loveseat and the other to the side. The air cleared, eventually. What a relief it was when the cat jumped up on the love seat to settle down on the back of the sofa for what I hoped would be sleep for both of us. But sleep was not to come quite yet. He began preening himself again and as he did, his body pushed against the mini-blind, causing it to bang against the wall. I listened to the banging. The ticker tape yielded this comforting thought, He will give his angels charge over you, to keep you in all your ways.

I reached for the cord and pulled it, and the blind went up. I tried to secure it, but it would not secure. Then I remembered seeing Mom wrap it around a hook to hold it up. I turned on a light, found the hook, secured the blind, turned out the light and hoped once again to sleep. I began feeling myself drift into a delicious, dreamy state when the last thought of the day passed through my mind, The Lord is my Shepherd, I shall not want. Sleep came at last.

In the wee hours, I woke to close the windows as protection from the cold, which the sheet didn't provide. Around five-thirty kitty-cat gently put his nose to mine followed by a soft brush of his paw against my cheek. It was time to wake up. Despite my sleep-deprived state, my waking thought energized me, today is the day Norm comes home!

Mom was up by seven, bright and chipper. Her symptoms of illness and tiredness were gone. I was pleased to see her so revived.

Chapter 50

California
July 1989

"Mom, would you like to take a shower this morning? We could wash your hair," I offered, knowing she hadn't showered for several days.

"Yeah, that'd be good" she answered, somewhat enthused. "Norm put a stool in the tub I set on." I helped her step over the edge of the small tub onto the stool where a hose with a showerhead came from the spigot.

"That feels about right," she finally said after my repeated efforts to adjust the temperature. I watched her enjoy the sensation of water against her skin as I let it cover her completely with its wetness. "I'm cold," she complained.

"Here," I said, handing her the showerhead. "You spray yourself with water. That will keep you warm while I soap you down."

I washed her back and legs carefully, but I didn't do a great job on her front side. When I washed where her legs met her body, I discovered a crusty line. That's probably been there for some time, I imagined. As I scrubbed a bit on the crusty line, images of Norm showering her went through my mind, Norm with his heavy belly and his aching back, struggling to help her into the shower; Norm trying to wash her with his stiff fingers.

"Hold your head back and I'll get your hair wet." I applied the spray of water to her hair and then lathered in the strange purple shampoo, not sure what she might look like when I had finished.

"I'm cold," she complained, for the third time.

"I'll rinse you all over one last time with warm water and you're done."

"Sit on the love seat, Mom." After she had dried, I put a blue robe on her. "I'll wrap you in your afghan to help warm you up." In a few moments, she was warm and comfortable.

"Can I fluff your hair with the towel, so it dries quicker?"

"That'd be good."

"Here's your comb." I handed it to her, then watched to see what she would do with it. "Well, Mom, you may have forgotten how to shampoo your hair, but you still remember how to comb it!" I teased.

"I can still comb my hair," she said with a smile on her face.

"While you comb your hair, I'll start the beef stew."

"Does this gas stove have a lighted pilot?" I asked.

"No, you hafta use that lighter Norm keeps by the stove."

If only they had electric instead of gas like I have, I groaned to myself after trying several times to light the burner before I succeeded. Thankfully, the crock-pot was where Norm said it would be, as well as the frying pan. I found the oil and the can opener, no problem. Soon, I had the beef stew cooking away in the crock-pot and the kitchen cleaned.

"I think we've joined the ranks of those helped by the presence of angels, like we saw on the TV last night," I joked with Mom. She gave me a little nod.

There it all was, just as I had imagined: a clean house with the delicious smell of stew coming from the crock-pot; mother safe and sound, sparkling clean and ready to pick up her man from the hospital.

"It's nine-thirty. Let's go out and sit on the porch to help pass the time," I suggested. It was pleasant sitting on the porch. Sunlight filtered through the trees. Neighbors were moving about slowly. A child was taking down a small tent. The activity gave Mom something to watch. This is an opportunity to talk with Mom again about her past, I thought as we sat alone on the porch. Another chance to get some answers to my questions.

Something held me back, probably yesterday's conversation. "Tell me about your mother, my grandma Pansie," I had encouraged, hoping to gain insight into Mom's experience of her mother. Mom had responded with an economy of words, "Momma wasn't much for hugging or giving kisses. Momma was quiet." Suddenly, after a brief pause, her had thoughts switched to her father. "Dad drank a lot."

For whatever reason, I hadn't asked her to elaborate, didn't probe further. Now I still wasn't able to approach the subject as we sat on the porch talking mostly trivia while we waited for a call from Norm. I allowed the golden opportunity to pass without really understanding why.

"Sure nice to talk to Jennifer this morning," Mom said, rocking gently back and forth.

"We were both tearful on the phone when we talked. I miss her so much. It's hard to be separated from her for so long, Mom." I got up to sweep more cobwebs from the side of the fifth wheel.

"I used to take care of all those things," Mom said as I watered a fern plant that sat on the picnic table.

"It must be difficult to watch someone else do it now. It's hard to be dependent on others." We talked of the difficulty in letting others do for us what we are no longer able to do for ourselves. I smiled at her, "Someday it'll be me sitting in the rocker while someone else does what I can't do. Phone's ringing," I said as I ran into the fifth wheel.

It was a little after ten so Mom and I both thought it would be Norm calling to say he was ready to come home. "Hello," I said somewhat out of breath.

"Hello, how's Norm doing? Does he get to come home today?"

It was my sister Verneda. I hadn't talked to her for five months, ever since our break-up in February. I was thankful that Mom was outside on the porch.

"Yes, he's supposed to come home between ten and eleven o'clock," I answered as if we had talked recently.

"Can I talk to Mom?" she asked with tenderness in her voice.

I stood there holding the phone while it seemed as if someone else spoke. I heard myself say, "Mom is feeling insecure about you and Norm. Could you call back later?"

"Me and Norm!" she exclaimed. "So that's what it is. She's been angry at me, and I didn't know why. Remember what I told you about Bud?" she asked. "How Mom thought of me as her rival when I was six years old!"

"Yes, I remember," I answered, but I was unable to relate to what she was saying. I hadn't talked with her for five months, and now suddenly we're on the phone, ignoring our personal issues with each other, heading straight into the thick of it by my disclosing what Mom had told me was between the two of us.

My anxiety level peaked, I fumbled for words, and blurted out something like, "Mom's waiting on the porch. I'm afraid she'll get upset if I tell her you're on the phone. Could you call back a little later?" I repeated.

"Okay," she said in a subdued tone.

What have I done, I asked myself when I hung up the phone. I told Mom I wouldn't share her concerns about Verneda and Norm with anyone. I went back out to the porch in a daze.

"Who was it?" Mom asked.

Oblivious to Mom, my mind raced back to Thursday afternoon in the hospital. Norm answered his ringing phone and began to carry on a quiet intimate conversation. I noticed the concern in my mother's face. "It's probably Susan, Mom," I suggested. This didn't sooth her, so I pushed on Norm's foot and asked, "Hey, we want to know who you're talking to."

"It's Susan," he answered. Mom relaxed. Norm's daughter was calling him from Kansas. We resumed our conversation after he said goodbye to Susan, but the ringing phone interrupted us a second time. Again, mother tensed. I knew she was afraid it was Verneda calling. I could tell from the conversation that it was Glenda. "It's Glenda, Mom." She relaxed and so did I.

Mom brought me back to the moment. "Who was it?" she asked, repeating her question.

"It was David wondering if we've heard anything." The lie came easily. I didn't want anything to upset her.

Weeks ago, when I was at Mom's, had Verneda called to talk with her. Mom responded minimally with grunted, angry words. I had dismissed it as Mom having one of her usual "angry days." Now I realized that her anger toward Verneda had persisted for many weeks. This experience shed light on what Norm had recently said, "Mother doesn't want to go to Terry's when I'm in the hospital."

I sat there thinking about Verneda. She knew Mom was angry with her, but she didn't know why. How much better it would be if Mom could talk about what bothers her instead of retreating into anger or silence which dumfounds the rest of us. If only she could talk about *why* she is angry, then we might work together toward a resolution. Instead, she isolates herself from us by retreating into anger or silence. I thought about what that did to me as a child. I'd ask myself, why is Mom angry with me? When most likely, I was not the source of her anger. I was just on the receiving end of it, like Verneda who had no clue as to why Mom had been so hateful and angry until I told her.

After Mom and I sat a while longer on the porch, I lied again. "I'm going to call Liz." But I had no intention of calling Liz. I went inside to call Verneda to relieve the extreme discomfort I felt over breaking my promise to Mom. The phone rang repeatedly with no answer. I redialed. Again, it rang over and over until a voice I didn't recognize said, "Hello."

"Hello, who is this?" I asked.

"Terry."

"I didn't recognize your voice."

She said something else, but the content was lost as I registered that she had been crying. My words stumbled out awkwardly, totally oblivious to my sister's state. "It's real important that you not say anything to anybody about Mom. Maybe she'll be better soon," I suggested hopefully. "I can't talk right now," I added quickly.

I went back out to Mom. "I'm ready to go inside. I'm gonna lay down on the sofa." She went over and curled up on the love seat. I decided to sit with her and stroke her legs and feet while we waited. It was a special time, being there alone with my mother, her legs across me as I stroked them. She was in my care, something I had longed for many times as a child.

Overcome with fatigue, I closed my eyes to rest a bit. My mind replayed what Mom had said as we drove past the Lake Elsinore Cemetery on our way to the hospital, "That's where we're gonna be."

"Yes mother, I know. I guess you don't remember that we went together to select the plots." I was excited to tell her, "I bought a silk tree and had it planted right next to the place you chose. It will bloom with beautiful pink blossoms in the spring," but she gave no response as I continued to stroke her legs.

After a few minutes of resting on the love seat, she said, "We've had a good life. We worked hard together." I knew she was talking about Norm and herself.

"Was it a good life, Mom?" I asked as I held her hand.

"We worked side by side, but it was good," she stated contentedly.

In the silence that followed, reflections of my mother drifted through my thoughts. Mom can look at a dress or even a picture of a dress, then cut a pattern from newspapers to sew yards of fabric into an exact replica. She probably never thought of this as a special gift because it was so easy for her to do. I started wondering about her childhood. What happened to her when she lived with her parents? Was there any effort to develop her mind or her abilities, especially her designing and sewing talent? Did she get recognition and praise to encourage her? Questions without answers, I told myself.

My analytical nature continued probing. I don't think Mom has much self-esteem. Her behavior, especially in the past, supports this idea, I thought. How could she do what she did if she valued herself? Then I had an insight that put a spot of salve on an old wound of mine. How could I expect her to instill in me a sense of my own self-worth if she had little or none of her own? Is it possible to give to others what we ourselves lack? I asked myself.

I contemplated the two activities that had dominated her life during my growing up years: drinking and sex. What's at the root of these behaviors? What caused them to be the focus of her life? What contributed to the life she chose to live? I really wanted to know.

I recalled, as I looked at her resting there on the love seat what she had said yesterday, "If Norm had beat me like Vern did, I don't know what I'd have done." Shocked to learn this for the first time, I questioned the accuracy of her account. Mom had lied to us about so many important things. But then I pondered the fearful look I had seen in her eyes yesterday. I can't dismiss the look in her eyes as a lie, I decided. Regret and sorrow, that's what I felt for her, as I sat imagining the beatings.

My awareness turned my thoughts in another direction. Unlike me, she had never learned to dream her way out of her situation, I decided. Probably she had no vision of a different way of life other than what she had experienced on the farm. Since she had the disadvantage of no books to read, no television to watch, no movies to view; since she knew no one she admired as a model to a different and better life, she accepted the lifestyle handed to her by her father and came to believe, as she had expressed to me, "I never thought I would have much or be much." I said to myself, sadly your belief has become the reality of your life, Mom. Now you're living out the last days of your life in a fifth wheel. Mom stirred a bit but continued resting peacefully.

So many questions without answers, I thought as I covered her feet with the blanket. Although I didn't have answers to many of my questions, my realization that she hadn't gotten what she needed as she was growing up bathed me in the sweet experience of forgiveness. I saw my mother's life from a clearer perspective that day. I also realized that her deficiencies had become glaring omissions in the life of my sister and me when we as children became embroiled in her complex life. The love that I felt for my mother that Saturday morning while we waited to hear from Norm was a deep healing love, rooted in forgiveness and understanding.

"Oh, you've decided to wake up, Mom," I teased. She lay quietly for a moment before precious, golden words came from her lips, words of recognition and love that I had starved for over the many years of my life as her daughter, "I can never repay you for what you've done for us."

The phone rang at eleven o'clock. "Come and get me," Norm called. At last, the long-awaited time had come. The nurse wheeled him to where Mom was happily waiting. She smiled at him ever so sweetly, I thought, before getting into the back seat of the car. The nurse helped Norm into the front seat.

As we pulled away, Norm complained, "I don't know why I can't drive."

"You can drive, Norm, but I didn't want to hear you call my car a piece of junk again so I'm driving." I had found a new boldness in relating to Norm.

"I need to stop at the drugstore to get my prescription filled," he told me.

"I'll go in," I volunteered.

"No, I'll go in. I know Jerry and he'll let me bring the stamps in later."

While Norm was in the drugstore Mom said, "My, you couldn't even tell he had anything done." We waited in silence for a time then she said, "I sure hope he's not gonna to go next door with that bunch when we get home." Norm usually drank beer with the neighbors during the day; he drank away the late afternoon and evening at home with mixed drinks of whiskey and anything else he fancied. Mom had been part of this routine until she learned she had cancer. For the first time in her life, she had finally stopped drinking.

Her words echoed in my thoughts, accompanied by the helpless tone in her voice: "I sure hope he's not gonna to go next door."

Maybe I need to rethink my belief that Mom is the dominant one in their relationship, I told myself. Because she was a powerful, dominant figure in my life when I was a child, I thought that she was the same in her relationship with Norm, powerful and dominant. After all, I had seen him cower many times when she directed her anger at him, as I did as a child. And even recently, when we were at a restaurant with Norm's son Bob, she had glared at Norm about something and told him, "Oh, shut up!" Still, I thought, maybe I'm wrong. She told me not long ago that it was Norm who wanted her to have his baby. I'd always thought it was *her* decision. Now I began to wonder, as we sat there waiting for him to come out of the drugstore, is it Norm who dominates the two of them? Maybe he's the reason that Mom didn't keep her promise to come and see me, the broken promise that caused seven years of silence between us.

Norm returned. As I backed away from the drugstore I asked, "Well Norm, do you think you'll be going over to visit the neighbors today?"

Before he could answer, Mom spoke up, "Why no; he's not gonna do that!"

Although I couldn't see her face, the sound of her voice told me she would like to clobber me for asking the question. I had thought to ask Norm about his plans so that Mom would know his intentions and then deal with it rather than seethe in the anxiety of not knowing. "No, I'm not going anywhere," Norm responded.

There, now I hope Mom can relax, I said to myself. If only she could talk about what bothers her.

As I was getting ready to go, Norm looked at me tenderly and said, "I can't thank you enough for taking care of mother."

"It was my privilege," I responded sincerely.

I was in a dash to get home to David and our life together; to talk of our upcoming trip to Seattle; to decide for sure if we would stop on our way through San Leandro to see Vern, to hear his side of the story between himself and Mom.

Chapter 51

San Leandro, California – Redlands, California
August 1989 – September 1989

San Leandro Next Exit, the sign read. "Do you remember how to get to his place, David?"

"I think I can find it." David had his own internal compass for any terrain he traveled, a sense of "how to get there from here." When we crossed the railroad tracks, even I knew we were close.

"I'm surprised Vern wants us to stop. When I called to let him know we'd be here in the early afternoon, his response was one word, 'Beautiful.'"

"Industry has really moved into this area," David observed.

"This is an old residential area. I'm not surprised it's changed so dramatically," I said, noticing the remaining modest homes sitting in a dilapidated condition.

"Vern's property looks smaller to me, much smaller than when we were here last," I commented as we walked to the front door.

"You're early!" Vern greeted us gruffly.

I saw something green on his tongue and teeth. "Oh, you're in the middle of lunch," I said. He ushered us to a seat at the dining-room table. He went to finish his lunch at a small table in the kitchen where he sat with his back to us.

I looked about. Signs of old age took the form of massive railings from the hall doorway into the living room where they took a turn and went across the front of the fireplace and the bookcase. This side of the room had belonged to Kae, I remembered. Now it was devoid of furniture with only the massive railing, which seemed to jail in the fireplace and the bookcase. The railing led to a wheelchair, which sat in the corner next to the dining room.

My attention went to the chair next to me. It held two pillows, one on the seat and one at the back. Even my seat had a bulging pillow. In front of me on the table sat an extremely large magnifying glass with a flashlight apparatus attached. My

437

assessment old age was suddenly interrupted by the appearance of age itself in the form of two grey-haired ladies arduously making the turn from the hallway into the living room, the younger lady supporting the older as they slowly moved toward the dining room table. I looked carefully, but at first, I couldn't see Kae in the face of either woman moving in our direction. Then I looked behind the inevitable ravages of age and recognized the more elderly of the two, the infamous Kae Hicks. She was still alive, still there to make her presence felt.

I crossed to her just as she reached the railing at the fireplace. Her nurse clucked something to her. "Who is she?" Kae's ancient voice questioned the nurse.

I leaned toward her, "I'm Vernetta."

"Who?" Kae asked.

"Vernetta."

The nurse was saying to me, "She doesn't know you," when Kae, with her face scrunched up as if she were about to burst into tears exclaimed, "I remember you!" She seemed happy and tearful at the same moment. With much ado, she was seated at the dining room table next to me.

Vern came in from the kitchen and handed me a small plate holding three pieces of cucumbers. "It's been thirteen years since you were here."

"Oh," I responded in surprise, "I thought it had been longer than that."

"No, it was nineteen seventy-six. Thirteen years!" Vern repeated, almost as if talking to himself. He looked at me then he began: "Now Vernetta, you want to know about me and your mother and what happened. Well, I'll tell you. She took you kids and went to Kansas and stayed gone for nine months. Not so much as a letter or a phone call. Nine months!"

"Why did she do that?" I asked, already sure of the answer. A long period of silence followed my question.

Finally, he looked at me and said, "There's the question, "Why?"

He probably hasn't considered that I already know quite a lot about his history with my mother from his own brothers and their wives, I imagined. But I wanted very much to hear his account of the history. I didn't mention the obvious reasons that had sent Mom running to Kansas with my sister and me: our home had been so badly burned by the fire that we couldn't live there; Vern provided no financial support; Vern no longer lived with Mom. After going back and forth between Mom and Kae, Kae was his final choice. People usually have good reasons when they take drastic measures, I reminded myself, but chose not to share that thought with Vern. I looked at him, remembering my mother's sincerity when she told me of the beatings he gave her when he got drunk.

"When you got drunk..." I began, but Vern's temper flared, his angry words interrupted me.

"My drinking is no one's business!"

"When you got drunk," I repeated looking straight into his hardened eyes, "I was told you would beat my mother."

His anger dissolved as quickly as it had arrived. Extinguished by the truth? I wondered.

The ambiance was favorable, so I continued, but thought it best to change the subject. "I don't know if you remember saying to your brother Clarence that 'you weren't going to let a couple of brats ruin your life,' meaning Verneda and me when we were very young children." He made a brief unconvincing indication of denial. "Until I was in sixth grade, I had never met you, never seen you in person. You never made contact with me in any way. Your silence supported what people were telling me, that you didn't care."

"How did I even know you were mine?" he retorted. "Might not be. You might belong to someone else. We'd have to have blood tests."

I was caught off guard. David, normally quiet and one to avoid confrontation, boldly declared, "Oh, she's yours."

Vern's eyes flashed, "I came clear to Hays, Kansas in nineteen forty-nine to see you."

"Yes, I remember. I sat between you and Kae in the car. You wanted to take me home with you, but Kae told you she had already raised three children and didn't want to go through that again."

Quiet settled on us as we continued to sit at the table until I said to Vern, "I'd like very much to hear stories of your life when you were a boy." I was hoping to learn about his childhood experience because, along with Freud, I believe childhood is a powerful force in the shaping of our lives.

"I don't want to talk about that," he responded immediately but followed with a brief accounting. "I was born in Otis, Kansas. There were eight of us children. We were very poor and lived on the farm. The crops failed several years in a row. The next year there was a bumper crop and instead of getting the dollar eighty-five, we were paid nineteen cents a bushel." The theme "Dust Blown in Kansas" was often repeated in his narrative. He changed the subject. "Yesterday was my birthday."

"Yes, I noticed you have a lot of birthday cards on your mantel," I remarked as I walked over to look at his cards.

He started talking, "I want to show you this Bulova watch Verneda sent me. I don't need it. I'm gonna keep it until I die, then she can have it back." He's still calling her Verneda as I do, I thought, instead of Terry as others do.

He brought out an album of pictures. "Verneda made that and brought it when she came to pick up the car I gave her," he said, handing it to me. "Verneda has grown into a mature woman," Vern noted, as I finished looking at the carefully prepared album with endearing notes written beside each photo. "I gave her a new life," he said of himself. I didn't ask him to elaborate on his perceived accomplishment.

Kae was still sitting in the chair at the dining room table, wearing a blanket about her shoulders for warmth. I couldn't tell how much she understood of our conversation.

"She's been sick for seven years," Vern declared, stressing the number seven.

"I'm eighty-seven," Kae told me.

Vern contradicted her, "She's eighty-five. I'm seventy-seven. If she dies first, I'll move to Idaho or Nevada, someplace where the taxes don't eat you up."

The time had come to leave Vern and Kae.

"You're welcome to stay the night," he said.

"We already have reservations," I responded. "But thank you for the offer."

When I moved passed him through the front door out onto the porch, I felt a kiss on my cheek. A tender gesture, I thought, from a man who had just told me that I wasn't his daughter. But how wonderful it was to feel no need for this man to love me. I was thankful that he had no power binding me to him. I walked toward the car with the belief in my heart that he had beaten my mother.

Ten years would pass before Kae's children, Al Hicks, and his sister Francine, would candidly tell me about living with Vern, sharing their experiences and their feelings about him, confirming that he had indeed beaten my mother:

"Vern was always a very cantankerous man. When Vern drank, his personality changed. He became violent. He beat up my mother many times. I especially remember one time seeing my mother hold up her hands in front of her face and crying, 'Please, Vern don't hit me again, please, Vern.' At the end of her life he was treating her very badly," Al told me sadly.

"Mom met him at a dance and started seeing him," Francine began. "He just walked away from his own little family into our family, and we hated him. He ruined our lives. He thought nothing of others and their needs. His was a self-centered existence. I have hatred in my heart for him to this day. I thought he was one of the meanest bastards I had ever met. Whether he drank or not, he was just a terrible-tempered person.

"When I was fifteen, he came into the kitchen where I was ironing and said, ''You don't like me, do you?' And I was scared to death. He was looking at me with those eyes so mean and intense and an awful look on his face. I didn't say anything so he just made his great big hands into a fist and hit me right square in my nose and knocked me over in the corner on a metal flour can. He broke my nose," Francine recounted bitterly.

As we drove away from San Leandro, thoughts of my sister swept me away from thoughts of Vern.

"How long has it been since you've talked with her?" David asked.

"Since February, about six months, not counting when we talked by accident at Mom's. Oh, by the way, that was a special moment for me when you told Vern I was his."

"I didn't like him saying that to you," David said. "What kind of thoughts are you having about Verneda?"

"*She* was *really* my mother," I said emphatically.

"What do you mean by that?" David asked.

"Well, in talking with Mac about the past and what Mom said and what I can remember, Verneda's the one who took care of me when I was growing up. She was more my mother in some ways than Mom was. Mom told me she went to work and left me in the care of five-year old Verneda almost all day, remember? I was just a baby! *And* it was my sister who was alone with me when the cabin caught fire. She saved our lives! But I shudder to think of what happened to us when Mom put Verneda in charge of me on that train ride from Idaho to Kansas when I was barely old enough to walk."

"That doesn't make sense to let a five-year old take care of a baby," David said.

"I have memories of us being alone a lot in Jarbidge. That's where Mom beat Verneda when she was only six. That reminds me of what Mac said, 'Children or adolescents in charge of little children can be very cruel.' Verneda told me a few months ago that she treated me the way Mom treated her. But I sometimes wonder if there's any connection between her and one of those terrifying body memories when I felt like I was going to die."

"It was different from the other body memories," David said.

"Yes. Different and very scary."

I looked out the window and watched the scenery go by as we drove for a time in silence, but thoughts of my sister were still going through my mind. "I have a clear memory of how Verneda treated me in Larned after grandma died. She needled me, goaded me, frustrated me and always, always got the best of me. To her, I was a non-person to do her bidding, like an appendage to herself that she could use and mistreat at will. I recall yelling at her after many of the times she had hit me, 'Someday I'm gonna grow up and I'll be bigger than you and I'll beat you up!'"

"And did you?" David teased.

"No, I never did, even though I grew several inches taller than she was." Both of us laughed. "But Verneda watched out for me. Bought me a piano! Mom never did anything like that. Came to my graduation but Mom didn't. Gave me a great gift, that cedar chest. I remember that for my sixteenth birthday she gave me a pair of book ends I still have."

"So, she wasn't all bad." David said.

"I'm realizing she's been there for me way more than Mom ever was. Maybe she's had more of an impact on my life than Mom."

"That's probably true. I think you still have a lot of issues you need to resolve with your sister."

"Do you think so? Probably true, but I don't like hearing that I might still have issues with her. I know I'm not ready to contact her. But there is something I can do. I can try to own my feelings by honestly admitting to myself how I feel about her. Mac told me that I've got to own my feelings if I ever hope to heal, not just about Verneda but in everything."

David continued to drive us further north. Thoughts of Verneda and Mom and Vern gave way to the pleasurable anticipation of taking the Winslow Ferry from Seattle to the Olympic Peninsula to visit Mal and Sylvia, our old friends from Berkeley days.

Five weeks later when we returned home from our vacation, I went right away to see Mom and Norm. Mom looked better than she had in a long time. After our visit when I kissed Mom goodbye, Norm quickly whispered to me, "I need to see David to talk with him about Mother." This piqued my curiosity, but I was unable to ask him to explain. I told Mom as I stood at the door to leave, "We'll probably be back on Saturday. David wants to come out to say hello and we can have a longer visit."

"Want to go to the store with me, David?" Norm asked on Saturday. It was Norm's clandestine way of getting David alone.

With the men gone, I had a few minutes of privacy with Mom to get my own question answered. "When I was here Thursday, you were trying to tell me something about Verneda, but Norm came back, and you stopped talking. I could see you were upset, and I thought something new had happened while I was on vacation."

Expletives began pouring from my mother's mouth, "Verneda's a slut, an asshole! I never want to see her again. I'll kill her!" I sat speechless. She continued, "I never thought..." she began, then seemed at a loss for words. She tried again, "I never thought..." but she was still unable to complete the sentence even on a second try. Fluency returned when she told me, "Norm and I have been so good together. Verneda came out here and brought the two little girls. She sat over there but I didn't even talk to her."

A scowl transformed her face and her eyes hardened as she looked at the spot where Verneda had sat. She made half-sentence attempts to express her painful feelings. Then I watched her face suddenly soften, her eyes warmed, and she said, "I always liked Terry." Without pausing, she made another abrupt shift as she flipped into my sister's given name. "She's got him. Verneda's got him! It's hard for me to go to sleep. Once when I was sick and went to bed at eight, I woke up at midnight and heard him talking with that bitch on the phone. I told him to get off the goddamned phone and get to bed!"

Mom is worse than when I left for vacation, I said to myself, realizing she needed relief from the agonizing pain of her obsession. "Are you still afraid if you die first Verneda will go after Norm?" I asked, in an attempt to help.

With an incredibly sad look on her face, she answered. "That's about the way it is."

"Then the only way you can take care of that is to outlive Norm," I responded stupidly. How can she possibly outlive Norm? My self-talk silently derided me; she has already lived well beyond the doctor's expectation.

But Mom answered me quietly, "That's right."

The door opened; Norm and David had returned. We drank juice, talked briefly and then David and I left for home.

"Norm wanted to tell me about your mom's insecurity," David said, as we drove away. "He doesn't know what to do about it. I encouraged him to take her everywhere with him. When she takes a nap, I suggested he stay in the fifth wheel with her until she wakes up, then they could visit the neighbors together." David shared a few more details of how he thought Norm could approach the problem.

"I like the suggestion you gave him because Mom said she doesn't worry if she can go everywhere with him. I sure hope it works. I wasn't any help, went brain dead, you'd never know I had a degree in counseling. She is so anxious about losing Norm to Verneda. But something else is wrong with her. She'll start talking but stops as if she's lost her train of thought. She's aware of it because she gets really frustrated. She was able to finish some of her sentences but a lot of them were fragmented."

Darkness began to drop around my vision, eventually leaving only a narrow tunnel of light. My legs went numb. My muscles occasionally contracted spontaneously as David took us safely home.

Chapter 52

California
September 1989 – November 1989

"This situation with Mom and Norm is so frustrating," I complained to David the next morning before he left for work. "Obviously, Norm is having difficulty dealing with Mom's insecurity and her probable memory loss. The time is coming when he won't be able to take care of her. It may be closer than we think."

"How can you help?" David asked.

"I can try to find out what kind of care is available for her, but I'd have to figure out a way to talk with Norm about it. Norm whispers behind her back; gets you alone on false pretenses. I wish we could sit with the two of them and talk about a solution that might be good for both of them, but Norm doesn't want to discuss it in front of her and it's impossible to talk with him alone!"

"It is frustrating but remember, 'Keep it light!'" David tried to tease me into a smile. "I've got to go to work," he said. "I'll call you later."

Mac advised against Mom living with me, for her sake as well as mine, I reminded myself after David left for work. Without Mac's advice, I reflected, I would probably tell Norm I'd take care of her. But I know I'm really not emotionally able to have her live with me; being with my mother turns me into an anxious, nervous person. It's almost impossible for me to function fully as an adult. When I finally accepted this fact, I decided to contact various agencies to learn what possibilities were available for Mom's care. As I looked out the window at the water flowing from the spa into our lap pool, I found myself wishing that I could take care of her myself.

Norm was distant and cold when I saw him after he'd gotten my letter describing possible options. Talking to Norm personally would have been far superior to a letter. We might have avoided the huff he's in, I told myself. I imagined that he was angry because he expected me to take care of Mom instead of offering a different plan. But he never verbalized the suggestion. For the time being, I had done what I could do but obviously it didn't sit well with Norm.

In an effort to maintain my personal life, I turned my attention away from Mom and Norm to focus on where David and I might relocate when he retired from practicing medicine. Homeward bound in early October from looking at potential retirement property in Pt. Ludlow, Marc and I were driving through the Bay Area when I told him, "Let's avoid the Nimitz Freeway because it's a very old freeway. I still have my fear of earthquakes when I get into this area. I guess my old fear from seeing that movie 'San Francisco' will always be with me."

"Well," Marc said, "you know that old saying."

"No, I don't. Tell me," I said.

"Even paranoids have something to fear," Marc said half seriously. Ten days later, a strong earthquake hit the Bay Area and portions of the Nimitz Freeway collapsed, trapping, or crushing to death many who were driving on the lower deck.

The media began constantly pounding the Southern California population with grim predictions: "The Big One could strike at any time." The media had assigned the name of "The Big One" to any earthquake of catastrophic proportions. They warned that it could occur on the San Andreas Fault, which ran only a few miles from where we lived, or on other faults running perpendicular to it. We lived in a hot zone.

The terror of being buried alive moved me to action as I watched televised images of the collapsed Nimitz Freeway and collapsed houses and apartment buildings. Mac and I had worked on my fear of being buried alive under rubble in an earthquake, but we hadn't successfully eradicated my fear or of identifying the psychological source of this persistent fear other than the impact of an old movie. If it related to some other trauma from my childhood, we hadn't been able to access it.

"I absolutely need to leave this area," I exclaimed to David. My fear eclipsed my concern for my mother, the little home I dearly loved, and the major change I proposed. However, I was keenly aware that our financial welfare was tied to David's current position.

"Let me look into the possibility of relocating to a medical group further north," David suggested. Within a short period of time, David was interviewed and given the promise of a position at a reduced salary in an area almost free of earthquake faults. "The board will meet the first of January to ratify the decision," the interviewing physician reported to David.

"That sounds too good to be true! Yippee, we're going to leave this area, if the board comes through for us, David."

"I was assured it won't be a problem. It's merely a formality for the board members to cast a final vote," David said.

"We're comin' down in November with Paul to go to Disneyland," Larry said when he surprised me with a phone call, around the time we listed our house in late October. "Rory's bringin Robin and the new baby. Tammy can't get away to come with us."

"Mom will really be excited," I told him. I couldn't believe it. Larry was coming back and bringing most of his family with him.

Ironically, Jennifer called right after Larry. "I'm planning to come home in November. I only have three days, but I want to come home."

"What a wonderful surprise! I just got a call from Larry. He's coming again in November with most of his family. Maybe you can be here at the same time and get to meet him."

"Give me the dates and I'll see what I can do," Jennifer agreed enthusiastically.

"Let's have a family picture taken while you're here," I suggested. "What do you think?"

"Good idea, Mumsy-Pooh," she said, using her favorite name for me. My children weren't allowed to call me Mom. While I hated the *name* Mom, I hadn't ever consciously thought "I hate Mom." But once I did scream at her, "I hate you," right after Elizabeth was born.

The visits were synchronized with Larry and his family arriving at the same time as Jennifer. We were in the middle of a board game when I said, "I hate to interrupt our good time, but we have an appointment for a family photo." Then an idea came to me. "Will you come to the studio with us, Larry? I'd love to have our picture taken together."

"Go on, Larry. Go with her to get your picture taken," Sherry encouraged. So, before the family picture was taken, Larry and I smiled into the camera's lens for our brother-sister photo.

Vernetta and Larry, 1989

After a loving farewell, Jennifer flew off to New England. Then Larry and his family followed me in their motor home to Lake Elsinore.

"Why don't we set outside," Norm said when we got there. He sat up on his little metal chair by the front door. Larry and his two sons, Rory and Paul, sat near him on the picnic bench. Mom, Sherry and Robin sat on the other side of the porch.

"Can I hold the baby?" Mom asked. Robin smiled and handed her Cody, her six-months-old son.

While Larry and Norm talked about trucks and motors, Sherry and I watched Mom play with the baby. I noticed there was almost no interaction between Mom and Larry. I was perplexed by her total absorption in the baby. She made no effort to speak directly to Larry, or to anyone else.

"You can park your motor home right here and stay the night," Norm suggested eagerly. "Plenty of RV spaces available."

"Thanks, but we're on our way to Disneyland," Larry said. "It's one of my favorite places."

"Gonna see Terry when you're down there?" Norm asked.

"Yeah, I think we'll drop by so she can meet my family."

The visit came to an end and Larry got up to leave. "Nice talkin to you, Norm," Larry said, then shook hands with Norm. He stopped in front of Mom, still seated. "Hope to see you again sometime," he said casually but made no physical gesture in her direction.

Sherry quickly moved to Mom, hugged her, and said, "We'll be sure to stop next time we come down."

"I'm goin in," Norm said after we watched them drive away.

"I have to go home, Mom." I gave her a kiss.

In a disgusted tone she voiced: "It's too late!"

Somewhat shocked, I asked her, "What's too late?"

"Larry. It's too late!" she repeated, her tone now edged with anger.

I wasn't able to say anything in answer to her simple statement, so heavy with meaning. I silently recoiled from her familiar negative response to the events in her life, her denial of finally being reunited with her son. She was probably oblivious to the feelings her words provoked in me.

Where is her joy? What effort did she make toward the son who came to see her? She sat playing with the baby! I thought these things but dared not express them to her. I had watched her and wondered from the expression on her face if Cody, the little six-months-old baby boy she held, brought back feelings and memories about Larry when she had given him up at about the same age. Maybe she got so overwhelmed with feelings, she hadn't been able to relate to *her* baby, who now sat as her grown son only a few feet away.

I hugged her and kissed her, "I'll see you soon, Mom." I drove away wishing I could have done more; burdened as usual with feelings of inadequacy, unable to relieve the agony of her unsatisfying life.

Chapter 53

California
December 1989 – April 1990

Escrow closed on our home one month before we learned that the Board did not ratify the decision offered in the initial interview but proposed a drastic financial change in their offer.

"We're not going, David. It would be foolish to risk our financial future by accepting their proposal."

"That makes sense, but I'm not sure why the Board didn't stand by the agreement!"

"At least we don't own property that can be damaged by an earthquake. We'll find an apartment that we like, and we'll continue to rent."

"I like that idea because then we're sitting on 'go,'" David said. "If another opportunity presents itself, we can move quickly."

We decided that it didn't seem wise to walk through a door just because it had partially opened. Still, it took a while for David to recover from the disappointment of not being able to give me what I wanted.

In my willingness to move away, I had carefully considered my mother, expressing to myself the same sentiment I often repeated: As long as she's with Norm, he'll take good care of her.

Included in my plan to leave the area, I had also thought of Glenda, who agreed to be completely responsible for Mom's and Norm's finances, maybe because she held almost twenty thousand dollars of their money in an account under her name, proceeds from the sale of their Kansas property. In addition, Norm had appointed Glenda as executor when my attorney prepared their wills and health directives. Somehow with Glenda named executor and placed in charge of their financial needs, I felt more comfortable in my willingness to move away. Norm had put Glenda in charge of everything.

"Mac can see you March sixth at one o'clock if that works for you," the secretary offered when I called. I hadn't seen Mac in months after terminating my sessions in anticipation of leaving the area.

"Yes, that works," I said. After I replaced the receiver, I sat momentarily wondering, how many years have I been seeing Mac? Typical of my aversion to math problems, I concluded, "quite a few years."

"I still have this tremendous fear of being buried alive in an earthquake, Mac. Those old images from television, of the collapsed Nimitz freeway with people trapped or dead, continue to terrify me." As soon as I finished talking, I began to have a spontaneous reaction of rhythmic contractions in my lower abdominal area involving my vagina. I heard myself scream. I tried to talk to Mac, but I had trouble forming the words. It came to a point where I couldn't talk even though I wanted to. Instead, I began coughing. Profuse amounts of bubbly saliva formed in my mouth. I had the sensation of "hair" in my mouth. I choked and spat up saliva, but more saliva formed. I spit the saliva into a Kleenex Max handed me as I experienced continuous contractions of my lower abdominal area. Blackness descended on my vision, "I can't see, Mac!" I screamed as I jumped up. Suddenly the saliva stopped pouring into my mouth and the contractions ceased. Shivers rippled through my body. I was cold even though the room was warm. Then I returned to normal.

"Do you remember ever being 'buried' as a child?" Mac asked gently.

"If it ever happened to me, it must have been in Jarbidge," I responded, surprised by my quick response. Then I remembered something. "Mac, when I asked Mom if she had ever shut me up in a dark place, she got a strange look on her face then told me in an innocent Grinch like voice, 'There was an outdoor cellar down in the ground in Jarbidge. It had a big heavy door on it. I lifted the door and told you I was gonna put you down there if you didn't stop peein' your pants.' But Mac, that doesn't seem to fit my fear of being buried by an earthquake." Mac agreed with me. We still lacked an answer.

At my next appointment on March thirteenth, the core of the session was almost identical to what had happened a week earlier but with added material at the beginning and the end. Black Monster brought darkness with her when she briefly appeared at the start of the session, making animal-like growling sounds. She quickly yielded to a crying Young Child, who repeatedly spat up bubbly saliva. I began to choke. Ripples of shivers ran methodically through my body. "I know I'm naked, Mac," I cried to him as I experienced the shivers. "I'm very cold." Then in the voice of a small child, I heard myself cry, "Someone is making fun of me. It's very dark in here. I have to be real quiet."

In our discussion at the end of the session I said, "I experienced myself as a very young child shut in a tiny dark space. Someone was being mean to me. It seemed urgent to be very quiet even though I didn't know why. I felt that 'no one likes me.'"

Mac made an important comment, "The order in which you experience the events, meaning the sequence of events, is all part of one memory recall."

Sometimes life thickens before it thins, I thought after I left Mac's office. That's what it feels like in this effort to heal from what happened to me when I was a child, and now I'm trying to survive my involvement with Mom. What else is going to come along to plump this thickening, I thought, wishing I could cut the cords to this "heavy bear who goes with me," sometimes "dragging me" unwillingly to places I'd rather not go.

March through early June threatened to consume me, or so it seemed. My stability and well-being were fragile, too delicate to be all that Mom and Norm wanted from me. One Tuesday in late March when I had gone to see them, Norm was grumpy and irritable as he repeatedly brought up Glenda, something he hadn't done before. When I returned on Sunday, Mom was snappy and hateful. I went home exhausted.

"These people have no concept of the impact their demands make on my life," I wailed to David. "Norm has been complaining about dizziness. He also said that when he reaches into the cupboard above his head, he feels faint. I don't know how to take care of Mom if he dies first," I complained. "It's so hard to be around Mom when she's hateful to me. No matter how much of myself I give, I always come out the 'asshole.'"

"What about your idea to let Glenda be more in charge?" David asked.

How easy it is to lose sight of a solution when emotion blinds the vision. But I began to see the issues more clearly. I'd been the only one helping them in spite of the fact that Glenda is their daughter. She rarely came to see them, and her involvement was minimal. I needed to step aside and maybe Glenda would get involved, I told myself. The old "easier said than done," I chided myself, getting lost in thoughts of Glenda. Perhaps working with them now at the end of their lives will benefit her. Besides, Norm is already talking about Glenda making plans with him. Although, I thought, I'm not sure what the plans are.

The first of April when I was visiting them, Norm said coldly, "I may need to go into the hospital; could you take care of mother. I'll pay you *fifty dollars* a day if you'll take care of her."

Where in the world is this coming from? I asked myself. Why would he offer me money? "I don't want your money, Norm. I'll be happy to take care of her."

When Mom got up to go to the bathroom, I whispered to Norm, "Have you thought about Braswell's as a long-term solution? It would only cost one hundred and nine dollars a month for Mom to stay at Braswell's."

Norm glared at me without saying a word.

Obviously, I'm not giving Norm what he wants so I'm a 'shit head,' I groaned in silence. He probably wants me to say I'll take care of Mom when he can't do it anymore.

But neither of us brought up this delicate issue. We sat awkwardly in silence until Mom returned and the subject turned comfortably to the cat.

A few days later, I drove Norm and Mom to the hospital where Norm stayed for the day to have various cardiac tests run. We entered the waiting room, which had visibility but no free access into the area where patients lay on gurneys ready to be taken for procedures.

"You and your mother can stay in the waiting room," the nurse directed when she took Norm into the gurney area. But a bit later, the nurse returned, looked straight at me, and said, "He would like to see you."

When I stood up, Mom stood up. I went through the locked door and heard it close behind me as I walked toward Norm. When I reached him on the gurney, I looked back to see if Mom was with me. But there she stood, still in the waiting room, her face red with rage and her mouth moving as she shook her fist at me. Oh dear, I thought, now she is threatened by me, too. Norm and I were totally in her view the entire few minutes I was with him.

Mom stood in the waiting room on the other side of the door. When I opened the door, she swung at me with her fist. I dodged the blow. She shouted at me, "Goddamn you, bitch…" then continued calling me names. I talked reassuringly to her. Equilibrium returned. We sat quietly, waiting.

When the trying ordeal with Mom and Norm had ended and I finally returned home, peace was not yet to be mine.

Chapter 54

California
May 1990 – June 1990

"Do you think you'll marry him?" I asked Jennifer, who called me from New Hampshire shortly after I got home from Lake Elsinore. I had asked this question on separate occasions twice before. She was still in a relationship with a man who, I believed, had the potential of destroying not only her life, but our family as well.

"No," she answered again, "I'm not going to marry him."

"Good decision," I said. "I think marrying him would be a grave mistake."

"Why do you think so?" she asked.

"Do you really want to know? I've told you some of it in my letters."

"Yes, please tell me. I'm running on 'no sleep' most of the time, fuzzy brained, so tell me."

"Well, for one thing, when you brought him home at Christmas, Daddy observed that he was quite possessive with you, and that concerned him," I told her.

"What do you think concerns Daddy?" she asked.

"I think both of us have the same concern, that he may eventually not even want to share you with your family. That's a big concern we have. Speaking of concerns, do you realize he has a lot of issues with his mother? When he and I talked in New Hampshire he shared a few things about their relationship. Seems to me there is a lot of anger and resentment there."

"I picked up on that when I met her and spent time with them," Jennifer said.

"He'll eventually have to work that anger out with his mother or a significant female in his life, and that could be you! Trust me, I know from living with my angry mother that life would be very difficult for you." That painful thought is probably why I changed subjects. "I think you said his father is a psychiatrist and his mother is a pediatrician, right?"

"That's right."

"Have you heard enough, because I have another concern I need to share, probably my last," I said.

"I want to hear it, go ahead."

"You know my background, living with an alcoholic mother. He told Daddy and me, when we took him to dinner that he likes to drink, but he stressed, only to the point of 'getting a buzz.' You don't drink and probably never will. That could become a real problem in the future, especially when you have children," I expressed. "But I think my greatest concern is your well-being."

"It would probably destroy me if I married him," Jennifer admitted.

After our conversation, I remained somewhat uneasy even though she told me, "No, I'm not going to marry him." Maybe, I considered, if only I weren't dealing with Mom and Norm, it wouldn't seem so serious; but what to do with these heavy feelings bearing down on me.

Three weeks later during the first week of May, Jennifer joined David and me on the Olympic Peninsula for a few precious days together. She waited until almost time for her to leave before disclosing, "I want you to know I'm considering the possibility of marrying him."

"I've felt there was something 'unsaid' between us these past few days, but I didn't know what!" I responded. "So, it seems that the long years of waiting for your soul mate may not yield to the evidence against the man."

"I'm considering it," she repeated.

Almost immediately, it seemed to me, she left for the East Coast. The miles between us didn't compare to the emotional distance I experienced. With the prospect of losing her from our family, I unknowingly misplaced my issues of abandonment onto Jennifer, instead of onto my mother where they belonged. This fear of loss lurked as a tyrant in my mind.

On returning home from the Olympic Peninsula, I tried to sleep, but sleep wouldn't come, only thoughts and more thoughts, connected like countless train cars, haunting me as I lay in the dark. Some of the thoughts repeated themselves relentlessly, random statements Jennifer had said at different times: "This may sound funny, but I don't really know him;" "He has some dark holes; said he has a dark side;" "He gave me the silent treatment and I told him, 'Look, I can't take this;'" "He wants me with him wherever he is all the time and wants us to be alone;" "He is a very private person."

Without my permission, Elizabeth's statements raked across my mind: "He's always belittling Jennifer;" "He rains on everybody's parade;" "He defies his mother over simple things."

The evidence against him continued to mount in my troubled thoughts. Nurses and fellow residents had expressed concerns to Jennifer. One of the nurses even gave her a book titled, "Dance of Anger!" Obsessive thoughts finally released me to sleep in the wee hours of morning.

On the following sleepless night, Depression became a tyrant tightly holding me in its grip. It obliterated my ability to reason. It dragged me deeply into the muck of my suicidal beliefs. When morning came, Depression and I drove to Davis, some four hundred fifty miles North. We got a room at the University Lodge. I took a sheet of stationary and began to write.

May 12, 1990

"The one thing that has kept me alive to this point was the deep belief that my mother was wrong in her evaluation of me. She considered me in the way, worthless, unlovable. She rejected me, the person I am. I've worked on top of these underlying feelings, trying to prove I have value, prove I belong, prove I am loveable.

David was a gift from heaven. With all my problems, he endured, is constant, expresses his love for me. I recently became aware he has been sacrificing much of himself for the sake of my well-being. At times he becomes kind of a non-person for my sake.

Then there is Jennifer. We were close. But then she went far, far away. I behaved abominably – lashing out in anger several times about him. Distance came between us over her relationship with him. She shut me out. She has reflected back to me an image of myself I detest. I seem to be breaking her heart. I want to be out of the way so she can make her choice freely. It was a great blow to give up the idea of having a family. When she marries him, he will want her to himself. It is more than I can tolerate. Life looks too alone again.

Thoughts of the many emotionally upsetting experiences I put my husband and my children through over the years are causing me grief as I see their lives today. Jennifer always chooses a demanding approach to life – over extended, stressed out; probably a result of trying to please me when she was a little girl. Now it is a monster on her back, driving her into the ground. I blame myself.

In addition, to all of these overwhelming reasons for ending my life, is the fact I am a bottomless pit filled with pain and ugly memories. There is no end to it except the one I bring to it.

Thank you for giving so much for so long. None of you failed. It was just I who was a mistake from the start. Mom was right."

When deep darkness descends upon us, threatening to consume our breath of life, what shall save us? I sat alone in the motel room, emotionally alone, longing to be relieved of my pain, half believing that death was my solution. The conflict raged within me; the choice was mine. I faltered. I hesitated. I argued with myself. I lay crying on the bed; sleep overcame me, took me safely into the hours of morning. When I awoke, I admitted to myself, "I want to live!"
Always, always in the past when I had made serious attempts on my life there rose up within me the desire to live. Now, once again, I wanted to hold on tightly to life. Surely this

desire came from God, the one who extracted me from my nightmare of despair then led me safely back home to David and Elizabeth and Marc.

"What were you thinking?" David asked as he held me. "Why would you want to kill yourself?" he wanted to know.

It took a minute before I could respond because, at the moment, it all seemed so absurd. "I think the final blow was believing that we were going to lose Jennifer when she married him. She would be lost to us and to herself. The constant stress of dealing with Mom along with Norm's hostility is a huge factor. But the body memories and experiences of myself that I keep having in Mac's office have worn me down. I'm weary of this personal battlefield to the point that recovery seems impossibly out of reach. I guess momentarily, my retreat into suicide held the promise of relief."

"Why did you drive all the way to Davis?" David asked.

"I didn't want to die in Southern California. I wanted to spare you any memory associated with my dying where you live; spare you the embarrassment as well."

The next day was Mother's Day. Newly fortified to meet my challenges, I purchased gifts to take to my mother. I wanted her to know that I loved her. I couldn't admit to myself how much I wanted to experience her love for me. I also purchased a package of dates for Norm. I sat with them in their fifth wheel after I gave each the gifts I had brought. Norm glared at me as he ate the dates.

"Has the doctor given you the results of your test?" I asked Norm, thinking that might be the reason for his attitude.

"My heart's fine. Said my symptoms are probably caused by stress," Norm said, without telling me what thoughts lurked behind his hateful look. I didn't ask. I expressed love to each of them as best I could, then left.

I presented myself at Mac's office the next week as a happy, peaceful person, making an effort to get on with my life.

"You seem to be in denial," he said, confronting me gently. "I think you are minimizing your suicide attempt. In my opinion, your life is at risk. You are in the life-threatening stage of therapy. I believe you are starting to face the Perpetrator."

"What do you mean?" I asked. I wasn't sure I understood his explanation, so I tried to put it into my own words. "The Perpetrator is a destructive force coming from within myself that threatens my life? Like having an enemy living within me?"

"Yes," Mac agreed. "This is either the last or next to last personality to emerge. This is the most life-threatening stage."

I sat there thinking of the "life-threatening situation" I had survived in Davis. "How is the Perpetrator any different from Black Monster or Angry Mother?" I asked.

When Mac couldn't give me a satisfying answer, I believe that he was struggling to understand what he may have theoretically learned recently. But he frightened me with his suggestion of the Perpetrator.

"You may want to see someone about medication as a means to help you through this," he gravely proposed.

"Mac, I don't want to be medicated," I said emphatically. "I'm not sure where I got my attitude toward medicine, but I don't want to take drugs that would interfere with the chemistry of my body, impact me with negative side effects, or alter my self-control."

I was grateful when Mac honored my position, but I left his office thinking of what he had told me, "Most people who talk about suicide and make attempts at suicide eventually kill themselves."

In the next few days, I uneasily pondered the eventual appearance of the Perpetrator. To fortify myself against the expected onslaught, I called Jennifer. "I need you to come home," I pleaded, offering a lengthy explanation behind my request.

"I need some time to think about it. Could I call you back tomorrow?" She requested.

She faithfully called back the next day. "I'm not able to interrupt my residency." Jennifer had gracefully said "no" to my request.

For a period of about two weeks, I experienced disappointment, anger, and vulnerability. I searched my motives for asking my daughter to come home. I had to admit that it was my way of trying to get her away from him. Oh, I was afraid of facing the Perpetrator without all my immediate family members present to surround me with their protecting love, but I couldn't deny my second motive.

I understood that Jennifer held a position of extreme significance in my life. After she said "no" to returning home, I became aware that I had transferred to Jennifer qualities that belonged to my mother rather than to her, so I worked carefully to untangle the two. To accomplish this task, I headed the page "Separating the Past from the Present" and made two columns, one titled "My Mother" the other titled "My Daughter. Under each heading I wrote similarities and differences of the two. Leaving out at least one significant comparison, here is a partial list:

Mother: sent me away or left me for a long time.
Jennifer: left me, moved to New Hampshire for three years.

Mother: emotionally unavailable.
Jennifer: physically unavailable; emotionally stressed with residency, unavailable.

Mother: unreliable caretaker. Hateful to me.
Jennifer: caregiver before she left. Loving. Patient. I had come to count on her.

Mother: The significant woman in my life when I was a child.
Jennifer: Became the significant woman in my life, so that I felt closer to her emotionally at times than to David.

After completing this task, I wrote a short note to myself. It started with, "Jennifer is not my mother. The events of her life have triggered my past. The anger I directed at her is the anger I feel toward my mother. It is misplaced anger." I experienced a deeper understanding after completing the task. I felt as if I had taken one more step toward mental well-being.

Chapter 55

New Hampshire
June 1990 – August 1990

"It's already June," David said, "If Jennifer is in agreement, why don't you leave as soon as you're ready. I'll join you later in August, if you're still there." Much to my delight, Jennifer was eager to have me join her in New Hampshire.

"Why didn't you come home to the West Coast when I needed you?" I asked sometime after my arrival.

"Because I hoped to find another solution. And your coming to Hanover was the perfect solution," she smiled as she gave me a hug.

"I can leave any time you need me," I reassured her. I reminded her of my position on marriage, "A woman separates herself from her family and becomes one with her husband. He comes first in her life and her heart." I looked into her loving eyes, then added, "But it has always been my dream that we can continue to be part of each other's lives," I purposely paused before continuing, "on the fringe, you understand." We laughed.

Toward mid-July Jennifer and I had regained the closeness we had before she entered her residency. I think we had actually strengthened our relationship.

"There's a wonderful hot air balloon show I'd like to see," Jennifer reported excitedly. "Also, there'll be a display of arts and crafts by local artists. Would you like to go?" she asked.

"I'd love to go."

"He won't be going with us. He said he didn't want to go," she volunteered before I could ask.

When we came to the top of the rise on the hillside, the sight of colorful hot air balloons all at different stages of inflation stretched over an expanse of green fields. One lifted up into the blue sky, hissing as it went. Others followed until the sky overflowed with their color.

"Let's go and see the crafts," Jennifer suggested after she had taken two rolls of film focused on the balloons. We meandered pleasantly down aisle after aisle of beautiful art.

"I like this picture," I said of a lovely painting on cloth. I bought one for each of us.

He came when we returned home. A black cloud came with him, giving his face a heavy serious expression that bode the coming of a storm. "You're late!" he said.

Jennifer bubbled over with excitement when she began to tell him of the hot air balloons. "You should have come with us! The hot air balloons were spectacular," she said as she reached to give him a kiss.

He pulled away. "I thought we were going to have dinner together," he said accusingly.

"We are," Jennifer answered, "I picked up fresh vegetables and I thought we could cook together." She said this because he enjoyed being in the kitchen with her. He shrugged his shoulders and silently remained seated on the couch, even though she tried to interest him in her purchases.

Silence, I told myself. Jennifer said this is often his choice when he's upset. I wanted to tell him, "You're pouting because you feel left out but you were invited. It was your choice not to go." The happiness we had experienced from the pleasure of the day was threatened by his cloudy presence.

By July twenty-eighth a month had passed, and I had made no contact with my mother. When I said goodbye before leaving for New Hampshire, I had no conscious intention of not staying in touch. Time continued to pass but still I didn't call. As I persisted on this course, so much time eventually passed that I considered it too late to call. I wasn't willing to face their imagined wrath. The explanations I gave myself were reasonable, but they didn't quiet my conflict in not being connected to my mother. There had always been a pull from part of me that didn't want to be connected to her and Norm, but I had overridden that urge by what I considered to be a more mature adult self who thought it best that I be connected.

What are my reasons for making contact? I asked myself, trying to resolve my inner conflict. I want to know what becomes of my mother. I love her. I don't want to abandon her.

This inner dialogue continued with a second voice that said, "Look how you've suffered because of her cruelty when you were a child. You're suffering now with all these body memories, sometimes wanting to die. You need to honor that part of you that doesn't want to be connected. And she tried to hit you when we were at the hospital with Norm. How can you *love* her? Besides, she abandoned you so many times. Why do you care? Oh, and don't forget how Norm glared at you when he was eating the dates you brought and how cold he's been."

The first voice came back with, "I know it's hard for you to believe that I love my mother, but I've *always* loved her. It's hard for you to believe or understand. And I know the pain of being abandoned. I'm not going to abandon her even if you don't understand."

The second voice said, "You've *always* loved her?" What about that time you yelled 'I hate you! I've *always* hated you?"

The first voice said, "I don't know who said that, but it wasn't me." I remembered the splintered parts of myself that Mac and I had worked to integrate. "As for me, I've always loved my mother, since I was a little girl."

The inner dialogue ceased. For a time, peace within was restored.

I continued to do nothing until August fifth. On that day, I made a list that I titled Pending Decisions. Included on my list was the question, "Shall I contact my mother?" My answer to myself was, "As long as she is with Norm she will be cared for. I'm not able to deal with Mom and Norm right now. I'm already totally challenged emotionally. I can't handle anymore." I decided to delay. I didn't contact her.

The time came for me to leave Jennifer and return home. I sat looking out the window at the passing landscape. Why did I take the train home to California? I asked myself. Because the distance from my daughter comes about slowly, gradually, I reflected, as the train moved in a direction away from Jennifer, but happily, in the direction of David.

Even after returning home, I resisted contacting my mother. Instead, I immersed myself in decorating our small apartment. But my priority was a letter to Jennifer, to summarize for the last time all that my heart wanted her to absorb regarding him.

Chapter 56

California
September 1990 – May 1991

"Adair Photography called to say you can pick up the photos," David said.

The photographer showed me the final prints of our family picture along with the ones taken with Larry last November. "Today, September twenty-first marks the second anniversary of finding my brother," I said to the disinterested clerk. When I got home, I looked at the pictures of Larry and me. I wish Larry didn't look so much like my mother, I thought. I was able to set the pictures aside, but I couldn't stop thinking about my mother.

"I'm going to the Lake Elsinore Cemetery to see if anyone is buried there yet. Maybe it's over. If it is, I can stop torturing myself about what to do," I announced to David when I woke on Sunday morning.

"I'll go with you," he offered. When we approached the cemetery, I became tense. David drove to the area where the plots were located. "Only the tree I planted is here," I remarked, feeling a small measure of relief.

"Once my mother dies, it will be finished," I had declared to David on a previous occasion. I stood looking at the empty plots. "It isn't finished," I said.

"Do you want to go see her?" David asked.

"No, I don't," I quickly answered, even though they were less than ten minutes away. I wanted to see Mom, but I wasn't willing to face her anger.

"Let's go home, David."

After a nap, I felt a need to talk with Marc about Mom. But a short time after I started talking with him, the body contractions started. I felt bathed in blackness as saliva poured into my mouth. I heaved several times. My head and torso shook. My vision was affected. When I finally came out of the body experience, I talked at length with Marc about family, about my mother and about Larry.

Then I tried to get up, but my legs wouldn't hold me. Suddenly it was as if someone had poured blackness mixed with terror over the top of me. I was being pulled in, sucked away.

"I need David," I cried. Marc called, and David came right away. Gripped by uncontrollable body contractions, covered by mysterious darkness, I heard myself scream as saliva profusely poured into my mouth. My frozen arms lay useless. My body shivered though I didn't experience myself as cold, a familiar ending to recent body memories.

"I feel better now," I commented to David and Marc.

"Are you aware it's been almost three hours since all of this started," Marc asked.

"It feels like forever ago," I answered.

During the body memory, I was able to consciously observe my own experience. I looked for images in the blackness that swallowed me whole. No images came, only the sound of screaming and the impression that I was inside the little house in Jarbidge.

"I think this body memory was about Verneda and Buddy, Jr. and me and something awful that happened in that little house in Jarbidge," I told David and Marc, "but my mind doesn't remember what it was."

Later Marc shared an article with me titled, "Your Inner Child." "This might give you some insights," he suggested.

"What's it about?" I asked.

"The theory is that we each have an inner child within us that we need to nurture. Let me put it differently. We each have a child within us that we need to facilitate and pay attention to. We need to understand the child's needs and try to meet them. At least that's what a few psychologists believe is one pathway to being healed."

"That's not new to me," I joked with Marc. "I have a number of "children within."

It was late October when I clearly heard sobbing and weeping within myself. Assuming it was a sobbing child, I sat down and wrote the following as an attempt to communicate with her:

"Are you the child who wants to see your mother?"
I felt as if I were talking to the unresponsive wall, but I kept writing.

"I've wondered why you love her to such an extent."
With no response, no impressions, my written confrontation continued.

"You haven't really let yourself separate from what she taught you about yourself. To believe she was a tyrant was more threatening to you than to believe the lies she told you about yourself. Why?" I wrote, awakened to an old forgotten awareness.

"Let me say this important point in a different way. Unwanted, disliked, you accepted the blame for being born, for being in the way. You tried to make up for being born! You gave up yourself to become someone you hoped she would love. You became acquiescent, submissive, disgustingly sweet.

Why was it safer for you to blame yourself for being born? Why did you accept as truth what mother taught you about yourself?"
Nothing happened beyond hearing myself breathe. I put the pencil down.

Well, I doubt I accomplished much by doing that exercise, I thought when the exercise brought *itself* to an end. I'll stick with my committee meeting as a way to work with my "children within," I decided when I sat back somewhat discombobulated by the activity.

In late November I awoke in an emotional panic. "David, my feeling of panic seems out of proportion. Mac said when I get overwhelming feelings that don't fit current circumstances they are most likely related to the past. He calls them feeling memories. These feelings I'm having are probably linked to the past."

A phrase came into my mind and repeated itself several times, "Bottom fell out. Bottom fell out." I searched through my memory for a time in my life when the "Bottom fell out." Two places emerged, Jarbidge and Larned, the same two places that had stayed lodged in my mind from childhood. As I started to think of Jarbidge, a familiar body memory came.

As usual, it started with contractions in my lower abdominal area, then darkness swallowed me as my mouth began profuse salivating followed this time by something new: I had a terrifying experience of being choked, unable to breath. Body shivers ended the memory.

"Did you have any cognitive memories with it this time?" David asked

"Nothing."

"I think the theory is that the trauma was so severe you'll never recover cognitive memories," David reminded me.

"It would sure help if my mind could remember what happened to me, not just my body releasing the traumatic memory," I admitted, feeling helpless. "Then maybe these body events would stop coming. If only I'd get cognitive memories with the body memories, I'd know who's hurting me and where it's happening and maybe it would all go away! Instead, my body remembers but my mind doesn't," I said.

The phone was ringing when I came into the apartment. "Hello," I answered.

"Hello mumsy-poo!" Jennifer said. "Have you thought about meeting me in Seattle in February for my interviews in Washington, Oregon and California?" she asked.

"Yes, I have. I'd love to join you if it will help."

We decided that the two of us would meet in Seattle toward the end of February and then drive together to her various appointments for a medical position when she completed her residency in June.

"I wish we could be together for Christmas," she said, just before our goodbye.

Christmas, I thought when I got off the phone, only a few days away and then Mother's birthday on the twenty-eighth.

Christmas came and went; the twenty-eighth came and went. "I probably will not be seeing my mother anymore," I told David. "I deal with guilt feelings about the lapse of months since I've seen her. I didn't mean to stop seeing her. Time went by and I didn't call. Then it seemed too late to call."

David offered a perspective I had been unable to see. "In the months that have passed, neither Norm nor your mom has called to ask how you are, to make sure that nothing has happened to you. They simply haven't called you. They have a part in the silence of the last few months."

"Why didn't I think of that? Amazing that it never entered my mind. Maybe that will give me some much needed guilt relief, I said.

Distracting me from thoughts of my mother was my emotional involvement with Jennifer. Yes, she was coming to the West Coast for interviews when residency ended, but she was also undecided if she would accept his invitation to follow him to Louisiana. Suspended and restless, I tried to turn my attention elsewhere but found it difficult.

When I went to pick Jennifer up in Seattle for her West Coast interviews, he was with her. Oh, I said to myself, she's going to go to Louisiana with him.

"He has business in Seattle," Jennifer said. He and I briefly exchanged a few words as he put Jennifer's luggage in the back of my Suburban. We said our goodbyes as we left him to his business in Seattle. As soon as we were buckled in and driving South Jennifer turned to me and said, "I'm not going to Louisiana."

Jennifer's decision to accept a medical position on the West Coast brought me to a pleasant, relaxed state at the end of May, just in time for the shocking information Norm's son Robert shared with me when we visited him the first week of June nineteen ninety-one.

Chapter 57

California
June 1991

"Let's stop by to see Robert and Judy when we're in the Huntington Beach area," I suggested to David on a Saturday afternoon drive along the coast.

"C'mon in," Robert said when he answered the door. "Judy isn't here. She won't be home until later." Robert and I had become close friends over the years. I felt fortunate to find him home but later reminded myself of what someone once said, "There are no coincidences..."

After we had talked for a while, Robert asked, "Did you know your mother is in a rest home?"

"What! She's in a rest home? How long has she been there?"

"Since February," he answered.

"February, but it's June! That was months ago, why didn't you tell me?"

"Glenda told me not to say anything, but I decided you have a right to know," he explained. "Glenda says she's outta her mind and doesn't know anyone."

"Oh my God," I murmured.

"No one goes to see her. Glenda says she swears and cusses at anyone who visits so no one goes."

"Oh my God," I repeated. "Where is she?"

"She's in Riverside someplace, just off the freeway."

"Can you find out from Norm or Glenda where she is? I need to go see her."

Robert agreed to help. Since Norm was his father and Glenda his half-sister, I thought he could easily learn where Mom was. Besides, he was still with the Long Beach Police Department; I assumed he had ways of finding answers that I couldn't.

"Robert made it sound like everyone has abandoned Mom, including Norm," I told David on the way home. I need to see her and find out for myself if she's out of her mind and doesn't recognize anyone. If she doesn't recognize me, then I'll

472

leave her in peace for the rest of her days if I'm satisfied with the care she's getting."

"I wonder why Robert waited so long to tell you?" David asked.

"Because Glenda told him not to tell me. I'm sure glad he changed his mind. Glenda lives more than an hour from Riverside, so why didn't she find a place for Mom close to her or close to Norm in Lake Elsinore? Why is Mom in Riverside?"

David didn't have the answer and neither did I.

"Did Glenda tell you where Mom is?" I asked Robert the next day.

"She doesn't want you to know where she is," Robert answered.

"I guess she's mad because I haven't been involved for a few months. Keep trying. Maybe Norm will tell you."

A week passed, "Have you found out where she is yet?" I asked, almost in desperation when I called Robert on Saturday morning.

"I'm searching the directory and I'm getting some information in the mail."

"Thanks, Robert, I can search the phone directories. But if you learn anything please let me know."

I went to the library to copy yellow pages from the Riverside phone directory for listings of Rest Homes, Homes, and Sanitariums. Nearly thirty listings under each heading. She has to be in *one* of these places, I assured myself. I found Larry and I'll find my mother.

When I got home, I complained to David "The number of places she might be is overwhelming!"

"You could start by calling them one at a time," he suggested, after I showed him the listings.

"Narrow the focus, good idea!" I looked at the first number on the first list. Military name, no need to call them, I decided. "You have reached a number that has been disconnected," I heard a computer voice say on my second call. I dialed the third number.

"Do you have a patient," I corrected myself, "a resident named Edna Hall?"

"Yes," the woman replied, "she's in room 229."

How could it be that I found her so easily? Could it be a mistake, not really be her? I sat wondering.

"David, I think I've found Mom after making only two phone calls by starting with the 'A' on the first list. It's like someone went to the directory and alphabetically picked the first place available! It's in Riverside about forty-five minutes from here, a place called Arlington Meadows. Do you want to go with me?" I asked.

"Sure, I'd like to go with you."

When we got there, David asked, "Do you mind if I stay in the car until you make sure she's here?"

"That's a good idea, because I want to find out if she recognizes me before I talk with her."

I don't want to announce my presence quite yet, I thought, so I quickly walked by the office, intent on finding my mother. Looks like the dining room; people having lunch, I noticed briefly, but continued to search the hallway for the stairs. Room 229 has to be on the second floor; I need to find the stairs.

This looks like a promising door I thought as I rushed through it. The door closed behind me. Panic struck. O dear God, am I locked in this small space? I took a step further into the space and caught sight of a stairway. Once on the second floor, I checked room numbers. Not even close to 229! I moved rapidly through the hallway to the next corridor where at first, I was frustrated to find that the numbers were too large. But as I continued, I realized that the numbers were getting smaller.

Finally, I stood at the door number 229. Without thinking, I slowly it. "Anyone here?" I called. No one answered. I walked into a room with two twin beds and two nightstands. I opened the drawer of one of the nightstands, looking for something to confirm that this was in fact my mother's room. There were cards and pictures in the drawer. One of the cards said something about Grandma and was signed, "Love, Mitzi." Not my mom's nightstand, I closed the drawer.

I looked across at the other nightstand. There was a bra tossed over a sheet of paper and nothing else on the stand. As I put the bra aside, a letter from the Social Security Administration now lay visibly in front of me, bearing my mother's name, Edna

Hall. I felt breathless. She's here, I said to myself, but where is she? Lunch. Maybe she's eating lunch.

Once I had found my way back to the dining room, I stood in the hallway looking through the windows that completely surrounded it. After searching many faces that filled the room but not seeing her, I looked again. One of the women who sat with her back to me caught my attention. "That could be her," I whispered. Careful not to enter her view, I moved to where I could see her face. Yes indeed, it is my mother! She looks lovely, I thought. The blue of her sweater complements the silver of soft curls outlining the peaceful look on her face.

In that moment, I decided to simply stand where she might see me when she came into the hallway. I watched, expectantly waiting, but she went with a woman out a different door. I tried to maneuver my way around people to reposition myself, but my mother and her companion got across the hall and into a room before I could reach them. I read the sign on the door where I saw them go, "Restroom." I stood leaning against the wall only a few feet from the door of the restroom. What is taking them so long, I wondered? A steady stream of people from the dining room crowded the hallway when the door of the restroom finally opened. Mother looked in my direction. Too many people between us; she didn't see me! I told myself as I watched her walk away. I moved in and out of the crowd of people in the hallway until I was beyond my mother and her companion. Then I stopped and waited. At first, she only glanced at me when our eyes met. Then she paused, turned, and looked directly at me, her gaze fixed.

"I know you," she said. "You're my daughter."

"Yes, I'm your daughter."

"I didn't think I'd ever see you again," she said in a sweet, quiet way that touched my heart.

Chapter 58

California
June 1991

"Can you take me home with you?" Mom asked.

Before I could respond her companion stepped forward. "I'm Norene, her roommate. Your mother doesn't have anyone, so I've been taking care of her."

"My mother is very fortunate," I began, but Mom interrupted me.

"Can you take me home with you?" she asked again, this time more urgently.

"Yes, Mom, I'd like to take you home with me, but I need to go to the office first, to make arrangements. Can you wait with Norene?"

"I wanna go with you," Mom said. She looks so frightened, I thought, but so would I if I'd been left here for over four months. She started to walk with me.

"You wait with Norene. I'll come right back." I assured her.

Why did Glenda lie to Robert? I wondered as I walked away from Mom. She recognized me! She's not out of her mind. What will Glenda and Norm do if they learn that I've found her? Somehow keep me from seeing her? With this anxious concern on my mind, I tried to appear calm when I approached the woman in the office.

"I'd like to take my mother Edna Hall home with me today for a few hours. Can that be arranged?"

"You really don't need to check at the office when you wish to take her with you," she informed me. "The residents are free to leave without signing out."

All the way back to Redlands, Mom talked constantly about coming to live with me or having a place of her own. Our time together went by in a blur.

"I have to take you back now, Mom."

"But I don't wanna go back," she protested. "Why can't I stay with you? I won't be *any* trouble. I don't like that place. I can sleep anywhere."

476

"Mom, I'm sorry but Glenda and Norm decide where you live, not me." I was uncertain if she understood.

She was quiet until we reached the car. "I kept ya with me when you was little, now it's your turn," she said in chilling, familiar mother tones.

Her unsettling comment, "I kept you with me," sent me plummeting into thoughts of our past history. She must have considered it an inconvenient sacrifice to go back and get me after giving me away to that "nice woman in Utica." It struck me as an obligation she labored to fulfill, keeping me with her.

The closer we got to Arlington Meadows, the more upset she became. "I don't wanna stay in that place," she kept repeating. I tried to explain why I had to take her back, but it was as if she didn't hear me. More than anything, she didn't want to be left at Arlington Meadows, but that's what I did the evening of the first day I found her there.

On my way home, I thought of our small apartment, six hundred fifty square feet, each room except the kitchen wall to wall with furniture. There might be space for a cot or a rollaway bed if we remove the table and chairs from the corner of the kitchen, I thought. Ironic, Mom sleeping in the kitchen where she often put me when I lived with her.

My cot in the kitchen idea began to slip away as I remembered Mac's words: "It would not be wise for you to have your mother live with you. It wouldn't be good for you, and it wouldn't be good for her." It's as if Mac had given me permission not to have Mom live with me, I considered, feeling a mixture of relief and guilt. But I reminded myself, her destiny is legally in the hands of Norm and Glenda; I'm not in charge. Obviously, I've alienated them by my absence over the last nine months, I thought. If I try to take control of my mother's circumstances, I'm not sure how they'll react.

"My anxiety is running high. I need courage to let Glenda or Norm know that I've found Mom," I said Thursday before David left for work. "I haven't been in touch with them for nine months. Not knowing what their attitude will be is scary!"

"Simply call Glenda and tell her, then you'll know what her response is."

"Better than calling Norm, I suppose."

"Much better," he said.

I picked up the phone, "I'll call her while you're still here and before she leaves for work."

"Hello," Glenda answered.

"Glenda, I know from talking to Robert, you don't want me to know where Mom is."

"That's right!" she responded adamantly. "I don't want you to know where she is!"

I wish I had asked her, "Why don't you want me to know where she is?" but instead I asked, "How would you feel if I could find Mom?"

"I wouldn't like that," she said coldly.

"Well, I've already found her, and I'd like to keep visiting her," I said as nicely as I could.

"You witch! I'll move her to a place where you'll never find her!" she yelled.

In a calm voice I said to her, "If you do that, it will be very hard on Mom and that would be on *your* head."

Glenda hung up.

"Glenda said she'll move Mom where I'll never find her! I know she's capable of making that happen," I cried to David.

"Trust me, that's *not* going to happen," he assured me. "You're letting them all off the hook by visiting your mom."

Within a short time, Robert called. "Glenda won't move your mom if your she doesn't get upset."

"Mother is already upset about being left there with no one coming to see her," I replied. "I still don't know why they left her there. The staff tells me no one comes to see her. Glenda doesn't come. Norm doesn't come. Even Verneda doesn't come to see her and I'm not sure why."

Robert didn't say much, but I had a measure of satisfaction that at least he knew the truth: Mom is not out of her mind; she recognized me; she is aware of being abandoned. My anxiety was greatly relieved once Glenda accepted that I had found mother.

The next day when I picked her up and we were walking to the car, I said, "You seem very tired today, Mom."

"There was men climbin' and crawlin' all over me in the night. That's an awful place," she complained as we drove toward Redlands.

"Mom, I feel really helpless," I said, believing that men may well have been in her unlocked room at night. "I don't know how I can get you out of there but I'm going to make it happen, somehow."

"I don't know what happened to me, how I got into that place."

"I don't know why or how that happened either, Mom. But I hope to find out. At least now, you get to come here every day," I told her as we approached the apartment.

"Yes, but I have to go back," she answered.

She had been quietly lying on the sofa when suddenly she told me, "That husband of mine doesn't love me, he doesn't care about me."

"Norm has always loved you. I'm sure he still loves you," I said, in an effort to comfort her. "Maybe something happened to him and that's why he doesn't come to see you," I suggested.

"No, he's still over there," she said with certainty.

"Mom, I know Norm was sick the last time I saw you. Maybe he is sick and not able to take care of you. But it isn't because he doesn't love you anymore. I'll find out what happened to him."

It was late in the day toward evening when we drove back to Arlington Meadows.

"I don't wanna stay in that place," she repeated over and over. She kept returning to her dreams: "I can get a little place of my own" and "I could live with you." When I turned into the parking lot she said, "I don't know why I have to come back here. I don't want to stay here."

"Mom, you don't understand." I started to cry, worn down by her pleadings, helpless to fulfill her needs and wants. "Norm and Glenda put you here, not me." My voice got louder, and tears ran down my cheeks. "I'm doing the best I can. For right now, you have to stay here but I'll keep coming to get you every day," I sobbed. "I feel bad about leaving you here but there's nothing I can do about it."

"That's okay, that's okay," she said softly, patting my shoulder.

"I'm so sorry you have to stay here. When we go in, do you want to say goodbye in the lounge or in your room?"

"In my room would be better." In previous days, she had put up a terrible fuss when I tried to leave her but not this time.

"I'll see you soon," I told her once she was in her room.

"I hope so," she said. I kissed her goodbye and as I looked back, she blew me kisses. I didn't remember this loving mother when I was a child, but something in me must have experienced her this way. Why else would I feel love for her and stay with her when others had not?

What is it that keeps me from taking her home with me permanently? I asked myself again. I'm so nervous when I'm with her, I answered. I feel emotionally fractured, unable to have her with me full time. For now, I'll continue to take her home daily, if I'm able, but she'll have to return to Arlington Meadows.

Only two days later, I was desperate for help when I saw Laurie in the hallway, an employee who had helped me once before during a difficult time of saying goodbye to Mom.

"Laurie, my mother is pretty upset. Could you come stay with her for a while after I leave?"

"Certainly. How are you, Edna?" she asked, putting her arm around Mom.

"Not so good," Mom told her.

"Laurie," I asked when I called later in the evening, "How was she when I left?"

"She went out one of the exterior doors and set off the alarm. She was hot and sweaty and very upset. I helped her get undressed and into bed."

"Thank you, Laurie, for being there for me and watching over my mother. I'll come tomorrow to pick her up," I said, feeling quite troubled by Laurie's report.

The start of Tuesday was almost identical to Monday, except that mom was wearing one house slipper and one brown shoe when I found her in the lounge to bring her home. She was exhausted, barely able to make it from the car to the apartment.

She fell asleep on the sofa and didn't wake until almost three o'clock.

She was silent in the car on the way back but when we arrived at Arlington Meadows, she turned to me and asked, "Why can't I go with you?"

What did I answer? I don't remember.

"You don't want me," she uttered sadly.

I clumsily countered her accusation but only the action of keeping her with me would have convinced her.

"Can you come in for a while?" she asked.

"Yes Mom, I certainly will."

On our way to her room, a black gal from the Salvation Army threw her arms around Mom and gave her a big hug. The hug probably did more for me than it did for Mom.

"I'll get away from this place. I don't want to stay here," Mom said when we got to her room.

I looked at my mother, sitting dejectedly on her bed. Mom, I said to myself, I wish I had the guts or whatever it takes to pack up your things and take you home with me for good. You probably have no idea how much I love you, a love that confounds me, regardless of what's happened between us in the past. I loathe this nightmare of our experience. Neither one of us fully understands my inability to find a better way through this mess.

"Here, Mom, before I leave, let me put some lotion on your hands." I reached for the bottle on her nightstand. "Mm, this has a nice fragrance," I said.

Mom sniffed the lotion. "That smells good." I slowly rubbed her hands with the lotion and watched as she began to relax.

After I put the lotion aside, I asked, "May I comb your hair?" She didn't protest. The only time I had been this close to her happened when Norm was in the hospital. Before that, I had almost never touched my mother, neither her hair nor her skin. Now I drew the comb through the curls of her silver hair. "You are a very pretty woman, Mom," I said sincerely. "I think a little lipstick is called for." I took my lipstick from my purse. "This will be the finishing touch."

"I have to go now, Mom, but I'll see you very soon," I promised when I kissed her goodbye.

"I'm not stayin' here. I'm gonna leave," I heard her threaten as I left the room.

"Your mother wasn't as upset today when you left as she was on Monday," Laurie said, when I called about two hours later. "I'll look in on her after dinner."

Laurie called back in the early evening, "I found your mom asleep in her clothes on her bed, so I woke her and put a gown on her then put her into bed. Your mother said, 'Thank you.'"

Chapter 59

California
June – July 1991

"The last two days of taking Mom back have been so traumatic; even more so than the first eleven days, if that's possible. She hates that place! I'm not very fond of it myself. It isn't the right place for her. She doesn't get the care or attention she needs," I ranted on as David listened. "She wore the same clothes every day the first week after I found her and recently, I learned that she even sleeps in them. I'm sure she's not drinking enough water because hours pass between bathroom trips. The employees come and go. If Laurie leaves, I won't have anyone to connect with."

"Take a few deep breaths," he said. "Think about what you can do to help."

"One thing I can do is find out my legal position to make decisions on her behalf. I'm not sure how to get a copy of Mom's Will. I'd especially like to get the Durable Power of Health Care and the Directive to Physicians. I think there's also a Durable Power of Attorney. If I'm indicated as having the legal power in those documents, I'll move her to a facility that will provide the care she needs and that is close to us, then Glenda's cooperation won't be necessary."

"I think that kind of action will get you out of the victim role. Let me know if there's anything I can do," David offered.

"I can see what's available just in case I can make this happen for her," I told him. "As usual, you've helped so much by listening to me vent my feelings."

"One step at a time, one positive step at a time, my dear."

That morning during my visit to the local retirement community of Plymouth Village to learn what levels of care might be available, the administrator said, "We recommend that you make an appointment with the San Bernardino Geriatric Assessment program to determine your mother's mental condition. This will assure she gets the proper placement for her care."

The next day, I was able to meet with Ann Rowe, a Nurse Practitioner with the Geriatric Assessment program. I was hoping that my face didn't show my feelings, as it usually does, when she informed me, "We will need her husband's signature in order to do the work-up. Please bring the signed papers to the next appointment."

I smiled at her. "Yes, I'll do that."

The following morning as David and I were driving to Lake Elsinore, I told him, "I'm glad you're free to come with me to see Norm today. It's been almost a year since I've seen him. I'm not sure how he'll act toward me. I'm hoping he'll sign this paper so I can get the Geriatric Assessment. I want to get this out of the way before we leave for Ashland on Friday."

"He probably won't give you any trouble," David said.

"I'm going to see if he'll let me be responsible for Mom's care and where she lives."

Norm's greeting was reserved, I thought, as he sat at the little table in the fifth wheel smoking his habitual cigarette. But his demeanor became friendly, even tender, once he understood why I had come.

"Do you have the copy of Mom's will and the rest of those documents?" I asked, after explaining why I wanted Mom to have the Geriatric Assessment and after he had signed the form.

"Yeah," he answered.

"I'd like to have them or make a copy. I may need the Directive to Physician, or the Health Care documents." He readily gave me the documents. "Arlington Meadows doesn't really provide the care Mom needs. I'd like to move her closer to me. Is that possible?"

"*Glenda's* in charge of where Mother lives!" Norm said emphatically before changing the subject. "I'm going to a potluck with the neighbors and Betty," he shared with an unfamiliar lilt in his tone.

"Betty? Is she the one whose husband Jerry died a couple of years ago, the one you and Mom used to be friends with?"

"Yeah, that Betty." Norm smiled, flicking off an ash of his cigarette.

"I see you have a new sofa and new pink curtains at the windows, Norm."

"Yeah, mother didn't want me to spend money for that stuff when she was here," Norm mumbled. My thoughts went to Betty. I wondered if the improvements had been to attract her to his nest.

"Have you been to see Mom?" I asked.

"No, she'd just throw a fit and want to come home with me and git angry. I collapsed in February and the doctor said I couldn't come home until I had someone else to take care of her. Glenda took care of her for me."

I didn't ask any more questions. He didn't ask me why I had stopped coming to see them, nor did he mention why he hadn't called me during the months of silence between us. We said our goodbye, as if the content of our encounter had been inconsequential.

"Did you hear his tone of voice when he told me, "Glenda's in charge of where mother lives?" I asked David.

"He was very definite about that. You'll need Glenda's cooperation if you want to move her."

On my drive to get Mom to bring her home with me the next day, I began to feel troubled. Today is July second. Only three more days and I'll be gone for ten days. Mom will somehow have to manage without me, I said to myself as I turned into the Arlington Meadows parking lot. Sitting there in the car, I asked myself, should I tell Mom I saw Norm yesterday? Images of pink curtains and a potluck with Betty helped make my decision. My thoughts turned to the upcoming assessment later in the month. Does she still remember how to write her name, I wondered?

"Mom, can you write your name for me?" I asked, handing her a pencil and piece of paper sometime after we had gotten back to my apartment. She took the pencil and wrote a short series of connected shapes that didn't resemble letters.

"Let me write it for you," I said. "See, that's your name. Can you write it by looking at what I wrote?"

"I think so," she responded. She tried but failed. I was surprised.

"What a good try, Mom!" I said, giving her a hug.

In the evening when we returned to Arlington Meadows, a confused old lady was sitting in Mom's room. "I'll be right back to help you," an employee said, after I'd seen her in the hall to alert her to our need.

We waited but she didn't return. I left Mom to go to the house phone in the hallway. "The phone doesn't work, Mom. I have to go downstairs to get someone to help us." We sat in Mom's room waiting and waiting until someone finally came to take the confused old lady back to her own room.

"Do you know what day this is, Mom?" I asked when I picked her up the next day.

The slight shrug of her shoulders and the blank expression in her eyes told me she did not.

"It's the fourth of July!"

"Oh," she said, as if she were surprised.

While I was taking out the ironing board, I started to explain that I would be going away. "Tomorrow, we leave for a trip to Ashland. Jennifer is returning to the West Coast to live. She's been in New England for three years and now she's coming home. We'll spend a few days together to celebrate."

Mom watched and listened as I ironed. "You need to be with your family," she said.

I was surprised at her response. I'm not sure she understands that I'll be gone for more than a week, I thought, and she'll probably forget what I told her.

It was a blessing that she wasn't upset when I took her back to Arlington Meadows. Fortunately, Laurie was on duty. "I'll be away until the fifteenth, Laurie. Please keep a careful watch over my mother. I'll remember you in a special way when I return."

I kissed Mom goodbye. It was a peaceful farewell, laden with concern for her. Mom will have to manage a few days without me, I told myself again. But as I left her, depression threatened to cast its shadow my way.

"How are you, Mom?" I asked when I called her from Ashland. "Did you remember I'm on vacation?"

"What day is it?" she asked. I didn't care that she didn't seem to understand my answer, but I did want to avoid her feeling abandoned.

"Laurie isn't here," a person at the facility said the following two times I called. She added, "Your Mom is doing fine."

On my return from Ashland, I found Mom in the lounge, sitting on the sofa between two male employees, watching television. When she saw me, she stood up and I gave her a big hug. "I'm so happy to see you." she said.

"Would you like to come home with me?" I asked.

"Yes, I want to go with you!" The sound of her voice left no doubt as to her wishes.

At the apartment we fell into our usual routine of simple conversation, lunch and Mom napping on the sofa. When we returned to Arlington Meadows, she walked up the stairs with me instead of going alone on the elevator. She stopped when we got to her room.

"I don't want to go in there."

"Shall we say goodbye in the lounge on this floor?" I asked.

"That'd be okay."

We sat together for a time in the almost empty space before I said, "Mom, I have to leave now but I'll come again real soon."

With a terrified expression, she asked somewhat frightfully, "Are you coming back?"

"I'll come back very soon," I said, kissing her goodbye. I didn't look back because I couldn't look back. She made no sound as I walked away wondering, why didn't she want to go into her room? Why didn't I ask her?

On leaving, I saw Vivien in the downstairs lounge, a woman who had befriended my mother while Norene was away. When I stopped to talk with her, I noticed she was wearing the earrings I'd given her. "I couldn't find anyone to be with my mother."

"I'll go right away to see her," Vivien replied, easing the difficulty of my departure.

Mom was asleep on a downstairs sofa the next day when I went to pick her up in the early afternoon.

"Mom, Mom," I said, trying to wake her.

"I'm very sick," she murmured. I held her for a few minutes.

"Do you think you can walk to the car?"

"I think I can make it," she said.

"Maybe you'll feel better after you eat lunch, Mom," I suggested when we got to my apartment.

Not only did she feel better after lunch, but she was also more present than usual. Now is a good time to talk with her about Norm, I decided.

"Mom, David and I went to see Norm. He told me that in February he became very ill. That's why he has been unable to take care of you." I gave myself the freedom to lie about the next thing I said, "That's why he doesn't come to see you, because he's sick. That's why you're in Arlington Meadows. Norm told me he loves you very much."

"I didn't know he's sick," is all she said before laying down on the sofa to rest.

"I want you to put in writing when you'll come to see me next time," she asked when she woke from her nap.

Her request surprised me, but I considered it related to my ten days away in Ashland. "What a good idea," I said. "I'll write you a note. It'll help you remember." After I had written it, I told her, "Let me fold it and put it in your pocket so you'll have it with you. Maybe Laurie can read it to you."

We had almost gotten back to Arlington Meadows when Mom said softly, "I think my time is gonna be soon. I guess I'm gettin' old."

"Are you feeling sick again?" I asked, surprised by her statement.

"Not too bad," she answered.

"I'll pick you up tomorrow morning. I want to make sure you're okay." I kissed Mom goodbye and watched her walk down the hall with Laurie.

Mom was surprised to see me the next morning even though I had promised I would come and had called to remind her. She had obviously forgotten. "You seem to be feeling well today. Do you feel well enough to do a little shopping?" I asked. "I'd like to buy you some new clothes."

Once inside the nearby Ross store, I sat her in a chair, then brought some blouses for her to see.

"I like that one and that one," she indicated.

"Good; then we'll buy these two for you."

"People don't like me," she kept telling me when we were driving to Redlands.

"Who doesn't like you," I asked. But she couldn't say.

"They don't care about me. They kick me."

"Kick you! Oh God! I can't stand the thought of someone kicking you, Mom." Maybe Norene's mistreating her, I thought. Since I've been coming to see Mom, Norene has changed toward her. Or maybe it's one of the employees. I was at a loss about what to do.

I thought of people I had seen responding to her in a caring way. The resident hairdresser I met on Wednesday said, "Your Mom told me that she had no one. Later she told me her daughter had found her." The hairdresser looked amazed when I confirmed this as true. I noticed that she was very kind to my mother. The exercise lady I met on Wednesday as we were leaving had a warm exchange with my mother. "Your mother is one of my best people," she said. I had noticed several other caring people, three of the female residents and two of the employees. "Maybe it's Norene who is unkind," I thought again.

"Let's put a new blouse on you," I suggested when Mom woke from her nap.

She seemed pleased, "It'll be nice to have a clean one." Her normal responses frequently surprised me.

"Yes, the one you're wearing is dirty and the seam of the sleeve has come out. It's almost time to go back," I said with a heavy heart.

"I know, and I'm dreading it," came her reply.

As we were driving back, she broke the silence with a question. "Is Betty with him?"

"Him?" I said, pretending not to understand. "Do you mean your husband Norm?"

"That's okay, never mind," she quickly added.

Earlier in the day I had asked her, "Do you miss Norm?"

"Not really, I never see him." Nothing more was said of Norm as we drove toward Arlington Meadows.

"I wish I lived closer to you," she told me.

"So do I, Mom. I'm trying to make that happen but it's taking time."

I felt anguished as I walked with my mother toward the front door of Arlington Meadows, her words echoing in my mind, "People don't like me; they don't care about me; they kick me." How can I leave her where others might abuse her? Who will keep her safe when I'm gone? In that desperate moment, I felt as if an angel hovered close to comfort me with a promise, "The Lord will provide."

When we entered the lobby, a young woman I didn't recognize came directly to my mother. With outstretched arms she embraced her saying, "How are you, Edna? Welcome back."

"My name is Tricia," she told me. "I'm very fond of Edna."

Her nametag caught my attention. She's an employee, I noted silently, but I've never seen her.

"I'll take you to dinner, Edna," Tricia offered. I hugged Mom and gave her a kiss goodbye. She was peaceful.

I breathed a silent prayer, "Thank you for sending Tricia."

"You still seem so peaceful today, Mom. And it looks like you're feeling well," I told her the next morning.

"I feel good," she said as she got into the car.

After lunch I asked her, "What's your name?'

She quickly answered, "Edna Ross."

Mother had given supplied the correct first name, but she had given me her maiden name rather than her married name of Hall.

"And what is my name?" I asked.

I saw the blank look in her eyes, "I don't know."

"I'm Vernetta and I'm your daughter and I love you very much." I hugged her. "Would you like to take a nap, Mom? You seem a little tired."

"That'd be nice." She slept for hours on the sofa.

"Well, sleepy head, it's almost six o'clock. That was a long nap! Would you like some dinner?"

"Yes, I'm hungry."

On the drive back I foolishly said something like, "…Arlington Meadows, where you live, Mom."

"I don't live there. I was put there," she said with a clarity that once again surprised me.

The first few weeks of returning her were hell, but Mom has gradually accepted our goodbye without protest, I reflected as I left her. Then found myself wondering if she has simply given up hope of ever leaving Arlington Meadows.

Chapter 60

California
July 1991

On Monday morning, after spending the weekend with Jennifer, I went to Arlington Meadows. Mom was sitting by herself on the organ bench with Norene nearby, slumped on the sofa.

"You're still wearing your new blouse from Friday. Maybe we should get a clean one," I suggested.

"I like this one," Mom quietly responded. I was noticing her black slacks were dirty when Norene suddenly stood up.

"Hello, Norene" I said, placing a kiss on her cheek and awaiting her unpredictable response.

"Hello. How are you?" she said affectionately, then quickly left the area.

"Are you ready?" I asked Mom. She was ready and eager. When we got to my apartment, she sat in a chair and promptly fell sleep, groaning now and then as she slept.

"I have to go to the bathroom," Mom said immediately upon waking from her nap.

"Are you all right?" I asked several minutes later from outside the bathroom door. "You've been in there a long time." I couldn't understand what she said so I opened the door. I gasped under my breath when I saw feces on her hands, some smeared on the toilet paper and some on her pants.

She was reaching for my towel saying, "Nasty stuff."

"Let's wash your hands in the sink first before you use the towel," I suggested. I ran water to wash her hands and watched her pick at the brown under one fingernail with the other. Her long nails should be cut, I thought as I watched, because they always have something under them, but cutting them would take away part of her identity, I suppose.

"Let's get you back to the sofa, Mom," I said, after we had gotten her cleaned from the bathroom ordeal. She quickly fell asleep again. I continued ironing as she slept but I noticed that her face seemed tense.

When she woke, she moaned, "I'm very sick."

"Maybe an aspirin?" I offered but thought the idea seemed totally inadequate.

"That might help," she said.

After a time, I asked, "How do you feel now?"

"Better," she answered.

"Mom, you have a red area on your thumb where your nail has broken. It looks like you have puss in it. Does it hurt?" I asked, thinking that it might be infected and causing her to feel sick.

"No, it doesn't hurt."

"I'm not sure if that needs attention. I'll check it tomorrow."

On the drive back, I noticed that she was contentedly enjoying the ride. When we got to Arlington Meadows, we walked into the lounge area where I saw Norene standing at a table talking with someone. "Why don't we sit on the sofa, Mom, until Norene finishes her conversation." I'm thankful she's a caring friend for Mom, I thought as we sat waiting.

"We'd love to have you join us, Norene," I called to her when the lady left.

"Your Mom and me don't get along at all. We fight all the time," she blurted out.

"Why don't you get along?" I asked, surprised to hear this disturbing news. "I thought you were friends."

Norene began to cry. "No one calls me. My mother doesn't call."

"Is your mother still alive?" I asked because Norene appeared to be in her late sixties.

She looked at me through tears, whimpering in a childlike voice, "I think so."

Perhaps Norene is struggling with dementia, I thought to myself, aware I'd never spent time talking with her because Mom had been my focus. Norene feels very alone, I realized. I've taken her companion away, my mother who once had no one except Norene, who never left Arlington Meadows until I innocently came between them well over a month ago. Is that why they don't get along, I wondered.

"Norene, Mom and I would love to take you to lunch sometime at a nearby Mexican cafe we found," I said, in my effort to help her feel included. She responded by leaving the room.

I kissed Mom goodbye, "I'll see you soon."

"See you soon," she echoed.

I'm deeply grateful for the blessing of peaceful goodbyes, I thought as I left my mom sitting in the lounge.

In the afternoon of the following day, I went to Arlington Meadows. At first, I couldn't find my mother. Then I saw her in the lounge, sleeping on the sofa. I put my hand on her shoulder, "Mom, Mom."

She opened her eyes and said, "I'm sick."

"I'm taking you with me if you can make it." As I got her up, I saw that her thumb looked more infected. A large puss pocket had formed inside a red circle.

I stopped at the front desk, "Do you have a resident doctor? My mother needs to be seen."

"He'll be here tomorrow," she said.

I managed to get my mother into my car. "I'm driving us to David's office, Mom. I'm concerned about your thumb."

David came out to the car and inspected her thumb. "The puss pocket will break soon. It isn't a serious problem. She'll be fine," he reassured me and gave me a kiss goodbye.

After arriving at my apartment, Mom and I went through the familiar routine of feeding her and then letting her sleep on the sofa.

"I feel better," she said on waking. Marc went back to Riverside with us, a pillar of support during these stressful times.

Early the next morning I went to bring Mom home. I stopped at the office to ask,

"What time will the doctor come today?"

"Oh, he delayed his visit until tomorrow," she told me.

I went to find my mother. She was sitting upright on the sofa, asleep.

"I'm sick," she said to me again when I woke her.

"I'm worried about you Mom, but I'm not sure what to do. The doctor won't be here until tomorrow." I looked at her thumb. It had drained just as David said it would.

After lunch and her nap she said, "I feel better. I need to go to the bathroom."

I waited for the flushing sound before I went in. "Let me help you wash your hands, Mom." As I cleaned the brown from under her fingernails the best I could, I had an awful realization. She's been using her fingernails to extract feces from her rectum.

Eventually, Mom and I took the drive back to Arlington Meadows. On the way I said, "When I return home, I'll make an appointment for you with Dr. Godfrey. Do you remember him?"

"No, who is he?" she asked, unable to remember that he was her oncologist.

"He took care of you in Sun City when you had your cancer treatment. He can help us find out why you feel so sick sometimes."

"Dr. Godfrey is on vacation. He'll return Monday," the appointment desk informed me.

"Could you please give me the earliest possible appointment?" I asked.

"He has Monday July twenty-ninth available, the first day of his return."

"Yes, I'll take that appointment time," I eagerly confirmed, but I was concerned about the four-day wait.

Early the next day I went to Arlington Meadows to stop by the office. "What time will the doctor come today?" I asked.

"He usually comes right after lunch, and he'll be here until five o'clock. He has about thirty patients to see," she informed me.

"Please put Edna Hall on the list of patients to be seen," I requested. "She's been ill, and I'd like to consult with him before the weekend."

Mom came home with me, but we returned shortly after lunch, early enough I thought for her to be seen by the in-house doctor. When I went to the office to inquire about his schedule, I was told, "He has already gone." Somehow Mom will have to make it through the weekend until Monday when we see Dr. Godfrey, I concluded, unless there's a crisis.

I woke very anxious on Saturday morning. "I'm worried about my mom. Would you be willing to postpone our plans? I'd like to check on her to see how she's feeling."

"We could go around noon, even bring her home with us for a few hours if you want," David said.

She was sitting in the dining room, asleep in front of a plate of food when I found her. I woke her.

"I'm happy to see you," she greeted me.

"Let's go home, Mom," I said as I got her up and took her to the car.

"How are you feeling now?" I asked after her nap.

"Pretty good," she answered.

On Sunday she said, "I'm feeling a little sick today."

"I'm taking you to see Dr. Godfrey tomorrow. I hope he can help you feel better."

Monday morning July twenty-ninth is here at last, I said to myself when I woke. Sure hope Mom can make it through two doctor appointments in the same day. I felt relieved that Marc had agreed to drive us to San Bernardino for Mother's first appointment in the Geriatric Assessment Center.

"Hello, I'm Dr. Randolph," he greeted my mother warmly. After a bit of friendly conversation, he asked her, "Can you tell me your name?"

She didn't say anything as she turned to me. I saw the face of a child who wasn't sure what the grown up wanted from her. I remained quiet, although it was difficult.

Mom turned back to Dr. Randolph, "I don't know."

"Do you want to be here?" he asked.

"Yes, I want to be here with *her*," she answered, pointing to me.

Dr. Randolph asked other questions such as "Who is the President of the United States?"; "What year is this?" "What state are we in?" But she didn't know the answer to any of his questions.

Later in the history-taking process Dr. Randolph said to me, "You are a loving, caring daughter."

I didn't feel like a loving, caring daughter. A loving, caring daughter would have snatched mother out of Arlington Meadows long ago no matter what the cost to herself, no matter the anger fired at her from Glenda or Norm. This is what I told myself. But I smiled back at Dr. Randolph and thanked him for his kindness.

After lunch, I woke her from her nap, "It's time to go see Dr. Godfrey, Mom." She moaned as if she was hurting. "Maybe we'll get some answers today."

Dr. Godfrey asked several questions, listened to her lungs and her heart, and then said, "I'll need to send her to the lab for some tests I want to run. Make an appointment with me for next week and we'll go over the results." He had nothing more to say about Mom's feeling ill almost every day.

"Mom, you came through with flying colors," I told her as we left the lab. "After I talk to the people in the business office, we're all done."

"Do you have your mother's Medicare card or her stickers?" the woman at the desk asked.

"No, but I'll give it to you the next time we come," I offered, hoping that my anxiety didn't show. I don't want to ask Glenda for Mom's card or her stickers, I declared to myself firmly as we walked to the car. The last time we talked, she threatened to move Mom where I couldn't find her. I don't want to stir up that hornet's nest! But what to do? Glenda has Mom's Medicare card and her stickers.

I went to see Shirley Goldberg in the office at Arlington Meadows after taking Mom to her room. "I wonder if you have my mother's Medicare card," I asked.

She searched her file. "I have a copy of it if that will help."

"Yes, could you make me a copy of it?" I left her office hoping a copy of the Medicare card would satisfy the needs of Dr. Godfrey's Office, because I didn't want to call Glenda. The long day is over, I told myself. I get to go home.

Chapter 61

California
End July 1991 – Early August 1991

"I'm giving myself the day off. I won't see Mom today," I told David when I kissed him goodbye as he left for work. After he had gone, I found myself thinking of Glenda. Tomorrow is her birthday, July thirty-first. I wonder what she'll think of the card and letter I mailed to her on Saturday. I took out a copy I had kept for myself and reread it:

Dear Glenda,
When all is said and done, the bottom line is we are both doing the best we can. I'm sure that's true for you; it's true for me.

Thank you for not moving Mother where I can't see her. I'm sorry for the hell you probably went through when you took her there. I'm hoping my visits with her might relieve you of some of the burden.

The first few times I brought her home she was upset when she had to return. Now she is able to come out for a visit and return without being upset. She still doesn't like to go back but at least she doesn't get upset.

David and I stopped by to see Norm. He seems to be getting along pretty good.

He asked me to call him once in a while. Be assured that if I do call or see him, I won't talk about Mother unless he brings up the subject. It may be best if I just stay away – I haven't decided.

If you'd like to talk, please feel free to call me

Anyway, however it all finally turns out, I wish you well. And,
Happy Birthday July 31.

Hmm, why didn't I tell her that Arlington Meadows didn't provide the kind of care and attention Mom needs? Then I reminded myself that my reason for the note and card was my effort to get past her anger towards me. That was my first important step toward my goal of establishing a working relationship with her regarding the care of my mother. It was hard enough to try to help Mother without the added stress of threats from family members who never came to see her. I didn't ask anything from her regarding the Medicare card or stickers because she might misinterpret the motive for my letter.

"How are you this morning?" I asked David the following day.
"Alive. Vomited most of the night, dealing with diarrhea."
"Will you be okay if I leave you alone? I have some important errands."
"I'll be fine, you go ahead."
"After my errands I'll pick Mom up and take her to the park or something instead of bringing her home, but I'll call you."
"No, don't call. I may be sleeping."

I duplicated the copy of the Medicare card and took one to the Geriatric Department in San Bernardino, which accepted the copy as sufficient. Next, I drove to Dr. Godfrey's office in Loma Linda. Much to my relief, the Billing Office accepted the copy as well. I felt wonderfully relieved but exhausted as I headed to Arlington Meadows.

"It's such a nice day, Mom, I think we'll go to Canyon Crest and have lunch."
"Let's sit outside," I suggested as I sat her at a table under an umbrella in front of a Mexican restaurant. "I'll go inside and

order the food. You stay here, okay?" She nodded her head but seemed far away in thought.

When I came back with the burritos she promptly asked, "Is Betty still out there?" I was surprised by her coherent question. She's thinking of Norm again, thinking maybe of him and Betty.

"I'm not sure. I don't go out there," I responded honestly.

The next morning, I didn't realize how frazzled I still was from the stress of the previous day until something simple catapulted my distressed feelings into an outburst. When I calmed down, David said to me, "I think you have such empathy, that you can't separate your identify from your mother's. I think you have internalized her physical experiences."

"You're probably right. I feel swallowed up. Thanks for your kind response to my outburst."

"You're worth it! Keep hanging in there."

"I think I have myself together enough now to go and pick up Mom," I told David when I kissed him goodbye. "So glad you're feeling better. I should be back before noon."

"You look like you're feeling pretty good today, Mom," I said when I saw her. She smiled. "You know that tomorrow you have an appointment with Dr. Randolph."

"Oh?" she said. Of course, she doesn't remember, I told myself.

By seven forty-five the next morning, very early for me, I was on my way to get mother, hoping to arrive at Dr. Randolph's office on time.

"Please have your mother undress. She can wear this gown," the assistant said as she handed me a hospital gown.

"I don't wanna take my clothes off," Mom objected. I persuaded her to cooperate. After Dr. Randolph gave her a physical examination he said, "You can get dressed now and then we'll talk."

Mother was dressed and sitting in a chair when Dr. Randolph came back. "I'll be giving you a test today," he told. I was wishing he hadn't used the anxiety-provoking word "test."

The first question he asked was the exact first question he had asked at the first interview:

"What is your name?"

"I don't know," she answered with little hesitation.

"What is your mother's name?"

Mom's face brightened, "Pansie."

It was an emotional moment for me to hear her recall her mother's name but not her own. She couldn't remember grandma's last name, but she remembered "Pansie."

Dr. Randolph continued to ask her question after question: Do you like your life? Where do you live? Unable to answer, mother became more anxious with each question posed. She looked at me, hoping I would answer for her, but I wasn't allowed.

Finally, we got to the very last thing he asked her to do. "I would like you to draw a rectangle box like the one already there." She picked up the pencil. She made several attempts to do as the doctor had asked but was unable to succeed. It was sad for me to observe my mother's reactions to her incapacity. She no longer knew her name. Even if she could remember her name, she wouldn't have been able to write it.

"Let's spend a little time together before I drive you back," I suggested to Mom.

"That'd be nice," she answered with one of her familiar brief responses.

"I hate this place," she said emotionally as I parked in front of Arlington Meadows.

"Where would you like to live Mom?" I stupidly asked. What did I expect her to say after she had asked so many times to stay with me.

"I don't know," she answered helplessly. I let silence fill the emptiness I felt. I sat quietly pierced with self-loathing for leaving her in a place she detested.

I decided to spend the next morning reading and doing a bit of nothing. In the afternoon, I prepared a statement about my mother for Dr. Randolph, with the first paragraph devoted to her background.

In February of 1991, Edna's husband Norman fainted and was taken to the hospital. Edna stayed a few days with her oldest daughter, Verneda, but it didn't "work out." When doctors determined that Norman's condition was due to stress, they advised him he must get help with Edna's care. This was done by Glenda, Edna and Norman's daughter. She placed Edna in a board and care.

Norman has not seen Edna since his hospitalization. He is taking care of himself emotionally by staying away.

The two daughters report that Edna swears at them when they come to see her; she pleads with them to take her out of the board and care. To avoid the conflict, they stay away.

Four single spaced pages later I looked at the report. A bit long, I told myself, but maybe the details will help Dr. Randolph and his staff with their assessment.

"After lunch today, we have an appointment with Dr. Godfrey to get the results of the lab work from eight days ago," I told Mom the following day. "Maybe we'll learn why you haven't been feeling well. David is coming home at noon to drive us to Oak Glen for chili and apple pie." She responded with the hint of a smile.
"Hmm, this is good," she said when eating her chili.
"Would you like a piece of apple pie?" I asked.
"That'd be good," she smiled and nodded. I complimented her, "What a wonderful job of eating you're doing today. No spilling." Our eyes met and we laughed.
Mom was tired when we got home. She fell asleep on the sofa and slept for an hour before I had to wake her. "It's time to go see Dr. Godfrey. Today we get the test results," I reminded her again. Mom gave me a faint smile.
Dr. Godfrey looked serious when he entered the exam room. "Her hemoglobin is very low. She needs a transfusion

today. She is in danger of going into heart failure. She will die without a transfusion."

His news stunned me. I looked at my exhausted mother whose life was in serious jeopardy. I thought of Norm and Glenda. "Perhaps the decision shouldn't be mine alone to make, Dr. Godfrey. I'm a bit overwhelmed. I understand what you're saying but I need to talk with her husband. Could we wait until tomorrow morning?"

"I wouldn't wait beyond tomorrow morning," he said.

"Do you understand what Dr. Godfrey told us, Mom?" I asked after we left his office and stopped in a hallway before leaving the building

"I think so," she answered. I explained again even though I wasn't sure she would understand. Then I told her, "Tomorrow morning I'll take you to the doctor and you'll have a blood transfusion."

That evening I pondered what to do. Should I go ahead with the transfusion without saying anything to Norm and Glenda? Would it be better to involve them? What if I didn't call and something went wrong, and she died? I was tired and decided to sleep on it.

I woke early. "It's clear to me that we should not consult Norm," David said.

"It's clear to me that I must contact Glenda before we proceed." I went to the phone immediately to call her before she left for work.

"Hello, Glenda! I have something I need to discuss with you."

I explained; she listened and then responded, "I visited Mom a couple weeks ago and had a hard time waking her. I asked Terry to have her blood checked. Terry said she would take care of it, but I guess she didn't." Glenda changed the subject to her dislike of Dr. Godfrey. "He didn't have a good answer when I asked him why he was giving her pain medication."

I tried to say without offending her, "The pain medication is intended to make her more comfortable. Norm relied on those pills to help Mom feel better. She does have bone cancer and Dr. Godfrey said that in the latter stages, the pain is tremendous. Would you like to go ahead and take care of the transfusion?" I asked, though I thought I knew what her answer would be. It was my way of helping her feel in control.

She immediately responded, "No, No. You go ahead."

"I will need her Medicare stickers," I told her.

"I'll send them to the office at Arlington Meadows. You can pick them up there." I expected to say goodbye at this point, but she continued, "Terry said your visit to Norm upset him and that you should stay away."

"Norm and I had an enjoyable visit, and he wasn't upset when I was there. He even asked me to call him, and I have."

"Hmm," she replied, "I'm getting different stories."

Chapter 62

California
August 1991

"I'll be ready for your mother at noon," Dr. Godfrey's nurse said when she called. By twelve thirty, mother was on a gurney with life-giving blood flowing through the IV into her arm. All seemed well until I noticed tears running down Mom's cheeks. Alarmed, I asked her, "What's the matter?" The nurse answered before Mom could say a word.

"She bent her arm. That has caused the blood to back up," the nurse grumbled. "She's in pain. The only thing I can do is stick her again, or we can try to get her arm warm. But she *must* keep that arm straight."

"I don't see how she can do that," I said. "I don't think she'll understand to keep it straight." The nurse made no reply as she reached for another needle.

"Mom," I said as I stroked her forehead, "it's hard to see you in so much pain." The next hour crept by slowly; gradually her pain gave way to reasonable comfort. I sat down in a chair next to the gurney. "Mom, I'm right here where you can see me and talk to me if you want."

"I'm cold," she complained an hour or so later, shivering when the nurse came to start the second pint of refrigerated blood.

"I'll get you a blanket," the nurse offered. She turned her attention to the IV then mumbled to herself in tones of disgust, probably not realizing I heard her say, "The IV clotted, left it too long, have to start another one." I too was disgusted. I couldn't stand to watch my mother endure more pain. I left the room.

When I returned, the new IV was functioning with the second unit in place. The nurse was attaching my mother's arm to an arm board. "This will keep her arm straight," she said without looking at me. You should have done that from the beginning, I wanted to yell at her, but didn't. If only I had known such things existed, I would have asked for one, I grumbled to myself.

It took a long time for Mom to receive the second unit of blood. She napped, a short while. For part of the time, she watched the unit as it emptied. It was four o'clock when the transfusion was complete.

"I never want to go through that again," Mother said to me when the needle was taken out.

The nurse put a pressure bandage on each wrist. "These need to be removed in a couple of hours."

I took Mom back to my apartment because I wanted to be sure she was all right. We talked for about an hour before I drove her back to Arlington Meadows. When we arrived, I went to the nurse station where I talked with Shirley and Ellen.

"My mother had a blood transfusion late this afternoon and these pressure bandages are to be removed in an hour. Will you make sure that happens?" I asked. They assured me my mother would be taken care of. Mom and I then went to the lounge where we sat together on the sofa before I kissed her goodbye. "I'll see you tomorrow," I told her.

"I'm getting a late start to pick up Mom today," I commented to David after lunch when he was ready to return to work.

"Better get going," he said.

The radio announcer gave the time as two o'clock when I turned into the parking lot at Arlington Meadows. "You're still wearing the pressure bandages," I almost screamed when I saw her. "Your arm is puffy! Let me get these off you Mom. Does your arm hurt?" I asked.

"No, it doesn't hurt," she answered.

"Unbelievable; this place is definitely not where you belong, Mom." My anger toward the nurses, who had promised to remove the bandages, left me upset.

At dinnertime, Marc rode with me when I drove her back to Riverside. We sat with Mom and two apparently normal ladies at a dining room table. Marion, who was confined to a wheelchair said to me, "Your mother wanders around in here as if she's lost."

I sat somewhat dismayed. I'm doing everything I can possibly do, but it isn't enough, I said to myself later when I kissed her goodbye.

"I'll see you on Sunday. Not tomorrow, but the next day, Mom."

After I took Marc home, thoughts of Mom wandering around lost disturbed me. I began debating with myself again: Shall I take Mom to see Norm? Norm might not want to see her. The result would probably be a horrific scene, I imagined. Norm might be happy to see her, but she couldn't stay with him. She'd have to leave again to go back to Arlington Meadows. What a mess that would be, I convinced myself.

A new line of thought comforted me. Norm's an adult. She is his wife. He made his decision, a decision to stay away. It's not my place to take her to see him. It simply isn't right for me to take her to him, I repeated, trying to convince myself. Despite my self-talk, I longed to put Mom in my car and drive her straight to Lake Elsinore to see Norm.

The phone rang on Sunday evening; it was Glenda. "How did it go?" she asked, referring to the transfusion that had taken place three days ago. I described out experience in detail.

Suddenly, without my solicitation, Glenda overflowed with guilt as she told her story of leaving Mom at Arlington Meadows. "That was a real hell for me. When Dad fainted and was taken to the hospital, I took Mom to see him after he was stable and had been put in a room. That was the last time she saw him. I couldn't leave Mom alone during the day when I went to work, so I left her with Terry. She didn't like being at Terry's. She kept threatening to run away. After only a few days, Terry said to me, 'I can't handle taking care of Mom.' So, I took Mom to Arlington Meadows. She knew what was happening the minute we got to the door, and refused to go in. We sat on a bench for a minute but then Mom started walking down the driveway. Finally, I tricked her into going inside. I had some tranquilizers with me. I got her some water and told her she needed to take her medicine, but she didn't know it was sleeping pills. I gave three to Mom and told her we were waiting for the car. When she got sleepy, I had her lay down on a bed in the room assigned to her. After she fell asleep, I left."

It was difficult to comfort Glenda, but I tried. She had chosen a course of action that weighed heavily on her heart.

"I didn't learn that Mom was in Arlington Meadows until early June," I told her.

"Really?" she asked in disbelief. "I thought Robert told you in February, when I put her there!"

"No, he didn't tell me until June. As soon as I learned what had happened, I went looking for her. I always thought she would be all right if Norm was taking care of her." I tried to explain to Glenda how I had come to stop seeing Norm and Mom for about nine months.

"I understand," she said. "All this time, I thought you knew Mom was at Arlington Meadows and that you didn't come to see her because you didn't care."

"No wonder you were angry with me when I called you the first time after I had found her!" I exclaimed. For a moment silence prevailed, as I believe we each absorbed this reconciling truth.

"Dad never once went to Arlington Meadows to see her. I think it was too hard for him," she suggested.

"You were close to Norm but not Mom?" I asked.

She didn't answer my question but began to sob softly. "Mom never told me she loved me."

"I don't know if it will help, Glenda, but Mom didn't tell you, Verneda or me that she loved us. For some reason, she just couldn't say that." I experienced Glenda in so much pain about Mom that probably even my best effort to help fell short.

My own guilt feelings were triggered by Glenda's story of how she left Mom at Arlington Meadows. If only I hadn't stayed away. If I had kept seeing Mom and Norm, I thought, maybe this sad conclusion to their lives could have been avoided. But on the phone with Glenda, I said nothing of my own guilt feelings. After my attempt to relieve her sorrow and pain, I heard a softness in her voice as she expressed her willingness to cooperate with me.

The following morning, I woke with feelings of dread about the day. "I really don't want to talk with Dr. Randolph about his conclusions on Mom's assessment," I said.

"You've gone through a lot to get this assessment. Why wouldn't you want to hear the results?" David asked.

"Because I think I already know what he's going to tell me." David and I attended the appointment in spite of my impulse to cancel it.

We sat across the table while Dr. Randolph began to go over his six-page Comprehensive Geriatric Consultation Report. I noticed when he got to page four that there were five points listed under the Impression section, but the first point presented as the most relevant, I thought: Progressive Dementia Syndrome, probably secondary to Alzheimer's. Cannot entirely rule out the contribution of Multiple Myeloma.

The Discussion section followed on page five beginning with: "The most important problem would seem to be the dementing illness. If this is Alzheimer's disease it will continue to progress in the next year or two. The Multiple Myeloma may make it worse at times because of the hematologic derangements that accompany her illness. *The dementia has progressed to a rather significant point* and there are risks to treatment and those risks and benefits of therapy should be discussed.

How could this report disappoint me, I asked myself, when it confirmed what I was anticipating. No place to hide now, I suppose, with the truth staring me in the face. "I'm not able to see Mom today," I said to David on the drive home from Dr. Randolph's office.

"Give yourself the day off. You deserve it," my loving husband urged.

Chapter 63

California
August 1991

David and I are usually away during the month of August, I thought wistfully when I woke up, remembering what life used to be like. Almost mid-August and we're still here. But there's no one I can turn to at Arlington Meadows when we leave on the twenty-first, no caregiver to watch over her while I'm away. She can't clean herself, she misses meals, and she needs special panties to catch the dribbles. I decided to call Glenda.

"We postponed our vacation once to take care of Mom, but I can't do it again. David needs a vacation. Can you look after Mom while we're away? Someone really needs to visit her regularly," I almost whined.

"Sure, I can check in on her," Glenda agreed.

I shared the assessment information with her and then talked of my ongoing concern. "Arlington Meadows doesn't provide the personal care she needs. Maybe we can make other arrangements when I return."

"Don't worry about Mom while you're gone. I'll take care of her. I'll look into other living arrangements for her while you're away."

While I was counting on Glenda to do as she agreed, I had trouble relying on her promise. I wish Laurie still worked there, I fretted. I could always count on her. But the personnel change so frequently that it's impossible to connect with one specific employee.

Afternoon arrived. Twice I made an effort to get myself out of the house to pick up Mom, but I couldn't do it. Instead, I ran away in sleep. I comforted myself with half a bag of Frito chips and almost a pint of ice cream. Television took me on fantasy trips away from my reality.

Three days have passed without my seeing my mother, I thought as I tried to fall asleep that night. Ironic, I'm so concerned about her while I'm away on vacation, yet I haven't gone to see her for three days. The coming of sleep relieved me of my thoughts.

"Two months ago, I found Mom at Arlington Meadows," I commented to David the next morning when I turned the calendar page to August fifteenth. "It feels like about two years ago."

"Are you able to see her today?" he asked.

"Yes, I'm up to it and eager," I declared.

The minute I appeared in the dining room door, Mom started waving and holding out her arms. She was so glad to see me. "I love you, Mom. How have you been?" I asked.

"Pretty good. I missed you."

"Do you want to go with me?"

"Yes, I want to go!"

As we were about to leave, I noticed her shoes. "Mom, you have your shoes on the wrong feet. Sit down and let me fix them for you." The tongues were crammed into the toes of her shoes and the socks didn't match.

As I worked with her shoes she said, "Terry never comes to see me." Mom frequently surprised me with such comments. I made excuses for my sister as best I could.

"There," I said. "Now we can go."

Norm was my mother's theme of the day. "I was in his way. He was angry with me. I don't think he loves me."

"He is very sick himself, Mom," I said, lying to ease her anguish. "I know he loves you very much."

"I never see him. He never comes."

Why didn't I call Norm and tell him, I want to bring Mom out to see you; she keeps asking about you. I could have driven her straight to Lake Elsinore directly to Norm. But I did not. Instead, I drove her back to Riverside, chastising myself again. Maybe Mom wouldn't be in this predicament if I had stayed in touch with her.

Mom sat dejected at my side when we returned to Arlington Meadows. I held her and tried to comfort her. I went inside with her. She softened a little as we sat at the dining table. She said quietly and earnestly, "I want to go home." An internal voice screamed, "Take her to see Norm!" But I still did not take her to see Norm.

The depression I felt in the evening yielded to the appearance of Frozen One with the coming of morning. Trapped in my body, I lay in bed staring out the window until David came home at noon.

"Do you have any idea what brought this on?" he asked. I wanted to respond, but I was unable to speak. David asked another question. "It might be wise to contact Mac. What do you think?"

David stroked my hair and my arm and spoke to me in loving tones. Slowly my body began to emerge from the paralyzing state that had held me captive.

"Maybe it's my extreme way of shutting down when I get overwhelmed," I was able to say to David. "It's kind of confusing, isn't it?"

"At least you're feeling better," he said when he kissed me goodbye.

"I'll give some thought to contacting Mac."

When I'm emotionally flooded my perspective is lost, I thought. I attempted to analyze the feelings that led to my depression and the appearance of Frozen One. Yesterday, I wanted to follow the demands of the voice that screamed at me, "Take your mother to see Norm!" But I wouldn't let myself do that. My lack of action turned against me in the form of depression fueled by the emotional fact that I didn't want to leave my mother while I went on vacation. I sat thinking on what I had just told myself. A comforting satisfaction confirmed my conclusion.

Maybe not taking Mom to see Norm is a bigger problem for me than leaving her to go on vacation. My thoughts turned to abandonment. I've told myself that Norm abandoned her after thirty years of marriage. Now I think I'm accusing myself of abandoning her by going on vacation. These raging conflicts caused my depression and my paralyzed state, I concluded.

What else is there to discover? I asked myself. That my life is no longer my own, I've given it to my mother. I'm living by what she taught me as a child: mother and her needs take priority in any and all situations. That's why I felt hopeless and helpless. I unconsciously became her little child again, allowing her needs to smother mine. It's too painful to be her little child again.

But what about contacting Mac? Why don't I call him to get help during these stressful times of dealing with my mother? It's been months since I've talked with him, I reminded myself. What are my reasons for not calling? I didn't have any answers, only resistance to more therapy.

I got up from my chair to leave my thoughts behind when the phone rang. "Would you like to go to a movie," Elizabeth asked.

"I'd love to go to a movie. I don't even care what we see!" I answered.

After taking Mom back to Arlington Meadows on Saturday, David and I discussed how I might help myself in the way I relate to her while still caring for her. Late Monday following Mom's return to Riverside, I captured in writing what I thought important to remember from our Saturday discussion.

How Can I Help Myself

Recognize that I am a distinct and separate person from my mother. Give myself permission to have my own life.

Accept that Norm will probably never come to see her.

The quality of her life will not be greatly improved by any sacrifice I make.

She is in a facility she sometimes likes and sometimes does not like.

Her life is not perfect, but whose life is. Sometimes she has shoes on the wrong feet but that will only hurt her, not kill her.

Be aware of the tremendous weight I give to the simple things, like her socks not matching. Put these little things into proper perspective.

I can feel sad about her life, but I must not be bound to her by pity.

Each statement provoked thought as I reread the list: "I am distinct and separate." Words, like enmeshment, co-dependent, and lack of boundaries come to mind. Yes, I thought. That's the swallowed up feeling I have. That's why I need to remember to give myself permission to be a person, a separate person from Mom with needs of my own. I went over each item on the list:

It's too painful to think that Mom will never see Norm. I want to take her to see him, but the result would probably be as painful as not taking her. Somehow, I need to get past this. I'm not sure how.

No, I don't agree with David, I told myself. The quality of Mom's life *has* changed since I found her. Maybe I should focus on the "not be greatly improved" part of his statement. But if I hadn't been there, she would be dead by now, without that blood transfusion.

I looked at the next three matter-of-fact statements. Yes, I admit she sometimes seems to like Arlington Meadows, but her life is far from perfect, and I think it could be better, like moving her to a facility that meets her needs. True, I probably overreact to the little things, but they simply trigger the bigger picture: she can't take care of herself; she has dementia; she's been abandoned; she hates Arlington Meadows. I'm not sure how to "accept the simple things, the little things" that to me aren't simple or little.

Pity, I agree, has permeated my interactions with her, rendering me dysfunctional at times. With awareness of what I'm doing, I hope I can change. I looked over the list once more, then put it away.

The next day I needed no reminder: this is the last day I'll spend with Mom before we leave for vacation. I wrote three notes with the same message:

> Please remind my mother that I'm on vacation. I leave August 21 and I'll return September 16. The office has my number where I may be reached.

When I arrived at Arlington Meadows, I placed a note above her bed and another on the back of her bedroom door. I gave the third one to Shirley Dominguez, an employee. "Will you please remind my mother I'm on vacation," I asked when handing her the note.

"I'll be happy to do that for you," Shirley said.

"Will you please remind my mother that I'm on vacation?" I asked the ladies playing games at the table when I passed around a plate filled with the cookies I had baked earlier in the morning.

I singled out one of them who, I noticed, had interacted kindly with Mom. "Is it possible that you might be able to have meals with my mother to make sure she is eating while I'm gone?"

"Well, I would, but you see I've been ill, and I may be going back into the hospital."

As Mom and I walked together from the lounge to the entry area to say our goodbye, she looked at me sweetly and asked, "Why couldn't I go with you?"

I had already considered the possibility of taking her with us, but she was too frail. "I don't think you're well enough to go, sweetie. We'll be driving for hours. You would get so tired." It seemed as if she accepted what I said. "I'll miss you so much. It's very hard for me to leave you. David needs a vacation, Mom, or I wouldn't leave you. Glenda and Marc promised me they would visit you."

"Give me kisses goodbye," she said. I kissed her again and again before my final farewell.

Twenty-six days of being away from her. Such a long time, I thought as I drove away with my heart aching. Glenda will visit while I'm gone, maybe Verneda too, I assured myself. Marc will visit her for sure.

Chapter 64

California
August 1991 – September 1991

For me, our trip to the Northwest *resembled* a vacation. But for David, a man who thrives on being out-of-doors engaged in physically demanding work, it was definitely a vacation. Away from the stress of practicing medicine, he was eager to explore and begin to groom our newly acquired five acres of virgin land.

When we arrived after dark, Larry and Sherry met us on the graveled driveway of their new home, still under construction. Fierce winds whipped the falling rain into a frenzy as Larry and David tried to negotiate our rented trailer into a resting spot where it could be plugged into a power source.

The agent's idea of a queen bed and mine differ, I thought, as I tried to sleep on the couch cushions that converted into a lumpy, cramped, and uncomfortable sleeping space. While David slept, I lay awake listening to the wind lash our trailer like a big angry tongue.

Rain filled the first two days. But despite the weather, David got up early each morning to work on land that had once been part of a large parcel farmed by the old gentleman who still lived across the road. Our acreage had a remarkable view of the bay. From a potential building site, we could see our pastureland down below, frequented by a herd of elk. A meandering stream flowed lazily across the property.

When I thought of my mother, I didn't want to be here and yet when I yielded to the tranquil beauty of this area, I didn't want to be anywhere else. In my heart I told myself, I know I need to be with my mother, but I need more to be here with my husband. I allowed the separation.

I called Mom on two or three occasions. When she finally came to the phone, she was confused, unable to understand anything I said to her. I wasn't even sure if she recognized she was talking to me, her daughter. I stopped calling her directly. Instead, I called Marc. "Have you visited my mother?"

"Yes, I've been to see her. She was just sitting looking about restlessly. Your Mom asked, 'Where is she?' I asked her, 'You mean your daughter, Vernetta?'

'Yes, where is she?' I told her, 'She's on vacation but she'll be back to see you.'"

"Where is she?" stuck in my thoughts after talking with Marc. Sometimes, I reflected, Mom seems normal, as when she said to me, "Is Betty still out there?" Or when she said, "Terry never comes to see me." Even the question, "Where is she?" suggests she knows I haven't been to see her.

It was a great relief when on Sunday evening the fifteenth of September, David and I returned to Redlands. At nine o'clock the next morning I walked in the front door of Arlington Meadows determined to drive Mom directly to Lake Elsinore to see Norm.

I found her sitting alone in the dining area, surrounded by empty tables. The only people present were two hair-netted Hispanic workers clearing dishes from the tables. Mother had her back to me, so she didn't see me coming but one of the workers looked at me as I approached her. He stopped what he was doing, "Is that your mother?" he asked.

"Yes," I responded.

"She doesn't eat. You need to come see her more often," he told me with concern in his voice.

When I bent to kiss her, I discovered she was missing the bottom plate of her teeth. "How can she be expected to eat without her teeth?" I mumbled under my breath in frustration. "I'm going to go upstairs to get your things," I told her. She sat motionless on the chair, almost catatonic.

Upon entering Mom's room, it became obvious to me that she didn't live there anymore. A strange lady lying on Mom's bed simply looked at me. Pictures of unknown people sat on Mom's nightstand. I looked in the closet. Nothing familiar hung there. Eventually, the lady told me, "Your mother moved to room two hundred fifty-nine.

Immediately I went to room two hundred fifty-nine. A fat ugly lady sat in her nightgown on the edge of a bed. "Who are you?" she demanded.

"I'm Edna's daughter. Are you her new roommate?" I asked.

"My name is Violet, but people call me Vi," she said, before launching into an angry outburst. "I want her out of here. I can't get any sleep. She talks all night. I feel like *hitting* her. I told her to shut up and she told me to shut up right back. She has a real gruff voice. Nobody likes her; nobody wants her, so they stuck her with me. What's wrong with her, anyway?"

"Well Vi, I've been away on vacation. My mother might do better now that I'm back. Let's wait and see," I suggested. I kept my explanation brief because I was eager to return to Mom. When I found the lower plate of teeth on the nightstand, I made a swift exit. Racing back to the dining room I thought, I don't want Mom to spend another minute with this hateful person, and I want to know why she was moved from her room with Norene.

In walking Mom to the car, I realized she was quite frail, and thinner than when I last saw her. I opened the car door, "Can you get into the car, Mom?" She was confused, almost as if she had forgotten how to get into a car. With great difficulty, I managed to ease her into the passenger seat.

We hadn't driven very far when I noticed that she clutched her neck at times or held her head in her hands, especially when I pulled away from a red light or went over a small bump. At other times, she winced in pain. Something is terribly wrong, I said to myself. I can't take her to Lake Elsinore to see Norm. I'm taking her to see Dr. Godfrey. I turned the car away from the direction of Lake Elsinore in the direction of Loma Linda.

Blessings fell from heaven. Dr. Godfrey could see her, but we would have to wait, and wait we did for a long time in a cold air-conditioned office. When we finally sat in the treatment room with Dr. Godfrey, he said, "She is probably having bone pain. She is fortunate she hasn't gotten into bone pain before now. I'm going to order blood tests and a bone-scan x-ray. I want to see her tomorrow."

I reluctantly brought her back for the night to Arlington Meadows. Except for my continuing to think about my mother and the noticeable changes in her condition, the long day ended when I arrived home in the evening. I decided to begin a daily journal of events to manage my own emotions in anticipation of the unknown:

Tuesday September 17.
When I went to Arlington Meadows, I couldn't find her. "She may be in the beauty parlor," an employee suggested.

"She'll be under the dryer for a few more minutes," Maria the hairdresser said, continuing to cut off my mother's long fingernails.

"My mother's fingernails have always been part of her identity," I said to Maria. "She has had long fingernails as long as I can remember."

"This will be better," Maria said with a smile.

I noticed that mother still had all her rings on her fingers, including her wedding ring. Maria's words broke through my thoughts. "Your mother was in pain when her neck lay back. When I scrubbed her head, she was in tears. That's never happened before."

"Yes, she was in a lot of pain yesterday. I took her to the doctor. This morning we're going back to see what the problem is." Maria is a sweet woman, I thought. She is fond of my mother or at least she seems to care.

We arrived late to the doctor's office, but it simply meant less of a wait. "Your mother needs another transfusion," were the first words out of Dr. Godfrey's mouth.

"But it's only been a month since her last transfusion," I said, somewhat alarmed.

He proceeded to explain the bone-scan to me. "Your mother has a fractured rib that is in the process of healing."

My thoughts went immediately to the fat ugly roommate, Vi. "How do you think that happened?" I asked.

"Her bones are riddled with holes, he explained. "She could simply have fallen against something, like a chest of drawers. It wouldn't take much."

Or be pushed, maybe by Norene, I said to myself, remembering her words, "we fight all the time."

"Bone pain is excruciating. I'm giving her a prescription for pain. Give her this as needed. Also," he continued, "she will need a laxative such as milk of magnesia because the medicine is constipating."

"The facility where she stays is unreliable. I can't count on them to take care of her, but that's my problem, not yours. Is it possible to give her the transfusion on Thursday?"

"Thursday will be fine," he answered.

After we left Dr. Godfrey, I took Mother to a quiet area a short distance down the hallway. "Mom, do you understand that you need another transfusion?"

She seemed to comprehend.

"The last time you got a transfusion, you told me you never wanted to have another one. But Dr. Godfrey said that you will die if you don't have another transfusion. What would you like to do?"

She smiled sweetly at me and said, "Whatever you think is best." She had left the decision to me.

That evening I called Glenda, the first time I had talked with her since returning from vacation. "Mother requires another transfusion."

"Norm fell and broke his hip on Labor Day. I've been caught up with him and his problem since you've been gone. I intended to get out to see Mom while you were gone, but I just didn't make it," Glenda said without emotion.

My insides tightened. No one except Marc had come to see mother while I was away. I had left on August twenty-one. Labor Day was on September two. In the twelve days before Norm broke his hip, Glenda had not been to see Mother. I pushed down my feelings to deal with the more immediate problems.

"She's in excruciating bone pain. Arlington Meadows can't be relied on to dispense her pain medicine, which will cause constipation. Her bowel activity must be monitored closely to determine when to give her a laxative. She needs to be moved to a facility that can give her the personal attention she needs."

I elaborated on the roommate situation then continued, "I plan to visit three facilities on Thursday that are closer to me. If you wish, we can have her moved closer to you." I knew what her choice would be, but I said it for other reasons. "Think about it and let's talk Thursday evening,"

She called back later, "I talked to Terry. We think Mom needs to be moved."

"Did you decide to locate a facility close to you?" I asked her.

"No, I think it's better if you can find something close to where you live," she answered immediately.

Just as I thought, I told myself. "I'll look into where she can get the care she needs and get back to you, Glenda."

Thursday September 19.

"You're going to get a transfusion today, Mom," I explained again. "It will help you feel better." We didn't have to wait at the clinic. Kathy, the nurse, was ready for us.

"I'm going to give her a sedative to make her more comfortable during the transfusion," Kathy said to me, unknowingly giving me a gift as well as my mother.

"Mom, I'll be leaving for a while once the nurse starts the transfusion. I won't be gone very long." I kissed her and she patted my arm.

This was my opportunity to check on three places to determine if one of them might suit our needs. All were located within fifteen minutes of my home. How wonderful it will be, I thought, to have her close to me instead of almost an hour away.

Of the three options, Heritage Gardens, a single-story building surrounded by beautifully kept gardens, was my preferred choice. As the administrator was giving me the tour of the convalescent section, I noticed the cleanliness of the facility, but I was equally impressed with how well it seemed to be managed.

The administrator stopped at one of the rooms. "This bed is available," he said, pointing to an empty bed.

"This is a lovely room," I said, noticing the attractive wood furniture and warm inviting carpet. Is it possible for you to put a hold on this bed for twenty-four hours?" I asked.

He hesitated before saying, "Yes, I can do that." I made a note, Room Six-hundred five, bed A. "If you'll come to my office, I'll give you a brochure that explains in more detail the care we offer."

"My mother is Dr. Godfrey's patient," I began. "She has multiple myeloma and I've just been told she, uh, her bones are…" I began to cry. My crying turned into sobs. He waited quietly after placing Kleenex nearby. Finally, I was able to continue informing him of her condition.

"I want you to take this and read it," he recommended, handing me a small brochure. 'It will tell you what you can do legally to assure that, when the time comes, your mother can die in peace." I learned that Dr. Godfrey follows his patients residing at Heritage Gardens.

I had checked on mother between visits to each of the potential places. She was doing well but I wasn't doing well after I got back from my search. The sights had impacted me negatively. I found it very difficult to ride the elevator to the third floor. Panic encompassed me. I called Marc.

"I'm having difficulty. Can you help me?" He came immediately. We talked together until the transfusion was finished and then he took Mom down the elevator, brought my car to where Mom and I waited, and returned to work.

"Mom, we'll go to my place, and I'll give you something to eat before I take you back to Arlington Meadows," I told her.

"That'd be good," she said.

On the way to my apartment she said, "I have to poop." I got her into my bathroom and left her for a time then returned to check on her. She was in distress.

"I can't go, and it hurts," she told me. I rubbed her back as she sat on the stool, hoping to relax her. I remembered her fingernails. If only she had her nails, I thought. But she doesn't and she can't help herself.

Rubbing her back didn't work. "I have a Fleets enema I can give you. Let's move you to my bed." I put down a towel and said, "There, lie down on the towel." I inserted the end of the enema, but I couldn't get the fluid to flow into her. I removed it and reinserted it in a different area. This time the liquid went in. It was a chore getting her back into the bathroom. The towel I put between her legs to catch the dribbles got tangled up as we tried to move. Liquid dribbled out onto the carpet, leaving a trail from the bedroom to the bathroom. Back on the stool she went. All the liquid whooshed out of her with a meager portion of feces.

The Fleets enema hadn't worked. We are still in trouble, I told myself. I called David to see what could be done. "Have her sit for a time. She can extract it with her finger, or you can extract it," he suggested. On my return to the bathroom, I heard her calling out, "Norm, Norm."

Maybe I can extract it, I reluctantly thought. I felt her dilated rectum and touched a huge mass. I recoiled in shocked surprise. We're in bigger trouble than I imagined, I said to myself.

What shall I do? I frantically asked myself while trying to remain calm. I called the Heritage Gardens Convalescent Hospital. I stammered something about having a bed on hold for my mother but that now she needed immediate unforeseen help after just having a blood transfusion. Could I please bring her to them?

The person was a bit confused with my request but answered, "Yes, please bring her. We'll be waiting."

Mother was standing in pain at the bathroom door, wearing only a blouse and wet socks. I struggled to dress her. She must have been absolutely miserable.

"We have to walk to the car," I told her, thinking it would be a miraculous accomplishment if we got there.

"I don't know if I can make it," she said. But laboriously we made our way to the car.

"How are you doing Mom?" I asked once I got her seated.

"Okay," she answered. Fortunately, I thought, the sedative from the transfusion is probably helping ease her discomfort.

The efficient nurses of Heritage Gardens whisked her into the bathroom connected to the lovely room I had found for her earlier. I stood in the hallway where I heard my mother cry out in pain as the nurses extracted the impacted feces from her rectum. She climbed wearily into bed when the ordeal had ended. Another crisis conquered. She was almost fast asleep when I kissed her goodbye.

Chapter 65

California
September 20, 1991 – October 18, 1991

Friday September 20.
"Life," a high school teacher once told me, is a series of problem-solving events."

When I arrived at Heritage Gardens to pick up my mother to take her home with me, she was sitting in a wheelchair in the hallway, next to the door of her room. "Look at this," she said in disgust as she pulled at the cloth around her waist that tied her to the chair.

I went to find a nurse to protest. She explained. "The hospital must report 'falls' to the state of California. We use the wheelchair to reduce the number of falls."

"My mother is able to walk. The administrator explained that people who can't walk are confined to the wheelchairs. I don't want her tied to a wheelchair."

"I suggest you talk with someone in the office," she said caringly.

"You signed the Restraint Form which allows us to confine her to a wheelchair when she is out of bed," the office woman said.

"I signed it because I thought she wouldn't be restrained as long as she was ambulatory," I explained.

At that moment there was nothing more I could do except untie mother and walk with her down the hall where we exited the building. I took her home with me for the rest of the day.

Sunday September 22.
I wrote a letter today:

Nursing staff of Heritage Gardens.
Re: Edna Hall, Room 605

Edna Hall is ambulatory. At this time, she will not need a wheelchair. For her safety and the hospital liability, she can be assisted by an attendant when she walks, if you choose. I would like to revoke the form I signed which states she can be restrained in a wheelchair. I misunderstood and thought this was hospital policy for all patients. You may need to involve Dr. Pollack, the in-house doctor assigned to her, to clear this. Please call me if there is any question.

My plan is to take her home with me for two to four hours per day until she makes a smooth adjustment to her new environment. I will be happy to assist you in any way with information regarding frequency of voiding and bowel movements on a daily report as you might need.

Edna was with me for several hours yesterday, Saturday the twenty-first and did not void, nor did her bowels move. She seems to go for hours without voiding.

When I returned her to Heritage Gardens yesterday, she was very accepting of being there. From this experience, I anticipate she will adjust fairly quickly. If there is anything I can do to be of help, please call me at any time of the day or night.

Monday September 23.
  Glenda called to tell me that she and Verneda would be coming to Heritage Gardens to see Mom. The last time they had visited Mother, I learned, was in July at Arlington Meadows.
  "If I knew when you're coming, I would meet you there," I told Glenda.
  At the estimated time she gave me for their arrival, I went to Heritage Gardens, anxious in anticipation of seeing my sister Verneda, whom I hadn't seen in over two years, but only Glenda was in the room with Mom.
  "She's asleep," Glenda said. "We brought her a blanket." I looked at the lovely soft blanket thankful for their thoughtfulness.
  "Where's Verneda?" I asked.
  "She went to the car." Glenda started moving toward the door. "Let's talk in the hallway." Once we were in the hall,

Glenda said, "Verneda is really upset. Right after we got here, Mom looked at her hatefully and said as she pointed her finger at Verneda, 'That one right there. She started the whole thing.' Verneda left and went to the car with her daughter."

It wasn't clear to me why Mom said what she did to Verneda.

Tuesday September 24.
Mother has an appointment with Dr. Godfrey today. I typed a list of items to discuss with him:

> Inform him that Dr. Adriana Pollack, a resident in Family Practice, has been assigned to Mother as the in-house doctor.
> Inform re her Bone Pain: Since returning from vacation September fifteenth, I have brought my mother home with me every day. She has indicated pain in the following locations: jaw, neck, shoulders, arms, ribs, back, left leg. Even with Tylenol #3 she is in pain.
>
> Inform re Mother signed a Directive to Physicians that was placed in her Sun City chart which reads, "No heroic measures": no tube or IV feedings, no CPR. I signed a "no-CPR" form at Heritage Gardens. Her comfort is the important factor.
>
> Ask: Is it safe to take her home with me for a few hours each day?
> I'm concerned about her pain and fragile bones.

After our visit, Dr. Godfrey wrote a letter to Peter Peabody, Administrator of Heritage Gardens Convalescent with a copy to me:

Dear Mr. Peabody,

I have discussed with Edna Hall's daughter the status of her mother and the fact that she is currently residing in your facility.

The patient has far advanced multiple myeloma. It is refractory to therapy, and as a consequence further follow-up of her blood work seems inappropriate at this point. It is my suggestion to you that blood transfusions are not in the patient's best interest, even though she may become severely anemic. In terms of her eating, what she can eat by mouth is satisfactory, and I would not think that tube feedings or IV feedings are appropriate in somebody terminally ill with cancer. The patient is no code, that is, no CPR.

I will be happy to work with Doctor Adriana Pollack regarding an appropriate program for her pain management.

Sincerely,

Thomas E. Godfrey, M.D.
Medical Oncology

Wednesday September 25.
In the morning, I wrote a letter to Glenda to inform her of the conclusions reached at Mother's appointment with Dr. Godfrey:

> "In the early stages of her illness she expressed she did not want to suffer. Unfortunately, she is now into the bone pain that usually comes with this form of cancer.
>
> The inability of her body to produce the red blood cells she needs, the loss of appetite and consequently the loss of weight are indications that her body is in the process of shutting down.

It might be possible to prolong her life with more transfusions and more tests but what would we gain? We would simply be giving her an extended life of pain that only the strongest medicines might relieve.

The pain, along with the condition of her mind, greatly reduces the quality of her life. If there were any hope of her getting better than we would want to do all or anything to save her. But this is not the case.

The conclusion Dr. Godfrey and I came to is to make her as comfortable as possible. That would mean no more needles, no procedures, no forced tube or IV feedings, no transfusions, no heroic measures.

Please discuss this with Verneda. Think about it. Let me know if you disagree or have a different way you want this handled…

Friday September 27.
I received an emergency call from a nurse at Heritage Gardens. "Your mother has fallen. She is very agitated."
I left immediately to get to her. When I arrived, the nurse said, "We've determined that she didn't fall. It seems that she got out of bed to go to the bathroom but because of the height of the bed, she was unable to get back into bed so that's why we found her lying on the floor."
I thanked the nurse and then I took Mom to the car. It was very difficult for her to get into the car. She was in terrible pain as we drove to my home. When we finally got into the apartment, she immediately wanted to lie down. After she woke from a short nap, she moved with great difficulty to sit in the easy chair.
"Where are you having pain," I asked her.
"My back hurts and my chest and my arms." We tried to talk. We watched some television, but she simply was in too much pain.

"I think I need to take you back so that we can get you some pain medicine, Mom."

She never protested about going back to Heritage Gardens.

Only one time when I sat with her in the cafeteria did she express her desire to be somewhere else. She sat at the table with her head hanging down, almost touching the plate of food sitting in front of her.

"Mom, you need to eat."

"I'm tired of these places," she said dejectedly.

I spoke softly in her ear, "I understand. I don't blame you for being tired of living in these places. I'm tired of them too. You're very sick and they are taking good care of you." In a moment she picked up her fork and began to eat.

Now, as we walked painstakingly to my car to return to Heritage Gardens, she said, "I guess I'm in my last days." Her understanding was clear and profound. Wellness dwells in part of her mind, I thought but it was too complex for me to comprehend.

One of the nurses approached me when we returned. "We are concerned that your mother may fall. Will you please allow us to constrain her?" I turned the decision to Dr. Pollack.

I understood that a fall would most assuredly result in a broken hip since her bones were now thin and weak. I talked to Mom and explained that she may no longer be able to walk the hallways of Heritage Gardens. "They may sit you in the wheelchair and move you about that way. It's better than not getting to move about at all," I tried to explain. She made no protests.

On returning Mom to Heritage Gardens, after talking to the nurse again about their concern of her falling, I decided that today would be the last that I would be able to bring mother home with me.

My desperate effort to run from my despair manifested itself in an internal conflict over wanting to "run away to school" by enrolling in classes, but after I had a written dialogue with myself, the conflict came to a halt. I'm not going to allow myself to be distracted from the experience of my mother dying.

October 4.

A few days ago, as I moved through the hall on my way to get a wheelchair to retrieve mother from the gazebo, a nurse called to me. "They will be moving your mother to the room next to her."

"Why?" I asked in surprise.

'To solve a problem between people in the next room."

"Mother is familiar with the room and the location of the bathroom. I think a move would be additionally traumatic for her. I'll speak with Mr. Peabody," I told the nurse. I sent a letter to the administration asking that she not be moved.

Today I wrote a letter to Glenda. Mostly I informed her about Dr. Pollack and her role in mother's care. I provided phone numbers where she could be reached. "She feels the same way about constraints that all of us do and they will not be used on Mother unless absolutely necessary."

"With regards to Mother being moved to another room, we have expressed our wishes that she continues to remain in the room where she is, but that is in the hands of the administration."

I left her with these thoughts: "It is very difficult to be part of this dying process. It seems there isn't anything else we can do to take care of her. With Dr. Pollack in charge to follow through with the guidelines for her care, working with Dr. Godfrey when needed, we can find some measure of comfort knowing we have given the very best in the face of difficult circumstances."

In the October days that followed, I visited my mother daily.

Friday October 18.

I was sitting at my desk mid-morning, enthused, and anticipating going out of town. The phone rang, "This is Shirley from Heritage Gardens. Your mother is bleeding from the mouth. We have removed her teeth. She will not be wearing them anymore. I'm calling to let you know so you understand when you come in." The nurse reported this to me in a matter-of-fact manner. Had she known that I visualized my mother bleeding profusely from her mouth, she might have provided more detail. My mind blurred as tears flowed; I was rendered unable to ask, "How much is she bleeding?"

I hung up the phone. I sobbed. I wandered around the house sobbing and feeling lost.

I wanted to call David, but I knew his schedule was usually filled with patients, so I called Marc instead. I sobbed into the phone as I repeated what the nurse had said.

"I'll come right over," he responded. By the time he arrived, my body had gone into a series of muscle contractions. I wept, "I don't know what's coming next. I'm frightened. I don't know what to expect. I can't go away for three days. We're supposed to leave tomorrow morning," I cried.

Once Marc had calmed me, I said, "I need to go and see her for myself."

"Ralph, Ralph, Ralph," I heard Mom calling, as I turned the corner into the hall leading directly into her room. Her brother Ralph had died earlier in the year, but I had chosen not to tell her. I believed she was already dealing with more than she could handle.

The curtain was drawn around the bed so that I had to pull it aside to see her. She was thrashing about; the hospital gown lay in folds about her neck and shoulders; the sheet had fallen away leaving her exposed. I didn't want to see her nudity. Thoughts flashed through my mind of her drunken states, of the men who had seen her nude, of the men who had slept with her. I pulled the sheet over her drawn up legs, which jerked and fell to the sides.

I saw spots of blood on her gown. Blood was not pouring from her mouth but had dried in a brownish shade, caked around her mouth. I was wiping it with a damp towel when Gloria the nurse came in with a special little pink sponge on a stick. She swirled it around in mother's mouth. A lollipop for the aged, I thought to myself. It came out slightly coated with blood.

Marc went away and the nurse went away. I sat holding mother's hand, watching, waiting. An hour later, David came from work. "I'm going to see if I can take a look at her chart.

I'll be right back." He returned with information. "The doctor has put a note in the chart, 'End stages of multiple myeloma.'"

Then David told me what I hadn't known before. "Not only is there a problem because the bone marrow can no longer make red blood cells, but it also doesn't make platelets. Platelets prevent us from bleeding," he explained. "Without platelets, random bleeding can begin anywhere: the brain, the gums, the lips, anywhere."

"What can I do with the horror of that information?" I whimpered. He took me to lunch then drove me home.

At two o'clock I returned to see Mom. She was semi-awake. I kissed her. I prayed with her. I held her hand.

"We were planning to go away three days this weekend, but with this new development, I'm thinking I should stay close," I told Shirley, a nurse who came into the room.

"Oh," she responded casually, "She could go on for ten years like this. Think of all the trips you'd miss. You should go."

In the evening, I went for the third time to be with Mom. Later, when I returned home, I informed Glenda of the day's event. "The blanket you and Verneda brought has disappeared. Mother needed a blanket today and the one you gave her was gone. Gloria is trying to locate it."

Glenda said, "It doesn't matter."

I cried, "It does matter."

Glenda asked, "Can you keep me informed? When I call to ask how she's doing they always say, 'Fine.'"

When I hung up something screamed inside me, "I don't want to keep her informed. I want this to be over."

Chapter 66

California
October 19, 1991 – October 29, 1991

Saturday October 19.

David and I decided to leave only for the day and night to stay at a golf resort near Laguna Beach, about an hour away.

"It's nice David," I said after we had been there awhile, but I'm not excited to be here. I have a lost empty feeling."

"Let's go for a walk," he suggested.

On our long walk, I felt as if my body had gaping holes blown through by harsh winds. "I wish I had a happy light spirit, David. I'm not much fun for you," I apologized.

"You're fine just the way you are. Why don't we go to a movie?"

Sunday October 20.

Mid-morning, I started to cry. "I'm not doing well. I need to go back."

"I'll take you home," he said tenderly.

When I went into Mother's room, she looked lovely sleeping in her pink gown. Her hair had been brushed. It's Sunday. She's been beautifully prepared for visitors. If only Norm would come to see her, I thought. Glenda has come only once, I thought. She didn't even come when I let her know that Mom was bleeding.

Towards the end of the long day, I returned again to see Mother. She was redressed in a hospital gown, sleeping. Her untouched dinner tray sat on the stand next to her bed. She woke. I stroked her hair and talked to her. I was happy to be with her instead of trying to celebrate my birthday somewhere else.

"Your mother was given a pain pill shortly before you came," Mary, the nurse told me when she came into the room.

"That must be why she's not very coherent and seems to be sleepy and drowsy," I responded.

"She may have tumors in her mouth, but she won't let us look inside so we can't tell. Your mother kept holding her bottom and we thought she might have a urinary tract infection. We catheterized her even though she didn't want us to. The results will be back soon." Mary left the room.

Monday October 21.
Since my loving husband had already taken the day off, I said, "I have an urge to go to Palm Springs for lunch and to do some shopping. What do you think?"

"I'm game to go to Palm Springs!" he said

The nurse was coming out of Mother's room when we returned. "I've just given her a pain pill."

Mom was drowsy but I leaned over and hugged her. She hugged me back.

"I love you, Mom."

"I love you," she echoed affectionately.

Tuesday October 22.
I went to see Mother in the afternoon. When I got there, she was in a neatly made bed, making noises as she slept very soundly. A nurse came and talked with me. "She gave me kisses and hugs this morning when I dressed her. Gloria and I are always able to get her to eat in the morning." This nurse actually seemed fond of mother, and I was thankful for her kindness. "It's best for her to sleep; that way she isn't in pain," the nurse told me. I sat quietly by myself for a time. God has people here who minister to her in ways I can't, I thought. I watched her sleep for a while, and then I walked away.

I feel myself suspended, waiting. How long can I wait? This haunting question lingered in my thoughts. Is it possible to go on with life even while she's in the process of dying? I asked myself. I'm not able to concentrate. It's hard to resist this strong urge I have to buy a house. I must not buy a house now and make a mess of things, I chided myself.

Wednesday October 23.

"Do you have the results of the urine test," I asked the nurse shortly after I arrived. "Mother is holding her abdomen and her bottom."

"I'll check the chart," she said before disappearing around the corner. "The results show that there is some bacteria in the urine. Antibiotics will be started this evening."

Thursday October 24.

When I entered Heritage Gardens, Mr. Peabody greeted me rather coldly. He always looks so sternly at me; I wonder what his thoughts are. Does he have feelings about how my mother acts; the room she's in; the choice we made for her treatment?

My thoughts of Mr. Peabody were interrupted by the appearance of Aida. I cringed at the sight of her. I cringe when I see her because she has power over which room Mother is in. I didn't want her to use that power to move Mom, but the decision wasn't mine.

"She's asleep again," I said to the nurse. I stayed only a few minutes but returned around dinnertime. Mary was on duty.

"Do you know if the antibiotics have been started," I asked Mary. Later in the evening she called me at home.

"Your mother is bleeding from the rectum and passing clots. This is probably the end. Shall we move her to the hospital?"

"I'm very upset. Please do nothing. My husband and I will be there in just a few minutes."

Mary came from behind the nurses' desk when she saw us. Standing in front of her I tearfully said, "The course of action has already been determined. The bleeding, I understand from talking with the doctors, is a consequence of the advanced stage of multiple myeloma and the doctor's advice against further blood transfusions. I don't want Mother moved to a hospital, but I do want her made as comfortable as possible."

Mary walked us to the room. "I see that mother is wearing diapers, Mary."

"It's our way of keeping track of the amount of bleeding. They're changed every hour," Mary said. How comforting her words were.

I looked at mother, uncertain if this was the end. "Will you be giving her morphine?" I asked.

"Her body is much too small for morphine. We'll be giving her another medicine IM. I'll contact Dr. Pollack."

Friday October 24.

Quite early in the morning, David and I went together to see Mother.

"Your mother is bleeding minimally," the nurse reported.

When we arrived at the room, mother was in a sitting position in the bed, semi-awake. A nurse was attempting to feed her by trying first one thing and then another. A second nurse came in to check her diaper.

"We'll wait in the hall," I told her. Mother began to make dreadful, painful sounds.

"Your mother has an impacted bowel," the nurse said as she whisked past me in the hall. Two nurses went in pairs into the room to work with her. "Push, push it out," they quietly kept telling her. Mother's screams shattered the silence of the hallway. I went fleeing from the area into the garden until the terror had subsided.

"Dr. Godfrey indicated she must have a laxative with the Tylenol Three because it causes constipation," I told the attending nurse on my return. "Above all, I want her to be as comfortable as possible. I want to avoid pain at all costs," I stressed to the listening nurse.

She left to check the chart. "The laxative is ordered but PRN," the nurse read from the chart, which means the patient has to communicate a desire or need for the medicine." I stood in a state of disbelief. The nurse quickly added, "Of course, your mother is unable to ask for it herself, so we will begin giving it to her regularly."

I was pleased with the care my mother was receiving, but how did this important need for a laxative and her inability to ask for it escape these efficient nurses? I walked to mother's bedside. She was sleeping peacefully. She was comfortable at last.

I returned in the afternoon, and again in the evening. From then forward, each time I visited her, I stroked her head. I brushed my hand across her face and her arm and whispered in her ear, "You are very sick. I'm sorry you're so sick. Remember, I'm your daughter, Vernetta who loves you very much.

Saturday October 26.
I was disappointed she was asleep when I came. I'll come early tomorrow, I told myself.

Sunday October 27.
"You're awake, Mom!" I said happily when I went to see her in the morning. I talked with her about little nothings for forty-five minutes. "I need to take Marc home. He wanted to see you."

Once I had dropped Marc at his home, I wished I had gone back to see her, but it was so difficult to go there and feel so helpless, to see her so sick, so tiny with a diaper and with no teeth and a bit of brown blood in the corners of her mouth. Instead, I numbly drove myself to Palm Springs.

Monday October 28.
Dr. Pollack called me: "I'll make sure your mother has the laxatives she needs. I've also ordered injections for pain relief to make her more comfortable."

I arrived at Heritage Gardens around eleven thirty, twenty minutes later than I'd planned, but to my joy, Mother was awake. We hugged and kissed. I prayed with her. Again, I had to leave before I wanted to, just like yesterday. David and I were to meet for lunch. Why didn't I call him to say, Mother's awake; I'll be here with her until she falls asleep again?

Tuesday October 29.

I awoke in the morning thinking of God. I turned my face heavenward and told Him, "It seems you're not here. I don't think I can endure much more. I feel a weight bearing down on me. I need to *know* you are here."

I got myself ready and left to go see my mother. "You're awake! How lucky can I be?" I said as I hugged her and kissed her. "I've come so many times to see you, but you were always asleep."

She seemed to understand. I prayed with her.

"You look like you're feeling better today, Mom," I said and gave her another kiss. I didn't tell her that the nurse said she's no longer bleeding from the rectum. At noon, I left to go home to have lunch with David. But at one o'clock, just one hour after I had left her, the phone rang.

"This is the nurse at Heritage Gardens," a soft voice said. "Vernetta, your mother is very sick. She is having trouble breathing, so we have put her on oxygen."

David and I drove to Heritage Gardens in separate cars.

Little plastic tubes came from Mother's nose and went around each ear. Her breathing was very labored. A deep breath, a pause, and then a deep breath. I sat in a chair as close to her bed as I could get.

"I'm so thankful the other bed in the room is empty, David." The curtain was pulled across the bottom of her bed giving her privacy. How delicious it was to have privacy at this time. I settled in. "I'll be all right. I know you're needed at work."

He left but returned about an hour later. "How are you doing?" he asked.

"You're special, darling," I said, appreciative of his attentive love.

I continued sitting with her until around three p.m.

"We're giving her injections for pain every four hours," the nurse told me aware of my need to have Mother as comfortable as possible.

"Thank you," I responded. "She hasn't changed for hours. I need some air. I'll be back soon," I told the nurse. I left for an hour and then returned. She was still the same.

I sat down once again in the chair next to her bed. I gazed out the window of her room at the trees and the late afternoon October sun. The days are shorter now, I said to myself.

I wanted to be closer to my mother than the chair would permit so I took the hairbrush from her nightstand and began gently brushing back her hair with slow repeated strokes. After laying the brush aside, I stood beside the bed to stroke her arm. I noticed the book I had left on the seat of my chair. I sought refuge in reading and copied interesting ideas onto a sheet of paper:

"The minute we begin withholding our thoughts from others, we've begun to isolate ourselves."

"People have to be in touch with themselves before they can make contact with others."

"Even the most exhilarating pursuit soon settles into a routine."

My reading was interrupted by a nurse who came to take Mother's pulse and blood pressure. "What is it?" I asked.

"Her pulse is 100 and her blood pressure is 100 over 60."

I made a note of it and the time, four forty-five p.m. When the nurse left, I sat and watched her breathe, listening to her breath as it moved in and out. Then my gaze went to the small pink flowers on the wallpaper. Gratitude filled my heart that my mother had not been moved from this lovely room. The carpet on the floor, the wood frame of the bed and the nightstand gave an added feeling of a home rather than a hospital. Occasionally my gaze fell on the picture I had placed on her nightstand: Mom with Norm sitting next to her and Glenda standing behind them.

I was weary as I sat there, alone but totally aware my mother's life was coming to a close. I didn't know what others do when death is near, yet uncertain of when it will come. I had seen her so often lately. I had experienced the panic of death when she had bled from her mouth, when she had bled from her rectum. I remembered the many times they told me she would not eat. I remembered the two horrible times her bowel had impacted. I remembered her anger and, as a result, the threat that she might be asked to leave Heritage Gardens. Now, she labored for breath.

Dr. Pollack came shortly after the nurse had taken mother's pulse and blood pressure. "Hello," she said pleasantly. "I would like to talk with you after I've finished examining your mother." She opened mother's eyes and shined a little light at them. Soon Dr. Pollack sat down on the empty bed and spoke with me. "There are many things I could do to keep your mother alive, but I agree with Dr. Godfrey's recommendation. Your mother is terminal with multiple myeloma. The quality of her life does not justify heroic measures. We would have to stick needles into her, this would cause her pain."

"I could not endure seeing her in more pain. She is so very thin, so very tiny now." I was glad the decision of how to proceed had been made long before this moment.

Dr. Pollack repeated herself, "I could keep your mother alive longer, but you have made a good decision. Her eyes are not responding to the light as I would hope." I didn't hear anything else until her voice broke through to me again when she said, "Now is the time to call the rest of the family members."

Chapter 67

California
October 29, 1991 – October 30, 1991

October 29, evening.

I was in a state of numbness when David suggested, "Let's get some dinner and then you can call Glenda," My thoughts went to the last time I called her, right before my birthday to tell her about mother bleeding. She didn't come. She didn't call me even once to ask how mother was doing. Maybe she's talking with the nurse at Heritage Gardens, I thought. Doubtful, I admitted to myself, since she told me that when she calls, they always say she's "fine."

After dinner, I dialed her number. It rang only twice. I was thankful when she answered. "Dr. Pollack suggested I let family members know that if you want to see Mother, the time to come is now. She isn't expected to live much longer. Will you please call Norm and Verneda?" She assured me she would call them but gave no indication that she planned to come.

David and Elizabeth left me at Heritage Gardens. It was just Mother and I, alone in her room. Darkness had fallen. I closed the blind and the drapes. She continued to breathe laboriously in and out until almost seven-thirty when her feet began to shake. The shaking moved up her legs into her torso until her entire body shook. When the shaking reached her head, her lips drew into a pucker. She stopped breathing; her eyes sprung open. Just for an instant, the cold staring quality of her gaze terrified the frightened child in me. For just an instant, she was the angry mother once again looking at me through eyes of hate.

Her body began to jerk rhythmically as if someone were sending intermittent electric shocks through her system. I ran into the hallway where a nurse saw my distress and quickly came to look at mother. Without a word, she went running out of the room, calling in the hallway "Mary, Mary."

Mother was almost at the end of her tremendous body quake when the second nurse arrived. She lay there with opened eyes. "Your Mother is taking her last breaths." Her eyes closed all by themselves; her labored breathing continued. Mary adjusted the oxygen level before leaving the room.

At eight-thirty, Mother's bed was changed, and she was placed on her right side with a pillow propped behind her. Two more times between then and midnight, the bed was changed, and she was turned.

"Thank you for keeping her dry and comfortable," I said to those attending her.

I sat waiting, watching, thankful that I had not gone home after dinner. About two hours later, her feet began to shake again. This time, knowing what to expect, I wasn't as frightened. I quickly got up to hold her hands. She held tightly as the shock went through her body. Her eyes opened but I didn't feel fearful. Her breathing stopped. I didn't know if it would begin again. Then slowly her eyes closed, and the methodical labored breathing returned. I sat back down in my chair.

Later, when a man came into the room wheeling an enormous tank to the side of her bed, I stepped into the empty hallway. As I looked down the stark white, brightly lighted corridor an experience of aloneness encompassed me, alone with Mother at the time of her death. Ironic, I thought. When I was a child, she always left me alone. She left me alone for hours, day and night, drinking and partying with her friends. Now at her death, she's alone, except for me. No husband is here, the one who I felt took what little of her I had when I was a child. Glenda, Mom and Norm's daughter, isn't here. Verneda, my sister isn't here. Only God and I for the final farewell.

I went to call David. "I really want to be with someone. Can you come back?"

I didn't call Marc because he had gotten very upset on Sunday. "I'm sorry," he had said, "but I'm into feelings and memories of my own mother's death." Elizabeth had gotten upset earlier in the evening when she came to see mother, so I didn't call her, and Jennifer was in Stockton. David gave me the impression he would come in a few minutes.

When I returned to the room, a nurse was trying to arouse Mother without success. "It's time for her injection of pain medication," the nurse indicated. I watched her closely to see if she would respond when the nurse pierced her skin with the needle, but there was no response.

For a while I sat listening to the laborious methodical breathing pattern of a breath followed by a pause, but now each breath came with sounds of congestion. I was remembering what the doctor had said, "She has fluid accumulating in her lungs," when for a third time, shaking started in her feet then traveled the entire course of her body to her head. There were no surprises as I observed it carefully. I calculated it to be less intense than the very first time. When her eyes opened, I slowly moved my hand in front of her eyes. There was absolutely no response. I knew she was no longer present. My mother had died.

A half hour later, David came into the room followed by a lovely foreign RN who came to talk with me. "Your mother could continue in this manner for hours longer. I encourage you to go home and get some rest," she kindly encouraged.

"I agree," David said. "She could continue like this for two days. Her mechanical breathing is a result of her autonomic nervous system. But it isn't an indication that she is still alive."

It was almost midnight. David looked tired; I was tired. My experience that mother had already died made it possible for me to go home.

I heard David say to the nurse, "If she dies before we return, please do not allow her to be taken away before Vernetta can see her." I breathed a sigh of gratitude for his foresight.

"We can leave your car here. I don't want you driving home alone," he said.

October 30, 1991.

Although I thought I would have trouble sleeping, I fell asleep quickly. At five a.m. I awoke abruptly, wanting to leave immediately to return to Heritage Gardens but because I didn't have my car, I thought I must wait for David to wake. I tried to go back to sleep but found it impossible. At five-thirty it occurred to me that I could drive his car and then return later for him. I was in the middle of brushing my teeth when the phone rang. It was the foreign nurse we had talked with at midnight. "Your mother has just closed her eyes," she said. It was five-forty a.m. Wednesday morning.

David and I left immediately for Heritage Gardens. When I stepped out of the car, I noticed the first rays of morning cast beams of light across the sky. With the beauty of the dawn came the thought of a new day with the promise of new beginnings.

Mother lay peacefully, as if asleep. I kissed her gently on her warm forehead. I stood gazing at her face, smooth and amazingly free of lines. You are still beautiful, I said to myself. I picked up the pictures I had placed on her nightstand a little over five weeks earlier, the pictures I had put there for others to see.

The nurse slowly pulled the sheet to cover her.

As David and I walked away, down the hall of Heritage Gardens, the scene of a black bag on a gurney went through my mind. "David, will you go back and ask the nurse to dress Mother in her pink gown set. I don't want them to put her nude into a black bag." He kindly obliged. I was still trying to take care of Mother, even after she had died.

EPILOGUE

Epilogue
People Identified

Al Johnston: Bud's oldest brother

Aunt Mary: Edna's younger sister

Aunt Emma: Pansie's Aunt, left her an inheritance

Aunt Evelyn: Edna's sister-in-law

Billy: Edna's nephew, son of Edna's brother Ralph

Blanche Johnston: Al's wife, Bud's sister-in-law

Bud Johnston: Edna's lover, father of her son Buddy, Jr. aka Larry

Buddy, Jr. aka Larry: son of Edna and Bud

Christie: youngest daughter of Verneda

Dewey Johnston: close brother of Bud

Glenda: Norm and Edna's only child

Grace: married to Dewey, brother of Bud

Grandpa: Lowell, Edna's Father

Grandma: Pansie, Edna's Mother

Larry aka Buddy, Jr.: son of Edna and Bud

Mac: Vernetta's therapist

Marc: family friend; vital support for Vernetta's healing process

Roy Lee: married to Vi, known to Buddy, Jr./Larry as Father

Sherry: married to Larry aka Buddy, Jr.

Terry aka Verneda: Edna's first daughter

Verneda aka Terry: Edna's first daughter

Vi Lee: sister to Bud, took and raised Buddy, Jr.; named him "Larry"

Aunt Mary   Vernetta
Hutchinson, Kansas 1992

Vernetta   Aunt Evelyn
Dighton, Kansas 1992

Within months of Mother's death, I had a burning need to begin a search for answers to the unanswered persistent question still clinging to me from childhood, "Why is Mother so angry?" I was driven to understand what had shaped who she became, because the life she lived almost extinguished mine. Not only my life, but my sister's life as well.

Edna Ross on the Healy Farm
1929, age 13

I turned first to Mother's closest living relatives: her sister Mary and her sister-in-law Evelyn, who had known the Ross family since she was twelve and had made her home with them on the Healy Farm for the first five years of her married life.

From California, I went to Dighton, Kansas to visit Aunt Evelyn, who was someone I had loved as a child. We hadn't been in contact for quite a long time but our years of separation were easily overcome in the first few minutes of conversation. Aunt Evelyn had an intelligence that supported the generous details she seemed to enjoy including in her answers to any questions I asked about the past.

"Mom told me she burned down the Ross family home in Healy when she was fifteen, Aunt Evelyn, but that's all I know. Do you know anything about it?" I asked.

"I certainly do," she began, "I can tell you exactly what happened because I was there. It was just before my 17th birthday, the evening of October 30, 1931. We was sittin' out on the North porch, me, Mary, Nettie and your Mom. The boys were gone. They were with Grandpa and Grandma Ross in Healy. Edna jumped up and said, 'The only way you can kill them goddamned son-of-a bitchin bedbugs is burn 'em!' "

"We had coal oil lamps with little glass bottoms for the oil. They had a wick and flue, kerosene lights for upstairs and downstairs and everywhere. Edna said to Mary, 'You carry Evelyn's clothes to the bathroom and tell her to come get 'em because the upstairs will be on fire.' And that was just what happened. She put oil on the beds of all three bedrooms; she put oil on the two single beds shoved up in the dormer windows. Then she lighted the fire in every place. That's just the way it happened."

"You know, Aunt Evelyn, it seems Mom must have had something going on with her before she decided to burn down the house. Can you imagine, you were sitting there and suddenly she jumped up to burn down the farmhouse? What was going on before that?"

"Edna's summer work was done, and she come back home. I think she was just disgusted with life in general, I really do," Aunt Evelyn answered.

Disgusted with life at age fifteen? I found that a mystifying comment. I thought about Aunt Evelyn's words, "She come back home." What was it about coming back home that had caused Mother to burn down the house?

By the time I began to wonder about the bedbugs, it was too late to ask Aunt Evelyn because I was miles from Dighton. So, when I talked with Aunt Mary I asked her, "Do you remember if the house had bedbugs?"

Aunt Mary responded quickly. "We didn't have no bedbugs."

A new question emerged: What was Mother's real motive for burning down the house if the bedbugs didn't exist? Nothing led me to an immediate answer. It unfolded gradually as I pursued information to learn what had shaped the person my mother became. From my counselor training I came to believe that the childhood one experiences has a profound impact on the adult one becomes. That's the reason I asked Aunt Mary about her father, who was my mother's father as well.

Aunt Mary said without reservation, "He was an old drunk." With great energy in her voice, she exclaimed, "He'd sleep with *anything* he'd get to lay down and spread out! Always tellin' dirty stories. He was mean even when he was sober. I was afraid of him. I remember him and my mother out in the yard. He had her down kickin' her. Once Momma had a coffee pot on the stove and Dad hit her. She picked up that pot and hit his bald head. Hot coffee poured down his face. He didn't touch her for a while after that."

Aunt Evelyn freely expressed her own experience of him. "Grandpa Ross was an alcoholic from the word go, made homebrew in the basement twenty-five gallons at a time. I think he drank up everything they had. Never got drunk but what he got MEAN. Grandpa beat the living daylights out of your grandma Pansie. Slap her and knock her across the house. I've seen him jump on Grandma's arms on a daybed and pour whiskey in her mouth to make her drink. One time, he lined all of us up, him drunk with a .38 pistol. Edna held Verneda in her arms. 'Which one's got it first?' he hollered when he waved the gun at us. And he kept us like that better than thirty-five minutes."

They described my grandfather as a person I hadn't known as a child. In the course of conversation, I came to know much more about Lowell and Pansie, my mother's parents. Lowell dominated the Ross family with his mean, angry, alcoholic behavior. He frightened his children and involved them in his alcoholic habit. Pansie, who didn't drink, went to church where she sang solos and played the piano. Frequently beaten by Lowell, she spent many of her days in bed. During her marriage to Lowell, she became a depressed and passive woman in the raising of her children. It was quite a disturbing revelation to learn what I hadn't known before about my mother's parents, my grandpa and my grandma.

Eventually the subject of incest was gently lofted into the conversation during a visit with Aunt Evelyn. "When your grandpa died, I had my hands fairly full of taking care of your Aunt Nettie. She was just hysterical. She lost her Daddy. Well, there was just as bad tales about Nettie and her own Daddy as there was about Ralph and Nettie and all."

"Who told you the story about Grandpa and Nettie?" I asked.

"Oh, everybody in the county talked about it."

I understood Aunt Evelyn's implied meaning. However, I'm grateful that Aunt Mary was much more direct when in whispered tones she exposed the incest. "I want to tell you. Nettie and your mother was *both* havin' sex with Poppa."

Momentarily I sank into a pleasantly insulating stupor that allowed no feelings to intrude. When I recovered, my thoughts went to what Mother had told me, "My Dad had me suck on a black hose to drink beer he made when I was a girl." I began thinking of my grandfather's motive for giving her beer at such a young age when suddenly it occurred to me *why* Mother may have burned down the house. It was an effort to free herself from a drunken father who satisfied himself sexually at her expense. Her fifteen-year-old mind may have reasoned that the only way of escape was to burn the beds.

It was four years after learning from Aunt Mary that "your mother was havin' sex with Poppa," that I returned to Kansas with Marc, to talk with her again to learn more about my grandpa and how far she believed his passions might have reached in satisfying his needs. Is it possible, I asked myself, that Grandpa had molested me when I was a child?

"Aunt Mary," I said, "my life was just full of sex when I was a child. Everything was sex, sex. Where did that come from?" I asked as she looked at some of Mother's old pictures taken at the Healy Farm I had brought for her to see. She looked at me for a moment then answered almost in a whisper, "My Dad. You see that's where that originated."

"Well, do you think there was a possibility he molested me?" I asked. Without a word, she returned to looking at the pictures, talking about them as if she hadn't heard my question.

She apparently isn't ready to approach the subject, I told myself. I'll try tomorrow.

That evening when Marc and I were having dinner, I shared with him what I had learned about my mother being molested by her father, but I didn't tell him I wanted to find out if he had molested me. Marc caught me by surprise when he said, "If he molested your mother, what about *you* being molested by him?"

Suddenly, muscles of my body started contracting. I had no control, no ability to stop the spasms. My mind went fuzzy. What to do? Here I was in a public place. Up to now, these things had happened to me only in private. Now, for the first time, I found myself in a public place. I don't know how long I sat there waiting to return to normal. Marc talked quietly to me until the experience passed.

The next day when I visited with Aunt Mary, I was determined to get an answer to my question: "Do you think Grandpa molested me?"

"Oh well I'm not surprised," she answered without emotion, speaking of his behavior as if it were a familiar known fact.

"You're not surprised!"

The pitch and volume of her voice escalated. "I'm not surprised at *anything* he would've done, Vernetta. I know he slept with Edna. Mm. That's the kind of man he was and still was doin' it when they was adults."

My attention was drawn to what she had said about Mom and Grandpa. Was I surprised to learn what Aunt Mary told me, "Still was doin it when they was adults?" Somehow this truth was known within me, deeply hidden among memories too painful to remember of those dark, drunken days in Larned, Kansas after my grandmother died. Other family members I eventually talked with confirmed that Aunt Mary had spoken the truth.

Awkward sentences streamed from my mouth to Aunt Mary in my effort to realize a more definitive answer. "Well, if he had sex with his daughters, I was thinking about when we lived with him after Grandma died. When I came here to talk with you four years ago, I didn't realize until then that I had blanked out the memories of living with my grandpa for those two years after Grandma died, and blanked out memories of him at other times we stayed with them. Psychologists think that's significant forgetting. Do you think Grandpa would molest me? He molested his own daughters and I think he molested Verneda and me."

"Wouldn't surprise me," she repeated. "Probably true."

Yes, I told myself, Grandpa molested me. Even though my mind chooses not to remember, my body remembers.

I thought of what Mac had told me. Some memories are so traumatic, they become shattered, fragmented pieces the mind seems unable to reassemble. There is no cognitive memory. However, the trauma can be stored in the body, recalled in muscles that involuntarily contract, often accompanied by piercing feelings of painful emotions attached to the physical recall of the actual trauma. Yes, cognitively I had no memories of the many times I had stayed with Grandpa when I was a little girl, especially the two years I lived with him after my grandmother died when I was a third and fourth grader, but for years now, my body had continued to release what my mind couldn't remember. Thankfully, over time, the intensity, duration and frequency of these experiences has gradually diminished into a whisper instead of the roaring, painful blackness I had experienced in the past.

This new awareness about my grandfather was a confounding revelation. This might help explain the scarring in my vagina discovered on my first GYN exam at nineteen, even though I was a virgin, and my incompetent cervix, which had to be sutured when I was pregnant. Early sexual trauma may have caused both.

When Mac concluded, after observing my earlier body memories, that I had been sexually violated, I found myself thinking that maybe it was some of the drunken strangers Mom brought home who had taken advantage of me, or maybe Wes who had molested Verneda. Uncle Ralph, Mom's brother, had molested two different twelve-year old girls in his sixties, possibly a repeated theme of his life. But had he molested *me*, I wondered as I remembered his two-year old son, Billy, asking me to suck his penis. Who had done this to Billy before, I asked myself: his father, my Uncle Ralph? Another thought hit me. If grandpa molested his daughters, did he also molest his sons? Does that explain Uncle Ralph's behavior? And had grandpa molested his granddaughters, my sister and me? It fit the facts, a startling possibility.

Questions became linked to answers. However, I hadn't yet directly asked Aunt Mary and Aunt Evelyn my persistent question from childhood, and I very much wanted to hear what each one would answer. "Why do you think Mom was such an angry Mother, Aunt Mary?"

"Well, she was just like my Dad and my brother Ralph," she said, "rough, gruff and outspoken. She was MEAN. She vented it on you kids even." Aunt Mary's voice became quiet. "She was a terrible mother. I remember her crunching you down in the high chair and haul off and shake you and bounce you down in that high chair hard enough to break your bones. I don't know why she done that. I never could understand that."

"When did she get mean?" I asked, ignoring the disturbing things she had just told me.

Aunt Mary sat quietly for a moment then said, "I don't know whether it was after she met your dad or whether or maybe these childhood things. Ralph and Jim was usin' her. But all of a sudden, she changed. She just went from worse to worse to worse. You never could talk with her and reason with her. Drunk and angry, drunk and angry."

I left Aunt Mary in Hutchinson and went to Dighton to ask my question of Aunt Evelyn. I listened as Aunt Evelyn talked of my mother, waiting to ask my question.

"Your Mom came to the basement house in Healy sometime after she sent Verneda and you alone on the train when you was barely walkin'," she said. "Edna was cruel to you when she come to the basement house. You'd come and sit on my lap for hours to be safe."

This hurtful information hit against my heart, but I remembered I wasn't a child anymore and then I was able to ask my question. "Why do you think Mom was so angry, Aunt Evelyn?"

"Not sure. Terrible resentment for some reason. Edna didn't talk much. I think she kept secrets to herself. Like Grandma Ross, she wasn't much of a talker."

When I left Aunt Mary and Aunt Evelyn in Kansas mid-March of 1996 to return to California, I felt quite certain that I understood why my mother was an angry person. But something still nagged at me. Did the loss of her son contribute to my mother's anger? Even though I thought I knew, I searched my transcribed interviews to see if any of them held the answer. Three relevant interviews were found, those of Blanche, Aunt Mary and Aunt Evelyn. Blanche had been a friend of my mother's in Jarbidge when Larry was born. She was Vi's sister-in-law.

"Vi and Roy wanted that baby so bad," Blanche said. "Bud and Edna was always goin' to dances and stuff and they couldn't take the little baby with 'em and oh he was kinda sick one time and Vi come and seen Bud and Edna and talked Edna into givin' the baby to them. Yeah, Bud and Edna would go out and party quite a bit 'cause they were always partying in the town, and she wanted to be with Bud."

Aunt Mary told me, "Edna wrote a letter to Momma. It was tellin' them that she had this little boy, but she was in serious bad trouble. She told Momma if I don't let them adopt and take my son, they're gonna cause me to lose Verneda and Vernetta. She had a hell of a choice there. That was a bad deal. And Momma wrote back, told her to give the boy away. I didn't think that was right."

Aunt Evelyn recounted what she knew. "Your Momma had a 'live in affair' in Jarbidge. Her boyfriend's sister Vi put it to her like this. She wanted that boy, the sister did. Well naturally Edna wanted to keep her own child. So the sister told Edna, "If you try to keep this boy, I'll prove you an unfit Mother and take your girls too." Edna sent you kids to your grandparents. Then later, Grandpa Ross sent for your mother, and she come home. And from that day on your mother just seemed to, oh I don't know, she just changed. And I put it all back to after your Daddy walked out on her for this other woman, she took up with this young guy. Edna told me he was younger, and she got pregnant."

"What changes did you see in Mom?" I asked, eager to hear Aunt Evelyn's answer.

"She was very quarrelsome when she was drinking and uh to the extent she didn't just argue. She'd just as soon hit you as look at you when she was drinking. Absolutely. She had a ferocious temper."

There it was, further insight into why my mother was so angry. The anger over the loss of her son had turned her existing anger into rage.

The thought came to me to review what Mom had told me about how the baby was raised by someone else. The first thing Mom said was, "February 27, 1941 is when they took him." "They took him" caught my attention, something I had missed before, but I quickly continued to read through her story. She had left the baby for a few days with Vi and Roy. When she came back to pick up the baby, Vi took her for a ride apparently for the purpose of persuading Mom to leave the baby with her, adding the promise that she could see him any time she wanted. Mom ended her story by saying, "So, I let her have him." Blanche said almost the same thing only more succinctly: "Vi and Roy wanted that baby so bad…Vi talked Edna into givin' the baby to them."

But what about Mom's opening statement, "they took him." It contradicts the rest of her story, but is supported by what Aunt Mary and Aunt Evelyn both report that Vi threatened to "take the girls too, if Mom didn't allow Vi and Roy to take and adopt her son."

I asked myself many questions. Did Mother willingly let Vi have the baby because of the promise made, that she could see him any time she wanted. Did Vi break her promise? With the promise broken, did Mother go to Vi later to get her baby back? Is that when Vi threatened to prove my mother unfit, threaten to take away her daughters? *When* were the threats made? Was it before or after the drunken trio (Mother, Grace and Dewey) went to get the baby back but failed?

I had no burning need to search further for the truth. But whatever the truth may be, the primary relevance is the fact that my mother was tremendously impacted the rest of her life by the loss of her son.

A semblance of relief and satisfaction came with the answers I had found. But my brief sanctuary of dealing with issues from the past was interrupted on April 2, 1996 when Glenda called.

Since moving to Northern California, I had little contact with Glenda and no contact at all with my sister Verneda, known also as Terry. The closest I had come to seeing her was when she came to visit Mother at Heritage Gardens, a month before Mother died. Now Glenda was on the phone.

"The reason I called is to tell you Terry called me. She told me she had just gotten out of jail. She said she had been in there for two months."

"What was she in *jail* for?" I asked, surprised by what she said.

"Drugs."

"Drugs, oh," I said somewhat dismayed. "Was she using or selling?"

"Both," Glenda said.

"Could you give me her number? I asked, thankful she had called.

Even though I hadn't spoken with my sister for seven years, I still cared about her. Learning that she had been in jail for two months saddened me.

I pushed the numbers on the keypad to call her. An annoying busy-beep was the result. Every five minutes when I tried again, I heard the same sound. I called the operator to report the problem. "The phone is off the hook," she said.

After lunch, I again attempted to call and absentmindedly leaned against the kitchen counter, expecting a busy signal. Oh my God, it's ringing, I suddenly realized. A voice said, "Hello." I wasn't certain if it was my sister's voice.

"Hello, this is Vernetta," I said.

"Is that you?" Is that really you?" Verneda sobbed quietly into the phone. "I love you. I didn't mean that I don't love you," she cried.

"I'm so glad you love me. I thought you might slam the phone down! I love you very much. Are you all right?" I asked.

"I'm all right. I was writing you a letter last night in my mind." Then she began to tell me her story.

She started with an explanation of how she had gotten on drugs. "When Christie moved away to school, I was depressed. A friend offered me something and I said, 'Okay,' and that was it, I was addicted. I always told her that I'm an alcoholic and if I ever started taking anything, I would be really addicted."

I wanted to ask *when* she started taking drugs. I thought there may have been a correlation to the way Mom had treated her in September at Heritage Gardens. But in the course of Verneda opening her heart to me, I listened, not wanting to interrupt the flow of her words.

"I had gone to my probation officer and he sent me for blood work and found that I was dirty and he put me in jail for fifty-seven days. I thought I was gonna die in there I was in so much pain. The nurse told me it was just old age. They called me grandma in there. Most of the women were nineteen and twenty."

Momentarily I was lost in thought, wondering why she had a probation officer.

"I was on speed," she said. "Man, when I was in jail, I found out the stuff that was in it and I didn't know it had all that junk in it. It changed my whole personality. I mean it really changed my personality! I brought home all this trash and stacked it up. I was buried in trash. When I was gone, the kids brought in a truck and loaded all the trash in it, cleaned up the place. You know, I was living in a room in my garage. They moved me into a room in the house."

My heart ached as I thought of her "buried in trash." We're both buried in trash, I thought, trash from our past that clutters up our psyche, impacts our functioning. But we need the help of others to clean out this crippling trash, we can't do it ourselves, experience has taught me that, I told myself.

"Fifty-seven days in jail," she said. "Took me that long to know I didn't want to do drugs." Ironic, I thought, does she realize her parole officer gave her vital help she needed, disguised as jail time? She went on to talk about an experience she had with an inmate.

"A lady got transferred in and had drugs on her. I told her, 'I saw you take drugs.'"

She said to me, "You better watch your back."

"What the fuck do you mean watch my back? I'll beat the fuck out of you!" I told her.

"Hey old lady," she said to me.

"What fat bitch," I said to her.

"You have to like me. You gotta like me."

"In there one of 'em threatened me and I told her, 'I've been beat by the biggest people in the world. I am ready to fight.' I layed on my bed later thinkin', why am I so mean? What is this rage?"

I was thankful she hadn't paused, because I was too dumfounded to respond. When she identified herself as mean and angry, I wondered if she had made any connection of "mean and angry" to our mother. Those were two of Mom's qualities Verneda repeatedly experienced during her childhood and experienced again in the last years of Mom's life. Maybe it would help her if she could search for answers to her questions, I thought. Then I recalled my inviting her years ago to see my therapist, Mac, at my expense. But she declined.

"In jail was the first time since I was fifteen, I wasn't under any drugs. No cigarettes, no alcohol, no marijuana, no speed. No threat of rape from anyone…" She continued to talk in detail about how people had waited on her because she had "commissary" and as a result, she had power. "No threat of rape from anyone," got buried in her avalanche of words, buried until I thought of it later. I regretted that I didn't interrupt her to ask that she elaborate on what she meant by "no threat of rape…" Left wondering, my imagination refused to explore possible details.

She quickly changed the subject to Vern. "You were right about him."

"Yes, but you needed to learn that for yourself," I said.

"I had blamed Mom all those years. I thought for years Mom was lying to me about my dad. I thought he was nice. I was angry at Mom over the loss of my father. I held it against Mom. I held the dream in my heart that Dad would come back and save me. I always had it in my mind that Dad was a saint." She talked about a few pleasant memories of Vern when she was a little child. Then she said, "But you were right about him. He was such a nasty man. He was mean. I was afraid of him. I'm glad he's dead."

"It's important that you found out for yourself what kind of man Vern was. Maybe it's even more important that you learned Mom had told the truth about him."

As the conversation finally came to an end, I said, "I'm scheduled for a seminar in Orange County in a few days, I'd like to see you then." Earlier in the conversation she had said, "I lost all of my teeth from taking speed. I don't want to see you until I get my teeth." But when I mentioned a second time that I wanted to see her, she didn't resist.

When I hung up the phone, part of me kicked and screamed, "I don't want to see her! I don't want to see her!" Probably the voice of my young child, I thought. Thankfully, the love I had for my sister fueled my desire to stay connected.

After Verneda and I had been reconciled for almost a year, she talked with me about Buddy, Jr. "I'd get drunk and I'd call trying to find Buddy, Jr." I remembered she had told me this before.

"How do you feel about Larry now?" I asked.

"I called him on his birthday. I talked to him about not being in touch with him because I was on drugs and that I didn't feel as good as other people. He said, 'Oh goodness, don't think anything about that, I used to drink and have done a lot of things.' He sent me a little valentine after that. It was real nice.

"But I don't feel like I need or want something from him. I just needed to know that he is okay. My part is over. I wanted Mother to see him before she died. I feel complete. Looking for him in my mind all those years, the weight is gone. He is Larry now, not Buddy, Jr."

At the time when I found Larry, she didn't say the precious words I longed for her to say, that her burden had been lifted. Instead, she treated me with animosity, denigrating my gift. But now, at last, I was privileged to hear from her heart, "the weight is gone."

What follows has been selected from the many things my sister told me during the years after our reconciliation.

"When Norm couldn't take care of her, Mom came to my place during the day while Glenda worked. I would have kept her with me but she was MEAN. She kept asking where Norm is. She threatened to walk out of here. I couldn't take care of her. That's when Glenda took Mom to Arlington Meadows in February and left her there."

"That was February of 1991, wasn't it?" I asked.

"Yes, I went there to see her at Easter. I fixed a real nice basket and bought a big stuffed bunny. When I gave it to her she said, 'What do I want with that thing!' "

"After taking her the Easter Basket, the next time and last time I saw her was in September in Loma Linda where you had her stay. I went with Glenda and Christie to visit Mom at Heritage Gardens. At first, she wouldn't even look at me. Then Mom got that look on her face. It was so evil. You couldn't see love there. You could see that hate. That ugly, ugly look that means horrible things. She pointed a finger at me and said, with that ugly look on her face and hate in her eyes, 'You, you're the one that started this whole thing.' She glared at me with that look. She hated me – that was really a hard thing to deal with."

Verneda began to cry softly when she said, "I'm not sure why Mom thought something was going on between me and Norm. Maybe he lied and told her there was something between us."

So why was Mom cruel to Verneda at Heritage Gardens? It seemed clear now. Mom's view of Verneda as a rival had persisted, separated them, revealed itself as hatred. And maybe Norm *had* lied.

"After Mother died, Verneda said, I decided to go see Norm. I used to always give each one of them a little kiss. So when I saw Norm, I started to give him a hello kiss. He grabbed me and stuck his tongue in my mouth. I didn't know what to do so I just acted like nothing happened. But I never went to see him after that. I did call him a couple of times when he was in the rest home at Loma Linda where you took him. He was happy there, he liked it."

Verneda never asked Norm, "Did you lie to Mom about you and me?" Something held the tongue of my outspoken sister.

Eventually, she reflected once more on her experience of going to jail.

"You know when they arrested me, I was in my front yard watering my lawn." She began to cry as she talked. "They handcuffed me. There were police cars everywhere. The neighbors all saw it. After I got out of jail, I couldn't go in my front yard. I thought people were looking at me and didn't like me. But I didn't really know how deep my feelings went until I got new lawn sod in my front yard. I was out there watering and the neighbors waved and smiled. People driving by waved and smiled, even the school bus driver waved and smiled. People stopped and talked.

"While I was out there, I saw a dove pick up an old dried twig from the dead grass area taking it to the garage to build a nest. As I watched, I thought, yes, the dove and the olive branch – the storm is over. I talked to God and asked him to help me experience the joy and excitement of living, like my little grandchildren do."

Because it had helped me to visit places in my past that held the most trauma, I suggested to Verneda that we plan a trip to Jarbidge, Nevada, a place that held a lot of traumatic memories for her. It was important, I thought, for Larry to join us since a portion of the trauma involved him. This is where we had lived for about six months after he was born.

It was something of a miracle when my sister, who was known to stay mostly in her room and infrequently leave her home, was willing to fly to Twin Falls, Idaho for us to pick her up.
With her willingness to join us, Larry and Sherry, David and I agreed to a trip that on our way, took us to Lakeview to visit his father, Roy then on to Boise where we visited with Grace who was Bud's sister-in-law, finally meeting Verneda in Twin Falls to travel together to Jarbidge.

We stopped for a short time to visit Roy, a kind person, pleasant to be with. I had visited him before in Lakeview, when he had told stories of knowing me as a child in Jarbidge. This visit allowed me to talk in detail with him about the mine in Jarbidge, which held a tender place in his Jarbidge experience.

I wasn't sure why Larry wanted to go to Boise to talk with Grace, but I was happy he wanted me along. Grace had been married to Bud's brother Dewey, before he died. A number of years ago I found her and Dewey in Washington and she said, "We don't know nothin' about nothin'."

The conversation with Grace warmed up on the subject of Vi, Bud's sister, who left poor blind Roy to run off with another woman's husband shortly after I had found Larry. I was surprised to hear what Larry said to Grace about his parents, Vi and Roy.

"It took me years to accept Mom leavin' Dad. I thought she did Dad wrong. But Dad's better off, believe it or not. She dominated his life. He couldn't breathe."

The conversation that followed was a lesson in what my mother was up against when she encountered Bud's sister Vi.

"Vi had her nose in there," Grace began, "got her nose in there where she shouldn't have and they gotcha. I don't know how they got their hands on you, but that wasn't right."

"Mom liked to run the show," Larry said. "She's very sharp with her mouth and her tongue. I love her dearly, but I didn't know Uncle Bud was my father until just recently. Didn't know that my mother was really my aunt," he said with a smile. "The only thing I regret is I never knew anything about my past." Larry paused, then said, "I think Mom had guilty feelings and she was too scared that I would abandon her if I found out the truth."

Why didn't anyone in the family come forward to tell Larry the truth, I wanted to ask Grace. Then I remembered what Vi's stepson Earnest Lee said, "I didn't say anything because of Vi's wrath."

"Bud tried several times to see Larry but Vi put a stop to it," Sherry said.

"I know that," Grace said. "Vi didn't allow Bud to see you as you got a little older. But they shouldn't have been getting their nose in it. I think Bud and Edna liked to go and have a beer or two and left you in the car or somehow or other when you were a little baby. I'm sure they didn't leave you so you would get hurt."

"But Dad said that I probably wouldn't have made it because I was sick when they got me," Larry said.

"Well, I don't think it was as bad as it was painted to be though. I really don't. I really don't think so."

With a lull in the conversation, I said to Grace, "I heard that you and Dewey went with my mother and tried to get Larry back from Vi."

"Ah yeah, we did," Grace admitted.

"Mom said Vi had her put in jail."

"We *all* went to jail. I don't tell it. I don't think my kids even know that. We all went down, Dewey, your mom and me. We was gonna raise cane. But we didn't get to first base!"

At least Mother wasn't alone when she tried to get her son from Vi, I thought when I learned for the first time that Vi had her own brother thrown in jail, along with Mom and Grace.

When we left Grace, I had a strong desire to talk with Vi. But for now, that desire must be set aside because soon, we would be in Twin Falls to pick up Verneda.

Our brief adventure in Twin involved Larry driving all of us around in his huge motor home to locate the small cinder block home where Verneda and I had stayed after Grandpa died.
And find it we did, still there but abandoned, left to itself in disrepair. The front door was wide open, we peeked inside. The living room was as small as I remembered with the stair case still in place. We didn't linger long, but there's something special about returning to a place that holds childhood memories.

Like the separation of Aunt Emma's gold watch from its chain, successfully united again with the passing of time, Verneda, "Buddy, Jr." and I walked together on the narrow dirt road through the town of Jarbidge after fifty-eight years of separation; after Vi got our brother, renamed him Larry and raised him as her own.

We had walked only a short distance from town when we found it. For a time, we stood in silence, looking at the tiny white house where the three of us had once lived. "I'm remembering one night when we were alone and I was scared," my sister began. 'Them cougars are comin' down out of the hills,' I heard the adults say. Well, I was scared because I thought cougars were gorillas. So that night I was so scared of cougars coming in the windows, I took us out to sit in the middle of the street under the street light where we would be safe."

My seven-year-old sister Verneda, alone and afraid in the dark, responsible for baby and me, had found comfort in the dim light of the street lamp.

Sherry handed Larry a blanket she was carrying. "Why don't you sit on this like you did back then," she said, "and I'll take your picture." Larry spread out the blanket on the dirt road in front of the house and sat between Verneda and me, pretending to suck his thumb. Healing laughter took away the distress of our yesterdays. Although she had smoked for fifty years, Verneda quit when she returned home from Jarbidge.

We said our goodbyes to Larry and Sherry. Verneda, David and I drove to Salt Lake City where she would take her flight back to California the next day. I was in her motel room saying goodnight, with my hand on the door handle when she asked me a question.

"Do you know the song, *The Wind Beneath My Wings?*"

"It's one of my favorites," I said. I have the CD."

"I've always looked up to you the way you are. You are the wind beneath my wings. Play that song when you get home."

Once again, my thoughts turned to my desire to talk with Vi. She had played a major role in my mother's life. I wanted more than ever to hear Vi tell me her version of how she became the one who raised Buddy, Jr. From the day I met Larry, it had been my desire to talk with Vi. But Vi had refused to talk with me when I had stood on her driveway in Lakeview and told her who I was, without mentioning that just days before I had found Larry. Now, ten years later and only a week after I had talked with Grace, Vi finally agreed to talk with me, in her home near Las Vegas, even allowing me to record our conversation.

It was my intention to be gracious to a woman who had the reputation of being ruthless and unpredictable; a woman who was in charge of those she allowed to be in her life; a woman who had left her husband Roy of many years for another woman's husband. I knew to be cautious. Larry had said of her, "You can't be around her too long, you know. You talk to her too long she's gonna cut you some way or another."

When we arrived at the doublewide manufactured home I was surprised at her appearance: a tiny thin woman with hair of apricot color, which framed a drawn wrinkled face bearing large tinted glasses. The smell of smoke on her clothes announced her habit.

Almost immediately she started talking about a letter I'd written to her months earlier in which I referred to the adoption papers,

"You said it wasn't your mother's handwriting."

"No, it wasn't my mother's handwriting," I said firmly but gently. "Her name wasn't even spelled correctly on the adoption papers."

"I know it wasn't," she said. Vi went on and on about the adoption papers, almost incoherently, but said nothing about the handwriting not being my mother's. However, she finished her long discourse with, "The lawyer probably misspelled her name."

"That may be the case, but I've seen the adoption papers and the signature is not my mother's signature," I repeated in a non-threatening tone of voice.

Vi's high-pitched voice dropped an octave or so, "Well the lawyer probably copied that in." Reenergized, she stated with finality, "We tore ours up. We tore it up, I guess about thirty years ago. No need keeping it as far as that's concerned." Immediately she got up and went to the kitchen to put a load of laundry in the dryer.

While I waited, I asked myself, why would anyone tear up papers that could prove a legal adoption, papers supposedly signed by my mother when giving up her baby? As I sat there, I realized that Vi has talked with me primarily about the adoption. It may have been her way of saying indirectly that Mother had agreed to give the baby to Vi and Roy to raise. I continued to listen carefully as Vi returned to talk with me, telling her truth as she probably had repeated it to herself over the years.

Truth, I have come to believe, is specific to the individual telling it. Usually, people believe their own truth. If it was a lie to begin with, but repeated often enough, I suppose the lie is eventually believed as truth.

Vi told me many things, but I sat on the edge of my chair when she related the details of what happened the day Mother,

Dewey and Grace came to get Buddy, Jr. "I went over, and I got Mom to celebrate Mother's Day," Vi began. "That evening about eight o'clock there was a knock at the door and it was my brother Dewey. I was so happy to see him. About that time in came Edna and in came my sister-in-law Grace, all three drunk as a skunk, and they come after that baby. I mean I got pushed up against the door. I yelled to Mom, "Call the police." I was in hysterics. I was hurt. Black eye and my hair pulled out by the roots. The police came and I swore out the warrant and they took 'em all three to jail: your mother, my crippled little brother Dewey and Grace, my sister-in-law. Away they went to jail. Well Mother's Day was on a Sunday. This happened on a Saturday instead of on Mother's Day, the next day. So they lay in jail, Saturday night and Sunday night. I had all three of 'em put under 'Bonds of Peace.' That means they just have to stay away. That was the end of that.

And truly that was "the end of that" because my mother never saw her baby again until he was forty-seven years old. But it wasn't only Mother who was separated from her baby. Verneda and I had each experienced the unexpected loss of him when we were children, a lingering loss.

One final loose end remained. My desire to see Bud (Vi's brother and Larry's biological father) wouldn't go away. Bud's brother Al had given me his location in a midwestern state near where we were traveling that summer.

On the twenty-mile drive from the motel, I considered what I might say when someone answered the door. From what Grace said and my own experience of the returned picture I had sent him, getting in the door to see Bud will be difficult. I settled on what I thought was a reasonable introduction. "I've just come from visiting Grace in Boise and we're on our way to visit my cousin but I wanted to stop to say hello."

After parking and walking across the street to the house bearing their number, I knocked lightly on the door. No answer. I noticed a vehicle parked at the corner of the house. They're home, I told myself. I played the little harp and jingled the bells that hung from the door on a thick ribbon. Still, no one came. Probably too soft for anyone to hear, I said to myself. This time I knocked louder. Still no response. Two lawn chairs next to the door caught my attention. I sat down and said to myself, I will sit here until someone comes. I'm not leaving until I see Bud.

I didn't have to wait long. The door opened. A small, pleasant woman came out of the house, cautiously closing the door behind her. I gave her my "just came from visiting Grace," introduction and she immediately invited me inside. My thrill of getting into the house yielded to my excitement at meeting Bud. We searched each other's faces. I saw in his face the Bud I had known as little girl.

We sat and talked briefly about Grace. Bud's wife was animated and friendly. At some point the conversation shifted from the little store they had on their property to Bud's talking about WWII. The rolled-up picture I had found on the back porch of Larned when I was in fourth grade came to mind – Bud on the deck of a big ship with masses of men lined up with him.

"I joined the Navy right after the Japs bombed Pearl Harbor."

"Why the Navy; did you enlist?" I asked.

"I enlisted; I wasn't drafted. I joined the Navy because I wanted to fly."

"And did you get to fly?"

"Yes, I was a gunner," he said proudly.

"Like in the movies, at the back of the plane?"

"Yes. We were shot down three times. Splashed down into the water."

"I guess you're lucky to be alive, Bud."

Bud continued telling me about himself, his black lung disease, and his experience working in the copper mines. I was perplexed at his personal revelations because I didn't think he knew who I was.

Indian jewelry somehow became a topic of conversation. After his wife had shown me several pieces she had for sale, I said, "I should be going. I don't want to keep you from your Sunday evening programs." Instantly, they both stood up and walked me to the front door. It closed behind me. Much to my surprise, there stood Bud. Unbelievable, I was alone with Bud. I looked at him and said:

"Bud, I'm Vernetta. I didn't mean to be deceptive, but I didn't want to upset your wife." Bud started walking toward a little building near his house.

"I knew who you was," he said. "I recognized you from that picture you sent."

He started walking toward the small building in front of us. "This is a little pueblo I built for the store we're about ready to open." He started to unlock the door but stopped. "You know, I wasn't with your Mom for very long. She told me to get lost," he said.

I didn't confront him with what I had been told, but said, "My friend Maxine said Vi came to Salt Lake City and took you back with her. I'm sure you had a hard time with all of it."

"The past is the past," he said as if to close the door on a discussion.

We entered his shop, where I began to look at items on display to sell. "Did you send Mom pictures of Larry? We have pictures of him until he was about three or four."

"No, I didn't send them," he answered. How can that be, I asked myself, who else might have sent them? I could think of no one.

I kept shoving aside the flood of thoughts about the past and the questions I wanted to ask as I selected items from his shop. His comment, "the past is the past" and the emotional moment of being with him, somehow prevented my asking anything more.

"Do you mind if I take your picture," I said when we left the store. Bud stood by his house. I snapped a picture. Almost immediately, his wife returned with my change and my purchases in a package, then quickly retreated into the house, unwilling to let me take her picture.

Bud and I stood quietly for a few moments. But our farewell held no observable drama, no expressed sentiment that might provoke a tearful goodbye.

When I left Bud, my mother's lover, the father of her son, I thought about the many people I've talked with who had tried to deal with their past by not dealing with it, that is, trying to avoid thinking or talking about it, still protecting secrets into the last years of their lives. I've discovered great healing from purposely digging into my past, purposely returning to places where I had lived as a child, purposely seeking to find and talk with significant people from my past. From my relentless pursuit, questions had become linked to answers with an unimagined result. A feeling of deep satisfaction filled my soul. I felt complete, whole. A golden-orange sunset filled the Western sky as I continued on my way back to David.

    The decisions each of us make are important to who we become. But when one is a child, important decisions are held in the hands of adults or older siblings. What happens when the decisions made are devastating to the child's well-being? Might it render the child incapable of making rectifying decisions as an adult? In my mother's case, I suggest that is what happened.

    Sexually violated by her father, as well as sexually used by her brothers from the time she was a young girl, seeds of helplessness, of anger began to germinate within her. Having a mother who didn't talk with her, didn't hug and kiss her, didn't tell her "I love you," it was easy for her to keep secrets about the "nasty things" that went on in the Healy, Kansas farmhouse. To me it was significant that my mother had poured kerosene on each one of the beds before setting fire to them. The beds where she had been overcome by "bedbugs." I interpreted this as a remarkable demonstration of her rage at being the victim of their sexual demands. Perhaps her rage was compounded by helplessly watching her angry, drunk father beat her mother, an apparently depressed woman. I believe that my mother began to identify with her father, the more aggressive of her parents. She eventually mirrored his destructive behaviors of sexual promiscuity, drunkenness and anger.

    Maybe she could have overcome these childhood traumas if she hadn't succumbed to Vern's advances. She probably didn't realize that, like her father, he also had a propensity to be sexually promiscuous. I prefer to believe that my mother didn't know Vern was an angry man who became violent when he drank and would beat her just as Lowell had beaten Pansie. But in my counseling degree program, I was introduced to the psychological theory that adults tend to repeat patterns of behavior, which were traumatic or distressing in earlier life. So, perhaps by marrying Vern, Mother had unknowingly chosen a man similar to her father, replicating in her adult life what she had experienced but couldn't resolve as a child.

Because she had grown up being exploited sexually, she continued to be easily exploited by men after Vern left her. She fell deeper and deeper into this behavior as her drinking escalated. I don't know how many men she gave in to before she left Red Getchel at the dance hall to go home with Bud in Jarbidge, but that was another giant downward step. These familiar behaviors, I imagine, helped her deal with her unresolved childhood issues and the heartbreaks she suffered in the loss of Vern, Bud and her son Buddy, Jr. but these behaviors didn't relieve her anger. My sister and I became a major outlet for her rage. But perhaps she directed most of the anger at herself in the self-destructive course she persistently pursued.

What else may happen to a daughter's psyche when she is having sex with her mother's husband, her own father. Might she come to fearfully believe that her oldest daughter is her rival. Mother had expressed this very fear to Verneda: "I was afraid you'd grow up and take Bud away from me." Verneda was only a first grader when Mother had this concern. In the last years of her life, she also demonstrated her fear of Verneda as a rival when she disclosed to me her concern of Verneda being "out to get Norm for herself." I believe there is a direct correlation between Mother's paranoia and the incest. Could her relationship with her father also explain the beatings she gave Verneda? Were the beatings a combination of Mother's fear and self-hatred, born of the incest, that she misplaced on her daughter?

When I was a child, I experienced my mother as a powerful woman. It wasn't until I was an adult that I experienced her as the victim she truly was. Her negative attitude permeated almost every aspect of her existence, which caused me to believe she experienced herself a victim of life itself. I came to know my mother as a woman of low self-esteem without a vision of what she might become. I'm satisfied that I now understand more clearly what shaped her most profoundly in who she became.

Mother struggled through life with her own set of special problems. My sister and I happened to be her children and her problems spilled over onto us. We had great gaping holes where love was meant to be, but then, so did she.

There were times during life with my mother that I wanted to walk away, run away and never turn back, including the last five years of her life. But I was drawn to her for reasons I didn't fully understand. Possibly there was a degree of pathology in the bond that held me to her. However, even though my love for her sometimes perplexed me, I truly loved her. For this, I give my Heavenly Father the often-unspoken credit.

TRAVEL PHOTOS OF 1999

Vernetta, Roy Lee, Larry Lee
Lakeview, Oregon 1999

Vernetta and Verneda
Twin Falls, Idaho location of where the shack burned

Vernetta and Verneda
Twin Falls, Idaho Uncle Clarence and Aunt Mae's old cinder block house.

Vernetta and Verneda
1999 on our way to Jarbidge, Nevada

Larry, Verneda, Vernetta
Jarbidge, Nevada

Vernetta, Larry, Verneda
Our home of 1941 Jarbidge, Nevada

Vernetta, Larry, Verneda
No longer afraid of "cougars in the night"

Verneda and Vernetta
SugarHouse, the first trailor park location
Salt Lake City

Maxine and Vernetta, Salt Lake City

Vernetta and Dale/Tudy, Salt Lake City

Bud, Colorado 1999

Vernetta and Bud's sister Vi, woman who raised Buddy, Jr./Larry
Nevada 1999

Made in the USA
Columbia, SC
21 October 2022